Towards Sustainable Aviation

Edited by

Paul Upham,
Janet Maughan,
David Raper and
Callum Thomas

Earthscan Publications Ltd
London • Sterling, VA

First published in the UK and USA in 2003
by Earthscan Publications Ltd

ISBN: 1 85383 818 7 (paperback)
        1 85383 817 9 (hardback)

Typesetting by Denis Dalinnik, Minsk, Belarus
Printed and bound in the UK by Creative Print and Design (Wales), Ebbw Vale
Cover design by Danny Gillespie

For a full list of publications please contact:

Earthscan Publications Ltd
120 Pentonville Road, London, N1 9JN, UK
Tel: +44 (0)20 7278 0433
Fax: +44 (0)20 7278 1142
Email: earthinfo@earthscan.co.uk
Web: **www.earthscan.co.uk**

22883 Quicksilver Drive, Sterling, VA 20166-2012, USA

A catalogue record for this book is available from the British Library

Library of Congress Cataloging-in-Publication Data applied for

Earthscan is an editorially independent subsidiary of Kogan Page Ltd and publishes in association with WWF-UK and the International Institute for Environment and Development

This book is printed on elemental chlorine free paper

Contents

List of Figures, Tables and Boxes   vii
List of Contributors   ix
Preface   xiv
List of Acronyms and Abbreviations   xvi

PART 1   TRENDS AND ISSUES

1 Introduction: perspectives on sustainability and aviation *Paul Upham*   3
2 Organizational and growth trends in air transport *Ian Humphreys*   19
×3 The social and economic benefits of aviation *Robert Caves*   36
×4 The human health impacts of aviation *Ken Hume and Adrian Watson*   48
5 The global atmospheric impacts of aviation *David Lee and David Raper*   77
6 Aircraft noise, community relations and stakeholder involvement
   Callum Thomas and Martin Lever   97

PART 2   MITIGATIONS AND POTENTIAL SOLUTIONS

7 Environmental management and the aviation industry *Paul Hooper,*
   Bridget Heath and Janet Maughan   115
8 The potential for modal substitution *Milan Janic*   131
9 Air freight and global supply chains: the environmental dimension
   David Gillingwater, Ian Humphreys and Robert Watson   149
10 The potential offered by aircraft and engine technologies *Jacquetta Lee*   162
11 Climate policy for civil aviation: actors, policy instruments and the
    potential for emissions reductions *Andreas Pastowski*   179

PART 3   MULTISECTOR COMMENTARIES

12 Multisector commentaries on sustainability and aviation   199

    Economic aspects of sustainability and UK aviation *Simon Bishop,*
       Institute for Public Policy Research   199
    Sustainable aviation: implications for economies in transition
       Delia Dimitriu, TAROM Romanian Air Transport   201
    Key issues in aviation environmental policy-making *Léonie Dobbie,*
       Partner, GreenAscent (former Director, Aviation Environment,
       IATA, 1996–2002)   204

Towards sustainable aviation? *Brian Graham, University of Ulster*   211

Aircraft noise: the NGO perspective *Tim Johnson, Aviation
    Environment Federation*   213

Environmental and economic factors in airport capacity *Joop Krul,
    Schiphol Airport*   218

Potential improvements to air traffic management *Arthur Lieuwen and
    Ted Elliff, EUROCONTROL*   220

Making aviation less unsustainable: some pointers to the way ahead
    Caroline Lucas, MEP   223

✗Sustainable aviation: what do you mean? *Mark McLellan, Partner,
    GreenAscent*   225

✗Sustainability and aviation: problems and solutions *Beatrice Schell, T&E*   229

Airlines and sustainable development *Hugh Somerville, British Airways*   232

The case for 'no growth' *John Whitelegg, Liverpool John Moores University*   234

13 Conclusion *Paul Upham*   239

    Index   242

List of Figures, Tables and Boxes

FIGURES

1.1	Key components of a contemporary aviation system	9
2.1	World annual air passenger traffic growth and forecast	20
2.2	Market power of hub-and-spoke networks	25
5.1	Radiative energy balance of the Earth's atmosphere	79
5.2	Global annual mean radiative forcing (Wm^{-2}) from a number of agents for the period from the pre-industrial (1750) to the present (2000)	80
5.3	Global annual mean radiative forcings from aircraft emissions for 1992 (a) and 2050, Scenario Fa1 (b) (Wm^{-2})	81
5.4	Spatial distribution of ANCAT/EC2 1991/1992 emissions of NO_x from civil aviation, vertically integrated between ground and 16km ($kg\ NO_2\ m^{-2}\ yr^{-1}$)	83
5.5	Vertical distribution of emissions of civil aviation NO_x, 1991/1992	83
5.6	Development over time of fuel usage and NO_x emissions from aviation	84
5.7	Representation of the production of ozone from methane, carbon monoxide and non-methane hydrocarbons	85
5.8	Change in temperature per ozone column amount (Dobson units) by altitude	85
5.9	(a) Modelled nitrogen dioxide concentrations in parts per trillion (ppt) and (b) ozone in parts per billion (ppb) from aircraft at cruise altitudes for 1992 and a 2050 scenario (Fe1)	86
7.1	The main drivers of environmental degradation	117
8.1	Evolution of train and aircraft speed	133
8.2	Development of the high-speed rail (HSR) network in Europe	134
8.3	Dependence of HSR traffic on the length of the HSR network in Europe	135
8.4	Dependence of the generalized user cost on the length of corridor/route	137
8.5	Market share of particular transport modes dependent upon the origin/destination travel distance	138
8.6a	The mutual influence of HSR and APT in selected French market corridors	138
8.6b	The mutual influence of HSR and APT in selected German market corridors	139
8.7	Generic schemes of possible complementarity between HSR and APT	140
9.1	An integrator's overnight short-haul network operation	151
9.2	Air-freight movements at East Midlands Airport: 20:00–07:00hrs	154
10.1	Aircraft noise	163

10.2	Noise trends	164
10.3	Fuel efficiency and specific fuel consumption (SFC)	165
10.4	Thermal efficiency variations	169
10.5	Trade-off between noise and fuel efficiency	169
10.6	Noise reduction programmes and technologies	170
10.7	Development of combustor technology	171
10.8	The More Electric Engine	174
10.9	The More Electric Aircraft	175
11.1	Long-term relative changes in transport activity, fuel consumption and unit fuel consumption for Swissair	184
11.2	Main actors in causing environmental problems and environmental policy	185
11.3	Domestic and international passengers by income per capita group of country of departure	187

TABLES

2.1	Trans-national global airline alliances	27
2.2	Major new airport projects	29
4.1	Reported risk factors for the development of DVT	50
4.2	Socio-economic status-adjusted relative risks for cancer incidence and mortality amongst flight personnel	55
5.1	Fuel, NO_x and emission index (EI) for NO_x for 1991/1992, 2015 and 2050 gridded data sets	82
7.1	Main differences between EMAS and ISO 14001	122
7.2	List of environmentally certified European airports as of 19 November 2001	123
7.3	Corporate reporting and measurement guidelines and standards	126
8.1	Examples of rail infrastructure at particular EU airports	142
11.1	Likely rebound effects of options for reducing aviation's climate impact	183
11.2	Objectives, options, direct actors and climate policy in civil aviation	186
11.3	Assessment of various instruments for climate policy in civil aviation	191

BOXES

1.1	Sustainability criteria in the OECD's *Environmental Strategy for the First Decade of the 21st Century*	8
1.2	Selected questions in the UK government's consultation on *The Future of Aviation*	13
2.1	Forms of airport ownership	31

List of Contributors

Simon Bishop is responsible for helping to develop the Sustainable Aviation 2030 project for the Institute for Public Policy Research (IPPR), a prominent UK think tank on the centre left. With the publication of a discussion document on sustainability and aviation in August 2001, IPPR worked closely with stakeholders in the aviation community to develop a policy options paper, published in spring 2002. Previously, Simon worked for the UK Department of Environment, Transport and the Regions (DETR) as an environmental economist.

Dr Robert Caves is Senior Lecturer in the Department of Civil and Building Engineering, Loughborough University. He has lectured internationally on transport technology and systems, operations analysis, air transport, aircraft technology and safety, aircraft operations and airport planning and management. He is European editor of the *Journal of Air Transport Management* and a member of the Transportation Research Board Committee on Airport System Planning.

Delia Dimitriu is Manager of Environment and Work Safety for the airline TAROM, Romanian Air Transport. She is a member of the international aviation/environment committees IATA-ENTAF and ICAO-CAEP-WG4 and is a LEAD Fellow (Leadership for Environment and Development). At the time of writing, Delia Dimitriu is on sabbatical in ARIC at Manchester Metropolitan University, where she is researching a PhD thesis on strategic environmental assessment entitled *Sustainability Aspects in Aviation Related Policies, Plans and Programmes: A Comparative Analysis of Economy in Transition Countries in Europe*.

Léonie Dobbie was recently Director of Environment for the International Air Transport Association (IATA). She has participated in the work of ICAO's Committee on Aviation Environmental Protection (CAEP) and was a lead author in the IPCC *Special Report on Aviation and the Global Atmosphere* (1999). Léonie Dobbie is an external lecturer on various university aviation courses, including IFURTA, University of Aix en Provence, and ENAC, Toulouse. She is now a Partner in the independent consultancy and think tank GreenAscent.

Ted Elliff has worked at EUROCONTROL since 1991 and has an in-depth understanding of modelling issues and application of flight data. Since forming the Environmental Studies cell at the Experimental Centre two years ago, he has been an active participant in several ICAO CAEP working groups and, latterly, has managed a study to estimate European fuel burn and emissions savings resulting from the implementation of EUROCONTROL's ATM2000+ strategy.

Dr David Gillingwater is Senior Lecturer and Director of Studies in Transport Planning and Management at Loughborough University. He is editor of the international journal *Transportation Planning and Technology*, and co-editor of the international book series *Transportation Studies*. He is also director of the internationally accredited short course programme for airport managers and planners, Airports and the Environment, which has been held annually at Loughborough since 1984.

Professor Brian Graham is based at the University of Ulster. He has published extensively on air transport issues, most recently on environmental capacity issues in the European Union and regional air services in the UK. Professor Graham is advisor to the Northern Ireland government on air transport matters.

Dr Bridget Heath is Senior Lecturer at Manchester Metropolitan University. With a PhD in gas desulphurization at power plants, she previously worked in consultancy as a principal environmental chemist, focusing on air pollution abatement and ground contamination. Dr Heath's lecturing and research interests include air quality, business and environment, sustainable energy policy and waste management.

Dr Paul Hooper is Senior Lecturer at Manchester Metropolitan University, with a PhD in industrial policy for clean technology (University of Manchester). His research interests include environmentally sustainable industrial policy and practice. Current research focuses on three aspects of aviation: waste management, public consultation associated with airport development and environmental management and reporting in the world airline industry. He has recently prepared best practice guidance on many of these issues for IATA in Geneva.

Dr Ken Hume is Principal Lecturer and Research Director in the Department of Biological Sciences at Manchester Metropolitan University. His research career has involved investigations of the disturbance of sleep patterns by aircraft noise and other causes. He works on a number of national and international committees/groups concerned with sleep disturbance and has been the Honourable Secretary of the British Sleep Society.

Dr Ian Humphreys is Lecturer in Air Transport Management at the Transport Studies Group, Loughborough University, and a member of the Performance Measurement Research Unit. He gained a PhD in airport marketing and management from Cardiff University in 1994 and his current research interests include performance measurement, airport planning, airport privatization policy and airport management.

Dr Milan Janic was Chief Researcher at the Institute of Transport, Ljubljana, Slovenia, during 1994–1997. Following research at Loughborough University and Manchester Metropolitan University, Dr Janic is now Senior Researcher in OTB Research Institute at Delft University in the Netherlands. He has considerable experience in air transport research, including modelling and planning for airports, airlines and air traffic control.

Tim Johnson is Director of the Aviation Environment Federation (AEF), a UK-based environmental association representing over 100 organizations and companies. He represents the AEF on government and European Commission policy working groups, and is a coordinator, and active working-group representative, of an international consortium of environmental NGOs granted observer status to the International Civil Aviation Organization (ICAO).

Joop Krul graduated in Urban Planning at the University of Amsterdam and has worked for Schiphol Airport in different roles since 1986. Currently, he is Director of Airport Development and is responsible for long-term planning and master planning. He is a member of Airports Council International Environmental Standing Committee, which has an advisory role to ICAO-CAEP on airport issues.

Dr David Lee is Technology Chief for Atmospheric Science in QinetiQ (formerly the UK Defence Evaluation and Research Agency, DERA), Visiting Reader at Manchester Metropolitan University, and Fellow of the Royal Meteorological Society and of the Institute of Energy. He is a participant in the current EU aviation-related projects TRADEOFF, PARTEMIS and AERONET and coordinates AERO2K. David Lee was a lead author for the IPCC report *Aviation and the Global Atmosphere* and has published widely on atmospheric science in scientific and technical journals.

Dr Jacquetta Lee was recently Principal Environmental Technologist – Products within the Environmental Strategy Team at Rolls-Royce plc. She is a member of the Technology Sub-group reporting to the Society of British Aerospace Companies (SBAC) Greener by Design Foresight Programme, sits on the British Standards Institute (BSI) panel developing a technical report entitled *Guidelines to Integrating Environmental Aspects into Product Development,* and is a judge for the Sustainable Engineering category of the Engineering Council Environment Awards. She is currently working in a consultative capacity.

Dr Martin Lever is Research Associate in ARIC at Manchester Metropolitan University, with a PhD on stakeholder participation in the context of forced migration. For a major airline, Martin Lever has critically evaluated methodologies used to determine compensation for noise-affected airport communities and has contributed to a EUROCONTROL-funded project on defining and assessing airport environmental capacity. Recent work relates to airport community involvement initiatives and community resistance strategies in relation to airport expansion.

Dr Arthur Lieuwen is EUROCONTROL's Agency Environmental Focal Point to ensure that all EUROCONTROL air traffic management work takes into account environmental considerations. Dr Lieuwen was a lead author of the Intergovernmental Panel for Climate Change (IPCC) Special Report on *Aviation and the Global Atmosphere* and represents EUROCONTROL in ICAO-CAEP and ECAC-ANCAT.

Dr Caroline Lucas is UK MEP for South-East Region Green party. In the European Parliament, she is a Member of the Committee for Trade, Industry, Energy and

Research, and a Member of the Committee for Regional Policy and Transport. She is Vice President of the Delegation to ACP (African Caribbean, and Pacific) countries, and of the Animal Welfare Intergroup. Dr Lucas has a professional background in research and policy analysis on trade, development and environmental issues for a major UK development agency.

Dr Janet Maughan is Research Fellow in ARIC, Manchester Metropolitan University, with a PhD in the dispersion of inorganic contaminants in the roadside environment, and consultancy experience in contaminated land and minerals application experience. She has lectured in environmental physics and has expertise in the management of noise and radiation. Currently, she is working on air quality dispersion modelling for UK airports.

Dr Mark McLellan recently established, and is a Partner in, GreenAscent, an independent consultancy and think tank, providing environmental services to the aviation industry and stakeholders. Previous to this, he was Head of Environment at London Luton Airport. He has served on the Airport Operators Association Environment Committee and Airports Council International (ACI) Europe Environmental Strategy Committee.

Dr Andreas Pastowski is Research Fellow with the Transport Division of the Wuppertal Institute for Climate, Environment and Energy. He is currently working on environmentally sustainable transport scenarios and policy instruments, particularly for aviation and freight. Andreas Pastowski has an extensive research background with German environment ministries and the Organization for Economic Cooperation and Development (OECD) and has lectured on Environmental Policy and Transport and Environment at several European Universities.

Dr David Raper is Reader in Environmental Science and Director of ARIC at Manchester Metropolitan University. His expertise relates to hydrocarbon and acidic gaseous emissions for vehicle, aircraft and fixed plant sources. Dr Raper was a lead author in the 1999 IPCC Special Report *Aviation and the Global Atmosphere*.

Beatrice Schell is Director of the European Federation for Transport and Environment (T&E), Europe's principal umbrella NGO for environmental NGOs working for sustainable transport. She is the porte-parole for the International Coalition for Sustainable Aviation, the delegation of environmental NGOs in ICAO. Beatrice represents T&E in fora that include the United Nations Framework Convention on Climate Change (UNFCCC), the OECD and the European Conference of Ministers of Transport.

Dr Hugh Somerville is Head of Environment at British Airways. He has served on the Confederation of British Industry's environment committee and has chaired environmental committees for IATA and the Association of European Airlines (AEA). He was involved in preparing the 1999 special report *Aviation and the Global Atmosphere* issued by the UN's Intergovernmental Panel on Climate Change.

Professor Callum Thomas is Professor of Sustainable Aviation in the Centre for Aviation, Transport and the Environment (CATE) at Manchester Metropolitan University and sits on a number of UK government and EU working parties. Callum Thomas has worked in the aviation industry for 15 years. His current position – Chair of Sustainable Aviation – is sponsored by Manchester Airport plc.

Dr Paul Upham is Research Associate in CATE at Manchester Metropolitan University. He previously worked with Lancashire Wildlife Trust and his PhD research for the UK National Centre for Business and Sustainability focused on the utility of the Natural Step approach to sustainability. Dr Upham's recent research relates to an environmental-and-operational strategic decision support tool for airports and his research interests focus on sustainability assessment at all levels, currently in relation to aviation.

Dr Adrian Watson is Senior Lecturer at Manchester Metropolitan University. His main research interest is in air quality management, specifically in the measurement and modelling of air quality and its impact upon human health. He is currently involved with several collaborative research projects working with local authorities and major medical research teams to assess air quality impact. He has assisted with creating public health action plans and assessing transport on air quality for the UK National Health Service.

Dr Robert Watson followed a career in freight transport before joining the Transport Studies Group at Loughborough University in 1999 as Lecturer in Logistics. His recent research has focused upon assessing the potential impact on the transport industry of impending European Union regulations that require noise mapping and noise reduction targets, and understanding the tensions that exist within integrated carriers undergoing rapid growth.

Professor John Whitelegg is leader of the Implementing Sustainability Group at the Stockholm Environment Institute, University of York. He is also Managing Director of the transport consultancy Eco-Logica. He presented evidence on sustainability and health to inquiries into Manchester Airport Runway 2, Heathrow Terminal 5 and new airports in Redhill and Finningley. He is editor of the journal *World Transport Policy and Practice*.

Preface

When, 100 years ago, the Wright Brothers undertook their first historic flight, they could no more have imagined the influence they would have on the development of humankind than did Alan Turing when he invented the world's first electronic computer in Manchester 50 years later. Today, aviation is one of the world's fastest-growing global industries. Demand for air travel is increasing due to the development of the global economy and increasing affluence. The effects of being linked to the rest of the world by a network of air routes are substantial: aviation promotes trade, inward investment, travel for leisure and education, tourism and much more. The ability of cities and regions to achieve maximum benefit from the global economy will depend, to a significant extent, upon the way in which aviation develops in the future. Indeed, along with the growth of information technology and, particularly, the Internet, the development of aviation and the global society go hand in hand.

The social and economic benefits that arise from the aviation industry can be substantial. However, the environmental and social costs of air travel are also significant and are increasing year on year. In the longer term, the continuing growth of civil aviation is unsustainable given current technologies and operating systems. Governments therefore face very major challenges in trying to meet air traffic demand in a sustainable manner.

This book considers how stakeholders, including society, governments and the aviation industry, need to respond to the issues of global climate change, aircraft noise disturbance, resource use and waste production. Moreover, it raises the issue of how a global aviation industry may develop in order to take account of both the aspirations of the developing world and the commercial demands of the developed world. One thing is clear: sustainability within the aviation industry will not be achieved through 'business as usual'.

This book has been edited and, to a large extent, produced by researchers affiliated to the Centre for Aviation, Transport and the Environment (CATE) at Manchester Metropolitan University, working with nationally and internationally recognized experts. These come from all sectors: universities, the aviation industry, the regulatory sector and environmental non-governmental organizations (NGOs). While sharing a common interest in the subject, there is only limited agreement between representatives of different sectors as to whether aviation can be made more sustainable or whether its current reliance on fossil fuels and the magnitude of its impacts will eventually limit its ability to continue to play such a broad and varied role in modern society. Sustainable development, industrial growth, climate change and globalization are all contentious issues that are subject to political debate.

The mission of CATE is to contribute to the attainment of a sustainable aviation industry through research and teaching, in partnership with stakeholders in academia, industry, government and NGOs. In this book we present a series of essays and commentaries that consider aspects of the issue of sustainability as it applies to the air transport industry. The objective has not been to produce an academic text-book in the wholly conventional sense, though the reader will find well-referenced material written by experts in their fields. Rather, the objective has been to produce a readable, informative and politically inclusive text that gives a voice to a range of opinions on the subject of sustainability and aviation, as well as providing a unique information resource. Inevitably with such an approach, there is a degree of thematic repetition among some of the pieces. Yet, what one gains in return is a sense of urgency. If authors writing from a variety of perspectives repeatedly refer to the same issues as problematic, is that not an indication that the issues require action?

We hope that this book will both educate and contribute to the debate on the environmental, social and economic implications of aviation, which are sure to feature increasingly prominently in political discussion. At the time of writing, in November 2002, the UK is entering the closing stages of its consultations on air service for a White Paper on the future of aviation. The White Paper will set a national framework for aviation for the next 30 years. *Towards Sustainable Aviation* will provide background information to not only the UK policy debate, so important nationally, but similar aviation-related debate around the world.

Paul Upham, Janet Maughan, David
Raper and Callum Thomas

Center for Aviation, Transport and
the Environment (CATE)
Manchester Metropolitan University

List of Acronyms and Abbreviations

ACI	Airports Council International
ACP	African, Caribbean and Pacific
AEA	Association of European Airlines
AEF	Aviation Environment Federation
AIDS	acquired immune deficiency syndrome
ANCAT	Committee on Abatement of Nuisance Caused by Air Transport
ANS	autonomic nervous system
APD	air passenger duty
APT	air passenger transport
APU	auxiliary power unit
ASHRAE	American Society of Heating, Refrigerating and Air-Conditioning Engineers
ATAG	Air Transport Action Group
ATC	air traffic control
ATFM	air traffic (flow) management
ATKs	available tonne kilometres
atm	atmospheres
ATM	air traffic management
ATM	air traffic movement
ATS	air traffic system
AVE	Alta Velocidad Espagñola (Spanish high-speed train)
BA	British Airways plc
BANANAS	build absolutely nothing anywhere near anybody
BOT	build, operate, transfer
BSI	British Standards Institute
BWB	blended wing body
CAA	Civil Aviation Authority (UK)
CAEP	Committee on Aviation and Environmental Protection (of ICAO)
CATE	Centre for Aviation, Transport and the Environment
CBA	cost–benefit analysis
CBI	Confederation of British Industry
CDA	continuous descent approaches
CDM	Clean Development Mechanism (Kyoto Protocol mechanism)
CEFIC	European Chemical Industry Council
CEPAA	Council on Economic Priorities Accreditation Agency
CER	corporate environmental report
CFCs	chlorofluorocarbons
CFD	computational fluid dynamics

CFMU	Central Flow Management Unit (European Airspace)
CH_4	methane
CLEAN	component validator for environmentally friendly aeroengine
CNEL	community noise equivalent level
CNS	communications, navigation and surveillance
CO	carbon monoxide
CO_2	carbon dioxide
2D	two dimensional
3D	three dimensional
DAC	double annular combustor
DB	Deutsche Bahn
dB	decibel (a unit of noise measurement scaled logarithmically to encompass the upper and lower limits of human hearing)
dB(A)	decibel noise unit (weighted with an 'A' filter to account for human hearing characteristics)
DEFRA	Department for Environment, Food and Rural Affairs (UK)
DEM	German Deutschmarks
DETR	Department of Environment, Transport and the Regions (UK) (now DEFRA)
Dp/Foo	ICAO regulatory parameter for gaseous emissions, expressed as the mass of pollutant emitted during the landing/take-off (LTO) cycle divided by the rated thrust (maximum take-off power) of the engine
DFW	Dallas/Fort Worth
DLR	Deutsches Zentrum für Luft- und Raumfahrt
DTI	Department for Trade and Industry (UK)
DTLR	Department for Transport, Local Government and the Regions (UK)
DU	Dobson Unit (a measure of ozone layer thickness; 1DU is equivalent to 0.01mm of ozone thickness at standard temperature and pressure)
DVT	deep vein thrombosis
EATMP	European Air Traffic Management Programme
EC	European Commission
ECAC	European Civil Aviation Conference (standing)
ECHR	European Court of Human Rights
ECS	environmental control systems (air conditioning etc)
Ecu	European Union currency
EEA	European Environment Agency
EEG	electroencephalography
EI	emissions index
EIA	environmental impact assessment
EIT	economies in transition
EMAS	Eco-management and Audit Scheme
EMS	environmental management system(s)
EPNdB	effective perceived noise level
EST	Environmentally Sustainable Transport (OECD programme)
EU	European Union
EURATOM	European Atomic Energy Community Treaty
FAA	Federal Aviation Administration (US)

FESG	Forecasting and Economic Analysis Sub-Group (of CAEP)
FRF	French francs
F-T	Fischer-Tropsch synthesis process
FTKs	freight tonne kilometres
FUA	flexible use of airspace
GCM	global climate model
GDP	gross domestic product
Gg	giga grams
GHG	greenhouse gas
GIS	geographic information system(s)
GNP	gross national product
GRI	Global Reporting Initiative
g/s/km	grams per second per kilometre
GWP	global warming potential
ha	hectare
HCs	hydrocarbons
HEPA	high-efficiency particulate air (filter)
HSE	Health, Safety and Environmental
HIC	high-income country
H_2O	water vapour
HO_2	hydroperoxy radical
HPA	hypothalamic pituitary adrenal
HSCT	high-speed civil transport
HSR	high-speed rail
IAS	International Accounting Standards
IASC	International Accounting Standards Committee
IATA	International Air Transport Association
ICAO	International Civil Aviation Organization (UN)
ICE	Intercity Express
ICR	inter-cooled recuperative cycle
ICRP	International Commission on Radiation Protection
ICSA	International Coalition for Sustainable Aviation
IISD	International Institute for Sustainable Development
IPCC	Intergovernmental Panel on Climate Change (UN)
IPPR	Institute for Public Policy Research (UK)
ISEA	Institute of Social and Ethical AccountAbility
ISO	International Standards Organization
JI	joint implementation (Kyoto Protocol mechanism)
JIT	just-in-time freight operations
JPY	Japanese yen
km/h	kilometres per hour
kwh/s-km	kilowatt hours per second-kilometre
LCA	life-cycle analysis
LEAD	Leadership for Environment and Development
Leq	equivalent sound level (long-term average noise exposure)
L/D	lift to drag ratio
LIC	low-income country

L*max*	maximum (A-weighted) sound level
LTO	landing and take-off
mSv y^{-1}	milli-Sieverts per year
μSV h^{-1}	micro-Sieverts per hour
MAGLEV	magnetic levitation transport system
MEA	More Electric Aircraft
MECU/km	million Ecus per kilometre
MEE	More Electric Engine
MEP	Member of the European Parliament
MIC	medium-income country
mppa	million passengers per annum
mu	micrometre (also called a micron and μ) (a millionth of a metre – 10^{-6}m)
N_2O	nitrous oxide
NAFC	North Atlantic Flight Corridor
NAFTA	North American Free Trade Area
NASA	National Aeronautics and Space Administration
NIMBY	not in my backyard
NLG	Netherlands guilder
NO	nitric oxide
NO_2	nitrogen dioxide
NGO	non-governmental organization
nm	nautical mile
NMHCs	non-methane hydrocarbons
NMVOC	non-methane volatile organic compound
NO_x	nitrogen oxide (the sum of $NO + NO_2$)
O	oxygen
O_3	ozone
O/D	origin/destination
OECD	Organization for Economic Cooperation and Development
OEF	Oxford Economic Forecasting
OEW	operating empty weight
OH	hydroxyl radical
OPR	overall pressure ratio
OTB	Research Institute for Housing, Urban and Mobility Studies (Delft, the Netherlands)
PM_{10}	particulate matter, with a mass median aerodynamic diameter of less than 10 micrometers
ppb	parts per billion
ppmv	parts per million by volume
ppt	parts per trillion
PSCs	polar stratospheric clouds
PSZ	public safety zone
R&D	research and development
RAIN	Reduction of Airframe and Installation Noise (a 50 per cent EC Framework 4-funded programme, completed April 2001)
RAT	Ram Air Turbine (air-driven backup pump for an aircraft hydraulic system)

RCEP	Royal Commission on Environmental Pollution (UK)
RESOUND	Reduction of Engine Source Noise through Understanding and Novel Design (a 50 per cent EC-funded research programme completed December 2000)
RNAV	area navigation
RPKs	revenue passenger kilometres
RR	relative risk
RTKs	revenue tonne kilometres
RVSM	reduced vertical separation minimum
SAD	surface aerosol density
SASS	Subsonic Assessment Programme (of NASA)
SBAC	Society of British Aerospace Companies
SBSTA	Subsidiary Body on Scientific and Technological Advice (UNFCCC)
SEA	strategic environmental assessment
SEL	sound exposure level (instantaneous peak)
SERAS	South-Eastern and East of England Regional Air Service Study
SILENCER	Significantly Lower Community Exposure to Aircraft Noise (due to start April 2001 and run for four years)
SMART	specific, measurable, achievable, realistic and time-bound targets
SNCF	French Railway
SNS	sympathetic nervous system
SO_2	sulphur dioxide
SPM–TAR	summary for policy-makers of the IPCC third assessment report
SRI	Strategic Resources Institute
SST	supersonic transport (aircraft)
T5	Heathrow's Terminal 5
TB	tuberculosis
T&E	European Federation for Transport and Environment
TENs	trans-European transport networks
TERM	Transport and Environment Reporting Mechanism
TET	turbine entry temperature
Tg	teragrams (10^6 tonnes)
TGV	Train à Grande Vitesse (High Speed Train)
TKP	tonne kilometres performed
TMA	terminal area (in air traffic management)
TRM	trans-rapid MAGLEV
TurboNoise	turbomachinery noise source CFD models for low-noise CFD aircraft designs (due for completion in February 2003)
UHCs	unburned hydrocarbons
UN	United Nations
UNCED	United Nations Conference on Environment and Development
UNEP	United Nations Environment Programme
UNFCCC	United Nations Framework Convention on Climate Change
USEPA	US Environmental Protection Agency
US GAO	United States General Audit Office
UV	ultra-violet radiation
UV-B	ultra-violet radiation of 0.29–0.32 micrometres wave length

VFR	visiting friends and relatives
VOC	volatile organic compound
WBCSD	World Business Council for Sustainable Development
WHO	World Health Organization
WRI	World Resources Institute
ZAR	South African rand

Part 1

Trends and Issues

Chapter 1

Introduction: perspectives on sustainability and aviation

Paul Upham

STRUCTURE OF THE BOOK

Towards Sustainable Aviation discusses notable trends and issues relating to sustainability and aviation from a variety of academic, industrial and political perspectives. The book is split into three parts. Part 1 is authored by UK academics involved in researching different aspects of the aviation industry. It sets out the main contemporary environmental, social and economic issues associated with aviation. Part 2, with a broader range of authors, describes some approaches to mitigating and reducing aviation–environment problems. Part 3 addresses the contentious nature of aviation growth. Where Parts 1 and 2 provide relatively extended comment on aviation and sustainability, Part 3 allows commentators from a range of sectors and perspectives to express their opinions more succinctly. In this way, we hope that readers will understand more, not only of some of the problems of aviation, together with some of the latest thinking on associated mitigations and perhaps even solutions, but also of the disparate opinion on the subject. By including the views of the industry and of representative non-governmental organizations (NGOs), we aim to have been as inclusive of the range of opinion as is reasonably possible. The remainder of this introductory chapter sets the scene by considering the implications for aviation of differing approaches to sustainability and to the regulation of aviation impacts.

THE SIGNIFICANCE OF AVIATION

During the course of the 20th century, air transport has become one of the world's most influential industries. Aviation is a major direct and indirect employer – it facilitates the expansion of world trade and provides opportunities for travel and tourism.

Few people would want a world without the possibility of air travel. While this is an unlikely prospect, a world of unlimited air travel is likely to be equally unacceptable. At issue is not whether or not there should be aviation, but at what point for different regions and nations the disadvantages of additional air capacity outweigh the advantages. How sufficiency should be determined in this context and who should determine it are also key issues.

In 1999, following a request from the United Nations (UN) International Civil Aviation Organization (ICAO) and the parties to the Montreal Protocol on Substances that Deplete the Ozone Layer, the UN Intergovernmental Panel on Climate Change (IPCC) published an important report on the atmospheric impacts of aviation (IPCC, 1999). The IPCC noted that aviation has experienced rapid expansion as the world economy has grown (IPCC, 1999). Passenger traffic (expressed as revenue passenger-kilometres) has grown since 1960 at nearly 9 per cent per year, 2.4 times the global average gross domestic product (GDP) growth rate. Freight traffic, approximately 80 per cent of which is carried by passenger aircraft, has also grown over the same time period. Although the rate of growth of passenger traffic has slowed to about 5 per cent in 1997 as the industry is maturing in some parts of the world, growth rates of 5 per cent per year are expected to continue for the next 10 to 15 years (IPCC, 1999).

As the GDP of a country increases, there tends to be a shift towards faster modes of passenger transportation (Schafer and Victor, in Clarke, 2001, p2). In the US, with no large-scale passenger rail infrastructure and little political will to construct infrastructure for high-speed rail, aviation is likely to continue to be the primary high-speed transportation mode for the foreseeable future (Clarke, 2001, p2). In smaller island states scattered throughout Asia, where the centres of commerce and trade are separated by stretches of ocean, aviation offers a means of transportation that is significantly faster than marine ship. Similarly, in Africa and South America, aviation offers a means of high-speed transportation that is independent of terrain for linking centres of commerce and trade. Similar comments might be made of China, the aviation market of which Boeing expects to grow at twice the average rate over the next 20 years (Anon, 2000). In general, then, as most economies develop and the GDP of these economies increase, there is likely to be increased passenger air transportation (Clarke, 2001, p2). This conclusion is supported by a second study that indicates that the travel growth for a country averages 1.7 per cent above the forecasts for economic growth as measured by the GDP (Anon, 2000).

The environmental consequences of contemporary aviation are significant. Of particular note at the global scale is the contribution of aviation to global climate change. Although global aviation emissions of carbon dioxide (CO_2) are a small percentage of carbon emissions worldwide, they are still roughly equivalent to the carbon emissions of industrialized countries such as Canada and the UK (US GAO, 2000). More locally, aircraft and airport operations generate noise from take-off and landings, engine testing, surface transport and construction, so that noise is widely considered to be one of the most serious environmental problems of aviation. Although perception of noise is subjective, it can contribute to sleep disturbance problems and other related physiological and psychological effects (Morrell et al, 1997; Bullinger et al, 1999). Other airport-related environmental issues include contaminated land, ground and surface water at airports arising from jet fuels, aircraft de-icing operations

(Turnbull and Bevan, 1995), waste generation and land take. Moreover, in the UK increases in the emissions of surface transport to airports may contribute to exceeding statutory air quality standards (Maughan and Raper, 2000). Several European airports already apply charges to aircraft gaseous emissions as a means of influencing air quality and noise impacts.

DISTINGUISHING ECO-EFFICIENCY AND SUSTAINABILITY

In the UK, a government (pre-legislative) White Paper on air transport aims to establish a framework that will ensure that the long-term development of aviation in the UK is sustainable (DETR, 2000a). This book covers two aspects of the associated debate. On one hand are themes of environmental efficiency and mitigation, in the sense of reducing environmental impact per unit of business performance – the latter, in this case, primarily being the number of people transported by air (though different parts of the aviation industry have differing, if related, business priorities). It is on this side of the debate that there is most common ground among the different constituents of the aviation industry, its consultants, regulators and NGOs. At the most general level, this side of the debate concerns 'doing more with less' (DETR, 1999) and echoes the injunctions for materials and energy efficiency of Factor 4 and beyond by von Weizsäcker et al (1998). Related to this are arguments for a more service-based, closed-loop economy motivated by capitalist ethics, exemplified in the natural capitalism espoused by Hawken et al (2000) and forming part of the rhetoric and substance of the Natural Step message (Robèrt et al, 1997; Natrass and Altomare, 1999).

Mitigation of the types of local environmental impact discussed by Callum Thomas and Martin Lever in Chapter 6 and the health impacts of aviation discussed by Ken Hume and Adrian Watson in Chapter 4 – impacts which form the most obvious downside of the socio-economic benefits discussed by Robert Caves in Chapter 3 – are likely to involve relatively consensual, site-specific enhancements of environmental efficiency. Reductions or stasis in the ambient noise around an airport, for example, may obviously be achieved through quieter aircraft. Technological advances may obviate the much more contentious option of fewer aircraft. If the number of aircraft rises – as it has generally – but noise is constant or reduced, this constitutes an environmental efficiency gain in terms of the specific indicator of near-airport noise. Many of the chapters and some of the commentaries in the book refer to environmental efficiency or mitigation of such localized impacts near or at airports: for example, Chapters 4 and 6 referred to above, the commentary on potential efficiency improvements to air traffic management by Arthur Lieuwen and Ted Elliff of EUROCONTROL in Chapter 12, the commentary on airline initiatives by Hugh Somerville in Chapter 12, and Chapter 9 on air freight and the implications of just-in-time logistics by David Gillingwater, Ian Humphreys and Robert Watson. Similarly, corporate environmental management as discussed in Chapter 7 by Paul Hooper, Bridget Heath and Janet Maughan is likely to lead to reductions in materials usage and waste production per unit of business output at an airport site or with respect to an airline's corporate boundary.

On the other hand is the issue of sustainability, the meaning and implications of which are intellectually and physically contested. Eco-efficiency and mitigation are relatively straightforward to observe with respect to an aspect of the environmental quality of a site (eg ambient noise near an airport), a single input (eg fuel) or a unit of business output (eg passengers entering a terminal). Moreover, pursuit of eco-efficiency does not imply a constraint on growth in the scale of an activity. Eco-efficiency is a win–win activity for corporate growth and 'the environment' if that environment is defined in only a few terms or with a narrow geographic focus.

Strictly defined, however, indicating environmental sustainability requires assessment of product and service life cycles, linked to protocols for allocating consumption and emission quotas (Upham, 2001). Only if such protocols exist for relating discrete activity to environmental systems can one reliably assess the sustainability of a sector, industry, business or other organization. In the absence of these, all that can be said is that an organization is increasing or reducing its environmental sustainability (Upham, 2001).

Drawing on ecological economic ideas (Georgescu-Roegen, 1971; Daly, 1977, 1992), early work on life-cycle analysis (Schmidt-Bleek, 1993) and an understanding of the Natural Step approach to sustainability (Upham, 2000a), a precautious approach to assessing environmental sustainability via measuring the flows of masses mobilized by the human economy through the biosphere implies that growth in the physical scale of aviation will generally entail movement *away* from conditions of environmental sustainability.

The adverse environmental impacts implicit in this general rule can be postponed to the extent that there are conventional materials and fuel efficiency savings through the entire life cycles of production and service processes supportive of aviation. At some point, however, the additional material (including fuel) needed to support growth would literally outweigh that saved by material efficiency, such that adverse impact would, in general, begin to rise again. Alternatively, the impact of growth could be reduced if it involved the replacement of mined and subsequently synthesized materials and fuels with use of biomass and renewable energy in such a way as to maintain or enhance vegetative soil cover and, preferably, biodiversity. Again, this replacement would need to be through the life cycles of production and service processes supportive of aviation (Upham, 2001).

Either way, it is the sheer scale of aviation growth – outlined in Chapter 2 by Ian Humphreys – that justifies special attention to its environmental impacts. In wider terms, the European Environment Agency (EEA) has drawn attention to the way in which the persistence of key environmental problems are a consequence of the overall scale of resource use (EEA, 2001a,b). These problems include global warming as discussed by David Lee and David Raper in Chapter 5. The EEA is of the view that if environmental and sustainability aims and targets, such as those proposed in the European Union's Sixth Environment Action Programme, are to be reached, higher efficiencies in the use of materials and energy will be necessary (EEA, 2001a,b). The precautious approach to environmental sustainability discussed above requires that those efficiencies must be achieved through the life cycles of a wide range of products and services, and that growth in material usage necessary for growth in the physical economy should not exceed efficiency gains.

More concretely, it implies that the environmental benefits of some of the mitigations and potential solutions to aviation impacts discussed in Part 2 of the book will, at some point, be offset by growth. This is also the case for modal substitution (see Chapter 8 by Milan Janic), and for aircraft and engine technology improvements (see Jacquetta Lee in Chapter 10).

Only one chapter in Part 2 (Chapter 11 by Andreas Pastowski) positively addresses the contentious issue of planning and policy instruments that could, in principle, place upper limits on aggregate levels of particular impact types, rather than, for example, per-aircraft engine emission certification standards applied by the UN International Civil Aviation Organization (ICAO) under Volume II of Annex 16 to the 1944 Convention on International Civil Aviation. Thus, greenhouse gas control policies, for example, could, in principle, be used to control the scale of a nation's aviation sector by placing an upper cap on tradeable CO_2 emissions permits. This said, both commentators and practitioners are well aware of the potential for aircraft noise emissions to limit aviation growth (see, in particular, Joop Krul's reference to Schiphol Airport's extrapolations in Chapter 12). Explicit advocation of limits to growth is left to commentators in the political sector (see several of the other commentaries in Chapter 12).

WIDER VIEWS OF SUSTAINABILITY

In terms of the criteria above, growth in contemporary aviation cannot but be unsustainable, and the same could be said of other transport sectors – indeed, of most economic sectors. Yet, the general term 'sustainability' clearly means different things to different people at the level of both principle and detail, and it is at the level of detail that consensus on its meaning is hardest to maintain (Upham, 2000b). This can be illustrated by comparing the application of the Organization for Economic Cooperation and Development's (OECD's) sustainability principles in Box 1.1 (OECD, 2001) to key components of contemporary aviation systems requiring manufacture and operation (see Figure 1.1), the application of UK government sustainability objectives (DETR, 1999).

The OECD principles selected are not unusual. They bear considerable similarity to the common elements of other environmental sustainability principles reviewed by Upham (2000b), which are:

- Waste emissions are within the absorptive capacity of the receiving media.
- Use of renewable resources is within self-regeneration capacity.
- Intra-generational equity is accounted for.

Alternatively phrased, the OECD principles effectively supplement these core principles with a substitutability element, such that they resemble Daly's seminal ecological economic sustainability principles (see, for example, Goodland and Daly, 1996). The following sections discuss aviation in relation to the OECD (2001) sustainability principles.

Box 1.1 *Sustainability criteria in the OECD's* Environmental Strategy for the First Decade of the 21st Century

I REGENERATION

Renewable resources shall be used efficiently and their use shall not be permitted to exceed their long-term rates of natural regeneration.

II SUBSTITUTABILITY

Non-renewable resources shall be used efficiently and their use limited to levels which can be offset by substitution by renewable resources or other forms of capital.

III ASSIMILATION

Releases of hazardous or polluting substances to the environment shall not exceed its assimilative capacity; concentrations shall be kept below established critical levels necessary for the protection of human health and the environment. When assimilative capacity is effectively zero (eg for hazardous substances that are persistent and/or bio-accumulative), effectively a zero release of such substances is required to avoid their accumulation in the environment.

IV AVOIDING IRREVERSIBILITY

Irreversible adverse effects of human activities on ecosystems and on biogeochemical and hydrological cycles shall be avoided. The natural processes capable of maintaining or restoring the integrity of ecosystems should be safeguarded from adverse impacts of human activities. The differing levels of resilience and carrying capacity of ecosystems must be considered in order to conserve their populations of threatened, endangered and critical species.

Source: OECD, 2001, p6

OECD sustainability principle I (renewables)

As part of an aviation system, aircraft are only one of a wide range of static and mobile infrastructure required to support passenger and freight air transport (see Figure 1.1). Each item of infrastructure requires manufacture and operation, entailing resource use and waste. With regard to OECD principle I, it is unlikely that significant use is being made of renewable resources except for foodstuffs.

OECD sustainability principle II (substitutes)

The most obvious and perhaps important violation of principle II (development of substitutes) in aviation – as in most economic sectors – is fossil fuel consumption. Discussing the implications for transport of a declining oil supply, Fleay (1999) refers to *The World's Oil Supply 1930–2050* by Campbell and Laherrere (1995), based on performance data from thousands of oil fields in 65 countries. Campbell and Laherrere concluded that the mid-point of ultimate conventional oil production would be reached by year 2000 and that decline would soon begin. They expected production post-peak would halve about every 25 years, an exponential decline of 2.5 to 2.9 per

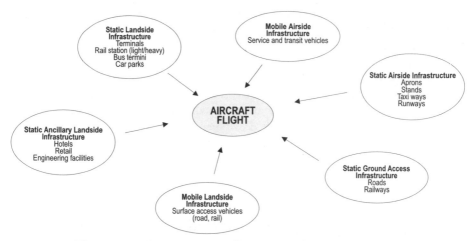

Figure 1.1 *Key components of a contemporary aviation system*

cent per annum (Campbell and Laherrere 1995, pp19, 27, in Fleay, 1999, p9). By 2050, Fleay (1999) expects the hydrocarbon era to be effectively finished. Whether one considers this an underestimation of technological capability or of medium-term significance for aviation (particularly given long research and development (R&D) lead times) will depend upon one's world-view. Either way, there is no obvious demand by airlines for the development of kerosene substitutes, despite the feasibility of biomass-derived fuel referred to in Chapter 10.

OECD sustainability principle III (assimilation)

The third OECD principle requires that assimilation rates in pollutant-receiving media are not exceeded. Although contingent on the effectiveness of environmental regulators, airports are likely to already be indirectly subject to emissions limits to air, water and land that are, at least in part, assimilation based. In Europe this would be via European Commission (EC) Directive 96/61/EC on integrated pollution prevention and control (EC, 1996). However, such regulation tends to be partial in its scope. Most notably, the quantity of CO_2 emissions at altitude are not regulated, despite anthropogenic climate change and rising atmospheric CO_2 levels (IPCC, 1999), indicating that the assimilation capacity of the climate system has been exceeded.

OECD sustainability principle IV (reversibility)

The fourth OECD principle requires that reversible adverse effects of human activities on ecosystems and on biogeochemical and hydrological cycles are avoided. Use of this principle as a decision-making criterion is complicated by issues of practicality and the way in which the large-scale climate system and related cycles (carbon, nitrogen, sulphur, metals) are not straightforward to relate to nations, let alone to individual businesses or sectors.

Regarding practicality, although land occupied by and for built aviation infrastructure may be reclaimable, it is lost to vegetative growth – and hence a role in environmental cycles – for many generations. Whether or not this loss should be

considered reversible depends upon the time period over which one considers revers-
ibility should be assessed, and whether the capital and labour will exist in future to
reclaim the land.

While there will be some adverse effect on large-scale environmental systems,
waiting for posited thresholds of irreversibility would be neither precautious nor
wise. Yet land-take for built infrastructure continues across economic sectors, of which
aviation is, of course, only one among many. It is this growth in the *scale* of the human
economy that has long been identified as potentially problematic environmentally
(Daly, 1977, 1992), and which regulators may now also be identifying as a key cause
of continuing environmental problems (EEA, 2001a, 2001b). At the heart of environmental and sustainability debate are differences in perception and response to
this growth in economic scale.

UK government sustainability objectives

Use of an even wider set of sustainability principles complicates the decision process
and makes the opportunity for disagreement more explicit. The UK government, for
example, has defined four broad objectives of sustainable development that it considers should be met at the same time, in the UK and the world as a whole (DETR,
1999):

- social progress that recognizes the needs of everyone;
- effective protection of the environment;
- prudent use of natural resources; and
- maintenance of high and stable levels of economic growth and employment.

These objectives are patently much broader in scope than the environmentally focused
OECD principles discussed above. Most importantly, they are neither necessarily
commensurate or compatible. In the first case, they are different in nature, and in
the second they are interrelated in such a way that the advancement of one is possible at the expense of another. In particular, inclusive social progress, environmental
protection and prudent use of natural resources may not only be sacrificed to high
and stable levels of economic growth and employment, but the latter may actually
require that sacrifice to the extent that material usage and inequity are not de-linked
from GDP growth. Perhaps a more critical issue is the extent to which high and stable levels of employment require continuously high levels of economic growth as a
result of productivity increases (Fleming, 1996). It is arguably the competitive drive
for the latter at a corporate and national level that is fuelling growth in environmental impact.

The ATAG/INFRAS approach to sustainable aviation

While aviation could be considered in terms of further sets of sustainability principles,
there is a particular study that merits reference here, namely the report *Sustainable
Aviation* by INFRAS (2000) for the Air Transport Action Group (ATAG). ATAG is
an industry lobby group and *Sustainable Aviation* is a collation and analysis of some
of the evidence that one might consider when relating sustainability to aviation.

Notably, INFRAS sees sustainability as an industry-friendly discourse:

> *Since the debate on aviation is very much environmentally dominated, the analysis of sustainable aviation allows a wider approach and will add some important arguments for the industry* (INFRAS, 2000, p1).

However, despite posing the central question: 'Is air transport sustainable?' (INFRAS, 2000, p7), the report does not answer the question directly, but rather judges that aviation compares reasonably well with other transport modes per revenue kilometre travelled (INFRAS, 2000, pp17–18).

In order to reach this assessment, the report first assumes that there are three main dimensions of sustainability – economic, social and environmental – as is usual. INFRAS then states that it will use the approach to sustainability assessment taken by the EEA's Transport and Environment Reporting Mechanism (TERM) project (EEA, 1999), which it understands to be an identification of the characteristics of the aviation sector in terms of (INFRAS, 2000, p4):

- global, regional and local impacts (economic, social and environmental);
- growth dynamics of the industry;
- uncertainties: economic, environmental and social;
- degree of intermodality of the industry;
- quality aspects and market segmentation.

From these, INFRAS (2000, pp10–11) infers further criteria and indicators, as outlined below.

Economic criteria

- Job creation and growth contribution (local, regional, global): labour per unit of output, multiplier effects in regard to income and job creation per unit of air transport.
- Access and travel time and speed (regional, global): improvement of accessibility between destinations, congestion and delays.
- Productivity (global): development of unit costs and unit prices respectively.
- Market distortions (regional, global): performance of the air transport sector with respect to liberalized market conditions.
- Cost recovery of (financially relevant) infrastructure costs (local, regional).

Social criteria

- Safety (regional, global): number of accidents, deaths per year and per unit of transport.
- Accessibility of remote areas (regional): number of flights between capitals and provinces within countries with low transport supply (eg Africa).
- Participation: local participation procedures in enlargement of airports, involvement of environmental groups, land-use planning procedures, etc.

- National participation procedures – notably, the involvement of the public within legal decisions – and international participation procedures – notably, access for NGOs within international decision-making fora.

Environmental criteria

The most important aspects are seen as:

- energy efficiency and climate change (global): CO_2 and nitrogen oxides (NO_x) emissions and other radiative-forcing substances;
- noise (local): noise nuisances in the surroundings of airports;
- air pollution (local): NO_x, volatile organic compound (VOC) and particulate matter (PM_{10}) emissions in the surroundings of airports;
- land use (local, regional): sealed surface area of airports.

Comment

The main issue to raise regarding INFRAS's approach is that it is not referenced to critical environmental thresholds, as TERM suggests should be done (EEA, 1999, p20). Whether or not aviation is performing reasonably in comparison with other transport modes is not the most important issue (nor is it satisfactorily evidenced in the INFRAS study in terms of environmental impact, since this requires comparison via life-cycle analysis). Comparative assessment can inform decision-making in relation to existing transport modes. For example, it can help policy-makers decide whether the environmental burden of aviation is unreasonably high in relative terms, particularly whether other transport modes should be preferred whenever possible. It is insufficient, however, when one or more aviation-related environmental impacts are considered to be already excessive – that is, when one or more absolute impacts need curbing. This is the case for aircraft noise in the view of many of those who experience severe aircraft noise. Moreover, it is the case for greenhouse gases emitted by the human economy as a whole (IPCC, 2001), including other transport modes dependent upon fossil fuels.

When total economic impacts are excessive, it is necessary to know not only how transport modes compare, but how best to reduce total impacts absolutely. Important issues therefore include identification of which sectors should be given which reduction targets. Since transportation is a means to an end and has significant greenhouse gas emissions growth rates, it would not be unreasonable to attempt major emissions reductions within the transport sector, and it would be difficult to justify the excuse of aviation as a case deserving special exemption.

IMPLICATIONS FOR DECISION-MAKING

The clash of differing views on economy and environment gives rise to policy and planning conflicts. This, in turn, raises the issue of how regulators should deal with the conflicts inherent in broad conceptions of sustainability and between the actual values of individuals. While complete resolution of conflicts relating to sustainability and aviation will rarely be possible, different procedural approaches to their management will influence the value and nature of the outcome in any given case.

Box 1.2 Selected questions in the UK government's consultation on
The Future of Aviation

GENERAL

How should the government ensure that aviation meets the external environmental costs for which it is responsible? Should greater emphasis be placed on regulation (at global, national or local level), economic instruments or voluntary agreements? If we should use a mix of approaches, what are the principles that should underlie the choice of approach for each issue?

ENVIRONMENTAL EFFECTS

Is a balance between mitigation and compensation the best approach for local impacts? Are there further steps the government could take to mitigate the environmental effects of aviation?

AIRPORT PLANNING

Could the concept of environmental capacity limits be applied successfully to UK airports? How would limits be set? Would these be alongside or instead of limits on passenger throughput?

Should the government encourage a system of voluntary environmental agreements between airports, airport users and local interests, which could provide an agreed framework for development and complement the statutory role of the planning system?

How should people best be compensated for the environmental impact of airports on their local area? Should the government encourage greater use of voluntary arrangements to compensate for, or mitigate the effects of, significant airport development?

Source: DETR, 2000a

Monetarization of environmental costs

Different options for procedures and outcomes are implicit in Box 1.2, which lists several of the UK government's consultative questions on the future of aviation (DETR, 2000a), mostly relating to airports. The government's first question in Box 1.2 implies decision-making on the basis of monetarized costs and benefits as a means of informing decisions on the extent and distribution of UK air traffic. As the government states:

> *Under the polluter pays principle, external costs should be reflected in costs incurred by the aviation industry, so that (in an ideal world) it fully meets its external costs* (DETR, 2000b, p3).

The government briefly reviews some of the literature on monetarization of noise, air quality and climate change impacts and considers the implications for aviation (DETR, 2000b). However, it explicitly declines to endorse any of the valuations, and refers to the way in which its appraisal framework for managing demand in the south-east of England (DETR, 2000c) uses physical as well as monetary indicators (DETR,

2000c). In fact, the environmental indicators used in the latter appraisal are non-monetary (DETR, 2000c, pp20–24): there is no attempt to reduce the various consequences of capacity expansion at different sites to the single measurement term.

There are good reasons for the government to be cautious about relying heavily on monetarization of environmental impacts for aviation and other policy domains. The main disadvantage of monetarizing non-marketed phenomena for cost–benefit analysis (CBA) is that such monetarization is not only highly contentious, but is particularly inappropriate in the case of irreplaceable environmental systems (Daly and Cobb, 1989). Use of surrogate market values (such as the damage cost approach, which uses the market cost of repairing environmental damage as an indicator of the full cost of that damage) may legitimately inform policy. However, neither this nor monetarized measures of the willingness to pay to avoid or accept damage are appropriate for valuation of systems that people cannot live well without. Relative climate stability is such a system, and the same principle applies to particular levels of local environmental quality, such as a healthy level of air quality and a quiet environment.

Although the attraction of extended CBA as a decision-making method is understood, it is not a reliable means of policy-making and the method should, at best, inform not determine policy. A healthy environment should arguably be sought for its own sake and for the benefits this brings, not on the condition that its monetarized benefits exceed monetarized costs. Environmental policy objectives should arguably continue to be informed by the values of the electorate, environmental science, technological capability and regulator judgement. While this is imprecise and is subject to political lobbying, as a variant on the traditional approach to policy-making it remains preferable to risking further damage by underestimating the value of critical environmental systems in valuation surveys.

Critical thresholds and environmental targets

Although environmental regulation of individual businesses is not informed simply by environmental science, knowledge of the environmental and human effects of different exposure levels typically plays an important role. However, relating climate change to individual businesses requires that targets are set in a way that avoids exceeding the critical threshold of the total climate system, not of administratively determined sections of water, land or air (Upham, 2001). As a result, there is a need for intra-national political negotiation on meeting national climate change targets that will facilitate stabilization of global atmospheric CO_2 concentrations at a maximum of 550 parts per million by volume (ppmv) (RCEP, 2000).

Instead of relying on CBA, governments need to consider the policy instruments referred to in subsequent chapters, particularly those in Chapter 11 for controlling greenhouse gases. The objective should be to meet national environmental quality standards and international treaty obligations, particularly those made at in Kyoto in 1997. Thereafter, concerted effort needs to be made to meet the minimum 60 per cent greenhouse gas reduction target of the UK's Royal Commission on Environmental Pollution (RCEP) (2000), relative to the global emissions level of 1990.

This is advocated with awareness of the magnitude of the political task. In the view of the RCEP, a standing advisory body to the UK government, 'an effective, enduring and equitable climate protocol will eventually require emission quotas to be allocated to nations on a simple and equal per capita basis' (RCEP, 2000, p56). In this scenario, national emission quotas would follow a contraction and convergence trajectory, with each nation's allocation gradually shifting from its current level of emissions towards a level set on a uniform per-capita basis (RCEP, 2000, p57). Quite what this would mean for airlines and airports has yet to be determined. For governments committed to stabilizing anthropogenic influence on climate change, the outcome for aviation will be particularly influenced by societal priorities for fossil fuel use and rates of technological change.

Local participation: airports

To date, no government has yet sought to reduce the volume of air traffic for reasons of avoiding anthropogenic influence on climate change. Rather, the emphasis has been on managing the local impacts of rising air traffic, particularly aircraft noise and – to a lesser extent – particular gaseous emissions. Accompanying the increase in traffic has been commercial pressure for, and the actuality of, providing new airports and associated infrastructure. Whether or not infrastructure or additional traffic are welcomed by people living near airports is likely to depend upon a range of factors, particularly the degree of local economic need for increased business activity.

In Europe, participation and consultation on expansion plans for major airport infrastructure is already required under European Commission (EC) environmental impact assessment law (EC, 1997). Yet development consultation can often be a cursory and unsatisfactory affair for affected residents. How better to strike the balance between commercial aviation interests, government aviation policy and local residents needs to be resolved, though some suggestions are outlined by Robert Caves in Chapter 3. Whatever solutions are devised, satisfactory ingredients are likely to include enforceable upper limits on environmental and operational factors and compensation for lost amenity, within a context of an explicit national policy for airport and air traffic distribution.

CONCLUSION

Whether or not one considers aviation trends to be sustainable depends, of course, upon one's definition of sustainability. The more environmentally precautious approaches to sustainability suggest that aviation, in common with other fossil-fuelled activity, is moving in an unsustainable direction due to absolute increases in environmental consumption and emissions. In the short to medium term, the degree to which sustainability poses a challenge for aviation will depend largely upon the ways in which electorates and policy-makers react to the noise impacts of increasing air traffic, remembering that this increase has historically been conditional on GDP growth.

In the longer term, increased frequency of more energetic weather events may lead to stricter control of carbon emissions across economies. Yet this in itself may not require an end to even kerosene-fuelled aviation growth. An internationally equitable contract and convergence trajectory for greenhouse gases would have different implications for different countries, with some countries more free to expand their aviation sector than others. Moreover, it may prove easier and more important to achieve low-carbon surface transport, industrial and energy sectors than a low-carbon aviation sector, given the technologies and relative carbon emissions involved.[1] Savings achieved in surface and energy sectors might, in principle, allow aviation to grow. That this would create a breathing space for aviation should not, however, lead to complacency with respect to carbon emissions. The scenario of ongoing aviation growth in a context of low-carbon economies presupposes that those forms of economy are actively developed. It also presupposes community protection from undue noise. Both conditions are far from being met.

The remainder of the book describes the relationship of contemporary aviation to its environmental impacts. It then considers some of the policy (and engineering) issues that may prove increasingly significant in the future. The book concludes by providing a forum for different commentators to put forward summaries of their own views on sustainability and aviation, and by suggesting directions for further research.

The text provides observers with an (admittedly somewhat Eurocentric) overview of the main issues in the sustainability and aviation debate, together with selected opinion. Our hope is that the book will go beyond this, to stimulate further research and action that shapes aviation and related transport policy in directions that are not just economically profitable and socially equitable, but are consistent with the sustenance of critical environmental systems.

NOTES

1   US GAO (2000, p14) reports that US Environmental Protection Agency figures for 1997 show greenhouse gas emissions from US aviation to have accounted for about 3 per cent of the total US greenhouse gas emissions from human sources, while the remainder of the transportation sector accounted for approximately 23 per cent. Passenger cars and light-duty trucks were responsible for well over half of the latter. Other industrial sectors accounted for approximately 41 per cent of the total US greenhouse gases from human sources, and other miscellaneous sources accounted for the remaining 33 per cent. It should be noted that while aviation carbon emissions similarly constitute 'only' some 3 per cent of the global total, this is equivalent to the carbon emissions of a country with an industrial economy the size of the UK or Canada (US GAO, 2000).

REFERENCES

Anon (2000) The Boeing Company, *Current Market Outlook*, available at www.boeing.com/commercial/cmo/index.html

Bullinger, M Hygge, S and Evans, G W (1999) 'The Psychological Cost of Aircraft Noise for Children', *Zentralblatt Für Hygiene Und Umweltmedizin*, vol 202(2–4), pp127–138

Campbell, C J and Laherrere, J H (1995) *The World's Oil Supply 1930–2050*, vol 1, Petroconsultants S A, Geneva

Clarke, J P (2001) 'The Role of Advanced Air Traffic Management in Reducing the Impact of Aircraft Noise and Enabling Aviation Growth', *Proceedings of the 1st SCAN UK International Conference – Environmental Capacity at Airports*, 2–3 April 2001, UK Sustainable Cities and Aviation Network, ARIC, Manchester Metropolitan University, Manchester, available at www.scan-uk.mmu.ac.uk

Daly, H E (1977; 1992) *Steady-State Economics*, Earthscan, London

Daly, H and Cobb, J (1989) *For the Common Good: Redirecting the Economy Toward Community, the Environment, and a Sustainable Future*, Beacon Press, Boston

DETR (1999) *A Better Quality of Life: A Strategy for Sustainable Development for the United Kingdom*, Department of the Environment, Transport and the Regions, Cm 4345, HMSO, London, available in full at www.environment.detr.gov.uk/sustainable/quality/life/index.htm and in brief summary at www.environment.detr.gov.uk/sustainable/consult2/index.htm

DETR (2000a) *The Future of Aviation. The Government's Consultation Document on Air Transport Policy*, Department of the Environment, Transport and the Regions, HMSO, London, available at www.aviation.detr.gov.uk/consult/future/index.htm

DETR (2000b) *Valuing the External Costs of Aviation*, Department of the Environment, Transport and the Regions, London

DETR (2000c) *Appraisal Framework for Airports in the South East and Eastern Regions of England: A Consultation Paper*, HMSO, London

EC (1996) 'Council Directive 96/61/EC of 24 September 1996 Concerning Integrated Pollution Prevention and Control', *Official Journal L 257*, 10 October, European Commission, Brussels, pp26–40

EC (1997) 'Council Directive 1997/11/EC of 3 March 1997 Amending Directive 1985/337/EEC on the Assessment of the Effects of Certain Public and Private Projects on the Environment', *Official Journal* L 073, 14 March 1997 pp5–15

EEA (1999) 'Towards a Transport and Environment Reporting Mechanism (TERM) for the EU. Part 1: TERM Concept and Process', *Technical Report No 18*, European Environment Agency, Copenhagen

EEA (2001a) *Environmental Signals 2001*, European Environment Agency Regular Indicator Report, EEA, Copenhagen, viewed at www.reports.eea.eu.int/signals-2001/en/signals2001 on 1 June 2001

EEA (2001b) 'Latest Environmental Signals Highlight Europe's Public Policy Challenge', European Environment Agency News Release, Copenhagen, 29 May 2001, viewed at www.org. eea.eu.int/documents/newsreleases/signals_2001-en, June 2001

Fleay, B J (1999) 'Climaxing Oil: How will Transport Adapt?', *Beyond Oil: Transport and Fuel for the Future*, Chartered Institute of Transport in Australia National Symposium, Launceston, Tasmania, 6–7 November 1998, available at www.istp.murdoch.edu.au/research/oilfleay/oil.html, June 2001

Fleming, D (1996) 'Beyond the Technical Fix' in Welford, R and Starkey, R (eds) *The Earthscan Reader in Business and the Environment*, Earthscan, London, pp145–168

Georgescu-Roegen, N (1971) *The Entropy Law and the Economic Process*, Harvard University Press, Cambridge, Massachusetts

Goodland, R and Daly, H (1996) 'Environmental Sustainability: Universal and Non-Negotiable', *Ecological Applications*, vol 6(4), pp1002–1017

Hawken, P, Lovins, A B and Lovins, L H (2000) *Natural Capitalism*, Earthscan, London

INFRAS (2000) *Sustainable Aviation – Pre-study*, for the Air Transport Action Group, INFRAS Consulting, Zurich and Bern

IPCC (1999) *Aviation and the Global Atmosphere*, Cambridge University Press, Cambridge

IPCC (2001) *Climate Change 2001: Synthesis Report. Summary for Policymakers*, Geneva, http://www.ipcc.ch/pub/SYRspm.pdf

Maughan, J and Raper, D (2000) 'Local Air Quality – Will Local Air Quality have an Impact on the Growth of the Aviation Industry?', *Aviation and Environment Conference*, Euromoney, 25–28 January, London

Morrell S, Taylor R and Lyle D (1997) 'A Review of Health Effects of Aircraft Noise', *Australian and New Zealand Journal of Public Health*, vol 21(2), pp221–236

Natrass, B and Altomare, M (1999) *The Natural Step for Business: Wealth, Ecology and the Evolutionary Corporation*, New Society Publishers, Gabriola Island, Canada

OECD (2001) *OECD Environmental Strategy for the First Decade of the 21st Century*, adopted by OECD Environment Ministers, 16 May 2001, Organization for Economic Cooperation and Development, Paris

RCEP (2000) *Energy – The Changing Climate*, Twenty-second Report of the Royal Commission on Environmental Pollution, Cm4749, HMSO, London; see www.rcep.org.uk/pdf/chp4.pdf

Robèrt, K-H, Daly, H, Hawken, P and Holmberg, J (1997) 'A Compass for Sustainable Development', *International Journal of Sustainable Development and World Ecology*, vol 4, pp79–92

Schafer, A and Victor, D G (2000) *The Future Mobility of the World Population*, Transportation Research (part A), vol 34(3), pp171–205

Schmidt-Bleek, F (1993) 'MIPS Re-visited', *Fresenius Environmental Bulletin*, vol 2, pp407–412

Turnbull, D A and Bevan, J R (1995) 'The Impact of Airport De-icing on a River – the Case of the Ouseburn, Newcastle upon Tyne', *Environmental Pollution*, vol 88(3), pp321–332

Upham, P (2000a) 'An Assessment of the Natural Step Theory of Sustainability', *Journal of Cleaner Production*, vol 8(6), pp445–454

Upham, P (2000b) 'Scientific Consensus on Sustainability: The Case of the Natural Step', *Sustainable Development*, vol 8, pp180–190

Upham, P (2001) 'A Comparison of Sustainability Theory with UK and European Airports Policy and Practice', *Journal of Environmental Management*, vol 63(3), pp237–248

US GAO (2000) *Aviation and the Environment – Aviation's Effects on the Global Atmosphere are Potentially Significant and Expected to Grow*, Report to the Honorable James L Oberstar, Ranking Democratic Member, Committee on Transportation and Infrastructure, House of Representatives, February 2000, GAO/RCED-00-57, United States General Accounting Office, Washington, DC

von Weizsäcker, E, Lovins, A B and Lovins, L H (1998) *Factor Four: Doubling Wealth – Halving Resource Use*, Earthscan, London

Chapter 2

Organizational and growth trends in air transport

Ian Humphreys

INTRODUCTION

The growth in air transport has been phenomenal since the first powered flight by the Wright Brothers on 17 December 1903, which did not remain airborne for longer than the length of a Boeing 747. Today there are over 18,000 commercial aircraft in service, around 1300 airlines, over 1192 airports open to international aviation and, worldwide, over 3 billion passenger kilometres were flown in 1999 (Endres, 2001; ICAO, 1999, 2000). In addition to the growth in terms of the scale of air transport, forces of market competition, liberalization and deregulation, privatization and globalization have had, and are having, a profound effect on airports and their surrounding communities, airlines, consumers, industry, governments and the physical environment.

The purpose of this chapter is to examine the main organizational and growth trends in air transport in order to provide the context for considering the sustainability issues covered in the following chapters.

HISTORICAL AND PROJECTED GROWTH IN AIR TRANSPORT

Passengers

Global air-passenger traffic is forecast to increase by an average of 4.6 to 4.9 per cent per annum between 1999 and 2020 (Boeing, 2001a; Airbus, 2000; ICAO, 2000). This represents an almost trebling of revenue passenger kilometres flown from 3 trillion in 1999 to 8 trillion in 2019.

Seen in the historical context of passenger growth, and the events of 11 September 2001 apparently having only a temporary effect on passenger numbers, these figures

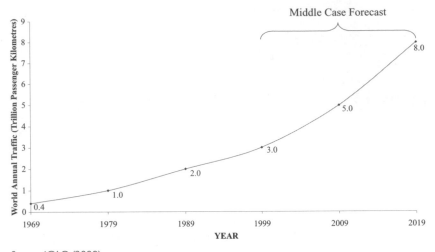

Source: ICAO (2000)

Figure 2.1 *World annual air passenger traffic growth and forecast*

are not unreasonable. Figure 2.1 shows that the number of passengers has doubled every 12–15 year period since the 1970s. There are a number of interrelated reasons for growth. Increased airframe and engine technology has improved efficiency in terms of the capability and economic performance of air transport with respect to speed, range and fuel economies. This has consequently led to the reduction in the unit cost per available seat kilometre flown, excluding the cost to the environment. The expansion of the global economy, rising levels of gross domestic product (GDP), package holidays, the falling price of air transport to the consumer, relative increase in wealth of the population and the new globalized structure of industry are further factors that have driven growth and are likely to continue to drive it in the future (Doganis, 1998; Airbus, 2000; Boeing, 2001a).

The proportion of passengers flying for leisure purposes varies by route. Generally speaking, in Europe 50 per cent of passengers are flying on leisure and 50 per cent on business; for Europe–North Atlantic routes it is estimated that 80 per cent fly on leisure and only 20 per cent on business. The geographical distribution of air transport activity reflects global economic wealth: North America and Europe account for around 70 per cent of world passengers; Asia currently accounts for 21 per cent and is likely to exhibit the strongest growth; Africa, Latin America, the Middle East and the Caribbean account for 9 per cent (ICAO, 2000). The pressure for expansion of infrastructure to accommodate growth is universal, and begs the question of how much more the industry can realistically continue to grow. The potential for growth in terms of passenger trips is massive given that only around 1 per cent of the world's population has ever flown.

Airport congestion

Forecasts typically and unrealistically assume an unconstrained availability of infrastructure to accommodate growth. Despite the scale of current and future development (see Figure 2.1), congestion, particularly at major airports in Europe and the US, is likely to continue.

There is growing political, social and environmental opposition to expansion. In the past the attitude of people and politicians to airport expansion was very much not in my backyard (NIMBY). Today a new attitude has emerged from the most capacity-constrained context of Northern Europe – people are going BANANAs (build absolutely nothing anywhere near anybody)! The 30-year saga from proposal to opening of a new Munich airport and the likely 15 years from proposal to opening of a fifth terminal at Heathrow are lead times that signal the great social and environmental sensitivities, mainly to localized noise and poor air quality. It is therefore highly likely that the forecast growth will not materialize in the numbers forecast due to a lack of capacity.

Airline behaviour

In order to understand the implications of the airline industry for society and the natural environment it is important to examine how the airlines intend to serve traffic growth in terms of aircraft sizes, numbers, routes and the distribution of air services across airports. Airlines have concentrated passenger traffic on the points that offer the most attractive market in terms of yield, and this pattern has been exacerbated by hub-and-spoke networks (discussed later). This is why 32 per cent of world passenger traffic passes through the 25 busiest passenger airports, 17 of which are in the US (ICAO, 1999). Economic pressure for concentration by airlines at key airports where the market is strongest has created continual pressure for capacity expansion at these points. Governments need to be aware of market forces and must balance the environmental, economic and social costs of development in the interests of their countries.

United and British Airways have both recognized the problems of future hub airport congestion and have proposed to operate business jet point-to-point-style operations in the future in order to supplement conventional services (Kelly, 2001). Over two years prior to this, plans were initiated to develop the F1, a six-seater aircraft for point-to-point services that offer the business traveller flights using local airfields in order to avoid hub congestion (Noble, 1999).

Historically, air traffic movements (ATMs) have grown at a slower rate than passenger numbers, as the average aircraft size has increased in response to better operating economics for airlines flying larger aircraft on longer routes with higher average load factors. The forecast is for these trends to continue, with 3.3 per cent growth of ATMs per annum 1999–2020 (Airbus, 2000). Average aircraft size, 179 seats in 1999, is forecast to grow to 217 seats by 2019 and average load factors are set to increase from 70–73.5 per cent over the same period in response to growth of low-fare markets and better yield management by the airlines (Airbus, 2000).

A recent counter-trend has been an increase in the numbers of shorter sectors flown by smaller aircraft. The introduction of 50–100 seat regional jets has made a range of new city pairs economically viable, and has slowed the growth in aircraft size, a trend particularly important for congestion at certain airports.

Freight

Currently, an estimated 40 per cent of global trade by value is moving by air. As logistics operations have become globalized and just-in-time (JIT) supply chains have required more rapid transport, airfreight volumes have rapidly increased. Industry forecasts predict that 'belly-hold' freight, traditionally the primary form of airfreight, will more than treble over the next ten years (Boeing, 2001b).

A significant development in the market has been the expansion of integrated carriers such as DHL, TNT, UPS and Fedex, who carry 9.2 per cent of the current global air freight market, and are forecast to grow at a staggering 13 per cent per annum and to take a global market share of 31 per cent by 2019 (Boeing, 2001b). For clients, the attractiveness of an integrated carrier is the single company point of contact for door-to-door global delivery of an ever-widening range of cargo types, to a majority of places within 48–72 hours, depending upon the distances involved.

In terms of environmental impact, the sustainability of current operations and forecast growth is of concern, particularly in Europe. The integrators' role in just-in-time networks is predicated on night flights – unpopular with local communities – in order to achieve close-of-business pick-ups and start-of-business deliveries. Opposition to night flights has led to a range of local night-time operating restrictions and, in several cases, outright bans on night flying that threaten the ability of the supply chain to deliver with the same response times as are currently achieved (Humphreys et al, 1999).

The traditional 'predict-and-provide' approach to airport capacity no longer seems acceptable given the lack of public and political support for unconstrained infrastructure expansion. The questions this raises are: what level of capacity provision is sustainable from an environmental, economic and social perspective and which segments of the air transport market should be accommodated?

AIRLINE MARKET LIBERALIZATION AND DEREGULATION

Air transport has moved away from being a highly regulated, government-owned and subsidized mode of travel run as a public utility, towards an industry where economic market regulations are being removed. Traditionally, low traffic volumes and unfavourable aircraft operating economics led governments to subsidize air transport for political and economic ends. Traffic growth and the fall of the cost per seat kilometre have improved the financial viability of airline operations: since 1994, International Air Transport Association (IATA) scheduled airlines have made an operating profit that in 1999 was 4.1 per cent of operating revenues. In response to this, many state-owned airlines have started to work to commercial objectives: some have sold shares to the private sector and a few have fully privatized.

The trend towards private-sector airline ownership is global. In the US most of the major airlines are privately owned and in Europe this includes the non-flag-carrier airlines and British Airways. By 2001 a number of governments had sold part of their airline and had announced aspirations to sell further shares. Examples include South African Airways, Air France, Singapore Airlines, China Airlines, Air Afrique, Air New Zealand and Kenya Airlines (Doganis, 2001). Many countries have seen the financial benefits of divesting themselves of airline ownership and are considering forms of privatization – for example, India, Jordan and Portugal. Aviation is increasingly striving to meet demands of private shareholders, whereas previously it had been operating to a solely public utility mandate.

Economic regulation and deregulation

Air services have traditionally been strictly regulated. Regulators have controlled safety, routes, timings of services, aircraft type, frequency and airports to be served. Internationally, fare levels were decided through collaboration in the form of IATA fare conferences. Inefficient airlines and poor levels of customer service were two of the key reasons for pressure to introduce market deregulation. Market forces were introduced first in the US with the Domestic Market Deregulation Act of 1978, which by the mid 1980s had removed restrictions on fares, frequencies and routes. Europe followed with liberalization of air services, a gradual introduction of market forces over three packages spanning 1988 to full implementation of the final package in 1997. European Union (EU) registered airlines are now free to fly on any intra- or inter-EU route, fly whatever capacity, frequency and times, and charge whatever fare they like provided that the airline is deemed safe, and financially and professionally sound by the relevant civil aviation authorities.

The example of profitable airlines that do not require a subsidy has led many governments to seek to subsidize their airlines less and to liberalize their international, bilateral air-service agreements. It should be noted that aviation internationally is still regulated on a route-by-route basis by over 200,000 bilateral air-service agreements negotiated between governments and controlling airline access to routes, fares, frequencies and, in some cases, revenue pooling.

The bilateral agreements between the US and countries in Europe have become increasingly liberal, and the US has negotiated a number of open skies agreements with the countries of Europe and is pushing to gain more liberal agreements worldwide. Strategically, this makes sense for the US because it has the largest, most wealthy domestic market in the world and can consolidate passengers at a single hub point. This allows favourable competition with foreign carriers who do not have access to the US domestic online feeder traffic (hubbing is explained further below). Interestingly, the US itself does not believe in free market forces within its domestic market for international carriers and has frequently refused to allow access to foreign carriers to this market.

The implications of liberalization and deregulation on the organization and structure of the air transport industry depend upon the specific context. Generally, competition has led to increased frequency, route network reorganization, duplication of services on busiest routes and lower load factors as a consequence of this and reduction of aircraft size as airlines have opted to give the market the increased frequency of service. These factors have resulted in increased fuel burn per passenger carried and raise a key question for the industry: how should the goal of competition be balanced against the goals of sustainable aviation? Long-term sustainability goals need government intervention in the market because airlines are increasingly governed by the short-term financial bottom line of their shareholders.

Low-cost airlines

A primary result of market deregulation and liberalization has been the birth of low-cost scheduled airlines. This was led by the model of Southwest Airlines of Texas, US, which began operations in the early 1970s. In Europe, the emergence of Ryannair, easyJet, Virgin Express, Go and Buzz since the late 1990s has introduced low-cost travel at low fares previously restricted by regulation. In 2000, low-cost operations began in Brazil and Australia, suggesting the potential for this model of airline operations to grow on a global basis.

In the UK, low-cost scheduled traffic is forecast to grow at 6.6 per cent per annum for the years 1998–2015 (DETR, 1998). Some of this growth is undoubtedly due to domestic low-cost air services attracting trips from land-based modes such as rail. Domestic air services between London and Scotland can be up to four times quicker than rail or car (city centre to city centre) and also cheaper. At the time of writing, the Ryannair website quotes one-way prices for London Stansted to Dublin for UK£8, Frankfurt for UK£5, Turin for UK£8, Brussels for UK£8, Glasgow for UK£8 and Stockholm for UK£8, a fraction of the fares available four years earlier (Ryannair, 2001).

Low-cost fares appear to have encouraged travel for the sake of it and certainly for leisure. This highlights the conflict between increased mobility affordable for lower-income groups as a result of market freedom, with sustainable use of resources by the aviation industry (Graham and Guyer, 1999). Graham (2001) is right to question the necessity of the degree of mobility low-cost airlines have introduced. Notably, consumer choices made now may limit the scope available for consumer choice in the future.

Hub-and-spoke networks

Another significant impact of US domestic airline deregulation that has had important repercussions for global airline networks is the change in airline network structure from point to point to hub and spoke. The reason for the rise of airline hubbing can be seen in Figure 2.2. If the network were connected by point-to-point route structure, four city pairs would be served. If the same points were connected using a hub, then 36 city pairs would be served. The impact of spokes (n) on city pairs served in a hub network, including the hub city, can be calculated by: total city pairs served = n (n + 1)/2. For example, if the number of spokes were doubled to 16, then the number of city pairs served in a hub network would be 136. In contrast, due to bilateral regulations, airline networks in countries outside the US were naturally focused upon key points, although the scheduling of flights to maximize connectivity between flights was not common practice (Dennis, 1994).

Hub-and-spoke networks minimize airline operating costs per seat kilometre flown in relation to the airports served in a network. A hub can be defined as a central airport location used as a transfer point for services from outlying spoke airports. Airlines schedule waves of flights into the hub and then back out to where they came from within a short time period. Passengers transfer between flights at the hub. This allows the airlines to maximize the number of marketable connections between points of the network for the lowest airline operating cost.

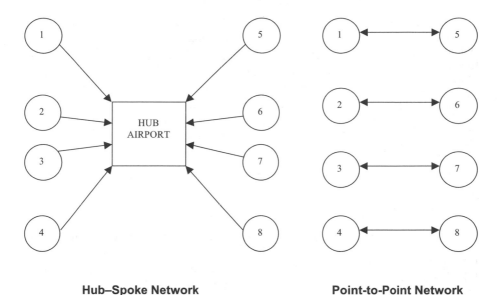

Hub–Spoke Network
36 city pairs

Point-to-Point Network
4 city pairs

Figure 2.2 *Market power of hub-and-spoke networks*

The hub acts as a consolidation point for passengers, thereby enabling higher frequencies to be operated with larger aircraft and seat occupancy rates, hence lowering the operating cost per seat kilometre. Airports and airlines become mutually dependent upon each other in this system: typically, as the share of flights operated by the hub airline increases, so does the number of transfer passengers. Examples include Delta at Atlanta where the airline has a 75 per cent share of departures and around 80 per cent of traffic is transfer; KLM, which has 58 per cent departures at Amsterdam; Lufthansa, which has around 60 per cent at Frankfurt; and American, which has 70 per cent of departures at Dallas Fort-Worth.

Hub-and-spoke operations have been criticized for reducing the number of direct point-to-point services available for the consumer, increasing the number of aircraft kilometres the customer has to fly via a hub and increasing trip times because of the need to change aircraft mid trip (Dempsey, 1989). The airlines try to counter these claims by pointing to the lower cost and increased frequency of services arising from hubbing economics. It should also be noted that consolidation of passengers onto larger aircraft might not be negative in terms of environmental and social sustainability.

Hub-and-spoke operations may be economically beneficial for the airlines; but they require an increase in airport infrastructure at certain locations in order to cope with more pronounced peak operating activity and revised internal terminal configuration to cater for much larger transfer passenger flows.

Airbus anticipate growth of the existing system of hub-and-spoke routes in which the growth of high-density long-haul routes requires the A380, an aircraft capable of conveying 600–1000 passengers. Boeing disagrees and predicts the erosion of the hub-dominated network structure and the growth of a more point-to-point route structure for medium-density long-haul services. These would be flown by a sonic cruiser 200–300 seat aircraft, capable of speeds up to Mach 0.95 that could cut up to four hours off a transatlantic rotation (Norris, 2001).

The two views of the future have different environmental implications. The A380 offers reduced energy consumed per seat kilometre, while the Sonic cruiser may burn half as much fuel again as a conventional aircraft (Norris, 2001) and may make high-altitude emissions, more damaging to the environment than those of a conventional aircraft. In its favour, the Sonic cruiser could allow travellers to fly from closer to home and would make better use of available non-hub airport capacity.

TRENDS IN THE GLOBALIZATION OF AIRLINE ACTIVITY

Airline consolidation

At a global level there is economic pressure for consolidation within the airline industry. This trend is not new on a national scale. Within a country (or single economic area in the case of the EU), commercial alliances, franchise agreements, code sharing and outright purchase of equity stakes have typified relationships between larger and smaller airlines.

In 1988 only two of the top 50 US regional carriers were independent, and today none are. This pattern, a response to domestic market deregulation, is being followed throughout the world where the majority of smaller scheduled airlines have either a franchise, code share, equity or marketing agreement link to a major carrier. Franchise agreements have been a means for the large airlines to gain access to feeder markets swiftly, for lower cost. In the US, eight airlines accounted for 65.7 per cent of the domestic market in 1981, airline consolidation since deregulation has led to six airlines accounting for 82 per cent of the market in 1998, and there are a number of proposals for further consolidation into possibly just three airline groups (Jasper, 2000a).

Code sharing

The most common form of cooperation between airlines from different countries is code sharing. Airlines offer a flight under two different codes, such that one aircraft is flown but seats are sold by partner airlines. This allows coordination and rationalization of capacity and schedules. For example, when KLM and Alitalia were in a close alliance for the service from Milan Malpensa to Sydney via Singapore, the airlines took joint responsibility for seat sales, took turns to operate the service, removed almost half the previous capacity and consolidated passenger loads for around half of the original costs. Alliances and code sharing should offer the world a more efficient set of airline network connections, consolidation of loads and a more efficient use of airport and aircraft capacity. Perhaps this is why the IATA load factor has begun to creep up from 63.5 per cent in 1994 to 70 per cent over the past six years and why the forecast is for it to rise to 73.5 per cent by 2019, despite competitive forces for increased frequencies in certain markets (IATA, 2000).

Global alliances

National ownership regulations prevented the airline industry from creating single global companies. The economic forces for globalization have not been deterred by these barriers, and during the late 1990s several global airline alliances have emerged, the main ones being Star Alliance (13 airlines, including Lufthansa, United, SAS, Varig, Thai and Singapore airlines), Oneworld (eight airlines, including British Airways, American, Qantas and Cathay Pacific airlines) and SkyTeam (Air France, Aeromexico, Delta and Korean), plus two smaller alliances, Qualifier (11 European airlines led by Swissair and Sabena) and Wings (KLM and Northwest) (see Table 2.1). Today the top three alliances account for 48.5 per cent of world revenue passenger kilometres (RPKs). If all five alliances are considered, then 61 per cent of all revenue passenger kilometres are carried by an alliance (Jasper, 2000b; Lewis, 2000) and that is before the traffic of over 100 regional carriers affiliated to these airlines is considered.

Table 2.1 *Trans-national global airline alliances*

Alliance	Star	Oneworld	SkyTeam	Wings	Qualifier
Operating revenues	US$63.1 billion	US$47.6 billion	US$30.4 billion	US$16.8 billion	US$16.2 billion
Annual passengers	296.4 million	209 million	174.3 million	71.6 million	52.3 million
Countries/destinations served	130/815	134/559	98/451	80/350	N/A/332
World share of RPKs	21.3%	16.4%	10.8%	9.9%	3.6%

Source: data from Jasper, 2000b; Lewis, 2000; KLM, 2000; Swissair 2000

Partners have been selected to try to gain coverage of global markets. Forms of co-operation range from equity stakes being held in partner airlines, through to code sharing, marketing and scheduling agreements between partner airlines. Airlines have entered into alliances for several reasons: to cut costs through the rationalization of air services; to increase network traffic by being able to offer more destinations through alliance partners; to increase marketing scope per unit cost; to maximize economies of scope; to increase purchasing power with suppliers; and to restrict the threat of effective competition.

This recent trend is likely to continue for the simple reason that the benefits of alliances reported so far appear to have had a positive impact upon the financial bottom line. Alliance carrier profits have increased faster than market share (Button et al, 1998). For example, evidence from Northwest Airlines presented to the General Accounting Office estimated in 1995 that their alliance with KLM has resulted in 200,000 extra passengers per annum and revenues of circa US$175 million (Doganis, 2001).

Alliance instability

Airline alliances are far from stable. Alliance partners can be promiscuous and are susceptible to altering their allegiance in order to maximize the financial bottom line for their airline as circumstances change over time. Over 80 per cent of alliances have failed within five years since 1990. For example, during the summer of 2000 KLM and Alitalia split up, weakening the Wings alliance considerably. British Airways

(BA) is currently in its third transatlantic alliance after links with United and US airlines failed.

The transient nature of airline alliances and their vulnerability poses a problem for airport infrastructure planning and utilization. Alliance partners in global groupings have begun to request co-location in terminals at airports in order to gain economies of ground handling and ease of connectivity between flights. This has affected a large number of major hub airports across the world. The fleet mix and nature of operations is often not compatible with the planned usage and design of particular aprons and terminals.

Airports can accommodate some change; but often there are losses in efficiency regarding the use of infrastructure. This places further pressure on capacity. There is now more of a need than ever before for flexible airport infrastructure planning to maximize the use of capacity under a range of different alliance behaviour scenarios.

Global airlines?

It is uncertain whether or not alliances could provide a more sustainable airline network. The continued development of global alliances depends upon national governments and their view of the benefits and drawbacks of multinational global airlines. Global airlines may represent a more sustainable air service network for the world if airlines coordinate the provision of air service capacity and create a network that needs fewer larger aircraft operating, that in turn may reduce the fuel consumed and emissions produced per revenue passenger kilometre. On the other hand, global airline competition may result in increased frequency competition between alliances that may increase environmental and airport capacity impacts per revenue passenger carried.

A further threat might be that global airlines will be able to play off one country against another, so that some parts of the world become peripheral to the air service network. Smaller nations might not receive an air service network that serves the economic and political interest of their countries. New hub locations may be selected according to airline interests, geographically skewing the economic benefits, and environmental and social problems associated with airport development.

It is interesting to note that governments have allowed three airlines to have global networks, these being integrated carriers Fedex, UPS and DHL. These airlines offer express door-to-door service for freight. Clauses in the bilateral air-service agreements related to freight are generally more open because countries do not have their own integrated carriers and can see the economic benefits for their nation of being included in the global network. Whether or not multinational global passenger airlines are permitted in the future depends upon whether governments lift regulation of airline nationality and of air-service agreements, which is only likely if they perceive the advantages to outweigh the disadvantages.

AIRPORT COMMERCIALIZATION AND PRIVATIZATION

Airports have traditionally been regarded as facilities to be publicly owned, operated and subsidized. Since the mid 1980s, there has been a significant shift in many countries towards airport development being funded by the private sector and being run on a commercial basis. The reason for this is primarily the need to finance expansion. Many of the key hub airports in Europe and the busiest in the US are congested now and will continue to be so in future, as the rapid growth of air traffic outstrips the supply of infrastructure. New large aircraft such as the Airbus A380 will require new investment and design of new or redeveloped facilities in order to cope with the processing of passenger loads of up to 1000 people.

Worldwide, it is estimated that US$500 billion will be required to fund future development to accommodate forecast traffic growth from 1999 up to 2020 (Momberger, 2001). Some examples of the major developments are listed in Table 2.2. Such pressures have led governments around the world to adopt or consider forms of privatization and commercialization in order to relieve themselves of the financial burden of airport ownership (Humphreys and Francis, 2000).

Table 2.2 *Major new airport projects*

Airport/terminal	Estimated investment	Opening date/major projects
Europe		
Amsterdam–Schiphol	US$18.7 billion (NLG 35 billion)	terminal expansion, fifth runway; new offshore airport after 2025 (project on hold)
Paris (third airport)	US$3.6 billion (FRF 20 billion)	new airport after 2015
Berlin–Schonefeld	US$3.2 billion (DEM 7 billion)	first-phase expansion until 2007
Frankfurt	US$2.3 billion (DEM 5 billion)	CargoCity South and pax terminal expansions: fourth runway
London Heathrow T5	US$2.3 billion (UK£1.46 billion)	complete by 2013? decision pending
Athens–Spata	US$2.3 billion (Ecu 2 billion)	March 2001 – complete by 2013
Middle East		
Tehran Imam Khomeini International	US$1 billion	completely new airport
Tel Aviv–Ben Gurion/Israel	US$950 million	Ben Gurion 2000; third terminal (phase 1)
Abu Dhabi/UAE	US$630 million	doubling of terminal capacity; new runway
North America		
New York–JFK	US$9.3 billion	by 2006; new terminals and terminal and infrastructure redevelopment, includes US$1.5 billion *AirTrain* rail link
Los Angeles International	US$8 billion	development under 15-year master plan
Miami International	US$5.5 billion	staged expansion of pax and cargo facilities

Table 2.2 *Major new airport projects (Continued)*

Airport/terminal	Estimated investment	Opening date/major projects
Chicago–O'Hare	US$3.7 billion	Worldgate Terminal redevelopment by 2005
Washington–Dulles International	US$3.4 billion	new runway, terminal, people-movers
South America		
Mexico City	US$5.5 billion	stage 1 of second airport for the capital
Buenos Aires	US$1.3 billion	Nueva Ezeisa project
Brazil	US$1.3 billion	modernization of Infraero airports (US$350 million)
Africa		
Johannesburg/Cape Town/ Durban; and Durban–La Mercy	US$765 million (ZAR 3 billion)	upgrading within the next three years in 2010
Khartoum	US$750 million	completely new airport planned
Dakar	US$580 million	complete rehabilitation of all facilities by 2005
Asia–Pacific		
Tokyo (third airport)	US$35 billion (with reclamation)	planned
Kansai (second runway, terminal)	US$14.6 billion (JPY1.56 trillion)	by 2007; construction under way
Inchon International (New Seoul Airport)	US$6.7 billion	phase I to open on January 2001
Nagoya–Chubu International, Japan	US$6.4 billion (JYP 786 billion)	by 2005 for World Expo at Nagoya

The UK provided the first example of full privatization when the seven airports of the British Airways Alliance were fully privatized in 1987 and 16 local-authority-owned airports were commercialized. To date, more than 60 countries across the world have introduced some kind of private-sector involvement into the ownership, financing and/or management of their airports. Examples include Australia, New Zealand, Canada, the UK, South Africa, the US, Italy, Germany, Denmark, Mexico, Uruguay, Japan, Hong Kong, Malaysia, Mexico, India, Vietnam, Austria, the Philippines, Singapore and Switzerland (GAO, 1998; Ashford, 1999). A diverse and dynamic pattern of airport ownership has begun to emerge that includes the forms listed in Box 2.1.

Box 2.1 *Forms of airport ownership*

- Airport fully owned and operated by a private company – for example, the airports of the BAA plc: Heathrow, Gatwick, Stansted and others.
- Airport owned by government and by private company – for example, Vienna, Copenhagen and some of the New Zealand airports.
- Airport owned and operated by government but set up as a separate entity, financially self-sufficient and working to commercial objectives – for example, Schiphol in Amsterdam; Aer Rianta Irish Airports; Manchester, UK.
- Airport owned by government but developed and operated by a private concession on a long-term lease basis. Examples include La Paz, Bolivia; Australian airports (17 airports on 50-year leases).
- Joint venture with airline to develop a terminal or part thereof – for example, Munich Airport has entered a joint venture where the two parties will develop, finance and operate a new terminal. Other examples include JFK Terminal 4; Eurohub, Birmingham, UK.
- Airport ground infrastructure owned by state government; terminals operated, leased, or developed by airlines. This is a common model in the US.
- Build, operate, transfer (BOT) – for example, the new Athens Airport, opened in 2001, was built by a consortium that included Hochtief and ABB.

IMPLICATIONS OF CHANGING OWNERSHIP OF AIRPORTS

Advantages and disadvantages

There are various advantages and disadvantages to different forms of airport ownership. Generally, the introduction of commercial objectives (such as maximization of revenue and minimization of costs) and the involvement of private firms to build, operate or own airports have relieved the public sector of the huge financial burden of investment and has enabled development to take place. The nature of the ownership structure determines who reaps the financial rewards and bears the operating and financial risks.

The pace and scale of airport development has been driven by the new ability of airport owners to invest and develop. There has also been a trend for management to seize development opportunities as they arise. This has placed increased pressure on the planning system and raises policy questions regarding the compatibility of development with plans for long-term capacity growth.

Increase in commercial activity

Commercial objectives have led to airports being viewed as revenue generators, a role beyond the traditional definition of an airport as a modal transfer point for airline, freight and passenger operation. The comment of a staff member at a European airport that the operation was no longer an airport but 'a shopping mall with a runway beside it' reflects this change of role (Humphreys, 1999). Airports have diversified their businesses and increased their focus on non-aeronautical sources of revenue (Barrett, 2000; Parker, 1999). In the future, airports may seek to maximize returns to their shareholders by diversifying into other activities in preference to expanding their existing facilities.

Of the 16 UK airports commercialized in 1987, the number of airports with over 30 per cent of their income from commercial sources rose from 40 per cent to 100 per cent between 1986–1999 (Humphreys et al, 2001). The UK example has shown that some small airports (less than 200,000 passengers per annum) traditionally believed to be unprofitable and unable to pay their way can be profitable through innovative diversification. Such commercial revenue streams include running hotels, operation of charter flights, business parks, increased retail, maintenance facilities, reservations centres, fire-fighting services selling training to other airports and even the bulk buying and selling-on of electricity (Humphreys et al, 2001).

Since privatization, BAA plc has raised the percentage of revenue from commercial sources at its London airports from 49.5 per cent during 1984–1985 to 71.5 per cent during 1998–1999 (CIPFA, 1986; CRI/CIPFA, 1999). Diversification of BAA plc's business has been partly stimulated by the UK regulator restricting the amount of revenue raised from aeronautical charges at its three London airports (Francis and Humphreys, 2001). Since 1987, BAA's activities have included operation of over 200 duty-free outlets across the world, duty-free operations for a number of airlines, buying and selling a freight forwarding business, managing shops in hospitals, buying, operating and selling hotels, buying Lynton Property development group and entering a joint venture with Macarthur Glen to manage out-of-town shopping centres (Parker, 1999; Starkie, 1998; Francis and Humphreys, 2001). Diversification on this scale is of concern in terms of its implications for management time and the impact that a downturn in non-core business might have on airport operations.

Loss of control of airports

Full privatization means that the government effectively loses control of the airport and its development. Even when the government owns the airport but allows private companies to develop and run the infrastructure there are a number of potential risks. These include buildings being constructed to last the length of the concession and no longer; cost minimization in construction processes; and the long-term capacity of site being compromised in favour of short-term revenue generation (Craig, 1999). The activities of private firms that are working to maximize their shareholder value may conflict with the needs of the community from a social, economic and environmental perspective.

The result of development pressures and their implications for the economic, social and environmental sustainability of airports will vary depending upon who owns the airports. This will determine the goals of the companies concerned, whether they are driven by profit alone or have the social and environmental interests of the population at heart, and whether they wish to develop the land and sell on at a profit. All of these issues may affect the long-term economic plans for a region. Perhaps airports with some form of state ownership could claim to work to the triple bottom line of environment, social and economic needs of the community/region (Humphreys, 1998).

A key policy question for governments is this: how can the interests of the nation or region be safeguarded if an airport is sold to the private sector? This issue has increased the significance of the nature and form of regulation in order to ensure that the outcomes are compatible with those desired by government.

Globalization of airport ownership

The global financial community has discovered that airports make 'excellent investments' (Momberger, 1998, p1) and a number of airport groups have begun to emerge. Global airport groups have started to engage in airport management, consultancy, construction and airport operation on a global scale. BAA plc, for example, has developed a diversified portfolio of global interests. It owns seven UK airports, including Heathrow, the busiest international airport in the world. It has ownership/management interests in seven foreign airports, two in Australia, three in the US, one in Italy and one in Mauritius (Humphreys and Francis, 2000).

Frankfurt has a presence at some 50 or so airport sites; consultants Hochtief and Bechtel are involved in a variety of airport projects; the French airport operator TBI has a role at over 40 airports; and Aer Rianta has a presence at more than 15 airports. Amsterdam owns and manages a number of airports around the world and during the late 1990s created the world's first airport alliance with Frankfurt to jointly offer their expertise to airports worldwide. Global airport companies will be more difficult to regulate and guide with respect to national or regional economic, social and environmental interests that are not likely to be congruent with commercial interests.

Airport regulation

The role of regulation will be crucial since it is one of the few policy levers that remain for governments to guide this dynamic industry, with all its economic, social and environmental implications. However, such regulation may have dysfunctional effects (Humphreys and Francis, 2000). For example, regulation of aeronautical charges at BAA London airports has made these airports some of the cheapest in the UK for the airlines to use. This conflicts with UK government policy goals to encourage direct air services from the regions and to minimize the concentration of environmental impact upon Heathrow. It also discourages the development of infrastructure because revenues generated from this are restricted (Francis and Humphreys, 2001). A wider stakeholder view of regulation is required that is consistent with wider policy goals and the implications for society as a whole.

CONCLUSION: FUTURE TRENDS AND ISSUES

While the implications for any specific market and its stakeholders will depend upon the particular context under examination, the general trend in the industry is one of growth in the demand for air travel, the supply of air services and the expansion of airport infrastructure. Control of the industry is moving away from governments towards large corporate players.

Traffic growth, privatization, commercialization, deregulation of markets, infrastructure congestion and globalization of airlines and alliances of airlines and airports are forces that are likely to increase. The challenge for governments is to determine what policies, if any, and what form of regulation could be adopted that ensure a sustainable balance of interests to a variety of stakeholders from an economic, social and environmental perspective at local, national and international levels.

ACKNOWLEDGEMENTS

The author gratefully acknowledges Graham Francis Open University Business School for comments and Pam Wilson and Caroline Neale, Loughborough University, for chapter figures.

REFERENCES

Airbus (2000) *Global Market Forecast 2000–2019*, Airbus, Blagnac Cedex

Ashford, N (1999) *Airport Finance,* Loughborough Airport Consultancy, Loughborough, UK

Barrett, S (2000) 'Airport competition in the deregulated European aviation market', *Journal of Air Transport Management,* vol 6, pp13–27

Boeing (2001a) *Current Market Outlook 2000*, Boeing, Seattle, available at www.boeing.com

Boeing (2001b) *World Air Cargo forecast 2000/2001*, Boeing, Seattle

Button, K et al (1998) *Flying into the Future,* Edward Elgar, Cheltenham

CIPFA (1986) *Local Authority Airports – Accounts and Statistics 1985–1986,* Chartered Institute of Public Finance and Accountancy, London

Craig, V (1999) *Risk and Due Diligence in Airport Privatisation,* ICAO Airport Privatization Paper, Guatemala City, Guatemala

CRI/CIPFA (1999) *The UK Airports Industry Airports Statistics 1998/99,* Centre for the Study of Regulated Industries, University of Bath, Bath

Dempsey, P (1989) *The Social and Economic Consequences of Deregulation: the Transportation Industry in Transition,* Quorum Books, London

Dennis, N (1994) 'Airline hub operations in Europe', *Journal of Transport Geography,* vol 2, pp219–233

Department of Transport and the Regions (DETR) (1998) *UK Air Traffic Forecasts,* DETR, London, www.detr.gov.uk

Doganis, R (1998) *Flying off Course,* Routledge, London

Doganis, R (2001) *The Airline Business in the 21st Century,* Routledge, London

Endres, G (2001) 'World Airlines', *Flight International,* vol 159, pp104–110

Francis, G and Humphreys, I (2001) 'Airport Regulation: reflecting on lessons from BAA', *Public Money and Management,* vol 21, pp49–52

GAO (1998) *Airport Financing: Funding Sources for Airport Development GAO/RCED-98-71,* GAO, Washington, DC

Graham, B (2001) *The Policy Context: The UK,* Paper for Directions in UK Air Transport, RGS/IBG, London

Graham, B and Guyer, C (1999) 'Environmental sustainability, airport capacity and European air transport liberalization: irreconcilable goals?', *Journal of Transport Geography,* vol 7, pp165–180

Humphreys, I (1998) 'Development and privatisation of Cardiff airport', *Contemporary Wales,* vol 10 pp81–102

Humphreys, I (1999) 'Privatisation and commercialisation: changes in UK airport ownership patterns', *Journal of Transport Geography,* vol 7 pp121–134

Humphreys, I and Francis, G (2000) 'Critical perspective on traditional airport performance indicators', *Transportation Research Record,* no 1703, pp24–30

Humphreys, I, Francis, G and Fry, J (2001) 'What are the lessons from airport privatization, commercialization and regulation in the UK?', *Proceedings of the 80th Annual Meeting of the Transportation Research Board,* Washington, DC, p31

Humphreys, I, Gillingwater, D and Watson, R (1999) 'Globalisation and logistics service providers: a strategic position analysis', *Proceedings of the Second International Conference on Managing Enterprises*, Newcastle, Australia, pp9–14

IATA (2000) *Annual Report*, IATA, Canada, available at www.IATA.org/ar00

ICAO (1999) *The World of Civil Aviation 1999–2002*, ICAO, Montreal, Canada

ICAO (2000) *Air Traffic Forecasts*, ICAO, Geneva, available at www.icao.int

Jasper, C (2000a) 'Slugging it out', *Flight International*, vol 157, pp34–42

Jasper, C (2000b) 'Restraint the key', *Flight International*, vol 158, pp46–52

Kelly, E (2001) 'United to lure business jet set', *Flight International*, vol 159, p6

Lewis, P (2000) 'SkyTeam sets its sights on Star', *Flight International*, vol 158, p8

KLM (2000) www.KLM.com, accessed May 2000

Momberger, M (1998) *Airport Privatisation*, ACI, Geneva

Momberger, M (2001) *Major New Airport Projects*, ACI, Geneva

Noble, R (1999) pers comm

Norris, G (2001) 'Boeing looks for sonic boom in aircraft market', *Flight International*, vol 159, p32

Parker, D (1999) 'The performance of BAA before and after privatisation. A DEA study', *Journal of Transport Economics and Policy*, vol 33, pp133–146

Ryannair (2001) www.Ryannair.com, accessed 25 May 2001

Starkie, D (1998) *Airport Regulation 1997–1998 CRI Regulatory Review*, CRI, University of Bath, Bath

Swissair (2000) www.swissair.com/qualiflyerguide/intro, accessed May 2000

Chapter 3

The social and economic benefits of aviation

Robert Caves

INTRODUCTION

Airport expansion policies are now being driven by the need for sustainability, as reflected in the UK government's recent consultation document (DETR, 2000a). This implies a correct balance between environmental, social and economic goals. There are many social and economic costs and benefits associated with airport expansion, and they fall unequally on local, regional, national and international communities. A given factor may be a benefit to one community and a cost to another. The communities impacted may be widely separated in space or may share the same space. The impacts also have a time dimension: the impacts during construction are of a different nature than those during operation, and the impacts during operation change over time due to changing traffic patterns and changing impacts per unit of traffic. The factors affecting communities close to an airport tend to be grouped according to whether they are seen mainly as a cost or mainly as a benefit.

The cost impacts generated by aircraft and the associated ground traffic are usually from adverse environmental impacts: noise, air pollution, the ecological balance, landscape, odour and groundwater contamination. There may also be many other causes of local concern such as urbanization, safety, severance and road congestion. Most have established metrics that are subject to criticism regarding their relevance. In particular, noise in the community is measured or estimated using metrics that result in poor predictions of the actual number and location of complaints, particularly night noise and the associated sleep disturbance. Such metrics may also be poor predictors of impacts on health; both they and criteria for assessing risk require further work. It has been realized that the market does not provide an efficient valuation of the costs of these externalities.

Public safety may well become the next main constraint on airport capacity. The UK government is instituting new public safety zone (PSZ) definitions as the result of studies into risk levels and the tolerability of risk. However, much more work is required in order to refine appropriate databases on accidents and the distribution of their location, the implications for casualties and their degree of acceptability before the public are likely to have confidence in the protection that these measures afford (Caves, 1996). In any case, the land-use controls that follow from the implementation of the new PSZs do not apply retrospectively.

Even when the economic growth itself is welcomed, the urbanization that inevitably accompanies major airport expansion (Breheny, 1987) may be less acceptable than the direct impacts of the airport. An example of concern about the consequences of too much economic activity, in this case tourism, is the Hawaiian island of Maui. While two other islands decided to extend their runways, Maui rejected the idea on the grounds of higher property prices, congestion, crime and a reduced sense of social responsibility (Fujii, Im and Mak, 1992). There may also be concerns about the potential overheating of local economies.

At the larger scales, both spatially and politically, the costs are seen more in terms of the global environment and resource depletion, while the benefits are seen more in terms of the contribution of aviation to regional and national economies and social welfare.

The main benefits are usually perceived to be job creation and economic growth, particularly in terms of regeneration and the structure of the economy, together with positive social consequences in terms of enhanced opportunities and choices. The benefits are also hard to measure in a way that is useful for policy-makers.

More difficult than the assessment of both the costs and the benefits is how they are used to make decisions and form policies for planning guidance. One part of the problem is the appreciation of the imperfections in the metrics and in the interpretation of their consequences. In the UK, both appear to be taken as read by the Department of Transport, Local Government and the Regions (DTLR – now simply the Department for Transport) in their ongoing south-east and regional studies for aviation planning. Another part is the uneven way in which the costs and benefits fall across the population, which could easily be underplayed in those studies. However, the larger problem is the lack of a rigorous and accepted method for balancing the unevenly distributed costs and benefits.

Other chapters address the environmental costs of aviation. The rest of this chapter reviews the benefits and then returns to the question of balancing interests.

BENEFITS

In the most advanced economies, society derives its aviation benefits primarily from the consumer and producer surpluses generated by users who choose aviation in free competition with other available modes of transport, as described by DETR (1999). Even in these countries, the case for competitive advantage in job creation and the stimulation of the economy through access to air transport is often also made. The user benefits are made self-evident by the revealed demand. They would normally include savings in cost, time and risk of accident (Brathen et al, 2000).

However, the benefits should not be overstated. They extend only to the difference in utility derived from using air transport rather than the next most convenient mode (Butler and Kiernan, 1988). Equally, the benefits should not be understated. Sometimes the whole utility of the activity could not be experienced if air transport did not offer a sufficiently low deterrence to travel.

A useful attempt to assess the economic benefits of additional airport capacity for users was presented in evidence to the Heathrow Terminal 5 inquiry (Coopers and Lybrand, 1995). The study estimated the effect on individual sectors of the UK economy. It did this by taking the Civil Aviation Authority (CAA) statistics of trip generation rates per sector, estimating the percentage of total expenditure per sector attributable to air travel, and estimating the increase in cost of travel associated with not satisfying demand at Heathrow. As a result, the percentage increase in the sectors' gross value added was calculated. The study concluded that the additional costs were equivalent to between 0.3 per cent and 1.1 per cent of a sector's gross added value, to which extent UK industry would be disadvantaged in competition with other countries' manufacturers. There would also be costs to foreign business and loss of inbound tourism.

Over and above the benefits to the users of air transport, society as a whole may benefit from the activities that become available when the deterrence to travel is sufficiently low. Once again, however, the benefits should not be overstated. Those benefits already counted as user benefits cannot justifiably be double counted on society's behalf. The economic benefits are often overstated by being in gross terms rather than net.

The benefits to users and to society may be economic or social. Most attention has been devoted to the economic benefits; but it is by no means certain that these are more valuable than the social benefits (Caves, 1994).

Economic activity

Attempts to derive a comprehensive measure of the economic benefits of aviation have tended to follow a methodology advocated by the Federal Aviation Administration (FAA) (Butler and Kiernan, 1986). This measures the contribution made to an economy by aviation by summing the costed direct, indirect and induced effects (impacts). Direct impacts are the consequences of the economic activity occurring at the airport. Indirect impacts are those that are directly attributable to, but occur away from, the airport. Induced impacts are generated by the direct and indirect expenditures triggering a chain reaction through the local economy through the so-called 'multiplier' effect. Thus, a study for the International Air Transport Association (IATA) by the Strategic Rescources Institute (SRI) (SRI, 1990) calculated that aviation's contribution to 22 countries in Europe was US$200 billion and 6.7 million jobs. In common with the many other studies using this methodology, nearly two-thirds of the contribution came from the induced effects. The implication drawn by SRI from this assessment was that if the traffic volume increased by 10 per cent less than for an unconstrained forecast, there would be US$10 billion less activity per year by the year 2000 (in other words, perhaps 3 per cent less than there would have been in the unconstrained situation).

A US airport advocacy group (USA-BIAS) has used a similar methodology to claim that daily service to a new US gateway from London would add at least US$268 million to the local US economy in the first year (Creedy, 1991). These estimates include stimulation of exports and foreign investment of US$139 million, in addition to the impacts derived using the FAA methodology. The Airports Council International (Europe) reports that between 350 and 1500 jobs are created at an airport site per million passengers per annum (mppa), the total employment being between 920 and 5130 per mppa (ACI, 1998). Again, the majority of the employment is associated with the indirect and induced effect due to the need for services ranging from taxi drivers to utilities. There is a clear difference between the total economic impact around small airports, where many of the services cannot be provided locally, and the major gateways and their associated regions. In the latter case, multipliers between 1.7 and 2.5 may be justified. Some analysts also add access-sensitive businesses to the indirect and induced employment estimates. This is similar to estimating the stimulation effect discussed below. Thus, it has been estimated that the Chicago airport system adds between 420,000 and 510,000 jobs to the local economy, and that an international passenger adds US$2,310 – over five times that of a domestic connecting passenger (Booz-Allen and Hamilton, 1998).

Social benefits

There is a general acceptance that there is a positive, mutually supportive relationship between aviation and the economy; at the same time, there is a general feeling that aviation is socially divisive. However, in many ways aviation allows similar social benefits to those derived from other transport modes. Moreover, it is the only mode that can provide these over long distances. Social benefits are self-evident when aviation is the only way to respond to disaster relief, medical evacuation, law enforcement or the protection of the environment (FAA, 1978). So are some of the other leisure benefits that are claimed by the FAA (FAA, 1978). Another example of a potential benefit to society, over and above the benefits to the individual, is that the world is becoming a global village in which people from different countries are made to feel like neighbours. Tourism has become a real force for peace in the world (Edgell, 1990). This type of intercultural tourism can only be accomplished, in practice, by air and only if it is conducted to ethical principles. British Airways (BA) has taken a lead in this (British Airways, 1996), and the pressure group Tourism Concern has issued a checklist to protect the interests of the local people (www.tourismconcern.org.uk).

The social advantages of aviation are more readily apparent in developing countries, in promoting cultural unity within a country and allowing cultural, ethnic and educational links with the industrialized world. The direct benefits from the support of industrial and social service activities are readily apparent in low-density situations and in the pre-industrial phase of an economy. However, it is perhaps the less direct benefits flowing from the transfer of technology that have the greater beneficial effect on a developing economy. The transfer process can be formalized as occurring at four levels of sophistication: appropriating, disseminating, utilizing knowledge and ongoing and interactive communication (Williams and Gibson, 1990). It would be very difficult to provide this latter most effective form of technology transfer without international aviation.

The establishment of airports and air services brings with it the need for technical support, which extends from governmental administration through to qualified mechanics. The training and quality-control requirements result in improved total industrial capability. This technological spin-off has a particular part to play around airports in developing regions, where the airport can form a base for local industry. Indeed, the airport is often the only place where clean water and a consistent supply of electrical power can be found. The effect of an airport can then be beneficial both technically and through increased job opportunities, and real meaning can be attached to the multiplier effect. The principal benefits are, however, unlikely to show up in the short term in calculations of economic contribution, input–output or cost–benefit analyses since they are embodied in the changes in local skills and perspectives.

Difficulties in quantifying benefits

Many criticisms have been levelled at the ways in which the impacts of airport activity have been quantified in applying the FAA methodology. This includes, first, the way in which all other sectors of the economy could claim corresponding indirect and induced effects. Second, this includes the way in which the multiplier argument can only be applied to self-contained regions that provide no alternative consumption (so that it can be assumed that if the consumer refrains from buying an air ticket, he or she will neither buy anything else nor invest it where it would be spent by someone else). Third, there is the way in which the indirect effects and multiplier effects can easily be double-counted (Karyd and Brobeck, 1992). The UK CAA has noted several of the more important objections (CAA, 1994), pointing out that there are cross effects of increased air transport on other modes, both by diversion from another mode and from increased loading of the airport access systems. More importantly, it is the additional impact of investment in airports over and above the impact that would accrue from alternative investments that matters. Also, trade and tourism operate in both directions. Not only is it the net effect which should be calculated; but the result depends upon how the denied passenger would have behaved.

These demand-side benefits may redistribute economic activity, and thus assist in regeneration, but they will not give an overall net long-term benefit to the national economy unless they are accompanied by supply-side improvements. These may arise through improving the level of competition; economies of scale (agglomeration economies); improved labour markets, productivity or skill levels; and locational effects (DETR, 1999). Improvement in the efficiency of production will be reflected in user benefits. The other net effects will vary in importance case by case, and are much harder to quantify. Even most of the benefits of regenerating an economy are likely to be captured in user benefits. Furthermore, the unit benefit probably reduces as activity expands, while the unit cost of additional infrastructure probably increases (Grayling, 2001). However, a positive sign is that aviation is a highly productive sector of the economy (Oxford Economic Forecasting, 1999).

Given the preponderance of UK holidaymakers among UK regional airport passengers, the net effect on the UK region's economy might well be negative, even though most of the holiday spending goes to UK airlines, airports and tour operators, rather than to foreign economies. On the other hand, the psychological impact of being deprived of sun and ski holidays could reduce enthusiasm and productivity, and increase time off for illness.

The most fundamental error associated with the use of the multiplier in assessing the aviation contribution to the economy is to imbue the resulting linkage as necessarily having a causal quality (ie that jobs at the airport cause jobs in the rest of the local economy). Also, given the derived nature of the demand for transport, the large claimed contribution to the gross domestic product (GDP) may also prompt the question whether an efficient economy should not run with a lower proportional spend on intermediate goods.

Stimulation of the economy

Given the lack of conviction and the limited relevance associated with the above measures of economic impact, it is important to understand how the presence of air services actually stimulates the local or regional economy, rather than simply being bound up with it. The FAA (FAA, 1978) suggests that this effect can be measured by asking firms how vital an airport was to their location decision or what would happen to the firm if an airport should close. The answers to these questions are obvious in most island and some tourist economies. Areas with intrinsic tourist potential usually only blossom into resorts after providing facilities for direct air services. In remote areas, the maintenance or revival of the economy may depend entirely upon the accessibility provided by aviation, whether it be by floatplane in Alaska or the conversion of a run-down coal-mining economy into a ski resort in Yampa Valley, Colorado (Cooper, 1990).

Tourism is sometimes shown by the statistics to grow strongly despite restrictive airline policies. Where tourism growth has been slow, the reasons often have little to do with airline policy. The tourism demand equation is multivariate, airline policy being but one of many important factors. Others include exchange rates, personal security, originating countries' policies with respect to foreign travel, the provision of hotel accommodation, the strengths of competing destinations, and policies on airport infrastructure, all of which can influence the apparent relationship between tourism and transport policy. Brazil, for example, had economic and security problems that were the predominant causes of the decline in tourism during the early 1990s.

In developing and isolated economies, air transport's more important contribution has been to enable production of specialized products such as fresh fruit and flowers from Africa. Even in these relatively clear-cut situations, however, the economic benefit to the local community may be small, although the tourist industry is big. In the Pacific micro-states (Britton and Kissling, 1984) and in Israel (Haitovsky, Salomon and Silman, 1987), the local economy often receives only 20–30 per cent of the total holiday price. This can be improved if the country's own airline brings in foreign exchange, although the aircraft investment can be daunting, being of the same order as the hotel investment (Wheatcroft, 1994).

It is clear from a survey of many studies (Caves and Gosling, 1999; DETR, 1999) that, in general, there is no consistent relationship between the provision of air services and the location of industry in developed economies. The explanation of the variation appears to be partly bound up with the richness of choice of transport available, partly with the nature of the economy and partly with specific constraints and distortions. The competition among UK regions for inward investment has led to large subsidies being offered in order to capture major investors, while lack of adequate sites can lose incoming multinationals (*Sunday Times*, 1996, p9).

Those industries with a particular need for air service, either for shipments of high value-to-weight items or to support just-in-time strategies or high-contact personnel, do seem to locate close to aviation facilities, and with good reason. Surveys of business parks near airports in the south-east of England show that tenants come mostly from the electronics, pharmaceutical, information technology and financial services sectors (Robertson, 1995). A survey in Austin, Texas, of high-technology industries (Mahmassani and Toft, 1985) showed a high value of US$333 per pound for surveying and drafting instruments, of which 48 per cent were air shipped, compared with a value of US$1.3 per pound for all commodities, of which only 2.8 per cent were shipped by air. The employees' propensity to fly per month, from the same survey, varied between 15 return flights for very small research and development (R&D) establishments to 0.07 return flights for large manufacturing branches (Mahmassani and Toft, 1985).

It can therefore be concluded that the introduction of new air service may generate new economic clusters, and overall national productivity may improve, as may the balance of invisible trade. There may also be social benefits from a redistribution of economic activity and wider benefits from tourism and visiting friends and relatives (VFR) traffic, over and above those reflected in the price of the ticket (eg international harmony and its spin-off benefits). However, each case has to be evaluated on its merits.

BALANCING DIFFERENT INTERESTS

Assuming that benefits can be identified as well as costs, and these benefits will be implicit (at least in the increased demand projections), the balance of interests still remains to be assessed before a decision on development proposals can be taken. This is normally handled through the political process, with great reliance on heuristic judgement. In this way, for example, Strasbourg refused a plan by the express air-freight carrier DHL for a courier hub that would create 1700 jobs, because of the environmental impacts (*ACI Communiqué*, 1996).

Local agreements

The UK displays two different aspects of the balance between local and non-local interests. Outside the south-east, the balance is between local communities and the region containing that local community. The scale is relatively modest, the local and regional need is recognized by the local communities (even if not to the extent of pacifying them), and the impact is largely local. It is becoming common practice for the balance to be struck by contracts, the so-called Section 106 Agreements, between the developer and the local governments, outlining acceptable levels of activity and operating procedures. Indeed, these contracts then make it possible to minimize the time taken for a public inquiry. Manchester's second runway inquiry took only three weeks after over 100 separate agreements had been signed, including an agreement for Manchester to be independently audited. The doubling of terminal capacity at Birmingham did not need an inquiry at all.

Though a similar agreement has been reached in the south-east for Gatwick to expand from 30 to 40 million passengers per annum (mppa) (Everitt, 2001), the inquiry into Heathrow's proposed Terminal 5 (T5) took four years, followed by 18 months for the inspector to file his report, and at least another 18 months for a min-isterial decision to be taken. The difficulties in the south-east include the huge scale of traffic (over 100 mppa now, with demand forecast to rise to over 300 mppa by 2030), the consequent huge scale of impact and the need to balance local interests with national ones because of the intercontinental nature of the traffic. The national need is generally not accepted by the local communities, the local effects are mostly negative, particularly at Heathrow, and they spread out far from the airports them-selves (partly due to the lack of airspace capacity).

In the UK, beyond and in addition to such voluntary agreements between an airport and its local community, the local balance of interests has been managed by ensuring that, if satisfactory contractual agreements cannot be achieved voluntarily, at least some minimum requirements are met. These typically derive from the out-come of an environmental impact assessment (EIA), from the expectation that the developer will be ISO 14001 compliant, from proper compensation for loss of value, from planning guidance or legislation on noise and emissions limits, and from local ordinances. They may also be imposed as a result of the inquiry recommendations. Unless at least this level of mitigation can be achieved, it is unlikely that permission for development would be granted. Even so, a considerable number of local people and members of national pressure groups will still feel aggrieved. Any remaining dif-ficulty may have to be resolved by ministerial approval of compulsory purchase orders if the minister judges it to be right for the greater good, whether they be local con-cerns or the nation's economic health.

However, judgement on the development is still largely based upon whether the mitigated impacts of a proposed development are tolerable for the local communities. There is, therefore, no overt attempt to achieve a balance. Rather, it is a question of imposing no less than minimum acceptable impacts on the local communities, and then allowing the developers and the other beneficiaries to take the surplus, as well as the minimum viable return on the development. The crucial balance between local and national issues has been increasingly decided after the inquiry by a group of government ministers and their advisors who weight the concerns in a much less transparent way, often resulting in decisions that bear little relationship to the inquiry proceedings. Yet, now that many airports are in private hands, it is more important that net benefits are shared equitably between the stakeholders, rather than being biased towards owners or the nation as a whole.

UK SERAS methodology

In the UK again, the South-Eastern and East of England Regional Air Service Study (SERAS) is considering development options for increasing London airport capac-ity. The appraisal methodology has been decided and made explicit (DETR, 2000b), treading a careful path between the transparency required to avoid accusations of covert decision-making and the blight and confusion that is often the consequence of a fully public process. The large number of possible site options is to be gradually reduced to three or four feasible packages through a process of four sifts. The eventual optional packages may consist of combinations of the previously considered single options. The team of government ministers will decide which schemes to carry forward to the next sift against a set of pre-determined objectives. The ministers will generate the weightings to be applied to the objectives. They will be assisted by two panels. One of the panels meets approximately monthly, consists of government officials and experts who advise the study, and has access to all pertinent information. The other panel meets less frequently, has a broader representation of interested parties, and does not share in the site-specific information. This reduces the possibility of needless scare stories causing local blight. The final packages will include a range of possible solutions, from a 'do nothing' option to a new mega-airport; the other packages have capacities between these two extremes. Once they are chosen, there will be full public consultation on these packages, the feedback being a vital element in determining government policy.

The SERAS appraisal framework deliberately has little to say about how to balance the interests of the various parties, either between environmental and economic objectives, between the different societal groups or between national and local interests. The weighting between these interests is still being left to ministers who will take on board the views of the officials and members of the advisory committees, augmented by public consultation in the last stage of the sifting of packages. It is expected that initiatives will also be taken within the planning process to allow a fairer balance to be struck through new forms of compensation, perhaps through local tax relief, cross transfer of taxes between jurisdictions, hypothecated noise charges or private deals.

Financial compensation

There is seldom an equal distribution of costs and benefits. In an ideal market economy, the price of transport would determine not only how each mode would be used but also how much travel was beneficial for society at large. In other words, the full social costs imposed by each unit of travel would be reflected in the cost of travel. It ought, in theory, to be possible to recycle the social costs of pollution. Some options are described by Grayling and Bishop (2001); but none of them is easy. Market forces operate with a decision rule that one dollar equates to one vote, while democracy operates on the basis that one person equates to one vote (Flyvbjerg, 1984). So, even if the price of transport accurately reflected the true long-term value of resources used, principles of social justice would still require additional judgements to be made. Ultimately, these judgements are made through the political process, but the judgements should be well informed.

An option for approaching the problem, if a fair market price can be established, is for the airport to buy out the property in the same way as would happen in the UK if a compulsory purchase order were to be obtained, with compensation for moving in compliance with the Land Compensation Act, 1973. British Rail offered to do this for properties within a 240 metre (m) wide corridor around the channel tunnel rail link in negotiation with Kent County Council, though it appears that the Department for Transport (DfT) is only prepared to allow up to UK£5000 as an additional 'solace' payment for houses within 100m of the track, compared with UK£30,000 for houses within 300m of the line of the M25 motorway (*Times of London*, 1997, p15). In the case of Dallas/Fort Worth (DFW), residents are offered a choice between buyout, the purchase of easements or the assurance of guaranteed sales, and US$125 million has been allocated to mitigate the effects on the city of Irving, relative to a likely project budget of US$3.5 billion.

The most satisfactory outcome must be when a win–win result can be obtained. This becomes more likely when a 'green–gold' coalition can be formed. A perhaps fortuitous example was the development of the high bypass turbofan engine that simultaneously cut noise and increased fuel efficiency. If the trade-offs can be correctly estimated, there must be scope for other technical and managerial win–win solutions to achieving sustainable growth in aviation, even though the result to each stakeholder may not be as advantageous as such stakeholders would have been anticipating in the absence of the need for cooperation. The air transport industry must still be educated in the need for sustainability (Everitt, 2001). A step in the right direction is the setting of targets by the Advisory Council for Aeronautics Research in Europe in order to halve fuel burn and perceived noise by 2020 (*Flight*, 2001, p6). However, it is likely to cost UK£100,000 to take an additional person out of noise contours, and it may be better to spend the money in the community than on technology (Ellis, 2001). The present capacity caps that are imposed upon movements at airports in response to their individual sensitivity to ecology, air pollution, water pollution, noise and social issues are somewhat crude attempts to preserve a balance based more upon 'do not lose too much' rather than the more palatable solutions that might be available from a system-wide assessment of the need for change.

CONCLUSION

Estimating the social and economic benefits of aviation is fraught with difficulty. Nevertheless, those benefits are as real as the costs, and some balance between the two is required. The essence is to seek consensus rather than compromise and commitment rather than agreement. This may be an unpalatable conclusion for the stakeholders in a system attempting to adjust to a new environment of untrammelled competition, coupled with freedom from government intervention. Equally, it does not help for Green representatives in the European Parliament to require that within 18 months the noise around airports be reduced to levels found in public libraries (*ACI Communiqué*, 2001). Yet, this search for new values through cooperation may be the only way to achieve a win–win solution, without which progress would not be made. The emphasis has to be on joint progress and mediation rather than conflict and confrontation.

REFERENCES

ACI (1998) *Creating Employment and Prosperity in Europe*, Airports Council International (Europe), Brussels, September
ACI Communiqué (1996) Brussels, November, p23
ACI Communiqué (2001) Brussels, February/March, p9

Booz-Allen and Hamilton (1998) 'Chicago aviation policy', Chicagoland Chamber of Commerce, November in TRB (2001) *Aviation Gridlock Phase II*, Circ ec032, May, Transportation Research Board, Washington, DC

Brathen, S, Eriksen, K S, Hjelle, H M and Killi, M (2000) 'Economic appraisal in Norwegian aviation', *Journal of Air Transport Management*, vol 6, pp153–166

Breheny, M J (1987) 'The urbanisation impacts of airport development', Lecture notes for short course in Airport Planning Procedures, Department of Transport Technology, Loughborough University, November

British Airways (1996) *Annual Environmental Report 1996: Report of Additional Environmental Data*, BA Report Number 9/96, London

Britton, S G and Kissling, C C (1984) 'Aviation and development constraints in South Pacific microstates' in Kissling, C C (ed) *Transport and Communication for Pacific Microstates*, The Institute for Pacific Studies, University of the South Pacific, Suva

Butler, S E and Kiernan, L J (1986) *Measuring the Regional Economic Significance of Airports*, US Department of Transportation, Federal Aviation Administration, October, Washington, DC

Butler, S E and Kiernan, L J (1988) 'Transport benefits from regional airports', *Airports Technology International*, pp 38–40

CAA (1994) *The Economic Impact of New Air Services*, CAP 638, UK Civil Aviation Authority, London, November

Caves, R E (1994) 'Aviation and society – redrawing the balance, part II', *Transportation Planning and Technology*, vol 18(1), pp21–36

Caves, R E (1996) 'Control of risk near airports', *Built Environment*, vol 22(3), pp223–233

Caves, R E and Gosling, G (1999) *Strategic Airport Planning*, Elsevier Science Ltd, Oxford

Cooper, R (1990) 'Airports and economic development: an overview', *Transportation Research Record 1274*, pp125–133

Coopers and Lybrand (1995) *Assessment of Wider Economic Benefits: Summary Report and Appendices*, British Airways Report BA 15 to Heathrow Airport Terminal 5 Inquiry, London, April

Creedy, K B (1991) 'The cost of realistic bilaterals', *Interavia*, March, pp19–21

DETR (1999) *Guidance on Methodologies for Assessing Economic Benefits from Airport Capacity Increases and New Air Services*, Department of the Environment, Transport and the Regions, December, UK

DETR, (2000a) *The Future of Aviation – The Government's Consultation Document on Air Transport Policy*, Department of the Environment, Transport and the Regions, December, UK

DETR, (2000b) *Appraisal Framework for Airports in South East and East of England*, Department of the Environment, Transport and the Regions, December, UK

Edgell, D L Sr (1990) *International Tourism Policy*, Van Nostrand, New York

Ellis, P (2001) 'The Airline Perspective: British Airways', Paper Presented to the Conference on Policy Directions in UK Air Transport: the Next Ten Years, Royal Geographical Society, 14 March, London

Everitt, R (2001) 'Airport Capacity and Congestion: the Southeast', Paper Presented to the Conference on Policy Directions in UK Air Transport: the Next Ten Years, Royal Geographical Society, 14 March, London

FAA (1978) *Aircraft and the Environment*, Report GA-300-104, US Department of Transportation, Federal Aviation Administration, Northwest Region, Boeing Field, Seattle

Flight, 6 February 2001, p6

Flyvbjerg, B (1984) 'Implementation and the choice of evaluation methods', *Transport Policy Decision Making*, vol 2, pp291–314

Fujii, E, Im, E and Mak, J (1992) 'The economies of direct flights', *Journal of Transport Economics and Policy*, vol XXVI, part 2, pp185–195

Grayling, A (2001) 'Air Transport Growth: The Macro Economic Viewpoint', Paper Presented to the Conference on Policy Directions in UK Air Transport: The Next Ten Years, Royal Geographical Society, 14 March, London

Grayling, A and Bishop, S (2001) *Sustainable Aviation 2030*, IPPR Discussion Paper, Institute for Public Policy Research, London

Haitovsky Y, Salomon, I and Silman, L A (1987) 'The economic impact of charter flights on tourism to Israel', *Journal of Transport Economics and Policy*, May, pp111–135

ICAO (1977) *Studies to Determine the Contribution that Civil Aviation Can Make to the Development of the National Economies of African States*, UNDP/ICAO Project RAF/74/021, March, International Civil Aviation Organization, Montreal

Karyd, A and Brobeck, H (1992) 'The delusion of social benefits', *Avmark Aviation Economist*, January, pp16–17

Mahmassani, H S and Toft, G S (1985) 'Transportation requirements for high technology industrial development', *Journal of Transportation Engineering*, vol 111(5), pp473–484

Oxford Economic Forecasting (1999) *The Economic Contribution of Aviation to the UK*, OEF, Oxford

Robertson, J A W (1995) 'Airports and economic regeneration', *Journal of Air Transport Management*, vol 2(2), pp81–88

SRI (1990) *A European Planning Strategy for Air Traffic to the Year 2010*, SRI International, for International Air Transport Association, Geneva

Sunday Times, 13 October 1996, London, Business Section, p9

The Times of London (1997) 2 May 1997, p15

The Times of London (1996), 27 July 1996, p27

Wheatcroft, S (1994) *Aviation and Tourism Policies: Balancing the Benefits*, World Tourism Organization/Routledge, London

Williams, F and Gibson, D V (eds) (1990) *Technology Transfer*, Sage Publishers, London

Chapter 4

The human health impacts of aviation

Ken Hume and Adrian Watson

INTRODUCTION

There are increasing pressures on the environment and human health due to world-wide growth of the transport industry. The aviation industry poses a unique set of health issues on a number of groups: passengers, aircrew, airport personnel and communities living around airports. These health impacts are set to increase with the global increase of aviation that has undergone rapid growth over the last decade and is predicted to double during the next 15 years. On very rare but tragic occasions the lives of passengers, aircrew and individuals, who may have no immediate connection with aviation, are at extreme risk from air accidents and hijacks – as demonstrated at Lockerbie and, more recently, New York.

There is a full range of health issues associated with aviation, from a 'reduction in physical and mental well-being', as included in the World Health Organization (WHO) definition of health, to acute serious medical conditions. For example, jet lag is a condition where the physical and mental condition of the sufferer is clearly compromised but not in a critical medical state, while a passenger with deep vein thrombosis (DVT) has a serious medical condition.

The groups of people affected and the situations in which their health is potentially put at risk by aviation are complex and not described by one simple list. Thus, jet lag can present a considerable physiological challenge after a flight from London to Sydney, crossing nine time zones, but is hardly an issue from London to Cape Town, where only one time zone is crossed.

In this chapter we will consider some aspects of the human health impact of aviation, but because of the breadth of the subject will focus on two topics, the aircraft cabin environment and the local community surrounding airports and, in particular, air and noise pollution.

THE AIRCRAFT CABIN ENVIRONMENT

As aircraft operators seek to reduce operating costs by operating at higher altitudes, thereby reducing fuel use, and increasing the capacity of seats within their aircraft fleet, a number of concerns have arisen amongst the medical profession, aircrew and passengers regarding the impacts of air travel that the aviation industry is being forced to address. As an example, the general cabin environment is, by necessity of flying at high altitude, pressurized. Hence, approximately 50 per cent of the air in the passenger cabin is recirculated, reprocessed cabin air, supplemented by external air. The recirculated atmosphere typically has low ventilation levels, a low cabin pressure of 0.74 atmospheres (atm), low humidity (15–20 per cent) and reduced levels of oxygen available to passengers for respiration. At the same time, elevated carbon dioxide (CO_2) levels and the presence of 'trace' contaminants such as bio-aerosols (despite the use of high-efficiency, particle-arresting filters, HEPAs), carbon monoxide, ozone, environmental tobacco smoke and other trace organic compounds have all been reported (Dechow et al, 1997; Hocking, 2000).[1] While all these levels are within acceptable guidelines, these factors can lead to airborne illness and this has led to agencies such as the American Society of Heating, Refrigerating and Air-Conditioning Engineers (ASHRAE), the Federal Aviation Administration (FAA) and the UK Civil Aviation Authority (CAA) to review various aspects, including both chemical and biological parameters, of the cabin environment.

The following sections outline the current major concerns regarding the impacts of the cabin environment upon health for both passengers and aircrew.

PASSENGERS

Deep vein thrombosis (DVT)

Perhaps the most controversial of in-flight health effects upon passengers is currently deep vein thrombosis (DVT). However, DVT is not a new phenomenon and the possibility of links between immobility and venous thromboembolism was recognized during 1940 by Simpson, who noted the high incidence (a sixfold increase) in pulmonary embolism amongst people sleeping overnight in deckchairs while sheltering from the London blitz – a phenomenon that subsequently disappeared when the deckchairs were replaced by bunks (Simpson, 1940). As long ago as 1954, Homans reported venous thrombosis in a 54-year-old doctor after a 14-hour flight, and suggested that prolonged sitting in airplane flights was able to bring on thrombosis in the deep veins of the legs (Homans, 1954). However, DVT events have recently gained high levels of media coverage due to high-profile deaths after long-haul flights, which – when combined with the threat of class-action lawsuits against airlines (an Australian law firm using three test cases launched legal action in July 2001 against KLM, Qantas Airways, British Airways and Australia's Civil Aviation Safety Authority) – make DVT a highly contentious issue.

DVT refers to the formation of a thrombosis (blood clot) within a deep vein, commonly within the thigh or calf. One cause of DVT is poor blood circulation associated with prolonged inactivity, such as is found in passengers on long-haul flights, although many other risk factors are known (see Table 4.1); but, as yet, the magnitude and independence of each risk factor is uncertain. The thrombosis can either partially or completely block the flow of blood in the vein, which in many cases causes no ill effects. However, there can be serious complications – most notably, formation of a pulmonary embolism. A pulmonary embolism can occur when the blood clot breaks free from the vein wall and travels to the lung, where it blocks an artery with potentially life-threatening consequences and requires immediate medical attention.

Table 4.1 *Reported risk factors for the development of DVT*

Patient-related risk factors	Cabin-related risk factors
Blood disorders affecting clotting tendency – thrombophilia	Flight duration or frequency of travel
Impairment of blood clotting mechanism, such as genetic clotting-factor abnormalities factor V Lieden[2] and prothrombin G20210A; these may explain up to 25% of all thrombotic events	Prolonged immobilization, especially in a seated position (particularly cross-legged)
Cardiovascular disease	Coach position
Presence of malignancy	Low air pressure
Recent trauma to lower limbs or abdomen (previous six weeks)	Relative hypoxia
Personal or family history of thrombosis	Low humidity
Recent minor surgery (previous three days) and major surgery (particularly leg surgery)	Dehydration – depletion of body fluids causing increased blood viscosity
Pregnancy or puerperium (the period from birth to the first six weeks postpartum)	
Women on oestrogen hormone replacement therapy, or oral contraceptives	
Increasing age above 40 years	
Obesity	
Smoking	
Varicose veins	

Source: Arfvidsson et al, 2000; Kesteven and Robinson, 2001

While DVT events have been recognized in many modes of transport, air travel is most typically associated with situations where the passenger is in a restricted position (ie immobilized for prolonged periods, such as on long-haul flights). Because of the 'cramped' seating arrangements associated with economy-class air travel, DVT was alternatively termed 'economy class syndrome' (Symington and Stack, 1977). However, many experts believe this to be a misconceived term suggesting the possibility that first and business class travellers need not concern themselves with the possibility of DVT, and the more appropriate term 'traveller's thrombosis' is now preferred (House of Lords, 2000).

The majority of commentators now agree that there is a connection between air travel and DVT, although the evidence is still largely circumstantial (Geroulakis, 2001). However, it is difficult to compare many of the medical studies because of differences in case selection and data presentation, and there are disagreements as to the true frequency of air-travel-related DVT events (Hirsch and O'Donnell, 2001). This is illustrated by recent studies that have ranged from showing no association between air travel (for travel more than five hours' duration) and DVT (Kraaijenhagen et al, 2000), a 3.8 times increased risk of venous thromboembolic disease for travel over four hours (Ferrarri et al, 1999), through to a 10 per cent risk of symptomless DVT occurring in long-haul flight passengers (travel over eight hours' duration) (Scurr et al, 2001). Thus, while a fair risk assessment of air travel and DVT has still to be performed, a rough estimate of travel-associated venous thromboembolism is 0.5–3 per 10,000 general population per annum (Kesteven, 2000).

There are two key reasons for the lack of data regarding the true frequency of DVT during long-haul flight. Firstly, many DVT events are symptomless and the traveller may have no cause to seek any medical attention; secondly, most travel-related venous thromboembolic disease is not recognized, as the patient can present many days or weeks after the journey in which the clot originally appeared.

As a result of the lack of conclusive data and the increasing public concern toward air travel and DVT, the WHO convened a meeting of international experts in March 2001 to review the existing state of evidence. It concluded that further research is necessary, identifying three priorities for further research that should be undertaken as soon as possible:

- The first priority is to establish whether or not traveller's thrombosis is a real entity and, in particular, is a link between DVT and air travel. This will be achieved through a set of multicentre international epidemiological studies, including a large prospective cohort study. If a link is to be proven, then the research would also offer answers as to the absolute risk of DVT in air passengers and the true scale of the problem, as well as providing clues to other causative factors.
- The second priority is to identify independent risk factors for flight-related DVT, both cabin related and behavioural, such as cabin air pressure, cabin oxygenation levels, excessive use of alcohol and lack of exercise. This will demonstrate how dangerous flying is compared to other forms of transport for the development of traveller's thrombosis.
- The third priority is an interventional study involving passengers prospectively using objective diagnostic methods and examining various interventional modes (ie in the event of a proven link, this will enable appropriate management of the syndrome).

Preventative measures

Despite the lack of reliable and conclusive data, there is increasing concern over DVT amongst the aviation industry, medical profession and general public. Since DVT is still potentially fatal, there is a perceived requirement for greater recognition of the syndrome so that preventative treatments can be adopted to promote healthy travel. In February 2001, the International Air Transport Association (IATA) advised all carriers to inform travellers of the risk of DVT when travellers make their reservation. Airlines such as Qantas, Air New Zealand and Singapore Airlines now offer advice on DVT on their main websites.[3] Others such as Japan Airlines, Lufthansa and KLM are also considering methods of informing travellers of the risks by updating passenger information material via in-flight magazines, audio and video programming or health leaflets attached to tickets.

Meanwhile, doctors recommend a variety of practices to prevent thrombotic events after airline travel, including leg exercises, walking around the cabin where possible within safety constraints, avoidance of alcohol and smoking, and drinking plenty of water. As a response to public attitudes, British Airways introduced an in-flight exercise programme in 2001, which primarily comprises stretching exercises that are designed to be carried out in the airline seat by passengers. Although not licensed for preventing travel-related DVT, many experts now advocate taking aspirin pre-flight for those passengers who have been determined to be at a moderate risk of thrombo-embolic disease (House of Lords, 2000). For those passengers with a case history of thrombotic disease, some experts have recommended wearing elasticated compression stockings (Scurr et al, 2001) or administering subcutaneous anti-coagulants, such as low-molecular weight heparin (Kesteven, 2000).

Finally, some commentators are calling for airlines to re-evaluate seating arrangements in some aircraft cabins that are not conducive to moving in and out of seats, particularly for large individuals. The storage of luggage under seats and the seat pitch (usually between 71–79cm or less) restricts leg room, and compression of the popliteal vein can be caused by the edge of the seat when sitting in cramped conditions for prolonged periods, which can lead to decreased venous blood flow (Hitosugi et al, 2000). However, any increase in economy passenger's room will be at a cost, with the improvements passed onto the consumer as higher ticket prices; in the absence of conclusive further medical study, there is no firm scientific foundation for such cost.

Airborne disease and infection (tuberculosis)

The increase in international travel and migration has also seen an increase in the spread of a number of infectious diseases such as AIDS and cholera; consequently, there is great interest in the role and mode of travel in disease transmission. As a result of the typical conditions associated with airline travel (ie a close and restricted confinement for many hours, combined with a high proportion of recirculated air), experts have expressed the concern that passengers are at an increased health risk from fellow passengers, particularly with regard to bio-aerosols and airborne infection. The bio-aerosol risk is believed to be primarily for contagious disease or for exacerbation of an existing asthma condition.

Studies on the concentration of micro-organisms in US airline cabin air found numbers of micro-organisms to be lower than in ordinary city locations and unlikely to be a contributor to the risk of transmission among passengers. The numbers found were comparable to typical indoor environments, particularly when in flight and when the aircraft environmental control systems are operating (Wick and Irvine, 1995). One reason for this is the use of high-efficiency particulate air (HEPA) filters in the air recirculation units, which can capture aerosol and particulate material as small as 0.3 microns.

For most biological agents, there is no data related to dose and response except for the case of tuberculosis (TB). TB is endemic in some countries (during 1996, 3.8 million new cases of TB were reported to the WHO), while it is relatively rare in others, and the potential for its transmission and introduction amongst disease-free areas is high. TB is the leading cause of death worldwide from infectious disease, and owing to the mode of transmission experts have raised particular concerns about exposure amongst passengers and aircrew. TB infection is acquired through inhalation of *Mycobacterium tuberculosis* in aerosolized respiratory secretions from an infectious person coughing, talking or sneezing. The risk of infection is related to the proximity and duration of exposure to the source patient. Decreased ventilation in crowded and confined environments is often a contributing risk factor. Although a single flight carries the risk of a relatively limited exposure, prolonged sojourn in a confined aircraft cabin may increase the risk of transmission of *Mycobacterium tuberculosis* (WHO, 1998).

During the past few years, several episodes of potential transmission of TB infection during air travel have been reported, some of which have raised great anxiety amongst the general population, health authorities, mass media and airline companies. No case of active TB has been identified as a result of exposure while on a commercial air flight; however, there is evidence that transmission of *Mycobacterium tuberculosis* may occur during long-haul flights (ie more than eight hours) from an infectious source to other passengers or crew members. Decreased ventilation and confined environment are risk factors. However, a single flight contains minimal risk of exposure, while prolonged travel may increase the risk of transmission (Driver et al, 1994; Anon, 1995; Kenyon et al, 1996).

The reason that transmission of TB appears to be rare is that most modern aircraft recirculate up to 50 per cent of the cabin air, with the remainder made up from fresh bleed air. *Mycobacterium tuberculosis* is between 0.5 and 1.0 microns; therefore, the HEPA filters used in recirculation (0.3 microns) should remove the tubercle bacilli from the cabin air during the recirculation process, providing the HEPA filters are well maintained. As a result, the potential risk from a person with infectious TB in an aircraft with recirculation should therefore be limited to droplet spread to a small number of seats in the immediate vicinity of the infected passenger before recirculation takes place (Ormerod, 2000).

Control and prevention of disease transmission

During 1998 the WHO produced guidelines for the control and prevention of TB transmission via air travel that would apply to all domestic and international airlines. The main guidelines were:

- Once informed by health authorities, airline companies should inform passengers and crew of possible infection and encourage the passengers to establish whether or not infection has occurred, and whether or not preventative treatment is required. To facilitate this, airlines should maintain complete passenger contact records.

- Maximum-efficiency air filters should be installed and properly maintained on all aircraft and ground delays kept to a minimum.
- Anyone with infectious TB should postpone travel until they become non-infectious. However, boarding can and should be denied to individuals known to have infectious TB.

Air travel does not seem to carry greater risk of infection with exposure to potentially infectious tuberculosis than other modes of transport; however, it is important that airlines follow the WHO guidelines in order to ensure that the transmission of disease is kept to a minimum.

FLIGHT CREWS

Occupationally, cockpit crews (and frequent flyers) are exposed to elevated levels of cosmic radiation, electromagnetic fields, sound, vibration, chemical substances, dry air, and viral/infective particles during flight operations. They also operate in conditions of mild hypoxia and circadian dysrhythmia. Work stress levels amongst cabin staff are high and have been strongly implicated in complaints about workplace (cabin) air quality.

Aircrew exposure to cosmic radiation

One of the most studied of the in-flight environmental parameters is the effect of cosmic radiation on aircrew. A common concern amongst aircrews is that the increasing total accumulated dose over time might be expected to cause an increased frequency of radiation-induced cancer. If this is the case, the cancer rate should increase with cumulative radiation exposure (ie number of flight hours per year, number of years of flying and higher flight altitude). It is believed that crew members who fly jets may receive a dose that is four to five times the average background radiation dose. While this is still a low radiation dose, high-altitude cosmic radiation has a large neutron radiation component which has a high impact owing to its biological effectiveness (10 to 100 times more effective than gamma rays). Hence, the radiation exposure offers grounds for concern.

Radiation dosage levels vary with levels of solar activity, flight duration, route of operation, latitude (increasing at higher magnetic latitudes) and altitude (increasing with altitude up to a maximum of around 20km). Despite practical difficulties associated with radiation dose measurements, owing to the high neutron content of the radiation, a number of studies have made assessments of radiation doses at a variety of latitudes and subsonic cruising altitudes, typically 9–13km, and suggest that aircrews are exposed to doses between 2 and 10 micro-Sieverts per hour (μSv h^{-1}) (Regulla and David, 1993; Schalch and Scharmann, 1993; Beaujean et al, 1998; O'Brien et al, 1998; Schrewe, 1999).[4] This equates to an annual average radiation dose in the region of 3–6 milli-Siverts per year (mSv yr^{-1}), assuming typical aircrew work patterns (Blettner et al, 1998; Hammer et al, 2000). Measurements on aircraft operating at higher altitudes, such as Concorde, suggested a higher received dose from 9–13μSv h^{-1} (Bagshaw, 1999).

Validated computer models are now available to estimate dosage that take into account changes in altitude and geographical location during a flight. One of the more commonly used is CARI–6 that was developed by the FAA Civil Aeromedical Institute in the US, and is freely available from the FAA via the Internet (www.cami.jccbi.gov/AAM-600/610/600Radio.html).

A number of studies have been performed that suggest a slightly increased risk of certain cancers (eg skin cancer: melanoma and basal-cell carcinoma) occurring on the trunk and limbs, prostrate cancer in pilots, brain cancer, breast cancer and acute myeloid leukaemia (see Table 4.2). Other cancers have also been reported but not at significant levels of incidence (eg cancers of the stomach, pancreas, colon, larynx, rectum and Hodgkin's disease) (Gundestrup and Storm, 1999; Ballard et al, 2000). Published studies still do not paint a clear picture, and most authors still interpret their results with great caution. Future studies are underway – in particular, the joint European cohort mortality study, which aims to standardize study protocol design across Europe and to provide a pooled analysis from the participating countries. The combined analysis should be the most powerful to date and provide much needed important information regarding the occupational cancer risk amongst aircrews (Blettner et al, 1998).

Table 4.2 *Socio-economic status-adjusted relative risks for cancer incidence and mortality amongst flight personnel*

	Relative risk (RR)	95% Confidence interval
Amongst male pilots		
Mortality from melanoma	1.97	1.02–3.82
Mortality from brain cancer	1.49	0.89–2.20
Incidence of prostrate cancer	1.65	1.19–2.29
Incidence of brain cancer	1.74	0.87–3.30
Amongst female flight attendants		
Incidence of all cancers	1.29	0.98–1.70
Incidence of melanoma	1.54	0.83–2.87
Incidence of breast cancer	1.35	1.00–1.83

Source: Ballard et al, 2000

Legislation relating to in-flight radiation exposure

In 1991 the International Commission on Radiation Protection (ICRP) (ICRP 60, 1991) published the recommendation that natural sources of radiation be classified as occupational exposures and recommended an occupational annual limit of 20mSv yr^{-1}, compared to a public limit of 1mSv yr^{-1}. Consequently, aircrews are considered to be one of the most highly exposed occupational groups, although their dosage is still typically less than half of the ICRP 60 recommended dose (ICRP 60, 1991). The recommendations of ICRP 60 were incorporated into European legislation, and requirements for the protection of aircraft crew are given in Article 42 of the European

Union Council Directive 96/29/EURATOM. While member states were required to transpose these provisions into national law by May 2000, there are wide variances between different member states' implementations of these new regulations (Bartlett, 1999; Courades, 1999).

The EURATOM legislation requires that:

- Exposure records must be kept for exposed aircrew.
- Appropriate measures should be undertaken in order to assess exposure to cosmic radiation of aircrew who are liable to be subject to cosmic radiation in excess of 1mSv yr^{-1}.
- Exposure should be taken into account when organizing work schedules to reduce the received dose.
- Workers must be informed of the occupational health risks.
- Additional provision should be made for pregnant aircrew (or breast-feeding aircrew) because of the increased risk of chromosomal damage to the foetus. Once pregnancy is declared, the employer is obliged to plan future occupational exposure to the foetus so that it is as low as reasonably achievable, and no greater than 1mSv yr^{-1}, for the remainder of the pregnancy. To achieve this legislation some aircraft operators have determined that pregnant crew members cease flying duties on declaration of pregnancy.[5]

Overall, flight personnel operate within an environment containing high levels of cosmic radiation and appear to be at an increased occupational risk for several types of cancer. While current legislation addresses this occupational risk, further studies are still required to establish the true nature of the risk, including the contribution of other occupational and non-occupational confounding factors.

FINAL CONSIDERATIONS REGARDING THE CABIN ENVIRONMENT

Despite all of the concerns regarding the in-flight cabin environment, air travel is still as safe (if not safer) a mode of transportation as any other, and most of the current issues mentioned previously relate to small and, as yet, often unproven health risks. However, the aircraft cabin is an example of a niche environment that is still to be fully characterized, and there is still the need for the appropriate professionals and airline companies to investigate in-flight health issues. Airlines need to exhibit caution with regard to the health of the cabin environment for a number of reasons. First, from a consumer perspective, passengers expect airlines to provide a safe and comfortable travel experience and will not support airlines that cannot offer this. Second, many health-affected passengers are now pursuing legal routes, and to avoid litigation airlines will need to be able to demonstrate transparency with regard to how they cater for the health of their passengers, rather than the obstacles to information access that many believe airlines currently have in place.

Ultimately, there is an onus on airlines, with the cooperation of scientists and medical professionals, in order to assess and inform the public and cabin staff about in-flight health risks, making sure they are put clearly into context so that travellers can make informed decisions regarding their health.

COMMUNITY HEALTH ISSUES

For most people, the potential health risk associated with aviation is part of a conscious voluntary act that is traded off against the benefits of air travel or employment. However, for many individuals living close to major airports, there are mainly the negative aspects of a close source of noise and air pollution. For airports near to urban centres, these can affect a considerable number of individuals. The main community health issues are associated with noise, air pollution and third-party risk.

Aircraft noise

It seems patently obvious, and has been clearly established, that aircraft noise adversely affects people living near airports. Loud aircraft noise is a source of irritation and annoyance that can disturb activities and interfere with communication (Berglund and Lindvall, 1995). For some vulnerable groups of individuals (those who are elderly, children, chronically ill, neurotic, or hospitalized) this could lead to chronic conditions of stress, maladaptation and ill health.

The disturbance caused by aircraft noise is the single most important environmental issue to affect the growth of airports in Europe (Berglund and Lindvall, 1995; Berglund, Lindvall and Schwela, 1999). Noise-related operational controls and limits have already significantly constrained the growth of some major European airports (ICAO, 1993). Aircraft noise technology is improving, but these benefits are being offset by the growth in air traffic. At the same time, residents of communities near airports are becoming more sensitive to issues such as noise disturbance and fear of crashes and have increasing expectations with regard to health, well-being and quality of life (Moss et al, 1997).

There is little evidence of direct auditory damage caused by aircraft noise in the community except in the most extreme cases. However, there are other less direct effects of noise, frequently described as non-auditory, that are considered by many authors to detract from the health and well-being of the recipient. Responses to aircraft noise that have been associated with possible health effects include:

- annoyance and complaint;
- sleep disturbance;
- stress.

It is obvious that the above are not mutually exclusive. For example, sleep disturbance could certainly lead to annoyance besides its more immediate physiological effects on the sleep process and become a source of stress. One of the first difficulties encountered in this research area is the lack of a common universal metric to describe the noise environment. There are two main types applied: single noise events or cumulative scores. Single noise events are usually described by $Lmax$ (maximum noise level experienced) or the peak sound exposure level (SEL), which measures the maximum instantaneous noise level experienced during a given brief period of time. Cumulative measurements usually consider noise on an energy averaged basis over a specific time period and can be differentiated into daytime, evening and night. The FAA in the US uses the community noise equivalent level (CNEL), while the UK commonly uses *Leq* as the long-term average noise exposure measure. Many authors are critical of cumulative noise measures and there is evidence that annoyance is more highly correlated with a measure of single extreme noise events rather than cumulative energy measures (Bjorkman and Rylander, 1995).

To explore the nature and extent of the potential damage to health and well-being, research in this area has included:

- attitudinal surveys of residents by questionnaires and focus groups;
- direct physiological monitoring of individuals in laboratories or field settings with actual or reproduced noise events;
- archival interrogation of medical records in affected localities compared with unaffected areas. Individuals may seek medication to relieve the general stress syndrome, which may express itself in a number of minor ailments or specifically as 'insomnia' due to night flights. This course of action has given researchers another investigative tool in the form of the prevalence of patients visiting local medical practitioners for hypnotics and sedatives.

Due to difficulties applying clear 'dose–response' relationships in the health domain, some authors and governments have looked at other disciplines to determine the extent of the perceived problem. For example, in order to derive an economic value of community disturbance, house price devaluation in noise-affected areas has been studied (Tomkins et al, 1998). This tendency to avoid moving into, or relocating out of, noisy areas presents a further confounding factor for research studies in that the study population is potentially self-selected, with coping survivors in the worst affected areas.

A recent approach has been to investigate the records of complaints made directly to the airports in relation to aspects of the airport's operations in an attempt to understand their objections, and any underlying patterns of complaining behaviour. This is an approach that has been suggested by a WHO task group (Berry and Jiggins, 1999), who included longitudinal studies in a list of research needs in order to investigate the causal connections between mental health effects, annoyance and spontaneous complaints.

In addition to noise exposure, there are numerous modifying factors – for example, personal benefits from the airport (employment or frequent use) – that can mask or modify the apparent adverse affects (Flindell and Stallen, 1999). This is a major confounding issue that can obscure relationships in many studies in this area.

Annoyance

Annoyance is a subjective reaction frequently reported in response to environmental noise. The reported level of annoyance is obviously influenced by many non-acoustical modifying factors – for example, attitudinal, personal and contextual factors (such as general health, attitude to the noise source or noise sensitivity) – that act to obscure attempts to investigate cause-and-effect relationships. Nevertheless, determining the extent of annoyance with airport operations by means of questionnaire surveys of local residents has been the main method of assessing non-acoustical responses to aircraft noise and has produced a rich source of data. Many early social survey studies investigating public perception of aircraft noise around airports showed that there were relatively high levels of reported annoyance due to aircraft noise, particularly at night (Brooker, 1978, 1985; Ollerhead et al, 1992). There is clear evidence for a dose–response relationship between aircraft noise and annoyance, with many psychological symptoms being positively related to annoyance (Morrell et al, 1997).

The advantage of using annoyance as a measure of disturbance is that it can act as a common indicator for many varied overt types of noise disturbance, such as being unable to get to sleep or hear a TV). On the other hand, covert risks such as air pollution and autonomic nervous system (ANS) activation are not usually perceived, do not enter the conscious psychological domain and hence cannot be readily appraised or reported by the recipient.

Annoyance with aircraft noise is greater (Morrell et al, 1997) in individuals who suffer from:

- sleep disturbance; and
- communication interference, such as telephone conversations;

and who:

- define themselves as noise sensitive;
- express a concern about the health effects of noise;
- harbour a fear of aircraft crashes.

The effects of noise are thought to be not simply caused by noise itself, and annoyance not simply governed by noise level (Fidell, 1999). Noise metrics on their own have failed to predict individual responses to noise, indicating that psychosocial modifying factors are involved. Hatfield et al (2001) found that expectations of future noise levels contribute to the physiological impact of the noise. It has also been suggested that fear of accidents is linked to increased sensitivity to noise and therefore leads to an increase in reported cases of annoyance (Reijneveld, 1994). Negative affectivity – a tendency to be sensitive to negative features of the environment and to be biased towards reporting negative outcomes – is another factor leading to perceptions that exposure to aircraft noise at night and noise sensitivity lead to poor health. This situation could be exacerbated by short- or long-term physical or mental problems or other stress in life, making it more likely to report health affected by aircraft noise at night (Diamond et al, 2000). There seems to be a link between annoyance with aircraft noise and mental health symptoms. Tarnopolsky et al (1980) found in a survey around Heathrow that symptoms, such as sleep problems, depression, irritability and tinnitus were more prevalent among those respondents who also reported high annoyance.

Of course, this raises the issue of causality: has noise caused psychological symptoms, or have psychological attributes led to noise annoyance? A person who is chronically very annoyed by aircraft noise has a clearly disturbed well-being, despite the fact that there is a lack of agreement on what measures constitute well-being. However, the missing evidence is a clear link between chronic extreme annoyance and higher rates of clinical morbidity and mortality. The main suggested pathway from annoyance to illness has been through a generalized stress response (Babisch, 1998); this is discussed in a later section 'Stress response'.

Recent results from a study around Schiphol Airport (Franssen et al, 1999) showed a higher than expected prevalence of serious aircraft noise annoyance in comparison with previous studies both at Schiphol and in other countries. The increased higher annoyance was explained by increased sensitivity to noise and concern about safety and the influence of the ongoing political and social debate about expansion of the airport.

Complaints

Besides indicating annoyance with aircraft noise by responding to noise pollution surveys, there are a number of more direct behavioural responses that give indications of residents' reduced well-being and quality of life. The potential direct action that residents can take includes (Gillen and Levesque, 1994):

* undertaking noise attenuation measures in the home;
* complaining to the airport and/or environmental health authorities;
* relocation;
* civil litigation;
* canvassing and media support;
* organizing political opposition.

One response to unwanted intrusive environmental noise is to complain about the cause of the annoyance. Concern about the impact of transportation noise on health and well-being, and the consequent restrictions on airport operations and developments, have been driven mainly by complainers and opposition from the communities affected. However, there has been apparently little effort to explore complaint data scientifically and to investigate the link between complaining, annoyance and ill health. A constant dilemma for regulatory bodies is how representative are certain vocal minorities of the population at large? Are complainers representative of the community and the 'tip of the iceberg' with a genuine complaint; or are they mainly composed of representatives of vulnerable groups or individuals from the community who readily complain about many issues? This is not a trivial matter as complainers and action groups sometimes have considerable leverage in terms of their ability to determine the outcome of official inquiries into planning applications for increases in airport infrastructure and operations.

There is some controversy about how useful complaints are in helping to quantify and provide insights into the problem. Some studies conclude that noise complaints do not sufficiently measure the community response to aircraft noise and, as a consequence, do not represent the size and scope of the problem (Luz et al, 1983; Borsky, 1979). However, other studies (Stockbridge and Lee, 1973; Gillen and Levesque, 1994; Bronzaft et al, 1998; van Wiechen et al, 2002; Hume et al, 2001a, b, c) conclude that complaints can provide useful insights into the problem of noise disturbance. The present authors consider that a well-structured complaints system operating in parallel with a computerized noise-monitoring system can provide very useful data to explore the relationship between aircraft noise and community annoyance.

Aggregate data on complaints per 1000 air movements at Pearson International Airport indicated that complaint activity increases with increased flights (Gillen and Levesque, 1994).

Studies carried out at Manchester Airport (Hume et al, 2001a, 2001b, 2001c), combining airport data on complaints with noise monitoring, found that:

- As expected, the louder the noise the more complaints were generated, with twice the complaints at 100L*max* decibel noise unit (dB(A)) compared with 65L*max* dB(A) (outdoor).
- Media interest, such as that generated by proposed airport developments, correlates with an increased level of complaints.
- Clear weekly and monthly patterns of complaint exist when the variation in flight densities is controlled for by calculating the complaints per 1000 flights (giving a reflection of sensitivity).
- There is a striking circadian pattern in the tendency to complain, with twice the tendency to complain between 23.00 pm and 07.00 am, and with the most sensitive time being between 24.00 pm and 01.00 am and the lowest between 14.00 pm and 15.00 pm.
- Most people complained a few times, while a few individuals, termed serial complainers, accounted for a considerable proportion of the complaints.

Sleep disturbance

Sleep disturbance is a common health issue in aviation. It is one of the main problems associated with jet lag in long-haul passengers and aircrew. Major airports operate over 24 hours, which requires night shifts with attendant sleep disturbance. Sleep disturbance is one of the main causes of complaint from communities living close to major airports who are subjected to aircraft noise at night.

A good night's sleep, in terms of adequate duration, depth and continuity, is a prerequisite for human health and well-being. It is a common experience that loud noise, such as over-flying aircraft, can disturb sleep. This is the basis of the recent judgement of the European Court of Human Rights (subsequently appealed against by the UK government) indicating that residents around Heathrow had a human right to a good night's sleep (Strasbourg, 2001).

Sleep disturbance due to aircraft noise is possibly the greatest cause of annoyance for residents near airports. This is not too surprising because insomnia, due to whatever cause, is a notable source of human misery. Studies have shown that noise causes a reduction in total sleep time and the pattern of sleep stages during the night. Vallet et al (1980) found that noisy conditions reduce sleep time and provoke brief EEG (electroencephalography – recordings of the electrical activity of the brain) arousal during all of the sleep stages. These findings are supported by the research of Wilkinson (1984) and Griefahn and Muzet (1978), who concluded that noise at night can lead to reduction of deep (slow-wave) sleep and possibly total sleep time.

It has been clearly established (Morrell et al, 1997) that high levels of aircraft noise are associated with sleep problems including:

- delayed sleep onset;
- increased awakenings from sleep;
- sleep loss;
- premature awakening at the end of the sleep;
- reduced reported quality of sleep.

It can also cause changes in the natural pattern of electrophysiologically defined sleep stages that humans display, reasonably consistently, each night. Noise can also evoke minor perturbations or brief arousals of the electroencephalogram recordings, which would not be consciously registered. Many of these brief arousals are associated with autonomic nervous system (ANS) activation, such as a temporary increase in heart rate (Muzet and Ehrhart, 1980; Whitehead et al, 1998). However, it is still unresolved how much such unwanted activation of the ANS contributes to pathological changes, as in cardiovascular disease.

Carter et al (1994a, b) carried out a laboratory study on a vulnerable group – nine heart-diseased subjects (cardiac arrhythmias). They found that road and air traffic noise (65–72dB(A)) increased arousals fivefold, while neither the rhythm defect nor the urinary catecholamine (a consequence of increased 'stress hormones') levels were significantly affected. There are further consequences with sleep disturbance. Sleep is the major time for rest and restitution of the brain and body, and when sleep is disturbed, one does not function optimally both mentally or physically during the following day, as the natural restorative processes have been impaired.

Carter (1996, 1998) has suggested that chronic noise-induced sleep disturbance could lead to several health disorders. They suggest a mechanism in which disturbance impairs the functions of sleep, which are largely unknown but are related to brain restoration, immune responses and other physiological systems. As sleep serves as a time of respite for the cardiovascular system, constant disturbance to sleep and the functions of sleep may have implications on long-term cardiovascular health (Carter, 1998). The slow-wave sleep that is affected by environmental noise is thought to be important to the immune system (Brown and Czeisler, 1992), and Carter (1996) states that the immune response of many people could be impaired by noise.

Many early studies on the assessment of noise-induced sleep disturbance were conducted in laboratories, as opposed to field studies where subjects are studied in their own homes. However, during the late 1980s, large discrepancies were becoming evident between laboratory and field studies, with far greater levels of sleep disturbance reported in the laboratory (Pearson et al, 1990, 1995).

During the early 1990s, a large field study (Ollerhead et al, 1992) was conducted in the UK to inform government decisions on night operations. The effects of night-time aircraft noise on the sleep of 400 residents living at eight sites adjacent to the four main airports in the UK was assessed. The main findings were that for aircraft noise below 80dB(A) Lmax outdoors (= 55dB(A) Lmax indoors) there was little disturbance, while for higher noise levels there was a chance of about 1 in 75 of being aroused from sleep (Horne et al, 1994). However, aircraft noise was found to be a relatively minor cause of sleep disturbance (about 5 per cent of reported awakenings), with domestic and other non-aircraft factors causing greater disturbance. In addition to the main technique of actimetry (measurement of limb movement), used for assessing sleep disturbance, the sleep of a sample (46) of the residents was recorded electrophysiologically. This showed that the lengths of sleep stages were similar to matched age and sex normal values quoted in the sleep research literature (eg Hume et al, 1998). However, finer analysis of the data (Hume et al, 2000) showed that there were clear but small effects within the subjects, with increased shifts to stage 1 (drowsy) sleep, wake and minor perturbations in association with aircraft noise events. Again, the health consequences of these minor perturbations of the ongoing sleep process due to aircraft noise are unknown.

Subsequent studies in the US (Fidell, 1995) using behavioural criteria in which subjects had to press a button to indicate awakening corroborated the UK study, indicating that, unlike laboratory studies, awakening in the home due to aircraft noise, except in the noisiest locations, is a rare event and only weakly correlated with the noise.

It should not be forgotten that mean values tend to obscure the considerable individual differences in noise sensitivity and sleep fragility. There was a large variation in the degree of sleep disturbance (2.5 times) between the least and most sensitive third of subjects who had EEG recorded (Hume et al, 2000; Van et al, 1993) in the Oller-head et al (1992) study.

The threshold for noise-induced awakening is usually quoted at about 55–60dB(A), but sleep stage changes and minor arousals without perceived awakening can occur at much lower noise levels (HCN, 1997; Berglund and Lindvall, 1995; Hume et al, 2000). It is also thought that intermittent noise is more disturbing to sleep than continuous noise, and leads to decreased time in slow-wave sleep (Carter, 1996). These findings corroborate Ohrstrom and Rylander (1982), who concluded that intermittent noise leads to poor performance and mood the following day. Fidell et al (1995) also found that individual noise intrusions were much more closely related to annoyance/awakenings than long-term noise exposure.

Porter et al (2000) reviewed the potential adverse effects of night-time aircraft noise as part of a continuing research effort by the UK government. Despite concluding that there was no hard scientific evidence of clinically significant health impairment, the possible existence of cause–effect relationships could not be rejected. A model of objective and subjective outcomes with linked chains of potential cause and effect was elaborated, which included:

- immediate physiological responses due to noise events that could lead to acute annoyance;
- total night effects as a sum of the immediate responses (eg sleep reduction and fragmentation);
- next-day effects, including increased sleepiness and reduced performance, causing perceived sleep disturbance, increased tiredness and annoyance;
- chronic effects that may be a deterioration of physical and mental health, with accompanying chronic annoyance and reduced quality of life.

The authors noted the potential confounding influence of modifying factors, such as attitude to the noise source, which could strongly influence the cause-and-effect chain within the model.

Everyday experience strongly suggests that a 'good' night's sleep is important for one's well-being. The evidence from field studies indicates that the level of sleep disturbance for most individuals is minor and, as such (given the strong homeostatic nature of sleep to compensate for disturbance), it appears difficult to deprive sleep sufficiently to produce adverse health effects in most situations. However, when noise pollution is so severe as to disturb sleep on a regular unrelenting basis, this would constitute a hazard to one's health. Critical questions that remain include what is the function of sleep and its benefit to health and how does sleep disturbance manifest itself in terms of ill health and well-being?

Stress response

There is considerable debate as to whether the non-auditory factors associated with noise could have detrimental health consequences due to a general stress syndrome. Such mechanisms are not new. Selye (1956) proposed a general adaptation syndrome for stress with three stages: alarm reaction, resistance and a stage of exhaustion. There are health consequences associated with the final stages of this schema. At the low to moderate levels of stress, where adaptation in the resistance stage can occur, there may still be a 'price to pay', including, for example, lowered resistance to infection, gastrointestinal ulcers and cardiovascular disease. Besides the reductionist biomedical models of stress-induced disease, there are other more recent models of stress that include psychological and social components, as well as biological components (ie the bio-psychosocial or psychosomatic model of disease that include the concepts of coping; Oken, 2000).

Noise, particularly loud and unexpected, is known to have an undesirable physiological effect on the recipient. How much this and the slower responses lead to a generalized stress response via the hypothalamic pituitary adrenal (HPA) axis, sympathetic (adrenomedullary) nervous system (SNS) and cardiovascular reactivity is controversial. The HPA axis and SNS have central roles in the ongoing homeostatic regulatory processes of the body in the face of the changing environmental stimuli that an individual encounters. This provides the body with the physiological survival mechanism commonly termed 'fight or flight', which can be activated in situations where the individual is unable to cope adequately with an extreme and potentially threatening set of stimuli. Furthermore, it has been suggested that excessive activation of this system, as with chronic noise exposure, can lead to patho-physiological processes, such as elevated blood pressure, high serum cholesterol, diabetes and cardiovascular disease.

It is known that noise can cause release of 'stress hormones' Babisch (1998, 2000), and Ising et al (1999) discovered that subjects exposed to noise show elevated levels of stress hormones in the blood. This is supported by Maschke et al (1993), who found that subjects exposed to aircraft noise with maximum levels of 55–65 dB(A) showed increased cortisol levels. The link between stress and cardiovascular disease is well documented – for example, Morrell et al (1997) report evidence for an association between perceived stress and fatal/non-fatal coronary artery events. This is supported by epidemiological evidence that chronic noise exposure increases the risk of ischaemic heart disease (Schwartz and Thompson, 1993).

The long-term activation of the HPA system and increased release of cortisol can result in a number of health problems, including immuno-suppression, insulin resistance, osteoporosis and intestinal problems. It is also thought that noise exposure can lead to increased systemic glycerol and non-sterified fatty acids, thus raising the risk of arteriosclerosis (hardening of the arteries) and myocardial infarction (death of a portion of the heart muscle due to loss of blood supply) (Ising et al, 1999).

Ising et al (1999) contend that noise is an important risk factor in cardiovascular disease, especially myocardial infarction. They envisage that chronic noise-induced stress accelerates the ageing of the myocardium, increasing the risk of infarct. The suggested mechanism is via increased stress hormones (catecholamines and cortisol) and an interaction with intracellular calcium and magnesium ion shifts. However, this is based partly upon animal studies, which have not always proved directly comparable to the situation in humans. Spreng (2000a, 2000b) studied the complex mechanisms involved in central nervous system activation by noise and suggests that chronic noise can lead to long-lasting activation of the HPA axis, which leads to disturbed hormonal balance and disease (eg immuno-suppression, diabetes, cardiovascular disease, osteoporosis and ulcers).

Important questions remain about the precise mechanisms or pathways by which environmental factors, such as noise, influence health outcomes (morbidity and mortality). Evidence of an increased risk of hypertension due to environmental noise is limited (Babisch, 1998). Babisch (2000), reviewing the potential links between traffic noise and cardiovascular disease, points out the limited number of epidemiological studies between traffic noise and cardiovascular disease, with no evidence of a relationship between noise exposure and blood pressure in adults. In children, noise-related rises in blood pressure have been found (Morrell et al, 1997). There is some evidence for an increased risk of ischaemic heart disease for subjects who live in noisy areas with outdoor levels greater than 65–70dB(A) (Berglund and Lindvall, 1995).

Stansfield et al (2000), reviewing the impact of environmental noise on mental health, found some evidence that exposure to high levels of environmental noise are associated with mental health symptoms and, possibly, raised anxiety and consumption of sedative medication, but little evidence of more serious effects. Several studies have reported no interaction between self-reported noise sensitivity and noise exposure to an increased vulnerability to mental ill health. Children exposed to chronic aircraft noise were not more susceptible to depression or anxiety despite having a reduced quality of life. These authors identified a need for more accurate and detailed noise measurement; careful consideration of other environmental stresses and confounding factors (eg socio-economic status); avoiding target communities where noise-sensitive individuals had moved away; and a wider use of standardized instruments to measure mental health outcomes and other related physiological outcomes, such as hormonal levels.

There are certain groups who are particularly vulnerable to the effects of environmental noise. For instance, Morrell et al (1997) indicated that annoyance reactions are greater in people who fear aircraft crashes. Patients in hospitals are also more vulnerable to noise. Children are also thought to be a particularly vulnerable group as it is believed that they are more susceptible to noise-induced hearing loss than adults.

In conclusion, it can be said that aviation noise has a number of health implications, both physiological and psychological. However, it can be seen that much of the research in this area is either inconclusive or contradictory. This is probably because there has not been sufficient expertise focused in this specialized area of environmental health, which will need to expand further in order to clarify some of the complex issues remaining. Generally, aviation does not pose a significant risk to the majority of people who are involved – particularly at low noise levels – and currently the benefits of modern and rapid transport outweigh the hazards. But concern for vulnerable groups in the community is an important future issue.

A recent report (Porter et al, 1998) explored the possibility of using existing knowledge on the potential health effects of environmental noise to define future noise targets and standards for the UK government. However, despite clear indications of a number of potential effects of noise on health in the literature, mainly regarding annoyance and sleep disturbance, the report concluded that, because of the confused state of knowledge of non-auditory health effects, it was not currently possible to use them as the base for noise standards. It seems that we have not moved far from the conclusions reached by an exhaustive review by Miller in 1974, in which the only conclusively established effect of noise on health was that of noise-induced hearing loss, though it was accepted that noise can disturb sleep, be a source of annoyance, interfere with communication and performance at complicated tasks, adversely influence mood and disturb relaxation. In short, the author concludes with the lines 'noise can affect the essential nature of human life – its quality' (Miller, 1974).

OUTDOOR AIR QUALITY

Many residents who live close to airports often regard the negative effect of pollution from aircraft and traffic exhaust as a concern. In a similar manner to noise, odours associated with aircraft movements and evaporative emissions can also increase anxieties regarding air quality amongst the general population. These air pollution issues often come to a head at the planning stages of airport expansion, and are typically one of the key issues within the airport's environmental impact statement (Abdel Aziz et al, 2000).

The primary locally problematic gaseous emissions from aircraft are nitrogen oxides (NO_x), carbon monoxide (CO) and non-methane volatile organic compounds (NMVOCs). NMVOC is a collective term for organic atmospheric compounds and includes materials found at airports such as benzene, polyaromatic hydrocarbons, kerosene, diesel fuel and de-icing compounds, such as ethylene glycol. NMVOCs will be the major contributor to the odour problems often associated with airports. Other air pollutants associated with the airport support traffic infrastructure are sulphur dioxide (SO_2), ozone (O_3) and particulates (PM_{10}). Overall air pollutant emissions tend to make a small contribution to the pollutants in a region. However, as this is highly localized, it can be significant with respect to the immediate vicinity of the airport, and it is likely, certainly in the vicinity of major international airports, that local air quality standards are exceeded.

The air pollution associated with airports has two major sources: first, the pollution generated by air transport movements and, second, the emissions from the transport infrastructure, which services the airport – road and rail, etc.

The main sources of air pollutants at airports are listed below.

Aircraft operations

Aircraft operations include movements in the landing and take-off (LTO) cycle – approach, climb out, taxi, take-off, landing and holding will have different emissions at different points in the cycle. Take-off has the highest emissions of NO_x with low emissions of NMVOCs and CO, while landing has higher emissions of NMVOCs and CO. Other emissions arise from fuel handling (evaporative losses and spillages) and operation of auxiliary power units.

Road traffic

Road traffic sources include emissions from airport access traffic, construction traffic, car parks, filling stations and air-side vehicles) For example, at any one time Heathrow Airport may have up to 350 diesel taxis waiting, the highest number of taxis waiting on a single site in the UK.

Other sources

Other sources include airport combustion plants (boiler houses), simulated fire exercises and paint shops, and other transport infrastructure (eg railway operations).

Emissions from aircraft are only considered to impact upon the local environment during the LTO cycle, which is normally treated as those operations at which the aircraft is below the atmospheric boundary layer (approximately 1000m height, although variable). Therefore, exposure in the general population can vary depending upon the direction of take-off and landing.

In common with the majority of air quality health studies, the main air-pollution-related health concerns that have been investigated around airports are respiratory complaints (eg chronic obstructive pulmonary disease, asthma, etc). Investigations into a broader range of health problems such as angina, bronchitis, anxiety and depression have been reported but have not demonstrated an association with living in the flight path area (Harrison et al, 2000).

Elevated concentrations of NO_x, SO_2, O_3, NMVOCs and PM_{10} have all been closely associated with respiratory-related admissions to hospital and mortality (COMEAP, 1998). However, a number of medical studies, such as hospital admission epidemiology, population health studies, measures of lung function and other questionnaire surveys, at airports such as Birmingham International, Schiphol and Heathrow have yet to show any evidence that airport operations are causing any additional respiratory effect that could not be explained by differences in lifestyle (Harrison et al, 2000; Franssen et al, 1999; Hillingdon Health Authority, 1997). An occupational study of airport workers who were more directly exposed to aviation fuels and jet exhaust did report an association with respiratory symptoms, although the authors could not draw strong conclusions as to the specific cause (Tunnicliffe at al, 1999).

Despite public concerns regarding the levels of NMVOCs and their cancer-causing properties, there have been few studies of cancer amongst the general population around airports. Studies have only shown slight elevations in certain types of cancer that, due to differences in lifestyle, such as smoking habits, cannot demonstrate an association between air traffic and increased cancer risk (Visser et al, 1997).

Occupational studies amongst airport personnel have shown low exposure to hydrocarbons and jet fuel derivatives, and while concentrations were typically under occupational exposure limits, the use of respirators amongst highly exposed workers has been recommended (Childers et al, 2000; Pleil et al, 2000). Examination of various biomarkers to show genotoxic endpoints in airport personnel showed no significant differences between airport workers and a control group (Pitarque et al, 1999).

In conclusion, although levels of air pollutants around airports are elevated, there is no clear evidence that air-traffic associated pollution from airports causes any additional respiratory health impact. However, the high localized air pollution levels around major airports associated with the total airport infrastructure are likely to have some health impact on airport neighbours. Measures to improve airport-related air pollution through improved infrastructure and cleaner engine technologies should still be made to try to meet local air quality standards with the resultant health benefits. Realistically, however, this is unlikely to be achieved during the next 15 to 20 years. The relationship between airports and their neighbours would be likely to improve if they were to reduce NMVOC odour-causing emissions through improved fuel handling procedures, etc, to reduce air quality anxieties in the surrounding population.

THIRD-PARTY RISK

A lesser but still significant health consideration is the third-party risk of a major aviation incident affecting the airport neighbourhood population. European concerns over third-party risk have been driven notably by the crash of the Boeing 747 at Amsterdam in 1992 that led to 39 third-party fatalities, although other events such as the Concorde crash at Paris in 2000 have kept third-party risk high on both the public and political agenda.

Airport growth is at a premium in densely populated and highly industrialized countries, where it is virtually impossible to reduce aviation-related third-party risks to zero. Therefore, authorities and the aviation industry had to face the task of how to control these risks effectively.

In the UK, the concept of public safety zones (PSZs), which refers to the area adjacent to the end of a runway where development is restricted, has existed since 1958, but until recently had relatively little scientific method to their derivation. However, since the early 1990s, both the UK and the Netherlands have taken leading roles in adopting a more scientific approach to public safety zones, which involves the generation of individual risk contours.

Both the UK and the Netherlands models focus primarily upon individual risk models where the individual risk is defined as the chance that a person staying at a fixed location permanently is killed as a result of an accident from the hazard. In the UK, the value of the upper limit to tolerable risk of death for third parties is taken to be the widely used value of a risk of death to any individual of 1 in 10,000 per year, as recommended by the Health and Safety Executive for other industries.

The calculation of individual risk for different locations around an airport allows a risk contour map to be created. The contours join points, which are subject to the same individual risk. The risk calculation requires three basic quantities, as outlined below.

Accident/crash probability

This concerns the annual probability of a crash occurring near a given airport. As aviation is a safe mode of transport per kilometre travelled, in order to achieve a statistically valid basis for a risk calculation at a particular airport this value is derived from historical information regarding crash rates per aircraft type from a number of world airports, which is then multiplied by annual aircraft movements at the airport under study (NATS, 2000). At Schiphol Airport, for example, risk analysis shows an accident probability of 0.4×10^{-6} per movement for take-off and 0.21×10^{-6} for landing (Ale and Piers, 2000).

Crash location model

This models the probability that the accident aircraft will end up at a particular location. A number of approaches have been developed for the crash location model using either runway referenced, traffic route referenced or non-dependent location probability models.

Crash accident consequence model

This determines the size of the crash area and the proportion of people likely to be killed within this area. For third-party risk analysis, the only consequences considered are fatal injuries to people on the ground. Consequence models should correctly reflect the influence of the aircraft, impact and environment-related parameters that affect the accident consequences (Ale and Piers, 2000).

Once defined, the risk contours can be used to control development in the areas surrounding the airport. While it is likely that there will be mandatory inclusion of third-party risks for environmental impact statements for airports, at present the risk assessments have only been applied where airports are undergoing reassessments regarding expansion plans. In these cases, the following measures are usually proposed for the UK:

- In the inner-contour zone where the level of risk is in excess of 1 in 10,000 per year (10^{-4}), existing housing and other developments occupied by third parties for a high proportion of the day should be removed.[6] Ale and Piers (2000) report that within the Schiphol risk assessment, a 5×10^{-5} risk contour is used for this inner zone.
- Where the risk is between 10^{-4} and 10^{-5} per year, new or more extensive development in this area, which would result in a higher density of human occupation, such as new housing and most types of new non-residential development including multistorey car parks and transport terminals, will be restricted. However, some non-residential development with a low density of human occupation, such as warehousing and surface-level car parking, may still be approved.
- The removal of existing development from outside the 10^{-4} contour is unnecessary because, on applying constrained cost–benefit analysis, the costs of doing so would be greater than the benefits.

One of the restrictions in performing individual risk assessments for airports is that such analyses may not fully address the public concerns raised by major accidents. From a societal risk perspective, the disaster potential posed through air traffic risk is substantial. However, the economic importance of airports is often seen by governments as outweighing societal risk, and these risks are usually accepted, although it is appreciated that there may be further safety measures that could be adopted even though not directly cost beneficial.

In conclusion, while the techniques used to calculate third-party risks have improved greatly since 1990, they are still prone to many uncertainties, such as the high growth rate of the aviation industry. Further improvements are still likely to be necessary to keep risk models up to par with the political challenges posed by the expected growth in aviation.

Conclusions on community health

The placement of airports in urban areas will, by necessity, involve environmental stresses on the local community. The clearly established, common stress indicators are high noise, frequent annoyance and sleep disturbance; poor air quality; and increased third-party risk. While studies have often highlighted these community issues, the consequent health problems must still be fully quantified. For example, however plausible the sequence of cause and effect seems theoretically, it has proved very difficult to demonstrate, objectively, physical or mental health impairment due to aircraft noise. In particular, those groups of the community who are more vulnerable to the stresses associated with the operation of the airport – particularly the elderly, chronically ill and children – need to be paid particular attention to in future studies.

For both the present operation and future development of airports, the health risks associated with their operations should be subjected on a regular basis to a fully integrated health-risk assessment. Airports should consider taking measures to reduce the negative impacts of environmental stresses, such as noise and air pollution, through greater integration of spatial planning policies, such as local transport infrastructure and land use. The integration of health risk assessments into airport operations still needs further study. Both airports and the local community would benefit from better relations if such assessments were planned and performed in an open and transparent manner.

CONCLUSIONS

Although this chapter has focused upon the negative aspects of the health impacts of aviation, it should not be forgotten that despite attracting more media attention, air travel is, historically, in terms of mortality and traumatic injury of passengers, far safer than road per kilometre travelled and has considerable benefits. The obvious positive aspects of air travel are its speed and directness, which facilitate economy of time and convenience for business and vacation travel. The economic advantages of an airport to the local economy, particularly in terms of employment and the regional economy, have been described elsewhere. It should be emphasized that employment itself has positive health, well-being and self-esteem benefits.

As yet, holistic studies on the balance of the positive and negative health benefits of aviation, which should also include the local and global environmental dimensions, such as ozone depletion and skin carcinomas, have yet to be reported. Until such studies are undertaken, it will be impossible to quantify precisely the full health risks associated with aviation, so that they can be considered within the industry's future sustainable development.

NOTES

1   A bio-aerosol is an air-borne particulate of biological origin (eg bacteria).
2   The Leiden mutation of blood coagulation factor V is the commonest genetic abnormality associated with venous thromboembolism, found in approximately 5 per cent of white people (Bertina et al, 1994; Bournameaux, 2000).
3   See, for example, www.qantas.com.au/flights/essentials/healthinflight.html.
4   Sv = Sievert, an international unit of measure for ionizing radiation that takes into account a measure of the biological effect of the ionizing radiation.
5   For comparison, the FAA recommends a maximum exposure to 20mSv yr^{-1}, averaged over five years, and a maximum limit for pregnant aircrew of 2mSv yr^{-1} until the end of the pregnancy, with a maximum of 0.5mSv per month.
6   Note that, in practice, the 10^{-4} individual risk contour is so close to airport runways that there is little or no development within it anyway.

REFERENCES

Abdel Aziz, M I, Radford, J and McCabe, J (2000) *Health Impact Statement*, Finningley Airport, September 2000, Doncaster Health Authority, UK
Ale, B J M, and Piers, M (2000) 'The assessment and management of third party risk around a major airport', *Journal of Hazardous Materials*, vol 71, pp1–16
Anon (1995) 'Exposure of passengers and flight crew to *Mycobacterium tuberculosis* on commercial aircraft, 1992–1995', *Morbidity and Mortality Weekly Report*, 3 March, vol 44(8), pp137–140
Arfvidsson, B, Eklof, B, Kistner, R L, Masuda, E M, and Sato, D T (2000) 'Risk factors for venous thromboembolism following prolonged air travel: coach class thrombosis', *Hematology/Oncology Clinics of North America*, April, vol 14(2), pp391–400
Babisch, W (1998) 'Epidemiological studies of the cardiovascular effects of occupational noise: a critical appraisal', *Noise and Health*, vol 1, pp24–39
Babisch W (2000) 'Traffic noise and cardiovascular disease: Epidemiological review and synthesis', *Noise and Health*, vol 8, pp9–32
Bagshaw, M (1999) 'Cosmic radiation measurements in airline service', *Radiation Protection Dosimetry*, vol 86(4), pp333–334
Ballard, T, Lagorio, S, De Angelis, G, and Verdecchia, A (2000) 'Cancer incidence and mortality among flight personnel: a meta-analysis', *Aviation, Space and Environmental Medicine*, vol 71, pp216–224
Bartlett, D T (1999) 'Radiation protection concepts and quantities for the occupational exposure to cosmic radiation', *Radiation Protection Dosimetry*, vol 86(4), pp263–268

Beaujean, R, Kopp, J, Roos, F and Reitz, G (1998) 'Measurements of radiation exposure in civil aircraft', *Acta Astronautica*, vol 43(3–6), pp271–275

Berglund, B and Lindvall, T (eds) (1995) 'Community noise', *Archive of the Centre for Sensory Research – Stockholm*, vol 2(1), pp86–104

Berglund, B, Lindvall, T and Schwela, D H (eds) (1999) *Guidelines for Community Noise*, World Health Organization, London

Berry, B F and Jiggins M (1999) *An Inventory of UK Research on Noise and Health, 1994–1999*, National Physics Laboratory, NPL Report CMAM 40, Teddington, UK

Bertina, R M, Koeleman, B P, Koster, T, Rosendaal, F R, Driven, R J, de Ronde, H, van der Velden, P A and Reitsma, P H (1994) 'Mutation in blood coagulation factor V association with resistance to activated protein C', *Nature*, vol 369, pp64–67

Bjorkman, M and Rylander, R (1995) 'Aircraft noise exposure units and reactions in humans', *Epidemiology*, vol 6, S27

Blettner, M, Grosche, B and Zeeb, H (1998) 'Occupational cancer risk in pilots and flight attendants: current epidemiological knowledge', *Radiation and Environmental Biophysics*, vol 37, pp75–80

Borsky, P N (1979) 'Sociopsychological factors affecting the human response to noise exposure', *Otolaryngologic Clinics of North America*, vol 12, pp521–535

Bournameaux, H (2000) 'Factor V Leiden paradox: risk of deep-vein thrombosis but not of pulmonary embolism', *Lancet*, vol 356, pp183–192

Bronzaft, A L, Ahern, K D, McGinn, R and Savino, B (1998) 'Aircraft noise: a potential health hazard', *Environment and Behaviour*, vol 30(1), pp101–113

Brooker, P (1978) *Noise and Sleep: A Survey of the Literature on Sleep Disturbance by Noise*, DORA (CAA) paper 780112, London

Brooker, P (1985) *Noise Disturbance at Night near Heathrow and Gatwick Airports*, CAA Report 8513, London

Brown, E N and Czeisler, C A (1992) 'The statistical analysis of circadian phase and amplitude in constant-routine core-temparature data', *Journal of Biological Rhythms*, vol 7(3), Fall 1992, pp177–202

Carter, N L (1996) 'Transportation noise, sleep, and possible after-effects', *Environment International*, vol 22(1), pp105–116

Carter, N L (1998) 'Cardiovascular response to environmental noise during sleep', *Proceedings of the 7th International Congress on Noise as a Public Health Problem*, Sydney, Australia, vol 2, pp439–444

Carter, N, Hunyor, S N, Crawford, G, Kelly, D and Smith, A J M (1994a) 'A study of arousals, cardiac arrhythmias and urinary catecholamines', *Sleep*, vol 17, pp927–942

Carter, N L, Ingham, P, Tran, K and Hunyor, S N (1994b) 'A field study of the effects of traffic noise on heart rate and cardiac arrhythmia during sleep', *Journal of Sound and Vibration*, 169(2), pp211–227

Childers, J W, Witherspoon, C L, Smith, L B and Pleil, J D (2000) 'Real-time and integrated measurement of potential human exposure to particle-bound polycyclic aromatic hydrocarbons (PAHs) from aircraft exhaust', *Environmental Health Perspectives*, September, vol 108(9), pp853–862

Committee on the Medical Effects of Air Pollutants (COMEAP) (1998) *Quantification of the Effects of Air Pollution on Health in the United Kingdom*, Department of Health, London

Council Directive 96/29/EURATOM of 13 May (1996) *Official Journal of the European Communities*, vol 19, L159, pp1–114

Courades, J-M (1999) 'European legislation on protection against cosmic radiation', *Radiation Protection Dosimetry*, vol 86(4), pp343–346

Dechow, M, Sohn, H and Steinhanses, J (1997) 'Concentrations of selected contaminants in cabin air of airbus aircrafts', *Chemosphere*, vol 35(1/2), pp21–31

Diamond, I, Sheppard, Z, Smith, A, Hayward, S, Heatherley, S, Raw, G and Stansfeld, S (2000) *Perceptions of Aircraft Noise, Sleep and Health*, Report to Civil Aviation Authority, December, University of Southampton

Driver, C R, Valway, S E, Morgan, W M, Onorato, I M and Castro, K G (1994) 'Transmission of *Mycobacterium tuberculosis* associated with air travel', *JAMA*, 5 October, vol 272(13), pp1031–1035

Ferrarri, E, Chevallier, T, Chapelier, A and Baudov, M (1999) 'Travel as a risk factor for venous thrombosis disease', *Chest*, vol 115, pp440–444

Fidell, S (1995) *Noise Induced Sleep Disturbance in Residences Near Two Civil Airports*, BBN Acoustic Technologies Division, NASA Contractor Report 198252, Washington, DC

Fidell, S (1999) 'Assessment of the effectiveness of aircraft noise regulation', *Noise and Health*, vol 3, pp17–25

Fidell, S, Pearsons, K, Tabachnick, B, Howe, R, Silvati, L and Barber, D S (1995) 'Field study of noise-induced sleep disturbance', *Journal of the Acoustical Society of America*, vol 98(2), pp1025–1033

Fidell, S, Pearsons, K, Tabachnick, B and Howe, R (2000) 'Effects on sleep disturbance of changes in aircraft noise near three airports', *Journal of the Acoustical Society of America*, vol 107(5), pp2535–2547

Flindell, I and Stallen, P J M (1999) 'Non-acoustical factors in environmental noise', *Noise and Health*, vol 3, pp11–16

Franssen, E A M, Lebret, E and Staatsen, B A M (1999) 'Health impact assessment Schiphol airport: overview of results until 1999', *National Institute of Public Health and the Environment RJVM Report 441520 012*, Netherlands

Geroulakis, G (2001) 'The risk of venous thromboembolism from air travel', *British Medical Journal*, vol 322, p188

Gillen, D W and Levesque, T J (1994) 'A socio-economic assessment of complaints about airport noise', *Transportation Planning Technology*, vol 18, pp45–55

Griefahn, B and Muzet, A (1978) 'Noise-induced sleep disturbances and their effects on health', *Journal of Sound and Vibration*, vol 59(1), pp99–106

Gundestrup, M and Storm, H H (1999) 'Radiation-induced acute myeloid leukaemia and other cancers in commercial jet cockpit crew: a population-based cohort study', *Lancet*, vol 354, pp2029–2031

Hammer, G P, Zeeb, H, Tveten, U and Blettner, M (2000) 'Comparing different methods of estimating cosmic radiation of airline personnel', *Radiation and Environmental Biophysics*, vol 39, pp227–231

Harrison, R M, Ayres, J, Walters, S, Somervaille, L, Saunders, P, Cook, S, Hopkins, K and Cotterill, S (2000) *Respiratory Disease around Birmingham International Airport Final Study Report*, University of Birmingham, Institute of Public and Environmental Health Internal Report, Birmingham

Hatfield, J, Job, R F S, Carter, N L, Peploe, P, Taylor, R and Morrell, S (2001) 'The influence of psychological factors on self-reported physiological effects of noise', *Noise and Health*, vol 3(10), pp1–13

HCN (1997) *Assessing Noise Exposure for Public Health Purposes*, Health Council of the Netherlands Report 23E, The Hague

Hillingdon Health Authority (1997) *Annual Public Health Report, Heathrow and Health*, Hillingdon Health Authority, UK

Hirsh, J and O'Donnell, M J (2001) 'Venous thromboembolism after long flights: are airlines to blame?', *Lancet*, vol 357, pp1461–1462

Hitosugi, M, Niwa, M and Takatsu, A (2000) 'Rheologic changes in venous blood during prolonged sitting', *Thrombosis Research* 1 Dec, vol 100(5), pp409–412

Hocking, M B (2000) 'Passenger aircraft cabin air quality: trends, effects, societal costs, proposals', *Chemosphere*, vol 41, pp603–615

Homans, J (1954) 'Thrombosis of the deep leg veins due to prolonged sitting', *New England Journal of Medicine*, vol 250, pp148–149

Horne, J A, Pankhurst, F L, Reyner, L A, Hume, K I and Diamond, I D (1994) 'A field study of sleep disturbance: effects of aircraft noise and other factors on 5742 nights of actimetrically monitored sleep in a large subject sample', *Sleep*, vol 17(2), pp146–159

House of Lords Select Committee on Science and Technology (2000) *Air Travel and Health, Session 1999–2000*, 5th Report, HL Paper 121-I, The Stationery Office, London

Hume, K, Terranova, D, Thomas, C and Gregg, M (2001a) 'A pilot study into complaints caused by aircraft operations: noise level and time of day', *Journal of Air Transport Management* (in press)

Hume, K, Terranova, D and Thomas, C (2001b) 'Complaints and annoyance caused by aircraft operations: temporal patterns and individual bias', NOPHER 2001 International Workshop on Noise Pollution and Health, Cambridge (*Noise and Health*, in press, vol 15)

Hume, K, Terranova, D, Thomas, C and Gregg, M (2001c) 'Can complaints about aircraft noise be used as an index of annoyance?', Presented at Inter-Noise 2001, The Hague

Hume K I, Van, F and Watson A (2000) *Effects of Aircraft Noise on Sleep: EEG based Measurements*, Unpublished Report, Manchester Metropolitan University, Manchester

Hume K I, Van, F and Watson, A (1998) 'A field study of age and gender differences in habitual adult sleep', *Journal of Sleep Research*, vol 7, pp85–94

ICAO (1993) 'International standards and recommended practices: environmental protection', *Aircraft Noise*, vol 1, annex 16, Montreal, Canada

ICRP 60 (1991) *The 1990 Recommendations of the International Commission on Radiological Protection*, Publication 60, Pergamon Press, Oxford

Ising, H, Babisch, W and Kruppa, B (1999) 'Noise induced endocrine effects and cardiovascular risk', *Noise and Health*, vol 4, pp37–48

Kenyon, T A, Valway, S E, Ihle, W W, Onorato, I M and Castro, K G (1996) 'Transmission of multidrug-resistant *Mycobacterium tuberculosis* during a long airplane flight', *New England Journal of Medicine*, 11 April, vol 334(15), pp933–938

Kesteven, P L J (2000) 'Traveller's thrombosis', *Thorax*, August, vol 55, supplement 1, ppS32–36

Kesteven, P L J and Robinson, B J (2001) 'Clinical risk factors for venous thrombosis associated with air travel', *Aviation, Space and Environmental Medicine*, February, vol 72(2), pp125–128

Kraaijenhagen, R A, Haverkamp, D, Koopman, M M W, Prandoni, P, Piovella, F and Büller, H R (2000) 'Travel and the risk of venous thrombosis', *Lancet*, vol 356(9240), pp1429–1493

Luz, G A, Raspet, R and Schomer, P D (1983) 'An analysis of community complaints to noise', *Journal of the Acoustical Society of America*, vol 105, pp3336–3340

Maschke, C, Breinl, S, Grimm, R and Ising, H (1993) 'The influence of nocturnal aircraft noise on sleep and on catecholamine secretion' in Ising, H and Kruppa, B (eds) *Noise and Disease*, Gustav Fisher, Stuttgart, pp402–407

Miller, J D (1974) 'Effects of noise on people', *Journal of the Acoustical Society of America*, vol 56(3), pp729–764

Morrell, S, Taylor, R and Lyle, D (1997) 'A review of health effects of aircraft noise', *Australian and New Zealand Journal of Public Health*, vol 21(2), pp221–236

Moss, D, Warnaby, G, Sykes, S and Thomas, C T (1997) 'The boundary spanning role of public relations in managing environmental organisational interaction', *Journal of Communication Management*, vol 2(4), pp320–334

Muzet, A and Ehrhart, J (1980) 'Habituation of heart rate and finger pulse responses to noise in sleep' in Tobias, J V, Jansen, G and Ward, W D (eds) *Noise as a Public Health Problem*, Rockville, US, ASHA Reports 10, pp401–404

National Air Traffic Services Ltd (NATS) (2000) *A Methodology for Calculating Individual Risk Due to Aircraft Accidents Near Airports*, R&D Report 0007, NATS, London

O'Brien, K, Friedburg, W, Smart, D F and Sauer, H H (1998) 'The atmospheric cosmic and solar energetic particle radiation environment at aircraft altitudes', *Advances in Space Research*, vol 21(12), pp1739–1748

Ohrstrom, E and Rylander, R (1982) 'Sleep disturbance effects of traffic noise – a laboratory study on after effects', *Journal of Sound and Vibration*, vol 84(1), pp87–103

Oken, D (2000) 'Multiaxial diagnosis and the psychosomatic model of disease', *Psychosomatic Medicine*, vol 62, pp171–175

Ollerhead, J B, Jones, C J, Cadoux, R E, Woodley, A, Atkinson, B J, Horne, J A, Pankhurst, F, Reyner, L, Hume, K I, Van, F, Watson, A, Diamond, I D, Egger, P, Holmes, D and McKean, J (1992) *Report of a Field Study of Aircraft Noise and Sleep Disturbance*, Department of Safety, Environment and Engineering, London

Ormerod, P (2000) 'Tuberculosis and travel', *Hospital Medicine,* March, vol 61(3), pp171–173

Pearson, K S, Barber, D S and Tabachnick, B G (1990) *Analyses of the Predictability of Noise Induced Sleep Disturbance*, US Air Force Report HSD-TR-89-029, USA

Pearson, K S, Barber, D S and Tabachnick, B G (1995) 'Predicting noise-induced sleep disturbance', *Journal of the Acoustical Society of America*, vol 97(1), pp331–338

Pitarque, M, Creus, A, Marcos, R, Hughes, J A and Anderson, D (1999) 'Examination of various biomarkers measuring genotoxic endpoints from Barcelona airport personnel', *Mutation Research,* 6 April, vol 440(2), pp195–204

Pleil, J D, Smith, L B and Zelnick, S D (2000) 'Personal exposure to JP-8 jet fuel vapors and exhaust at air force bases', *Environmental Health Perspectives,* March, vol 108(3), pp183–192

Porter N, Flindell, I H and Berry, B F (1998) *Health Effect Based Noise Assessment Methods: A Review and Feasibility Study,* National Physics Laboratory, NPL Report CMAM 16, Teddington, UK

Porter N, Kershaw, A and Ollerhead, J B (2000) *Adverse Effects of Night-Time Aircraft Noise,* NATS R&D Report 9964, London, UK

Regulla, D and David, J (1993) 'Measurements of cosmic radiation on board Lufthansa aircraft on the major intercontinental flight routes', *Radiation Protection Dosimetry,* vol 48(1), p 65–72

Reijneveld, S A (1994) 'The impact of the Amsterdam aircraft disaster on reported annoyance by aircraft noise and on psychiatric disorders', *International Journal of Epidemiology,* vol 23(2), pp333–340

Schalch, D and Scharmann, A (1993) 'In-flight measurements at high latitudes: fast neutron doses to aircrew', *Radiation Protection Dosimetry,* vol 48(1), pp85–91

Schrewe, U J (1999) 'Radiation exposure monitoring in civil aircraft', *Nuclear Instruments and Methods. Physics Research A,* vol 422 pp621–25

Schwartz, T J and Thompson, S J (1993) 'Research on non-auditory physiological effects of noise since 1988: review and perspective' in Vallet, M (ed) *Noise as a Public Health Problem,* INRETS, Cedex France, vol 2, pp497–500

Scurr, J H, Machin, S J, Bailey-King, S, Mackie, I J, McDonald, S and Coleridge Smith, P D (2001) 'Frequency and prevention of symptomless deep-vein thrombosis in long haul flights: a randomised trial', *Lancet,* vol 357, pp1485–1489

Selye, H (1956) *The Stress of Life,* McGraw-Hill, New York

Simpson, K (1940) 'Shelter deaths from pulmonary embolism', *Lancet* vol 2, p744

Spreng, M (2000a) 'Central nervous system activation by noise', *Noise and Health*, vol 7, pp49–57

Spreng, M (2000b) 'Possible health effects of noise induced cortisol increase', *Noise and Health*, vol 7, pp59–63

Stansfield, S A, Haines, M M, Burr, B, Berry, B and Lercher, P (2000) 'A review of aircraft noise and mental health', *Noise and Health*, vol 8, pp1–8

Stockbridge, H C W and Lee, M (1973) 'The psychosocial consequences of aircraft noise', *Applied Ergonomics*, vol 4, pp44–45

Strasbourg (2001) Court of Human Rights – Application No 36022/97: Case of Hatton et al versus UK

Symington, I S and Stack, B H (1977) 'Pulmonary thromboembolism after travel', *British Journal of Diseases of the Chest*, April, vol 71(2), pp138–140

Tarnopolsky, A, Watkins, G and Hand, D J (1980) 'Aircraft noise and mental health: prevalence of individual symptoms', *Psychological Medicine*, vol 10, pp683–698

Tomkins, J, Topham, N, Twomey, J and Ward, R (1998) 'Noise versus access: the impact of an airport in an urban property market', *Urban Studies*, vol 35(2), pp243–258

Tunnicliffe, W S, O'Hickey, S P, Fletcher, T J, Miles, J F, Burge, P S and Ayres, J G (1999) 'Pulmonary function and respiratory symptoms in a population of airport workers', *Occupational and Environmental Medicine*, vol 56, pp118–123

Vallet, M, Gagneux, J M and Simmonet, F (1980) 'Effects of aircraft noise: an in situ experience' in Tobias, J V, Jansen, G and Ward, W D (eds) *Noise as a Public Health Problem*, Rockville, US, ASHA Reports 10, pp391–396

Van, F, Hume, K I and Watson, A (1993) 'EEG-based responses to aircraft noise in "noise-sensitive" and "less noise-sensitive" subjects' in Vallet, M (ed) *Noise as a Public Health Problem, INRETS*, vol 2, pp569–573, Cedex, France

van Wiechan, C M A G, Franssen, E A M, de Jong, R G and Lebret E (2002) 'Aircraft noise exposure from Schiphol airport: a relation with complaints', Paper submitted to *Noise and Health*, not published

Visser, O, van Wijnen, J H, Benraadt, J and van Leeuwen, F E (1997) 'Cancer incidence in the Schiphol area in 1988-1993', *Ned Tijdschr Geneeskd*, 8 March, vol 14(10), pp468–473

Whitehead, C J, Hume, K I and Muzet, A (1998) 'Cardiovascular responses to aircraft noises in sleeping subjects', *Noise Effects*, vol 7, pp141–144

WHO (1998) *Tuberculosis and Air Travel: Guidelines for Prevention and Control*, WHO/TB/98.356, World Health Authority, Geneva (also available from http://www.who.int/gtb/publications/aircraft/PDF/98_256.pdf)

Wick, R L Jr and Irvine, L A (1995) 'The microbiological composition of airliner cabin air', *Aviation, Space and Environmental Medicine*, vol 66(3), pp220–224

Wilkinson, R T (1984) 'Disturbance of sleep by noise: individual differences', *Journal of Sound Vibration*, vol 95, pp55–63

Wilkinson, R T and Campbell, K B (1984) 'Effects of traffic noise on quality of sleep', *Journal of the Acoustical Society of America*, vol 75(2), pp468–475

Chapter 5

The global atmospheric impacts of aviation

David Lee and David Raper

INTRODUCTION

The effects of civil aviation emissions on the atmosphere have been under discussion for some time and are certainly not a 'new' subject. Indeed, the easily observed dark plumes from early turbojets gave rise to concern over local air quality, prompting the US Environmental Protection Agency (USEPA) to legislate against aircraft emissions during the 1970s. This early legislation, local to the US, later gave rise to the engine emission certification requirements of the International Civil Aviation Organization (ICAO) (ICAO, 1995) on unburned hydrocarbons (UHCs), nitrogen oxides (NO$_x$, the sum of NO+NO$_2$) and carbon monoxide (CO).

Concern over the effects of aircraft emissions on the upper atmosphere developed a little later during the 1970s when a fleet of supersonic aircraft that would fly in the stratosphere was proposed. Crutzen (1971) and Johnston (1971) postulated significant stratospheric ozone (O$_3$) depletion as a result of the potential NO$_x$ emissions. In the event, only a limited fleet was developed by the UK and France in the form of Concorde. The only other civil supersonic aircraft developed was the Tupulov 144, which saw only one year's active civilian transport service after a chequered history of two catastrophic crashes: one at the Paris air show in 1973 and another in Russia in 1978.

Renewed interest in the potential effects of aircraft emissions ensued during the late 1980s and early 1990s, this time on climate from subsonic aircraft emissions (Schumann, 1990), rather than stratospheric O$_3$ depletion. Initially, the attention was focused upon the potential effects of aircraft NO$_x$ emissions on the production of tropospheric O$_3$. Whereas O$_3$ in the mid to upper stratosphere (~15 to 50km) provides a protective 'shield' against harmful ultraviolet radiation (UV), O$_3$ in the upper troposphere and lower stratosphere acts as a powerful 'greenhouse gas', potentially contributing to climate warming. However, more recently, other effects such as those of contrails (condensation trails) have been studied intensively. Contrails are line-shaped ice clouds caused by the emission of water vapour and particles from the aircraft exhaust. Depending (principally) upon the particular conditions of temperature and humidity, contrails may be very short lived or persistent, sometimes spreading by wind shear, sedimentation and diffusion into cirrus-like clouds that are ultimately unrecognizable as having been caused by aircraft. Other effects on climate from associated particle emissions and the enhancement of cirrus clouds have also been discussed.

Research into the potential effects of aviation on the upper atmosphere was recently synthesized in a special report of the Intergovernmental Panel on Climate Change (IPCC) – *Aviation and the Global Atmosphere* (IPCC, 1999). This report was a landmark in that it was the first sectoral examination by the IPCC and that estimates of radiative forcing of climate from various aircraft emissions and their effects were made.

Besides the IPCC report, other assessments and syntheses have been made (eg Brasseur et al, 1998; Friedl et al, 1997; Rogers et al, 2002; Schumann, 1994). This chapter does not attempt to duplicate such reviews; rather, it provides the non-specialist with an overview of the global impacts of aircraft emissions and points the way to more detailed literature for the interested reader. In the next section, a very brief overview of climate change in relation to aircraft is given. Following this, we briefly review aircraft emissions and their development over time, and the effects of subsonic and supersonic aviation. Lastly, more recent research since the publication of the IPCC (1999) report is reviewed and an overall chapter summary is provided.

CLIMATE CHANGE

Given that much recent discussion has focused upon the estimates of radiative forcing from aircraft emissions given by IPCC (1999) for 1992 and 2050, it is pertinent to introduce some of the basic concepts of climate change. In such a short chapter, a complete and comprehensive overview is impossible, but the basic concepts and suitable references are provided.

'Climate' is, of course, different to 'weather', weather being the more-or-less instantaneous meteorological conditions, whereas climate describes weather conditions typical of a region or site (eg McIlveen, 1992). Climate *change* is a long-term systematic change. That climate has changed over the last 100 years or so is almost beyond doubt, although some of the scientific issues remain contentious. The IPCC was set up jointly by the World Meteorological Organization and the United Nations Environment Programme (UNEP) in order to provide authoritative international statements of scientific opinion on climate change, and it has delivered major reports in 1990, 1995 and 2001.

In order to describe climate change quantitatively, some sort of metric is required. The components of climate that change as a result of external or varying influences are multifarious. However, the most often – and, indeed, obvious – cited manifestation is surface temperature. However, it is extremely difficult to simulate or predict changes in surface temperature except with highly sophisticated three-dimensional climate models (for an overview, see McGuffie and Henderson-Sellers, 1997; IPCC, 1997). Initially, the concept of global warming potentials (GWPs) was introduced (IPCC, 1990), which was an index that allowed the climate effects of emissions to be compared, relative to those of carbon dioxide (CO_2). However, the limitations of GWPs became obvious for influences other than long-lived gases, such as CO_2, methane (CH_4) and the halocarbons. Subsequently, the concept of *radiative forcing of climate* was commonly used as a metric of climate change by the IPCC in its special report (IPCC, 1995) for the first meeting of the Conference of Parties to the Convention (United Nations Framework Convention on Climate Change) and the second assessment report of working group 1 of the IPCC (IPCC, 1996).

Radiative forcing may be defined as a measure of the importance of perturbations to the planetary radiation balance and is measured in watts per square metre (Wm^{-2}). One of the main reasons for its use as a convenient metric is that there is an approximately linear relationship between the change in global mean radiative forcing (ΔF) and the global mean surface temperature change (ΔT_s):

$$\Delta T_s \approx \lambda \Delta F \qquad (1)$$

where λ is the climate sensitivity parameter ($K(Wm^{-2})^{-1}$) (eg Shine and Forster, 1999).

Consequently, it can be seen that it is a very convenient metric, but nonetheless a proxy for climate change. It is worthwhile putting values of radiative forcing in context. Figure 5.1 summarizes the energy balance of the Earth's atmosphere system. This shows that incoming and outgoing radiation is balanced (as a global average) at $343Wm^{-2}$. It should therefore be appreciated that relatively small perturbations can make measurable and significant impacts on climate.

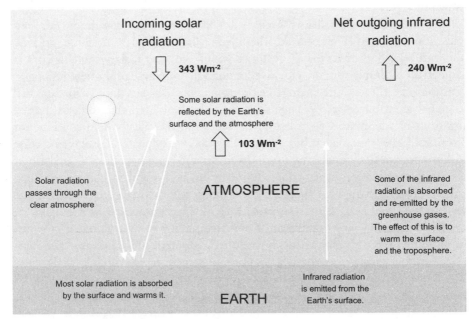

Figure 5.1 *Radiative energy balance of the Earth's atmosphere*

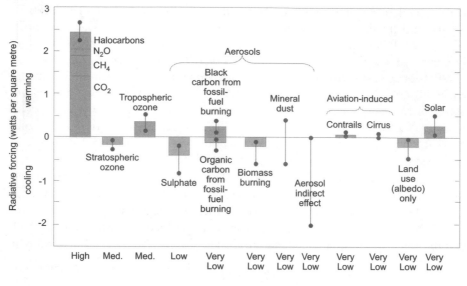

Source: IPCC, 2001
Figure 5.2 *Global annual mean radiative forcing (Wm^{-2}) from a number of agents for the period from the pre-industrial (1750) to the present (2000)*

The recent summary for policy-makers of the third assessment report (SPM–TAR) of the IPCC working group 1 (IPCC, 2001) provides the most up-to-date assessment of radiative forcing of climate that may be conveniently given in one figure, shown in Figure 5.2.

Figure 5.2 shows the radiative forcing from different components: the aircraft 'contrails' and 'enhanced cloudiness' are identified as they are signatures unique to aviation, other aviation effects being subsumed within the other radiative forcing bars. It is incorrect to simply sum the radiative forcing values because of shorter- or longer-lasting effects. The radiative forcings are from a number of agents since 1750, expressed as global annual averages. Some species are more long-lived than others; thus, if emissions of a long-lived species stopped tomorrow, the effect would continue for centuries. Other effects are shorter term – for example, sulphate aerosol would cease within approximately one or two months under the same hypothetical scenario of the complete cessation of emissions. Nonetheless, it is useful to point out a total radiative forcing of approximately 2.5Wm^{-2} from the long-lived greenhouse gases in the first bar (ie CO_2, CH_4, nitrous oxide (N_2O), chlorofluorocarbons (CFCs)).

Before moving on to estimates of radiative forcing from aviation, it is worth considering the question of what this total perturbation of climate means. The summary for policy-makers for the IPCC's third assessment report (IPCC, 2001) states that the increase in global average surface temperature over the 20th century was 0.6 ± 0.2 °C. From a range of emissions scenarios and model assessments, the globally averaged surface temperature is projected to further increase by between 1.4 and 5.8 °C from 1990 to 2100, depending upon the scenario assumed.

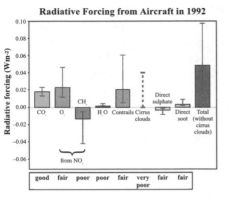
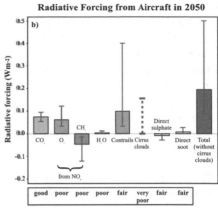

Source: IPCC SPM, 1999, and Deutschen Zentrum für Luft- und Raumfahrt (DLR) website at www.dlr.de/ipa

Figure 5.3 *Global annual mean radiative forcings from aircraft emissions for 1992 (a) and 2050, scenario Fa1 (b) (Wm^{-2})*

Having set the scene with the overall influences on climate and radiative forcing, we move on to illustrate the effects of subsonic aviation in 1992 and 2050, as estimated by the IPCC (1999), shown in Figure 5.3. Here, we see an overall forcing of $0.05\mathrm{Wm}^{-2}$ in 1992, approximately 3.5 per cent of the overall radiative forcing (as estimated in the IPCC's second assessment report; IPCC, 1996), and an overall forcing of $0.19\mathrm{Wm}^{-2}$ in 2050, 5 per cent of all climate forcings for a central scenario. The full range of 2050 scenarios studied imply forcings of 0.13 to $0.56\mathrm{Wm}^{-2}$ (ie 2.6 to 11 times the value in 1992).

Figure 5.3 shows the large uncertainties associated with contrail and cirrus effects (the two being linked): as is quite clear, the contrail and cirrus effects are relatively large and rather uncertain, the latter having no best estimate associated with it.

EMISSIONS FROM CURRENT AND FUTURE AVIATION

A number of attempts at estimating global aviation emissions have been made and are conveniently summarized by Henderson et al (1999). For present-day emissions (actually, early 1990s), three data sets are in common use: the ANCAT/EC2 data set (Gardner et al, 1998); the DLR-2 data set (Schmitt and Brunner, 1997); and the NASA data set (Baughcum et al, 1996). Furthermore, there are emission forecasts available for 2015 (Gardner et al, 1998; Baughcum et al, 1998) and scenarios for 2050 (FESG, 1998; Newton and Falk, 1997). Here, we focus upon the ANCAT/EC2 data sets and derivatives, and the FESG 2050 scenarios.

These aforementioned emission data sets all provide three-dimensional (3D) gridded data and have simplifying assumptions. The essential components include an aircraft movements database; a representation of the global fleet in terms of aircraft and engines; a fuel-flow model; calculation of emissions at altitude from fuel flow; and landing and take-off (LTO) emissions data.

The global fuel and NO_x data for 1991/1992, 2015 and 2050 are given in Table 5.1. The estimated global emission of NO_x (as NO_2) from civil and military aviation for the base year of 1991/1992 is 1.81teragrams (10^6 tonnes) of nitrogen dioxide per year (Tg NO_2 yr^{-1}) and the fuel burned 131Tg yr^{-1}. Military emissions, although more uncertain than the civil estimates, are approximately 11 per cent of the total, and for climate effects other than CO_2, are less important as most emissions are at much lower altitudes than those from civil aircraft. The spatial and vertical structure of emissions is shown in Figures 5.4 and 5.5, respectively. It can be seen that much of the emissions occur in the Northern Hemisphere and at altitudes of between 10km and 12km.

Table 5.1 *Fuel, NO_x and emission index (EI) for NO_x for 1991/1992, 2015 and 2050 gridded data sets*

Data set	Fuel Tg yr^{-1}	NO_x (as NO_2) Tg yr^{-1}	EI for NO_x	Reference
ANCAT/EC2 – 1991/1992	131.3	1.81	13.8	Gardner et al, 1998
ANCAT/EC2 – 2015	286.9	3.53	12.3	Gardner et al, 1998
DTI – 2050	633	4.43	7	Newton and Falk, 1997
Fa1 – 2050	471.0	7.2	15.2	FESG, 1998
Fa2 – 2050	487.6	5.5	11.4	FESG, 1998
Fc1 – 2050	268.2	4.0	15.0	FESG, 1998
Fc2 – 2050	277.2	3.1	11.3	FESG, 1998
Fe1 – 2050	744.3	11.4	15.3	FESG, 1998
Fe2 – 2050	772.1	8.8	11.4	FESG, 1998

By 2015, it is forecast that emissions of NO_x (as NO_2) from civil aviation will have grown by a factor of nearly 2, to 3.53Tg NO_2 yr^{-1} with a fuel burn of 287Tg yr^{-1}. It is important to discriminate between forecasts and scenarios. Here, we adopt a definition of a forecast as a situation that is the result of extrapolation of current and foreseen technologies and aviation growth. For scenarios, the assumptions are greater and the approach, while similar in some respects, tends to be driven 'top down'.

For 2050, the most commonly used gridded data sets are those generated by the forecasting and economic subgroup of ICAO (FESG, 1998). These scenarios were based upon a relationship between revenue passenger kilometres and gross domestic product (GDP). The GDP scenarios were the IPCC 'IS92a, c and e' scenarios (Leggett et al, 1992).[1] In addition, two technology scenarios for fuel and NO_x were assumed: one ambitious, one less so, giving six scenarios in total. The nomenclature adopted was, by example, Fa1 – *F*ESG IS92*a* Technology Scenario *1*. Fuel usages ranged from 268 to 772Tg yr^{-1} and NO_x emissions from 3.1 to 11.4Tg NO_2 yr^{-1}; these estimates equate to factors of approximately 2 to 6 on fuel and NO_x emissions over early 1990s data.

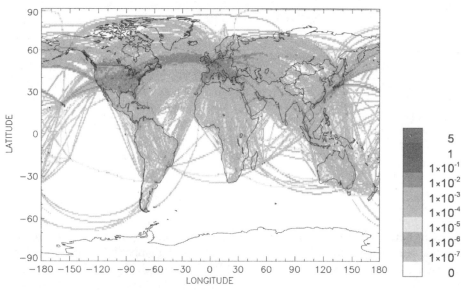

Source: Gardner et al, 1998, and Lee et al, 2002a

Figure 5.4 *Spatial distribution of ANCAT/EC2 1991/1992 emissions of NO_x from civil aviation, vertically integrated between ground and 16km (kg NO_2 m^{-2} yr^{-1})*

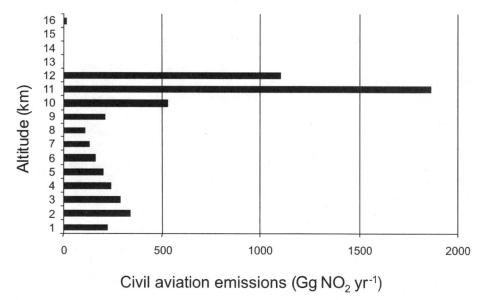

Source: Gardner et al, 1998, and Lee et al, 2002a

Figure 5.5 *Vertical distribution of emissions of civil aviation NO_x, 1991/1992*

This potential dramatic increase is illustrated in Figure 5.6. By 2050, it is clear that assumptions in GDP growth are critical to the overall emission, the technology assumptions having a second-order effect. In contrast to this overall pattern, the Department of Trade and Industry (DTI) 2050 scenario assumes a fuel usage (from traffic

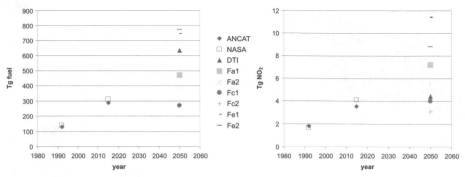

Source: IPCC, 1999, and Lee et al, 2002a

Figure 5.6 *Development over time of fuel usage and NO$_x$ emissions from aviation*

growth) between the Fa and Fe scenarios (mid- and upper-growth scenarios, respectively), but an aggressive NO$_x$ reduction, resulting in a global NO$_x$ emission closer to the Fc scenario (lowest growth of the FESG scenarios). For the DTI 2050 scenario, the global fuel consumption was estimated to be 633Tg, with 4.43Tg of NO$_x$ (as NO$_2$), produced as a consequence of a fleet emissions index (EI) of 7.

EFFECTS OF SUBSONIC AVIATION

Effects of NO$_x$ emissions from aircraft

Emissions of NO$_x$ arise from the combustion of aviation fuel (kerosene) and are a complex function of combustion temperature, pressure and combustor design. These emissions are primarily nitric oxide (NO) but are quickly converted to nitrogen dioxide (NO$_2$) in the atmosphere.

Emissions of NO$_x$ result in the catalytic production of tropospheric O$_3$ via a number of complex chemical processes (for a review, see IPCC, 1999, Chapter 2). Essentially, oxidation of methane (CH$_4$), carbon monoxide (CO) and non-methane hydrocarbons (NMHCs) results in the production of the hydroperoxy radical (HO$_2$). This HO$_2$ then reacts with NO to form NO$_2$, which may subsequently photodissociate, reforming NO and liberating the highly reactive atomic oxygen (O). Atomic oxygen reacts with O$_2$, forming O$_3$. This chemical process occurs in the natural atmosphere, but the introduction of extra NO$_x$ catalytically enhances the production rate of O$_3$. This is summarized in Figure 5.7, in which the catalytic role of NO$_x$ is shown, forming and recycling hydroxyl radicals (OH) and hydroperoxy radicals (HO$_2$).

The production of O$_3$ at altitudes at which subsonic aircraft typically fly (10–12km) is rather efficient and it is not so readily removed from the atmosphere as it is at the ground (by dry deposition), thus resulting in a residence time of weeks. Moreover, the temperature response for a change in O$_3$ is altitudinally dependent, as shown in Figure 5.8. This is because O$_3$ absorbs both incoming solar radiation and outgoing infrared radiation. At around the tropopause level, the sensitivity is greatest as the radiative forcing is proportional to the difference in the temperatures at

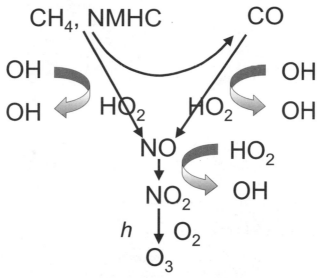

Figure 5.7 *Representation of the production of ozone from methane, carbon monoxide and non-methane hydrocarbons*

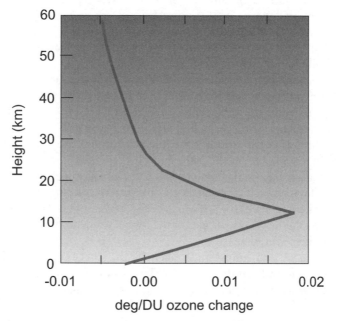

Source: adapted from Lacis et al, 1990

Figure 5.8 *Change in temperature per ozone column amount (Dobson Units – DU) by altitude*

which infrared radiation is emitted and absorbed by O_3. The maximum occurs at the tropopause, where temperatures are at a minimum.

Using 3D inventories of aircraft emissions, such as that shown in Figure 5.4, it is possible with a 3D chemical/transport model of the global atmosphere to calculate

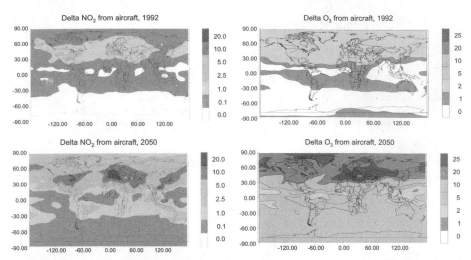

Figure 5.9 *(a) Modelled nitrogen dioxide concentrations in parts per trillion (ppt) and (b) ozone in parts per billion (ppb) from aircraft at cruise altitudes for 1992 and a 2050 scenario (Fe1)*

the perturbation induced by aircraft. Such a model typically divides the global atmosphere into grid boxes in three-dimensional space; wind fields are used to 'drive' the model with a typical time interval of six hours to transport the source gases around, over which period chemical reactions are calculated over shorter time periods, typically 5 to 30 minutes.

Perturbations attributable to aviation NO_x emissions and the resultant O_3 formed are shown from our own modelling studies (Lee and Kingdon, 2002) in Figures 5.9a and 5.9b. These figures show the contribution ('delta') of NO_2 (in parts per trillion (10^{-12}), ppt) and O_3 (in parts per billion (10^{-9}), ppb) for 1992 emissions and a sample 2050 scenario at cruise altitudes for July conditions. The NO_2 concentrations show a marked resemblance to the pattern of NO_x emissions, with some smoothing, the NO_2 having a residence time of a few days at these altitudes. By contrast, the O_3 perturbation shows a much more 'smeared-out' pattern, varying across the Northern Hemisphere, where much of the emissions occur, with tongues of ozone being transported across the hemispheres because of the longer residence time of approximately one month at these altitudes.

From equivalent simulations undertaken for the IPCC report (see IPCC, 1999, Chapter 4), it was found that the aircraft NO_x emissions resulted in a chain of chemical reactions that reduced ambient concentrations of methane (CH_4) emitted from other sources; CH_4 is itself a powerful greenhouse gas. The cause of this effect is rather complex and the magnitude of it was something of a surprise, as previous simulations with two-dimensional (2D) chemical/transport models of the atmosphere (latitude by height) had demonstrated such an effect but at a much smaller magnitude (eg Fuglestvedt et al, 1996). Essentially, aircraft NO_x emissions result in an enhancement of OH concentrations, which then reduce CH_4 concentrations via several chemical reactions and transport processes. Thus, aircraft NO_x emissions ultimately result in an enhancement of O_3 in the source regions – primarily the Northern Hemisphere – and an almost uniform reduction in CH_4 concentrations across both hemispheres. The enhancement of O_3 results in a positive globally averaged radiative forcing and a reduction in radiative forcing from reduced CH_4 concentrations (reduced by approximately 2–4 per cent).

That the globally averaged O_3 radiative forcing has an approximately equal and opposite magnitude to the reduction of CH_4 radiative forcing has resulted in the erroneous conclusion, in many quarters, that there is no climate effect, despite the fact that the IPCC report clearly stated otherwise (IPCC, 1999, section 6.5.1). It would be more correct to postulate a partial cancellation of the CO_2 radiative forcing induced by aircraft as both CO_2 and CH_4 are, more or less, well mixed across the hemispheres because of long lifetimes. This is a theme picked up in the concluding section of this chapter.

Effects of CO_2 emissions

The effects of CO_2 are much easier to assess than other aircraft emissions, since they are a simple function of fuel burn. Moreover, there is no difference between the emissions of CO_2 from aircraft or any other source in terms of radiative effect. Since CO_2 has an atmospheric residence time of many decades, it is well mixed in the atmosphere and can be treated as an additional CO_2 source in climate model simulations. The calculated radiative forcing in 1992 was $0.018 Wm^{-2}$, with an uncertainty of ±30 per cent that arises from uncertainties in the carbon cycle and the radiative transfer calculations themselves (IPCC, 1999).

Effects of water vapour emissions

Water vapour, *per se*, is a strong greenhouse gas; without it, the temperature of the Earth's atmosphere could not sustain life. The troposphere has relatively high concentrations of water vapour as a result of the natural hydrological cycle. The upper troposphere and lower stratosphere tends to be drier, and the mid to upper stratosphere very dry. Thus, any introduction of water into the stratosphere tends to warm the atmosphere. Subsonic aircraft introduce some water vapour from the combustion of kerosene; but this perturbation has been found to have a small effect, as the background concentrations of water vapour are rather high in the lower stratosphere, relative to the amount of water introduced by current and projected subsonic aircraft fleets. Thus, the radiative forcing is small, of the order $0.0015 Wm^{-2}$ (IPCC, 1999). Similarly, Ponater et al (1996) and Rind et al (1996) conducted studies of the direct effects of water vapour from aircraft using global climate models and concluded that the direct radiative effect was negligible. Emissions of water vapour into the stratosphere, particularly the mid–upper stratosphere, have a different effect, which is discussed later.

Effects of particle emissions on contrails and cirrus clouds

One of the impacts of aircraft on climate that has stimulated much interest and recent research is that of contrails and cirrus clouds. The idea that contrails can affect climate is not new: potential climate effects of contrails were discussed between the late 1960s and the early 1980s (eg Appleman, 1966; Chagnon, 1981). However, these studies of contrails did not receive much attention. The potential effects of contrails were subsequently discussed by Schumann and Wendling (1990); but the efforts made towards the IPCC report brought this issue to the fore.

Contrails form on particles that are emitted directly from the engine, such as soot, and sulphate particles that form in the plume and perhaps in the engine itself. The number density of sulphate particles in the plume is approximately one to two orders of magnitude greater than that of soot particles (Anderson et al, 1998; Schröder et al, 1998).

The formation of contrails arises from the increase in relative humidity that occurs during the mixing of the warm and moist exhaust gases from the aircraft engines with the colder and less humid ambient air. A contrail forms when saturation with respect to liquid water is reached or surpassed in the plume. For contrails to be persistent, the air mass through which the aircraft flies needs to be supersaturated with respect to ice. Thus, the critical factors in persistent contrail formation are water vapour and particles from the engine exhaust, and particular environmental conditions of temperature and humidity. In effect, since the engine exhaust conditions are not so variable at cruise, it is the environmental parameters that dictate whether a persistent contrail will form or not. Excellent reviews of contrail formation and their dependencies have been provided by Schumann (1996), Kärcher (1999) and IPCC (1999, Chapter 3).

The review and synthesis efforts associated with the IPCC (1999) report showed that the radiative effects of persistent contrails and the enhancement of cirrus cloudiness were potentially large (see Figure 5.3). Sausen et al (1998) calculated the potential global coverage of persistent contrails for 1991/1992 and Gierens et al (1999) for 2050. These coverages were utilized by Minnis et al (1999) to calculate radiative forcing using a simple radiative transfer model for these two timelines. The globally averaged radiative forcing from line-shaped contrails was shown to be ~0.02Wm^{-2} in 1992 and ~0.1Wm^{-2} in 2050 for the central Fa1 scenario (Minnis et al, 1999).

The other issue associated with contrails is the enhancement of cirrus clouds. Cirrus clouds can have a powerful effect on surface temperatures (Liou, 1986; Lohmann and Roeckner, 1995) and are a major source of uncertainty in global climate-modelling studies. The above-mentioned estimation of radiative forcing is for line-shaped persistent contrails only. As can be easily observed, persistent contrails may spread by diffusion and wind-shear to give a cirrus-like cloud coverage that cannot be ultimately recognized as having originated from contrails. Moreover, contrails and cirrus clouds (in common with all clouds) must nucleate on particles, typically submicron in size, and aircraft introduce such particles from soot and sulphate particles in the plume. It is possible that these condensation nuclei can trigger cirrus cloud formation long after the aircraft has passed, perhaps when temperature and ice supersaturation conditions are more favourable for cirrus formation.

Boucher (1999) showed a correlation between increases of air traffic in the North Atlantic Flight Corridor (NAFC) and increases in cirrus cloud coverage. A possible relationship between the two was postulated, but it was acknowledged that other causes could be contributory in a multicomponent way. Extending analyses of possible cirrus cloud increases, IPCC (1999, Chapter 3) concluded that 'a possible relationship between air traffic and cirrus formation' may exist. However, the uncertainties were so large in the IPCC's analysis that a best estimate of radiative forcing could not be given, only an uncertainty estimate that ranged from 0 (no effect) through to

$\sim0.04Wm^{-2}$ for 1992. There are several major sources of uncertainty in the radiative forcing estimates for line-shaped persistent contrails and enhanced cirrus cloudiness: contrail coverage calculations, optical depths of the clouds and ice crystal size distributions are all critical factors (Lee et al, 2000).

EFFECTS OF SUPERSONIC AVIATION

It has been suggested over the past 30 years or so that a significant fleet of supersonic transports (SSTs) would become economically and technically feasible. Most recently, the NASA high-speed civil transport (HSCT) research programme investigated technological and environmental possibilities and constraints. Ambitious technological goals were set in the HSCT programme, including an overall emissions index (EI) for NO_x of 5, under the supposition that the principal environmental effect would potentially be stratospheric O_3 depletion via NO_x chemistry.

Hypothetical fleet and emissions scenarios were designed that included different fleet sizes (500 and 1000) and SO_2 to particle conversion efficiencies. The aircraft were assumed to cruise at altitudes of approximately 17–20km. Although sulphur is only present in fuel at very low concentrations, much of it is thought to be converted to SO_2, which subsequently oxidizes to H_2SO_4, forming particles. Polar O_3 depletion is dominated by heterogeneous chemistry on polar stratospheric clouds (PSCs). This process is therefore highly dependent upon the surface area density of aerosols. As such, future SO_2 emissions may increase the surface area density and therefore possibly lead to further O_3 loss.

The calculation of the above effects is usually done in chemical/transport models of the stratosphere, treating the troposphere as a lower boundary condition. Models are often 2D (latitude versus height), although some more advanced 3D models are being developed and used (eg Rogers et al, 2000).

In the IPCC (1999) report, a major stratospheric modelling effort was made to assess supersonic potential aviation impacts (see IPCC, 1999, Chapter 4). Two significant results emerged from these studies: first, for the particular scenarios studied, the maximum ozone column change under scenario Fa1H (2050, 1000 SSTs, EI of NO_x of 5) was -0.4 per cent (-1.3 and +0.9 per cent from supersonic and subsonic aircraft, respectively); second, the most significant effect of supersonic aircraft on the atmosphere was from emissions of water vapour. The change in O_3 column was smaller than previously calculated and had only a small effect on increased UV-B penetration to the Earth's surface. The substantial increase in radiative forcing from water vapour was something of a surprise. Increases in H_2O of 0.4–0.7 parts per million (ppm) were found in the Northern Hemisphere, compared to background values of 3–4 ppm. However, these calculations were assessed to have large uncertainties.

RECENT ACTIVITIES AND FUTURE DIRECTIONS

That the IPCC (1999) report *Aviation and the Global Atmosphere* was a landmark, there can be no doubt. Since, and during, its writing and publication, there have been a number of significant events. NASA has ceased support of the HSCT research efforts as Boeing withdrew its intention to develop a large civil SST. At the same time, NASA dramatically reduced its funding of research into effects of subsonic aircraft in its Subsonic Assessment Programme (SASS). In Europe, however, there has been a strong research programme put into place both in the environment and technology areas, particularly regarding the areas of emissions, particle and contrail effects, and potential trade-offs. Other recent events in technology development include the intention of Airbus Industries to develop and build the A380, a competitor product to the Boeing 747, and Boeing's announcement of the development of the Sonic Cruiser. The environmental impacts of such developments have not yet been assessed.

The policy response to the IPCC report is effected mainly through ICAO's Committee on Aviation and Environmental Protection (CAEP) work programmes. Currently, only domestic aviation emissions of CO_2 are accounted for in greenhouse gas emission inventories and therefore in the Kyoto Protocol. However, the Kyoto Protocol makes allowance for inclusion of international aviation and the United Nations Framework Convention on Climate Change (UNFCCC), through its Subsidiary Body on Scientific and Technological Advice (SBSTA), has requested that ICAO's CAEP look at methods by which international aviation may be brought under the Kyoto Protocol. One favoured route is through CO_2 emissions trading (Gander and Helme, 1999). However, this ignores that fact that aviation has effects other than CO_2 on climate (see Figure 5.3) and that purchases by the aviation industry may *increase* total radiative forcing, not decrease it (Lee and Sausen, 2000).

In parallel to the issue of emissions trading is that of emissions allocations. Since aviation is, by its nature, international, the allocation of emissions is not so straightforward – though a number of allocation methodologies have been suggested by the UNFCCC (1996). Before emissions of CO_2 can be traded, there must be some sort of allocation. Currently, these allocations are not known, although initial work has begun (D S Lee, 2002, pers comm), which shows that approximately 40 per cent of global civil aircraft emissions in 1992 were domestic and 60 per cent were international. Attribution by country by two of the commonly accepted allocation methodologies is also calculated in this work.

There is much work yet to be done before we can have higher confidence in assessments of the impacts of aviation on climate and establish methods by which these effects might be ameliorated. Trade-offs between the different effects is the theme of a major European Commission research effort. In this project (TRADEOFF) climate impacts are being examined, as well as those of simple changes in operational practices.[2] For example, it has already been shown by Sausen et al (1998) that flying 1km lower or higher affects contrails in different ways, increasing contrail coverage for a 1km downwards shift in parts of Eurasia and the NAFC, but decreasing it in the tropics and North America. However, the effects on fuel efficiency and NO_x emissions were not considered. It has been calculated that a 2km shift downwards may increase CO_2 and NO_x emissions by approximately 4 per cent (Lee et al, 2002b). A downward shift in cruise altitudes may decrease O_3 production, and thus radiative forcing (Grewe et al, 2002); however, contrails at lower altitudes may have stronger radiative properties because of their higher water content (Meerkötter et al, 1999). Thus, it can be seen that potential operational changes have complex environmental responses that are not yet fully understood. It is premature to even begin thinking through the economic and technological consequences of changing operational practices for environmental purposes until studies are scientifically defensible and robust (Lee et al, 2000).

A more radical proposition is the development of a fleet of liquid hydrogen-fuelled aircraft. Experimental aircraft have been built and a major European Commission research programme, CRYOPLANE, is examining the technological feasibility and potential environmental impacts. A first study has been made of a hypothetical fleet of cryoplanes by Marquart et al (2001), who found that contrail formation could be a significant factor but were unable to give an overall prognosis of the environmental benefits or otherwise.

Contrails and cirrus cloudiness remain an important issue. More research is currently being committed to understanding the basic physics of contrail formation through measurement programmes such as the European Union (EU) project INCA and the German project PAZI.[3] The formation of particles in the plume and the engine itself are only incompletely understood and the EU project PARTEMIS (coordinated by QinetiQ) deals specifically with this issue. Since the IPCC (1999) report, a further assessment of the radiative forcing of line-shaped contrails has been performed using a global climate model (GCM), rather than an off-line radiative transfer model (Ponater et al, 2002). This study showed a much smaller radiative forcing of $0.004Wm^{-2}$, compared with the estimate of Minnis et al (1999), who derived a figure of $0.02Wm^{-2}$. The reasons for the differences were difficult to ascribe comprehensively; but, in effect, the uncertainty on contrail radiative forcing has increased.

Finally, we return to one of the issues that initiated much of the research into the effects of subsonic aviation: NO_x emissions and O_3 production. The fallacy of O_3 positive radiative forcing 'cancellation' by negative CH_4 forcing from aircraft NO_x emissions has already been referred to. Radiative forcing by aircraft-induced O_3 tends to occur strongly in the Northern Hemisphere and the resulting negative forcing (ie a reduction in overall forcing) from CH_4 is spread across the hemispheres. The real climate impact of opposing homogeneous and inhomogeneous forcings is not known. Remembering that radiative forcing is a *metric* (and proxy) for climate change, it is necessary to understand the limits of its applicability. The IPCC (1999) report broached the issue of the adequacy of radiative forcing as a metric for aircraft climate impacts. There are two issues relevant to this discussion: firstly, the temperature response to inhomogeneous forcings; and, secondly, the temperature response to O_3 forcings at different altitudes.

Central to the metric of radiative forcing is the assumption that the climate sensitivity parameter in equation (1), λ, is a constant. While λ is expected to be model dependent, it is implicitly assumed that it is constant in the model. However, in a number of GCM experiments, for the same increase of O_3 at different model layers, significant variation in λ has been found (eg Hansen et al, 1997). The parameter λ was found to vary significantly for different instantaneous radiative forcings for small aircraft O_3 responses by Ponater et al (1999). Stuber et al (2001) have subsequently found that surface temperature was more sensitive to aircraft-induced O_3 perturbations than an equivalent CO_2 perturbation using the stratosphere-adjusted radiative forcing, a forcing judged to be more reliable than the instantaneous forcing. There are some indications that inhomogeneous forcings produce a stronger climate effect in terms of surface temperature than equivalent homogeneous forcings

(Stuber et al, 2000). Thus, emissions of aviation NO_x and their effect on tropospheric O_3 production and radiative forcing remain an issue.

CONCLUSIONS

Much of this overview draws upon the IPCC 1999 assessment *Aviation and the Global Atmosphere*, which will be viewed as the benchmark for some years to come. However, a significant amount of research has continued past the IPCC assessment and important new results have been published, some of which are reviewed here. One of the most interesting developments is the commencement of 'what-if' scenarios that address operational issues. It should be stressed that these are in their infancy as the model tools with which aviation impacts are currently assessed are not yet mature enough, nor sufficiently convergent in their answers, to provide definitive recommendations on how aviation might minimize its climate impacts. Recent technological developments and proposals, notably the Airbus A380, Boeing Sonic Cruiser and a possible European-built large SST expand the scope of questions and the challenges for atmospheric science to provide robust environmental assessments.

ACKNOWLEDGEMENTS

This overview draws upon research commissioned by the UK Department of Transport, Local Government and the Regions (DTLR, Aviation Environmental Division), the Department of Trade and Industry (DTI, Engineering Directorate, Civil Aviation Issues) and the European Commission (EC). We would like to express our appreciation to Mike Crompton (DTLR), Peter Newton (DTI), Dr Reiner Dunker (EC), Dr Georgios Amanatides (EC) and Dr Helen Rogers (University of Cambridge, European Ozone Research Coordinating Unit). Figure 5.3 was downloaded from the Deutsches Zentrum für Luft- und Raumfahrt (DLR) website.

NOTES

1   Note that the IPCC IS92 scenarios have subsequently been replaced by the SRES scenarios; see IPCC (2000).
2   See www.ozone-sec.ch.cam.ac.uk/clusters/Corsaire_Website/corsaire_euproj.htm.
3   See www.op.dlr.de/ipa and above website for more details of aviation-related EU and national research projects.

REFERENCES

Anderson, B E, Cofer, W R, Barrick, J W, Bagwell D R, Hudgins, C H and Nowicki, G D (1998) 'Airborne observations of aircraft aerosol emissions: 1. Total and nonvolatile particle emission indices', *Geophysical Research Letters*, vol 25, pp1689–1692
Appleman, H S (1966) 'Effect of supersonic aircraft on cirrus formation and climate', American Meteorological Society and American Institute of Aeronautics and Astronautics,

Conference on Aerospace Meteorology, Los Angeles, California, 28–31 March, 1966, AIAA Paper 66–369

Baughcum, S L, Henderson, S C and Sutkus, D J (1998) *Scheduled Civil Aircraft Emission Inventories Projected for 2015: Database Development and Analysis*, NASA/CR-1998-207638, NASA Langley Research Center, US

Baughcum, S L, Tritz, T G, Henderson, S C and Pickett, D C (1996) *Scheduled Civil Aircraft Emissions Inventories for 1992: Database Development and Analysis*, NASA Contractor Report 4700, NASA Langley Research Center, US

Boucher, O (1999) 'Air traffic may increase cirrus cloudiness', *Nature*, vol 397, pp30–31

Brasseur, G P, Cox, R A, Hauglustaine D, Isaksen, I, Lelieveld, J, Lister, D H, Sausen R, Schumann, U, Wahner, A and Wiesen, P (1998) 'European scientific assessment of the atmospheric effects of aircraft emissions', *Atmospheric Environment*, vol 32, pp2329–2418

Chagnon, S A (1981) 'Midwestern cloud, sunshine and temperature trends since 1901: possible evidence of jet contrail effects', *Journal of Applied Meteorology*, vol 20, 496–508

Crutzen, P J (1971) 'Ozone production rate in an oxygen-hydrogen-nitrogen atmosphere', *Journal of Geophysical Research*, vol 76, pp7311–7327

FESG (1998) *Report 4: Report of the Forecasting and Economic Analysis Sub-Group (FESG): Long-Range Scenarios*, International Civil Aviation Organization Committee on Aviation Environmental Protection Steering Group Meeting, Canberra, Australia, January 1998

Friedl, R R, Baughcum, S L, Anderson, B, Hallett, J, Liou, K-N, Rasch, P, Rind, D, Sassen, K, Singh, H, Williams, L and Wuebbles, D (1997) *Atmospheric Effects of Subsonic Aircraft: Interim Assessment of the Advanced Subsonic Assessment Program*, NASA Reference Publication 1400, Washington, DC

Fuglestvedt, J S, Isaksen, I and Wang, W-C (1996) 'Estimates of indirect global warming potentials for CH_4, CO and NO_x', *Climatic Change*, vol 34, pp405–437

Gander, S and Helme, N (1999) 'Emissions trading is an effective, proven policy tool for solving air pollution problems', *ICAO Journal*, vol 54, pp12–14, 28

Gardner, R M, Adams, J K, Cook, T, ten Have, H, Larson, L G, Falk, R S, Fleuti, E, Förtsch, W, Lecht, M, Lee, D S, Leech, M V, Lister, D H, Massé, B, Morris, K, Newton, P J, Owen, A, Parker, E, Schmitt, A and Vandenberghe, C (1998) *ANCAT/EC2 Aircraft Emissions Inventories for 1991/1992 and 2015: Final Report*, ECAC/ANCAT and EC Working Group, European Civil Aviation Conference

Gierens, K, Sausen, R and Schumann, U (1999) 'A diagnostic study of the global distribution of contrails part II: future air traffic scenarios', *Theoretical and Applied Climatology*, vol 63, pp1–9

Grewe, V, Dameris, M, Fichter, C and Lee, D S (2002) 'Impact of aircraft NO_x emissions. Part 2: effects of lowering the flight altitude', *Meteorologische Zeitschrift*, vol 11, pp197–205

Hansen, J E, Sato, M and Ruedy, R (1997) 'Radiative forcing and climate response', *Journal of Geophysical Research*, vol 102, pp6831–6884

Henderson, S C, Wickrama, U K, Baughcum, S L, Begin, J L, Franco, F, Greene, D L, Lee, D S, Mclaren, M L, Mortlock, A K, Newton, P J, Schmitt, A, Sutkus, D J, Vedantham, A and Wuebbles, D J (1999) 'Aircraft emissions: current inventories and future scenarios' in Penner, J E, Lister, D H, Griggs, D J, Dokken, D J and McFarland, M (eds) *Aviation and the Global Atmosphere*, special report of IPCC working groups I and III in collaboration with the scientific assessment panel to the Montreal Protocol on Substances that Deplete the Ozone Layer, Chapter 9, Intergovernmental Panel on Climate Change, Cambridge University Press, Cambridge

ICAO (1995) *Engine Exhaust Emissions Databank*, first edition, ICAO Doc 9646-AN/943, International Civil Aviation Organization, Montreal

IPCC (1990) *Climate Change: The IPCC Scientific Assessment*, report prepared for IPCC by Working Group 1, Houghton, J T, Jenkins, G J and Ephraums, J J (eds), Cambridge University Press, Cambridge

IPCC (1995) *Climate Change 1994: Radiative Forcing of Climate Change and an Evaluation of the IPCC IS92 Emission Scenarios*, reports of Working Groups I and III of the Intergovernmental Panel on Climate Change, forming part of the IPCC Special Report to the first session of the Conference of the Parties to the UN Framework Convention on Climate Change, Houghton, J T, Meira Filho, L G, Bruce, J, Hoesung L, Callander, B A, Haites, E, Harris, N and Maskell, K (eds), Cambridge University Press, Cambridge

IPCC (1996) *Climate Change 1995, the Science of Climate Change*, contribution of Working Group I to the Second Assessment Report of the Intergovernmental Panel on Climate Change, Houghton, J T, Meira Filho, L G, Callander, B A, Haites, E, Harris, N, Kattenberg, A and Maskell, K (eds), Cambridge University Press, Cambridge

IPCC (1997) *An Introduction to Simple Climate Models Used in the IPCC Second Assessment Report*, IPCC Technical Paper II, Houghton, J T, Meira Filho, L G, Griggs, D J and Maskell, K (eds), Intergovernmental Panel on Climate Change, Switzerland

IPCC (1999) *Aviation and the Global Atmosphere*, special report of IPCC working groups I and III in collaboration with the scientific assessment panel to the Montreal Protocol on Substances that Deplete the Ozone Layer, Penner, J E, Lister, D H, Griggs, D J, Dokken, D J and McFarland, M (eds) Intergovernmental Panel on Climate Change, Cambridge University Press, Cambridge

IPCC SPM (1999) *Aviation and the Global Atmosphere: Summary for Policymakers*, special report of IPCC working groups I and III in collaboration with the scientific assessment panel to the Montreal Protocol on Substances that Deplete the Ozone Layer, Penner, J E, Lister, D H, Griggs, D J, Dokken, D J and McFarland, M (eds), Intergovernmental Panel on Climate Change, Geneva

IPCC (2000) *Emission Scenarios*, special report of working group III of the Intergovernmental Panel on Climate Change, Cambridge University Press, Cambridge

IPCC (2001) *Climate Change 2001, the Scientific Basis*, summary for policy-makers and technical summary of the working group I report, Cambridge University Press, Cambridge

Johnston, H S (1971) 'Reduction of stratospheric ozone by nitrogen dioxide catalysts from supersonic transport exhaust', *Science*, vol 173, pp517–522

Kärcher, B (1999) 'Aviation-produced aerosols and contrails', *Surveys in Geophysics*, vol 20, pp113–167

Lacis, A A, Wuebbles, D J and Logan, J A (1990) 'Radiative forcing of climate by changes in the vertical distribution of ozone', *Journal of Geophysical Research*, vol 95, pp9971–9981

Lee, D S (2002) 'Allocating international civil aviation emissions', *Climatic Change*

Lee, D S, Clare, P E, Haywood, J, Kärcher, B, Lunnon, R W, Pilling, I, Slingo, A and Tilston, J R (2000) *Identifying the Uncertainties in Radiative Forcing of Climate from Aviation Contrails and Aviation-Induced Cirrus*, DERA/AS/PTD/CR000103, DERA, Pyestock

Lee, D S and Sausen, R (2000) 'New directions: assessing the real impact of CO_2 emissions trading by the aviation industry', *Atmospheric Environment*, vol 34, pp5337–5338

Lee, D S, Brunner B, Döpelheuer, A, Falk, R S, Gardner, R M, Lecht, M, Leech, M, Lister, D H and Newton, P J (2002a) 'Aviation emissions: present-day and future', *Meteorologische Zeitschrift*, vol 11

Lee, D S and Kingdon, RD (2002) 'Development of a semi-Lagrangian model of the global atmosphere and application to present-day and future aviation emission scenarios', *Meteorologische Zeitschrift* (in preparation)

Lee, D S, Sausen, R, Marquart, S and Norman, P D (2002b) 'The effect of changing cruise altitudes on contrails and emissions of NO_x and CO_2 for the global civil aircraft fleet', *Atmospheric Environment* (in preparation)

Leggett J, Pepper, W J and Swart, R J (1992) 'Emissions scenarios for the IPCC: an update' in Houghton, J T, Callander, B A and Varney, S K (eds), *Climate Change 1992: The Supplementary Report to the IPCC Scientific Assessment*, Cambridge University Press, Cambridge, pp69–95

Liou, K N (1986) 'Influence of cirrus clouds on weather and climate processes: a global perspective', *Monthly Weather Review*, vol 114, pp1167–1199

Lohmann, U and Roeckner, E (1995) 'Influence of cirrus cloud radiative forcing on climate and climate sensitivity in a general circulation model', *Journal of Geophysical Research*, vol 100, pp16305–16323

Marquart, S, Sausen, R, Ponater, M and Grewe, V (2001) 'Estimate of the climate impact of cryoplanes', *Aerospace Science and Technology*, vol 5, 73–84

McGuffie, K and Henderson-Sellers, A (1997) *A Climate Modelling Primer*, John Wiley & Sons, Chichester

McIlveen, R (1992) *Fundamentals of Weather and Climate*, Chapman and Hall, London

Meerkötter, R, Schumann U, Dölling, D R, Minnis, P and Nakajima, T (1999) 'Radiative Forcing by Contrails', *Annales Geophysicae*, vol 17, pp1080–1094

Minnis, P, Schumann, U, Doelling, D R, Gierens, K R and Fahey, D W (1999) 'Global distribution of contrail radiative forcing', *Geophysical Research Letters*, vol 26, pp1853–1856

Newton, P J and Falk, R S (1997) *DTI Forecast of Fuel Consumption and Emissions from Civil Aircraft in 2050 Based on ANCAT/EC2 1992 Data*, DTI Report No DTI/ADI3c/199701/1.0

Ponater, M, Brinkop, S, Sausen, R and Schumann, U (1996) 'Simulating the global atmospheric response to aircraft water vapour emissions and contrails: a first approach using a GCM', *Annales Geophysicae*, vol 14, pp941–960

Ponater M, Marquart, S and Sausen, R (2002) 'Contrails in a comprehensive global climate model: parameterisation and radiative forcing results', *Journal of Geophysical Research*, vol D107, S ACL 2-1-ACL 2-15

Ponater, M, Sausen, R, Feneberg, B and Roeckner, E (1999) 'Climate effect of ozone changes caused by present and future air traffic', *Climate Dynamics*, vol 15, pp631–642

Rind, D, Lonergan, P and Shah, K (1996) 'Climatic effect of water vapour release into the upper troposphere', *Journal of Geophysical Research*, vol 100, pp7381–7396

Rogers, H L, Chipperfield, M P, Bekki, S and Pyle, J A (2000) 'The effects of future supersonic aircraft on stratospheric chemistry modelled with varying meteorology', *Journal of Geophysical Research*, vol 105, pp29359–29367

Rogers, H L, Lee, D S, Raper, D W, de Forster, P M, Wilson, C W and Newton, P J (2002) 'The impacts of aviation on the atmosphere', *Journal of the Royal Aeronautical Society* (in press)

Sausen, R, Gierens, K, Ponater, M and Schumann, U (1998) 'A diagnostic study of the global distribution of contrails part I: present day climate', *Theoretical and Applied Climatology*, vol 61, pp127–141

Schmitt, A and Brunner, B (1997) 'Emissions from aviation and their development over time' Schumann, U, Chlond, A, Ebel, A, Kärcher, B, Pak, H, Schlager, H, Schmitt, A and Wendling, P (eds), in *Final Report on the BMBF Verbundprogramm Schadstoffe in der Luftfahrt*, DLR Mitteilung, 97-04, Oberpfaffenhofen and Cologne, Germany

Schröder F, Kärcher, B, Petzold, A, Baumann, R, Busen, R, Hoell, C and Schumann, U (1998) 'Ultrafine aerosol particles in aircraft plumes: in situ observations', *Geophysical Research Letters*, vol 25, pp2789–2792

Schumann, U (1990) *Air Traffic and the Environment*, Lecture Notes in Engineering 60, Schumann, U (ed), Springer-Verlag, Berlin

Schumann, U (1994) 'On the effect of emissions from aircraft engines on the state of the atmosphere', *Annales Geophysicae*, vol 12, pp365–384

Schumann, U (1996) 'On conditions for contrail formation from aircraft exhausts', *Meteorologische Zeitschrift*, vol 5, pp4–23

Schumann, U and Wendling, P (1990) 'Determination of contrails from satellite data and observational results' in Schumann, U (ed) *Air Traffic and the Environment – Background, Tendencies and Potential Global Atmospheric Effects*, Springer-Verlag, Heidelberg, pp138–153

Shine, K P and Forster, P M D (1999) 'The effect of human activity on radiative forcing of climate change: a review of recent developments', *Global and Planetary Change*, vol 20, pp205–225

Stuber, N, Sausen, R and Ponater, M (2000) 'Towards a more reliable metric of climate change', presentation at the European Geophysical Society General Assembly, Nice, April 2000

Stuber, N, Sausen, R and Ponater, M (2001) 'Stratosphere adjusted radiative forcing calculations in a comprehensive climate model', *Theoretical and Applied Climatology*, vol 68, pp125–135

UNFCCC (1996) *Communications from Parties Included in Annex 1 to the Convention: Guidelines, Schedules, and Process for Consideration*, Secretariat Note FCCC/SBSTA/1996/9/Add.1, United Nations Framework Convention on Climate Change, 8 July 1996, Geneva

Chapter 6

Aircraft noise, community relations and stakeholder involvement

Callum Thomas and Martin Lever

INTRODUCTION

It is widely accepted that the most significant local environment impact associated with the operation of airports arises from the noise generated by aircraft. Over the past 40 years, very significant improvements in airframe and engine technology have been achieved, as manufacturers and airlines have seen commercial advantages in improving noise performance. International regulation by the world body for aviation – the International Civil Aviation Organization (ICAO) – has supported this by setting noise targets for future aircraft types and programmes for the phase-out of operations by older, noisier aircraft. As a consequence, despite a very significant increase in air traffic, the number of people exposed to high levels of noise disturbance has actually reduced around major airports over the last 10 to 20 years. However, poor land-use planning in many countries and a failure to prevent urban encroachment upon airports have negated the benefits of improved technology, with the result that millions of people living near airports and their approach and departure routes continue to be exposed on a daily basis to high levels of aircraft noise.

Three important factors are exacerbating the level of disturbance faced by these people. The first relates to the fact that while the noise of individual aircraft movements has declined, traffic has increased, with the result that the balance of nuisance at some larger airports is moving away from the disturbance caused by each aircraft to the frequency with which people are overflown. The second, as explained below, relates to the fact that, given new noise certification regulations recently announced by the ICAO and the anticipated rates of growth in the industry, noise exposure around many airports is likely to grow in the future. The third factor is linked to the fact that disturbance is a subjective issue that is related to perception or tolerance of nuisance and that this, in turn, declines with increasing affluence. As a result, levels of disturbance that were 'acceptable' in the past will no longer be considered so in the future.

This is of major significance to the air transport industry as disturbance or increasing nuisance will lead to increased levels of community opposition and, in turn, will act as a barrier to airport growth. This chapter links noise and capacity issues with community and stakeholder concerns and goes on to outline recent regulatory developments that are likely to influence airport noise policies in the short to medium term.

AIRPORT NOISE CAPACITY CONSTRAINTS

The level of traffic an airport can handle during a particular period of time is dependent upon a variety of factors, primarily:

- the capacity of its infrastructure – including runways, taxi ways, aprons, terminals and ground transport access;
- the capacity of the air traffic management system that serves the airport; and
- the skill with which the airport and the air traffic system is managed.

However, the disturbance caused by aircraft noise has the potential to further reduce an airport's operating capacity due to the imposition of noise restrictions, such that today there are many examples of airports throughout the world that are subject to noise-related constraints. A number of major airports (eg Schiphol) have reached their 'noise capacity' before having made full use of their runway and terminal infrastructure (ICAO, 1993). Others have failed to gain planning approval for further development as a result of the noise implications of future traffic growth, despite the proven demand. In the extreme case are examples of brand new airports (eg F J Strauss Airport in Munich and Hong Kong Airport) that have been constructed on greenfield sites, partially in response to noise problems at previously existing sites.

AIRCRAFT NOISE AND ITS EFFECTS

The physics of sound can be described in terms of changes in air pressure, wavelength frequency, amplitude or purity (Sekuler and Blake, 1994; Veitch and Arkkelin, 1995). However, while these describe how sound is transmitted through the air to the ear, they do not measure the level of disturbance caused in response to hearing that sound. Noise is generally defined as a sound that has an undesirable effect upon people (Berglund and Lindvall, 1995). Prolonged exposure to high levels of noise has been shown to cause serious psychological and physiological effects upon the human body, including hearing impairment or loss and sleep deprivation leading to stress and immunological problems (Veitch and Arkkelin, 1995).

There is unequivocal evidence that the auditory system can be damaged by exposure to extremely high levels of noise. However, despite considerable research into the possible non-auditory health effects of noise, the results are often contradictory. The broader World Health Organization (WHO) definition of health helps to resolve this apparent paradox. This definition (WHO, 1999) states that health is a state of complete physical, mental and social well-being, and not merely the absence of disease and infirmity. The inclusion of well-being in the definition expands the concept of health beyond clinical significance to encompass a number of effects of aircraft noise that are well known (annoyance, sleep disturbance, interference with speech communication, cognitive and performance effects).

The problem of aircraft noise disturbance involves the complex interaction of a number of physical, biological, psychological and sociological processes (Schultz, 1978). The relevant physical factors include those associated with noise generation: aircraft type, mode of operation and the resulting noise level. The other critical components are the human factors, which include the basic biological systems of audition followed by the psychological processes that interpret these signals and can include health status, annoyance and stress (Job, 1996). The further interpretation of noise disturbance can be influenced by social conditions that may include factors such as socio-economic status and cultural and lifestyle differences. Finally, although individuals may complain about the 'noise' of aircraft, a variety of other factors, such as fear of air accidents or disturbance from other airport activities, can be involved in the underlying causes of annoyance (Moss et al, 1997).

The level of perceived nuisance is therefore only, in part, a function of the frequency and noisiness of aircraft movements. Noise perception is also affected by:

• the variation in affluence, attitude, culture and lifestyle that affect perceptions of disturbance or annoyance arising from aircraft noise in different communities;
• an awareness of the social and economic consequences of constraining airport growth upon the local and regional communities they serve;
• the considerable variation in socio-economic need and the need for air route development in different regions of the world; and
• the level of public debate or opposition to airport development and the extent to which democratic systems are responsive to such action.

Noise metrics do not take account of the fact that less affluent residents of communities surrounding airports are likely to be more tolerant of aircraft noise and, at the same time, stand to gain additional employment from the continued growth of those airports. It is exactly for these reasons that there has been an inability of acoustic variables on their own to satisfactorily predict self-reported annoyance due to environmental noise.

MEASURING NOISE EXPOSURE

As a result of the above difficulties in precisely determining the effect of (or response to) aircraft noise, authorities have settled for the easier option of quantifying overall noise exposure. The level of exposure to aircraft noise can be, and is, measured in a variety of ways (reviewed in Ollerhead et al, 1992), such that there is no universal measure of exposure at the present time, although efforts to standardize metrics are taking place – for example, across the European Community through EC Directive 2002/49/EC (Assessment and Management of Environmental Noise) (European

Commission, 2002). The most commonly used approach to measuring noise exposure involves the calculation of the average amount of noise exposure experienced at a particular location over a specific period of time (eg 8 hours, 12 hours or 16 hours) and is a function of the number of aircraft movements and the noise made by each. A number of reports compare these noise exposure measures with the results of social surveys relating to levels of perceived disturbance in areas of different noise exposure. Some argue, and it is evident from noise complaints received by airports, that as traffic has increased and aircraft have become quieter, the frequency of exposure is becoming a more important cause of nuisance (Janic, 1999). All this would suggest that conventional noise-assessment metrics alone may not be adequate as an indicator of disturbance around airports.

THE SUSTAINABLE DEVELOPMENT CHALLENGE

Increasing global affluence is likely to lead to growth in air traffic demand. In part, this will be associated with the development of a global society, increasing trade, changing patterns of consumption and the maintenance of increasingly disparate social and family networks. A significant additional factor will, however, be an increasing demand for leisure travel.

These same drivers that fuel demand will also be associated with an increasing expectation of quality of environment, increasing concern for public health and a declining tolerance of nuisance, all of which will lead to increasing opposition to growth. The problem posed by this paradox is made worse by the fact that current forecasts indicate, as will be explained, that the anticipated growth in air traffic demand for the next 20 to 30 years will continue to outstrip improvements in aircraft noise technology. The result will be that the noise climate around many airports throughout the world is likely to deteriorate in the future. The sustainable development challenge for the air transport industry is to meet increasing demand for air travel, while at the same time constraining or even reducing the number of people exposed to 'unacceptable levels' of nuisance from aircraft noise.

The control of aircraft noise

A wide variety of measures are used to minimize the number of people exposed to aircraft noise and, hence, the level of nuisance they face.

Technological improvement

There is no question that significant improvements have been made in aircraft engine and airframe technologies over the past 20 to 30 years that have dramatically reduced the level of, and the area of exposure to, noise generated by modern aircraft. However, it would appear that the potential for further improvement is becoming more difficult. No step change in technology is on the horizon, and it can be anticipated that any such development would be exceedingly costly.

Even when new technologies have been developed, it takes many years for certification and airworthiness approval mechanisms to take effect. It then takes even longer for aircraft to progressively enter the airline fleet, if only because of the very high costs of buying or leasing new aircraft. Airlines and aircraft leasing companies already own large numbers of very expensive aircraft that are completely airworthy. They are understandably unwilling to take them out of service and invest in new models simply for environmental reasons, although such action is becoming increasingly necessary to ensure continuing access to noise-constrained or noise-sensitive airports.

A less costly approach would involve the retrofitting of existing aircraft with new or 'hush-kitted' engines. This has been achieved in the past, although the noise benefits have been far less dramatic than those that could be achieved through replacement with new aircraft.

Operational improvements

A wide variety of operating practices have been developed by airlines in order to reduce the noise generated by their flights. Continuous descent approaches reduce arrival noise. Quiet take-off procedures, which involve throttling back the aircraft engines once a safe height has been reached, minimize departure noise. Minimum noise routes for arriving and departing traffic can ensure that, as far as possible, aircraft are routed away from built-up areas. On the ground, air-traffic management procedures can ensure that aircraft are held in locations where noise propagation does not affect local residents.

Infrastructure developments

At airports, purpose-built engine-test facilities can contain the noise generated during ground maintenance procedures. The construction of noise mounds or walls can prevent localized noise exposure – for example, the domestic terminal at Copenhagen Airport has been designed to incorporate and act as a noise wall that protects local housing from apron noise. In the most extreme examples, entirely new airports have been built in remote and even off-shore locations in order to address, in part, the potential constraints caused by aircraft noise (eg Munich, Hong Kong and Kansai).

Noise charges and penalties

Differential charges based upon noise emissions encourage the use of quieter aircraft and discourage noisy operations. This tool can be adjusted to reflect varying sensitivity at different times of the day and night. Noise penalties, imposed upon aircraft that exceed agreed noise levels on take-off or landing, also put pressure on pilots to adopt the quietest operating procedures.

Operating restrictions and limits

Operating restrictions related to noise exposure have been introduced at airports throughout the world. In the main, these tend to relate to night flying, where convention has it that a limit is imposed upon the numbers and types of aircraft that can take off or land during the night-time hours. Many airports also close at night, though the definition of what is considered 'night time' varies between countries and individual airports. Some airports have restrictions on the use of particular runways at sensitive times. Others have agreed to, or have been forced to adopt, movement capacity limits during the day time, often as part of a planning agreement designed to enable future infrastructure growth. Another common constraint is a limit upon the noise that can be generated over a given period of time, such that once the limit is reached, further growth can only be ensured by action to encourage the use of increasingly quieter aircraft.

Land-use planning

The implementation of land-use planning around airports can ensure that the minimum number of people work or live in high-noise areas. Inadequate planning controls in many countries have led to domestic properties still being built close to airports. Even in the limited number of countries where adequate controls exist, they are not always implemented with sufficient vigour for a variety of reasons – in particular, because the growth of airports encourages urban development in its proximity. Many companies wish to locate close to airports. Airports require ancillary and support services and a workforce that is more conveniently provided locally. This drives up potential land values and leads to political pressure to permit development.

Even where land-use planning laws exist, many airports are already surrounded by urban conurbations close to their runways and arrival and departure routes, built before their existence. Finally, the growth of aviation over the last 20 to 30 years has been so rapid that even in countries where land-use planning controls have been in place for a long time, housing developments that were approved as late as the 1960s would be refused today.

There is an implicit tension between the needs of airports to surround themselves with a land buffer to prevent noise disturbance and the resultant increase in land value (particularly for some commercial developments), arising from that same proximity to an aviation gateway.

Buy out, compensation and sound insulation

A side effect of the disturbance caused by aircraft noise is a generally held belief that aircraft noise adversely affects values of properties in close proximity to airports and flight paths. A number of studies compare the value of properties affected by aircraft noise with similar properties in non-noise-affected areas (Feitelson et al, 1998; Tomkins et al, 1998). In recent years, airports have adopted a variety of measures to address this issue and enable continued growth, at the same time negating growing disquiet amongst noise-affected airport communities.

Evidence from the US suggests that land and property acquisition can be a successful though expensive means of reducing opposition to airport noise. Airport proprietors may acquire land surrounding an airport or an interest in that land through voluntary sales or compulsory purchase. After it has acquired the land, the airport will often use the property for airport-related uses, such as hotels and restaurants, or suitable non-airport-related functions (Falzone, 1999). Such land acquisition programmes often include measures for the relocation of residents and businesses.

While there is evidence that aircraft noise adversely affects property values, Tomkins et al (1998) suggest that noise nuisance is not the sole determining factor. Other factors that impact negatively and positively upon property values include location, local amenities, transport links and crime.

In some localities, compensation payments are made to nearby residents in recognition of the adverse effects of aircraft noise. Setting the level of compensation is, however, a complex task. Valuations tend to draw upon a number of variables including, for example, household income, period of residence and the value of a property. Place-specific, socio-economic factors can also influence mitigation and compensation initiatives.

Finally, it should be noted that airports provide positive as well as negative effects on property values. Positive development benefits in terms of access and employment were noted in a study by Tomkins et al (1998) that focused upon the impact of Manchester Airport on its nearby property market.

Sound-proofing of homes, public buildings and businesses in close proximity to an airport is one tool widely used by airports in mitigating against aircraft noise. However, while sound-proofing provides immediate relief against aircraft noise disturbance, its effectiveness is limited. Firstly, such projects require large expenditure that, depending upon the age of the building, may not be economically feasible. In addition, while the sound level is significantly reduced within a building, it may be ineffective in residential situations, especially during the summer months when individuals open windows and spend more time outdoors.

INTERNATIONAL REGULATION OF AIRCRAFT NOISE – THE GLOBAL PERSPECTIVE

The principles of sustainable development implicitly acknowledge limits to growth or, at least, limits to the environmental consequences of growth. In terms of aircraft noise and airport development, this will relate primarily to the level and nature of air traffic, the proximity and size of neighbouring communities and the level of perceived nuisance within those communities. Accordingly, future growth in air traffic, coupled with increased intolerance to disturbance caused by aircraft noise, must be offset by continuing and sustained improvements in aircraft noise technology and a rolling airline-fleet replacement programme. Regulation should therefore seek to drive the development and adoption of quieter technologies and the phase-out of noisier aircraft.

The ICAO is the United Nations (UN) body that governs the civil air transport industry. ICAO's remit extends to providing the regulatory framework within which aircraft noise is controlled at a global level. ICAO regulation has been a major driver for the introduction into service of improved aircraft noise technology – first, by setting noise performance targets for aircraft to be licensed to fly and, second, through the introduction of targets for the phase-out of operations by older, noisier aircraft.

Following increasing community opposition to aircraft noise and significant improvements in airframe and engine technologies, all aircraft must meet the standards set by the ICAO, which are contained in volume I of Annex 16 to the Convention on International Civil Aviation. For jet-powered aircraft, there are three levels of stringency in the standards. Stage 2 (Chapter 2) of Annex 16, volume I, contains the standards that are applicable to jet aircraft designed before October 1977 and stage 3 (Chapter 3) contains more stringent standards applicable to those designed after that date. In

September 2001, ICAO agreed new and more stringent Chapter 4 requirements that would be applied to aircraft certified for introduction after 1 January 2006.

Currently, all Chapter 2 aircraft must be phased out not later than 1 April 2002 (completed in the US at the end of 1999). After this date, Chapter 2 aircraft will have to be retired or recertificated to meet the Chapter 3 requirements. In recognition of the particular social and economic conditions in developing nations, derogations were made for certain aircraft to be allowed to continue operating. ICAO did not, however, adopt a phase-out programme for Chapter 3 aircraft. It chose, instead, to call for the adoption of what it termed a 'balanced approach' to dealing with the issue of aircraft noise disturbance, involving reduction in noise at source, land-use planning, operational constraints and noise-abatement procedures.

ICAO is responsible to all the UN member states and has to act in accordance with their wishes. The speed with which ICAO certification regulation moves forward, the level of increased stringency adopted at each stage and the inclusion of a provision for the phase-out of existing aircraft result from the resolution of the following significant and sometimes conflicting pressures.

The environmental perspective

The rate of the development and introduction of improved aircraft noise technology should be fast enough to offset the effects of growth in air transport. Even this will be a minimum requirement as sensitivity to disturbance increases.

The manufacturers' perspective

Noise certification standards have to reflect what can be achieved in technological terms. Progress in developing quieter aircraft is becoming more difficult and more expensive to achieve, and this will affect the rate at which aircraft are introduced into the airline fleet.

The airline perspective

Airlines continue to invest in very expensive aircraft that can be forced out of service by phase-out requirements, thereby reducing the operational life of their fleet and, hence, the value of the company.

The economic and social implications for different countries

Countries and the airports within them differ significantly in terms of traffic levels, number of people exposed to noise, need for air transport growth and levels of perceived opposition to noise in local communities. In some regions, especially remote and island communities, aviation has a particularly important role to play. In others, maintaining and developing air routes to key cities are critical to national economic development. National governments will also take account of the interests of their airlines, airports and aircraft manufacturers.

The growth perspective

The growth of the air transport industry increases the use of the existing airline fleet, while also driving more rapid fleet replacement. The phase-out of noisy but air-worthy aircraft can create a shortage of aircraft to serve the market.

The case of economies in transition in Central and Eastern Europe with plans to accede to the European Union (EU), illustrates the significant conflicting demands resulting from the need to grow their air route networks, while modernizing their airline fleets. On the one hand, they have had to rapidly phase out the use of noisy Russian aircraft, which used to operate primarily within Central and Eastern Europe, and replace them with modern, quiet aircraft in order to gain access to EU airports. On the other hand, they are unable to develop those routes because they have a significantly reduced airline fleet. In consequence, Central and Eastern European countries are at risk of losing or failing to gain significant market share to EU airlines, which will have the advantage of developing the wider European air route network.

It is self-evident that as aviation is a global industry, it should have common global regulations. However, it is exactly this that makes the processes of ICAO so very slow. Extensive time is required for consultation and agreement by governments, non-governmental organizations (NGOs) and the industry. The need for action to reduce noise emissions and exposure, and the ability to modernize the airline fleet varies across the world. Aviation demand is greatest in more developed regions such as Europe: those same areas where opposition to aircraft noise is highest and where the air transport industry is best able to undertake fleet modernization. In contrast, there are many hundreds of airports and, indeed, entire countries where there is currently no imperative to seek improvements in aircraft noise. However, even amongst developing nation airlines there is still a need for ongoing fleet replacement in the short term in order to gain access to developed nation airports, and in the long term to minimize the risk of community opposition at their own airports.

The challenge for ICAO in resolving the above tensions is obviously enormous. These tensions lead to significant delays in the time taken to agree and implement new certification standards and any phase-out requirements. Given the ongoing and strong growth of the industry and improvements in aircraft technology, such delays negate the value of the regulatory improvements. Furthermore, the need to develop regulation that meets such different national interests can lead to the adoption of the 'lowest common denominator'. Given the rapid growth of aviation, there is a need to develop this regulatory system so that it promotes continual improvement and the adoption of 'best practice', in keeping with the principles underlying sustainable development.

The response of the EU to the decisions made by the ICAO in September 2001 provides one illustration of how global regulation has been interpreted in a particularly affluent part of the world.

THE EUROPEAN SITUATION

Sensitivity to aircraft noise is particularly acute within Europe because of high population density, the size of the aviation industry and the fact that Europe comprises a comparatively affluent population in well-educated democracies with a high expectation of quality of life and a low tolerance of nuisance.

A draft report to the European Parliament in 2000 (European Parliament, 2000) stated that as many as one in three Europeans complain about noise from transport and industrial sources and that particular concern is related to noise at night. The report set out an EU noise policy that included a number of proposals of significance to the air transport industry including:

- the harmonization of methods of measuring noise exposure;
- the differentiation of 'night' and 'day' noise-exposure levels;
- the development of noise-exposure maps for the whole of the EU;
- the adoption of medium- and long-term goals for reducing the number of people affected by specific noise sources; and
- a specific directive dealing with noise from aircraft near airports, including requirements for noise action plans and targets to be achieved over 10 to 20 years.

Being a global regulatory body, it is perhaps unreasonable to expect that the ICAO could deliver new regulations that would meet the needs of residents living around Europe's airports who are amongst the most 'noise-sensitive' individuals in the world. It was not unexpected, therefore, that the 2001 ICAO Assembly failed to deliver the level of increased stringency for Chapter 4 aircraft and the phase-out programme for Chapter 3 aircraft that had been called for by the EU and, separately, by a number of European states. This result would make it more difficult for the EU to achieve some very significant noise policy objectives, and also for many of Europe's major airports to manage their noise impact while meeting air traffic demand.

The EU states have recognized the challenge that noise disturbance poses to the development of the European air transport system. They support the 'balanced approach' to noise control proposed by the 33rd ICAO Assembly, and are developing a draft directive (2002/30/EC) relating to land-use planning in member states. Furthermore, significant research and development (R&D) funding for improved airframe and engine technology has been set aside. The 'balanced approach' concept of aircraft noise management comprises four principal elements and requires stringent assessment of all options for noise mitigation, including reduction of airplane noise at source, land-use planning and management measures, noise-abatement operational procedures and operating restrictions (European Commission, 2002). While remaining committed to the role of ICAO in laying down global regulation, the EU does, however, acknowledge the need for a degree of regional and local flexibility to reflect particular conditions. While a significant number of airports suffer from noise-related capacity constraints, others, due to their particular geographical or social and economic situation, face little opposition and enjoy local community support for growth. The European Commission (EC) acknowledges, however, the need to avoid a 'free for all' emerging with the proliferation of local controls and restrictions across this region, and has proposed a common framework of rules and procedures to support airports in developing their noise action plans (Directive 2002/30/EC). Important amongst these are items designed to:

- enable noise-sensitive airports to apply to take action to exclude the noisiest Chapter 3 aircraft, since no phase-out is proposed by ICAO for Chapter 3 aircraft;
- establish a framework within which European airports would implement common noise-related charging regimes designed to encourage the use of quieter aircraft and discourage operations by noisier types;
- establish a European framework within which operational restrictions would be applied to different aircraft; and
- select appropriate mitigation measures available, with the goal of achieving the maximum environmental benefit most cost effectively.

The EU has, therefore, established a regional regulatory framework that is designed to facilitate aviation growth and acknowledge the needs of different parts of the EU and different airports and communities, while at the same time seeking to facilitate a longer-term objective of reducing the number of people exposed to noise. This EU regulatory framework is incorporated into national law and enforced by member states within the European Community.

Impact upon airport communities

While stringent measures to reduce and contain the negative effects of aircraft noise are being sought on a Europe-wide basis, wide disparities still exist within individual states' regulatory frameworks. These wide variations in regulating aircraft noise and vibration differentially affect the health and quality of life of people living in close proximity to airports (Koppert, 1993). Thus, the Europe-wide regulation of noise seems set to remain high on the agenda of policy-makers.

In all parts of the world, regulatory policy tends to target improvements in technology or to limit exposure to aircraft noise through land-use planning (Gillen, 2000). Positive examples of spatial planning and control of land use in the vicinity of airports can be seen – for example, at Paris Charles de Gaulle and at Amsterdam Schiphol airports. However, overall, policies have had a limited effect on reducing noise nuisance. Differing planning regulations in each country, together with nationally prescriptive procedures for managing land use, have made standardization of noise exposure controls extremely difficult in Europe. Moreover, each airport possesses its own specific social, economic and political context, as well as history and physical geography (Janic, 1999). These factors should not be overlooked. Indeed, it is these factors and the way in which airports take account of them that will determine levels of community opposition to noise.

The growth of the aviation sector in recent years has created something of a dilemma for airport managers. While, on the one hand, aviation brings economic benefits to regions and to some communities surrounding airports, on the other hand, the negative social and environmental impacts of airport expansion are borne exclusively by local communities and have led to increasing levels of opposition to airport expansion plans.

In the UK, for example, the lengthy London Heathrow Terminal 5 public inquiry highlighted growing public disquiet at the negative social and environmental externalities that have become a feature of life for communities residing close to major airports. While it is widely recognized that airports have made significant progress in addressing environmental issues, a number of emergent social issues might signifi-cantly delay or constrain airports' expansion plans if not managed effectively. In par-ticular, increasing levels of noise disturbance and increasing traffic congestion are seen as major potential constraints. Many airports have been forced to address these issues through active engagement with local communities in an attempt to maintain or enhance capacity, while at the same time satisfying government, local authorities and community stakeholders.

At the local level, achieving sustainability means balancing social, environmental and economic criteria in a framework that manages growth, while targeting benefits to the most adversely affected communities, or those greatest in need (Manchester Airport, 2000). Sustainability issues will continue to dominate airport operations in a future where growth can only occur in a balanced and inclusive environment. Accountability is another facet of a modern democracy and it is likely, therefore, that governments will require that community stakeholders participate in decision-making processes if airports are to achieve balanced growth that offsets social and environmental externalities (DETR, 2000).

Aviation actors will argue that it is airports that should take the lead role in pro-moting these issues and be given the necessary powers and support to drive forward programmes of environmental management and community affairs, while involving a range of partners. On the other side of the same coin, community groups will insist on checks and balances to constrain exponential growth. With government, they will look for open, accountable business practices that balance the needs of all stake-holders. Sustainability, then, will depend upon the ability of airports to provide and manage long-term development strategies that enjoy the active support of key stake-holders. Such is the impact of major airports upon their local communities that many have highly developed public consultation systems. These are used to assist the development of existing facilities and operations and also the design of new infrastructure.

Engaging airport stakeholders

Social inclusion is a fundamental component of a sustainable society, allowing every-one to share the benefits of increased prosperity. Airports can be drivers in this pro-cess by providing, for example, equality in employment and through sponsorship of education programmes that increase the employment prospects of low- to middle-income social groups.

The purpose of airport development is to facilitate airport growth and enhance the economic and social well-being of the local and national community. This means fully taking into account the views of the local community on airport development plans and how they are to be achieved. Participation is a question of both principle and practice. In terms of principle, people should be involved in determining the outcomes of issues that concern themselves and the society in which they live. In terms of practice, the effectiveness and sustainability of airport development depends, in part, upon the commitment of interested stakeholders. Thus, participation is a cen-tral element in achieving airport development objectives.

Participation contributes to the chances of airport development being sustain-able because:

- in drawing upon a wide range of interested parties, prospects for appropriate development and a mutually beneficial commitment to achieving objectives is likely to be maximized;
- it is more sustainable: people brought into the process feel part of the development, thus gaining their consensus for future development;
- development is seen as more transparent, responsive and accountable by local communities.

There is no all-encompassing model or tool kit for effective stakeholder participation. Effective stakeholder participation depends upon a variety of place-specific social, economic and environmental criteria. Nevertheless, stakeholder analysis is a tool that may help an airport discover its key stakeholders. It is the first step in helping to decide who should be encouraged and assisted in participating. Stakeholder analysis aims to:

- identify and define the characteristics of key stakeholders;
- assess the manner in which they might affect or be affected by development/ expansion;
- understand the relations between stakeholders, including an assessment of the real and potential conflicts of interest and expectation between stakeholders; and
- assess the different capacity of stakeholders to participate.

Key airport stakeholders

The main stakeholder groups with an interest in airports are as follows:

- government;
- airport company;
- employees;
- airport service partners (especially airlines);
- local authorities;
- the travelling public;
- communities affected by airport operations;
- NGOs, such as environmental bodies;
- business, commerce, tourism, arts, sports and education organizations;
- providers of other transport services in the area; and
- airport suppliers.

The main interests of airport stakeholders?

The multiplicity of interests that exist within airport stakeholder environments suggests that a number of divergent agendas need to be satisfied. The following list of questions may help to inform future stakeholder analyses, with the objective of enhancing airport community relations:

- What social and economic benefits of the airport accrue to each stakeholder group?
- Are they being optimized/maximized?
- What are the costs of the airport's operation and development to each?

- Are they being kept to a sustainable minimum?
- What are the interdependencies between groups?
- Is there any link between costs and benefits within groups?
- Can such links be established?
- What are attitudes of primary and secondary stakeholders to the airport?
- What are attitudes of the airport to primary and secondary stakeholders?
- Are all stakeholders brought together in any forum?
- How is the above affected by geographic proximity to the airport?
- Where there is conflict between stakeholder needs, how is this resolved?

Stakeholder representation

Balancing the needs of different groups of stakeholders is difficult, and different stakeholders have differing concerns and interests. Goyder (1998) declares that by engaging with stakeholder groups, organizational benefits can be derived. Airport managers are increasingly interested in identifying methods, institutional arrangements and policy environments that promote negotiations among stakeholders, leading to partnerships and, it is hoped, to sustainable management (Edmunds and Wollenberg, 2001). Three related issues are also of concern in the ongoing social responsibility debate. The first is whether airports pursue stakeholder interests for economic reasons or because doing so has intrinsic merit. Second, can airport managers successfully balance the needs of a variety of stakeholders; and, third, is a forum other than that organized by the airport necessary? Resolving the tensions that exist between different stakeholders is a challenging and complex task. As Harrison and Freeman (1999) argue, the issue is that economic effects are also social, and social effects are also economic. To balance the needs of different interests, airports should consider the multiple interactions that exist in stakeholder environments (Rowley, 1997).

The way in which different stakeholders are engaged will vary and, in some cases, will be far less formal than for others. In the absence of formal systems, increasing numbers of members of the public will attempt to deal directly with the airport company to put forward their own concerns. This is often the case where pressure groups and other interest groups are concerned. It has been noted in recent years, for example, that anti-airport-development pressure groups have become more organized, dealing not only with airport managers, but presenting their case via media contacts and worldwide campaigning networks. This raises questions about the validity of the current stakeholder framework in many countries, in that it bypasses a number of important stakeholder groups. The challenge is to bring these groups into the development process by understanding and responding to their concerns through providing a platform in which airport development would be viewed by government and community groups as more participatory and inclusive.

CONCLUSION

The disturbance caused by aircraft noise is, and will remain, the single most significant local environmental impact resulting from the operation of airports. Aircraft noise affects the daily lives of many millions of people throughout the world with the result that noise impacts are already the major environmental constraint upon the potential for growth at many larger airports in all regions.

The level of annoyance or opposition caused within neighbouring communities and its potential to act as a constraint upon airport growth will, however, vary significantly with the social and economic needs of those communities. Critically, the residents of communities surrounding airports who serve less affluent populations are likely to be more tolerant of aircraft noise or feel unable to express opposition. Opposition would be further reduced or tolerance increased if local residents benefited (eg by employment) from the continued growth of those airports.

The experience of the states within the European Union provides an example of how future noise policy could emerge in other parts of the world. Europeans are relatively noise sensitive and the issue of aircraft noise is high on the political agenda of every nation state within the EU. The EC has responded to this through adopting a policy objective that seeks, in the medium to longer term, to reduce the number of people exposed to noise. Growth in air traffic is strong, while many European airports are already noise constrained. Others, however, face little or no community opposition. This provides the background against which Europe has to address the issue of aircraft noise, particularly in response to the regulatory framework established by ICAO in 2001, a framework considered inadequate by many in Europe.

The longer-term growth of the air transport industry will depend, to a very significant degree, upon a continuing and credible reduction in aircraft noise at source through improved airframe and engine technology. The ability of airports to meet future growth in passenger and cargo demand will be constrained if growth continues to outstrip technological and operational improvements, with a consequential increase in noise levels around airports. Growing affluence and democracy will further drive an increase in the level of nuisance and opposition within local communities. This will affect all airports, even those without local noise problems, if they are unable to maintain or expand air services to noise-sensitive airports due to these constraints. Such constraints could have significant implications in terms of development if, for example, the air route network serving a particular airport cannot be extended to bring in new services to economically important destinations.

Clearly, reducing noise exposure can only be part of the solution to reducing opposition to airport growth. In the future, it is likely that shared liability for damage caused by aircraft noise, reviewing the methodologies for determining levels of compensation, and more funding for noise mitigation projects need to be addressed if the growing airport noise-pollution problem is to be satisfactorily mediated. Furthermore, the dialogue established between airports and their surrounding communities will be critical in determining the way in which airports identify and address issues of local concern. This, in turn, will affect the ability of airports to grow and meet air traffic demand where and when it arises.

REFERENCES

Berglund, B and Lindvall, T (eds) (1995) 'Community Noise', *Archive of the Centre for Sensory Research – Stockholm*, vol 2(1), pp86–104

DETR (2000) *The Future of Aviation: The Government's Consultation Document on Air Transport Policy*, Department of the Environment, Transport and the Regions, www.aviation. detr.gov.uk/consult/future/12.htm

Edmunds, D and Wollenberg, E (2001) 'A Strategic Approach to Multistakeholder Negotiations', *Development and Change*, vol 32, pp231–253

European Commission (2002) Directive 2002/49/EC of the European Parliament and of the Council of 25 June 2002 relating to the assessment and management of environmental noise, *Official Journal of the European Communities*, L189/12

European Parliament (2000) *Draft Report on the Proposal for a European Parliament and Council Directive on the Assessment and Management of Environmental Noise*, Provisional 2000/ 0194(COD), Committee on the Environment, Public Health and Consumer Policy

Falzone, K L (1999) 'Airport Noise Pollution: Is there a Solution in Sight?', *Environmental Affairs*, vol 26, pp769–807

Feitelson, E I, Hurd, R E and Mudge, R R (1996) 'The Impact of Noise on Willingness to Pay for Residences', *Transportation Research D*, vol 1(1), pp1–14

Gillen, D (2000) 'Measuring the Benefits and Costs of Alternative Noise Mitigation Strategies' in Immelmann, T, Mayer, O G, Niemer, H M and Pfähler, W (eds) *Aviation v Environment*, Proceedings of the 2nd Hamburg Aviation Conference, Hamburg

Goyder, M (1998) *Living Tomorrow's Company*, Gower, Hampshire

Harrison, J S and Freeman, R E (1999) 'Stakeholders, Social Responsibility, and Performance: Empirical Evidence and Theoretical Perspectives', *Academy of Management Journal*, vol 42(5), pp479–485

ICAO (1993) *International Standards and Recommended Practices, Environmental Protection: Annex 16 to the Convention on International Civil Aviation*, International Civil Aviation Organization, Montreal

Janic, M (1999) 'Aviation and Externalities: The Accomplishments and Problems', *Transportation Research D*, vol 4(3), pp159–180

Job, R F S (1996) 'The Influence of Subjective Reactions to Noise on Health Effects of Noise', *Environmental International*, vol 22, pp105–116

Koppert, A J (1993) *A Study on Measures to Protect the Environment in and around Airports against Aircraft Noise*, Ministerie van Verkeer en Waterstaat (Directoraat-Generaal Rijksluchtvaartdienst), the Netherlands

Manchester Airport (2000) *Sustainability Report 1999–2000*, Manchester Airport plc, Manchester

Moss, D, Warnaby, G, Sykes, S and Thomas, C S (1997) 'Manchester Airport's Second Runway Campaign: The Boundary Spanning Role of Public Relations in Managing Environmental Organisational Interaction', *Journal of Communication Management*, vol 2(4), pp320–334

Ollerhead, J B, Jones, C J, Cadoux, R E, Woodley, A, Atkinson, B J, Horne, J A, Pankhurst, F, Reyner, L, Hume, K I, Van, F, Watson, A, Diamond, I D, Egger, P, Homes, D and McKean, J (1992) *A Field Study of Aircraft Noise and Sleep Disturbance*, Department of Transport, London

Rowley, T J (1997) 'Moving Beyond Dyadic Ties: A Network Theory of Stakeholder Influences', *Academy of Management Review*, vol 22(4), pp887–910

Schultz, T J (1978) 'Synthesis of Social Surveys on Noise Annoyance', *Journal of the Acoustical Society of America*, vol 64, pp377–405

Sekuler, R and Blake, R (1994) *Perception*, McGraw-Hill, New York

Tomkins J, Topham N, Twomey, J and Ward, R (1998) 'Noise versus Access: The Impact of an Airport in an Urban Property Market', *Urban Studies*, vol 35(2), pp243–258

Veitch, R and Arkkelin, D (1995) *Environmental Psychology: An Interdisciplinary Approach*, Prentice Hall, Englewood Cliffs, New Jersey

World Health Organization (WHO) (1999) *Guidelines for Community Noise*, WTO, Geneva

Part 2

Mitigations and Potential Solutions

Chapter 7

Environmental management and the aviation industry

Paul Hooper, Bridget Heath and Janet Maughan

AVIATION AND THE ENVIRONMENT

Aviation is one of the world's fastest growing industries with demand doubling in size over the last seven to eight years and predicted to double again during the next 10 to 12 years (IATA, 2000). This increase is principally due to the development of the global economy and increased affluence. The benefits of being linked to the rest of the world by a network of air routes are significant as aviation promotes trade, inward investment, travel for leisure and education and tourism. Unfortunately, this growth has resulted in significant environmental impacts given the infrastructure requirements of air transport and the fundamental dependence upon fossil fuel.

The primary environmental impacts generated by the aviation industry that give increasing cause for concern are:

- Noise: disturbance by aircraft noise is the single most important environmental issue acting at a local level that has the potential to constrain the growth of airports and thus the wider aviation industry.
- Emissions: air pollution arising from airline and airport operations has a variety of sources, including aircraft engines, apron vehicles, ground transportation, re-fuelling and power generation equipment. These can pose a problem at a local scale, where increasingly stringent environmental quality standards are being imposed, and at a global level, where increasing concern is being expressed about the significance of the contribution of aircraft engine emissions to the problem of global warming (see, for example, IPCC, 1999).
- Water quality: a range of aviation industry activities – including terminal services, aircraft de-icing, engineering, maintenance and refuelling – has the potential to

cause considerable ground contamination and thus poses a threat to surface and groundwater. If not dealt with properly, this pollution can, ultimately, affect drinking water supplies and agricultural land, which has clear implications for human health. Consequently, if not addressed effectively, the legacy of groundwater pollution can cost millions of dollars to clean up.

- Waste: airports and airlines generate significant amounts of solid waste from in-flight catering and cabin services, along with engineering, maintenance, office-based activities and terminal facilities. Some of this waste is of a hazardous nature, posing a threat to human health and the environment if not handled in specific ways. Even the relatively benign solid waste stream (for example, packaging, paper and food waste) has important environmental implications arising from the need to utilize disposal routes, such as landfill and incineration.

Given the breadth of these environmental impacts, it is hardly surprising that the growth of the aviation sector is often seen to be at odds with the goal of sustainable development. On the other hand, as an important source of economic growth, aviation has a key role to play in illustrating how sustainability can be addressed in practice. As a contribution to understanding how – and to what extent – environment and economy might be reconciled, this chapter reviews the sustainable development debate and the nature of environmental management systems (EMS) and their potential within the aviation industry. The chapter presents the results of an international survey of airline environmental management and EMS usage.

SUSTAINABLE DEVELOPMENT: COMPENSATING FOR GROWTH

The term 'sustainable development' came to prominence following the publication of *Our Common Future*, a report into the key development issues facing the planet and commissioned by the United Nations (UN) in 1984 (WCED, 1987). Popularly known as the Brundtland Report, after the chair of the commission, the publication coined the most widely accepted definition of sustainable development: 'Sustainable development meets the needs of the present without compromising the ability of future generations to meet their own needs' (WCED, 1987, p43).

While this definition has been criticized for being open to a wide array of interpretations, this very quality has also been welcomed as it allows scope for forging a consensus to promote sustainable development (Cairncross, 1991). The first major attempt to arrive at such a political consensus on mechanisms by which to achieve more sustainable forms of development occurred at the 1992 United Nations Conference on Environment and Development (UNEP) in Rio, otherwise known as the Earth Summit. At this conference, many of the key findings of the Brundtland Report were endorsed; in particular, it was acknowledged that:

- Poverty is a major cause of environmental degradation, and thus any sustainable future would need to address the social and economic factors underpinning world poverty.

- Past economic growth was responsible for substantial improvements in the quality of life for many of the world's citizens; however, this has been achieved at a considerable cost to the natural environment.
- Solutions to the development problems identified would require action by all of the peoples of the planet at every organizational and regional level, given the interrelated and interdependent nature of many of the environmental, economic, social and political challenges presented.

Without going into any great depth, what emerged from the conference, in the form of a Declaration on Environment and Development and an Agenda for the 21st century (popularly known as Agenda 21), was a commitment to continued economic growth – to combat poverty and facilitate further increases in the quality of life – and a recognition of the need to ameliorate any adverse consequences associated with this growth. This *Green growth* strategy, therefore, calls for the decoupling of economic growth from environmental resource utilization and degradation in order to maintain the capacity for future development.

As key drivers behind this economic growth, the business community clearly has a fundamental role to play in achieving a more sustainable pattern of development. Some idea of the scale of the challenge facing the sector can be gained from a brief examination of the key factors influencing environmental degradation. A simple formula often used by researchers to describe the drivers behind environmental degradation is that presented in Figure 7.1 (Heaton et al, 1991; Hooper and Gibbs, 1995).

$$\text{Population} \times \frac{\text{GNP per capita}}{} \times \frac{\text{Environmental degradation per unit GNP}}{} = \frac{\text{Total environmental degradation}}{}$$

Figure 7.1 *The main drivers of environmental degradation*

Assuming that the world's population will at least double in size between 1980 and 2030–2040 (Meadows et al, 1992), in order to maintain environmental degradation at its present unsustainable levels, while preserving per capita income levels, a twofold reduction in environmental damage per unit output will be required. Superimposing aspirations of 2.5–5 fold increases in world average per capita income, as advocated in the Brundtland Report, generates a requirement for a 5–10 fold reduction in environmental damage per unit output over the next 50 to 60 years.

The feasibility of this challenge has been examined in more recent years in a number of landmark texts. For example, Factor Four presents a series of case studies, which demonstrate that at least fourfold increases in resource productivity can be achieved, indicating that people could live twice as well, using half as much material and energy (Von Weizsäcker et al, 1997). In *Natural Capitalism*, Hawken et al (1999) address a wider agenda, but nevertheless regard 'radically increased resource productivity' as the 'cornerstone' of attempts to move towards a more sustainable future (Hawken et al, 1999, p10). Since the vast majority of the activity determining resource productivity is undertaken by business, it is hardly surprising that these and other texts urge the private sector to move to the vanguard of environmental solutions. The commercial benefits of environmental management are considered in the following section.

Commercial benefits of environmental management

In order to encourage businesses to rise to the challenge of compensating for growth, many commentators point to the range of commercial benefits that can accrue from the preventative approaches to environmental protection that underpin productivity gains. In particular, researchers have highlighted the following direct commercial benefits:

• reduced costs of raw materials and energy;
• potential to exploit new market possibilities (due to new or improved products);
• reduced costs of pollution abatement and waste disposal.

Indirect commercial benefits include:

• improved relationship with regulators, given regulatory compliance;
• public relations benefits associated with improved corporate citizenship;
• maximized capacity for growth by reducing environmental constraints.

These commercial advantages and environmental benefits arising from increased resource productivity – namely, reduced rates of resource depletion and levels of pollution – have prompted researchers to emphasize the environment–business 'win–win' potential of preventative approaches to environmental protection. This, in turn, has encouraged government officials, planners, academics and business people across the world to take up the challenge of Factor Four and even Factor Ten levels of environmental improvement.[1]

ENVIRONMENTAL MANAGEMENT: A ROLE IN COMPENSATING FOR GROWTH

The increasing impetus behind the compensation for growth arguments is reflected in the changing business agendas in boardrooms around the world. The aviation industry is no exception. In a recent survey of the airline sector commissioned by the International Air Transport Association (IATA) and undertaken by researchers in ARIC at Manchester Metropolitan University (Dobbie and Hooper, 2001), company representatives were found to rate the importance of a range of social and environmental issues on a par with commercial issues (such as improving airline ticket-sales distribution networks, building new alliances and increasing the number of links from the home airport). Significantly, average importance ratings were highest for those environmental issues associated with direct impacts (eg noise, water pollution and emissions from aircraft) or the most obvious commercial and environmental 'win–win' situations (eg fuel and energy efficiency) (for more detail, see Dobbie and Hooper, 2001). That said, it is one thing to acknowledge the importance of improving eco-efficiencies and quite another to achieve that goal.

Reduction in environmental damage per unit of business output requires business organizations to move beyond the regulatory compliance strategies that have traditionally dominated corporate responses to the environment. In essence, there is a need to devise commercially efficient and environmentally effective solutions to the particular environmental challenges faced by each organization. This, in turn, requires a systematic approach to environmental issues, which allows for the:

- identification and prioritization of environmental liabilities;
- derivation of environmental policy objectives and more specific targets in the light of the strengths and weakness identified above;
- allocation of appropriate levels of human, financial and technical resources to achieve policy targets;
- development of accountable management structures to ensure the most effective use of allocated resources;
- review of performance and appropriate modification to the policy and processes outlined above.

These priorities, which form the basis of an embryonic environmental management system, have been adopted by a number of airports and airlines wishing to limit environmental liabilities and exploit the commercial advantages to be derived from a proactive environmental stance. Exactly how environmental management systems help build this capacity for environmental improvement is reviewed in the following section.

ENVIRONMENTAL MANAGEMENT SYSTEMS

An environmental management system (EMS) is a tool that potentially enables an organization to effectively control the impact of its operations upon the environment in an efficient and cost-effective manner. EMS is a structured approach to improving environmental performance, where the rate of progression and extent of improvement are determined by the individual company (CTC, 2000). A major benefit of EMS is the contribution it can make in ensuring that a company complies with environmental legislation, thereby avoiding any associated fines, prosecution or bad publicity. An effective system allows a company to prioritize its responses to such legislation and assess its means of achieving further environmental improvements. Associated with this is a multitude of other benefits, including scope for reducing costs; increased efficiency and profitability; enhanced public image; and greater competitive advantage. Furthermore, since companies are increasingly subjected to stakeholder pressure in order to operate in an environmentally and socially responsible manner, the implementation of an EMS is an ideal way of demonstrating such a commitment. It should be noted, however, that while EMS essentially creates the potential for environmental improvement, it does not guarantee that environmental improvements will take place. It is recognized that there is a danger that organizations may use certification as a display of their commitment to environmental protection without actually requiring any major improvements to take place (Pringle et al, 1998). In other words, the user determines the effectiveness of EMS as a tool for controlling environmental impacts.

During the past 30 years, there has been considerable growth in awareness and understanding of the environmental interactions with, and effects of, business operations at all levels. This growth in awareness has been accompanied by an increase in concern over the adverse effects of business upon the environment; as a consequence of this, a rapid expansion of legislation aimed at protecting the environment has occurred in most industrialized countries. In addition, the environmental issues themselves have become more complex and greater in scale. For example, concerns over localized urban smoke emissions have largely been replaced by international issues, such as global climate change and stratospheric ozone depletion (Howes et al, 1997).

The result of this has been that many businesses are facing increasing pressure to reduce the impacts resulting from their operations. The activities of greatest concern are generally those related to waste disposal, effluent discharge and energy use. In the UK, failure to address these issues and comply with the ever-tightening legislation places businesses at risk from financial penalties. Under the European regulatory regime of integrated pollution prevention and control (EC, 1996), penalties to UK companies may include revocation of operating licences and imprisonment of managers. This can result in unequivocal damage to corporate image and a decline in productivity such that, in extreme cases, companies may go out of business. In order to avoid such consequences, company managers and directors are increasingly turning towards EMS to help them improve their environmental performance and operate in accordance with environmental legislation.

The key elements of an EMS are summarized below:

- Management commitment: the first step towards implementing a successful EMS involves obtaining the support and commitment from senior management in order to ensure that appropriate time and resources will be made available.
- Environmental review: this involves a systematic and comprehensive identification and assessment of the environmental impacts resulting from all company activities, past, present and predicted. This 'stocktake' should be quantitative, as far as possible, and forms the baseline against which future progress is measured.
- Environmental policy: this is a short written statement of intent that indicates a commitment to continuous improvement in environmental performance and compliance with all relevant environmental legislation and regulations. It sets out the company's intentions regarding environmentally related aspects of the business. For maximum effectiveness, it should be publicly available and regularly reviewed.
- Legal and regulatory requirements: a register detailing all relevant environmental legislation and regulations should be produced and regularly updated. Knowing what the legal requirements are is the first step towards compliance. Such a register is likely to be compiled as part of the environmental review process.
- Environmental objectives and targets: the significance of each of the environmental impacts identified by the environmental review needs to be assessed. Typically, this is achieved by applying a ranking system to prioritize them. Environmental objectives are then established for reducing the most significant effects, together with quantitative targets and schedules for their achievement. Ideally, targets should be specific, measurable, achievable, realistic and time bound (ie SMART) (Sheldon and Yoxon, 1999).

- Environmental programme: the environmental programme sets out the means by which the environmental policy is to be implemented and the environmental objectives and targets achieved. It indicates who is responsible for what and includes strategies for measuring and improving environmental performance.
- Environmental management system: this is the implementation stage. Responsibility for this stage may be that of a dedicated environmental manager, most likely supported by a team of 'environmental champions', depending upon company size. Appropriate staff training and effective communication are central to the successful implementation of an EMS (IWM, 1998).
- Environmental management system audit: an EMS audit provides an ongoing check of environmental performance. It determines whether or not the environmental policy is being adhered to and the extent to which the objectives and targets have been met. It also verifies compliance with relevant legislation. Furthermore, it includes advisory information for the company indicating how further improvements in environmental performance can be made. EMS audits must be repeated periodically, typically every one to three years.
- Environmental reporting: the findings of an EMS audit should be documented and made available to staff so that the recommendations and advice can be implemented. In some cases, companies publish a separate environmental statement detailing their environmental policy, objectives, targets and performance (see following section on 'Formalized standards for environmental management'). Certainly, in the UK there is growing pressure, from the government, the European Commission (EC) and other sources, for businesses to publish reports of their environmental performance to enable stakeholders to assess the level of environmental responsibility, and so that companies can give an indication of their environmental liabilities (DETR, 2000; ENDS, 2001a).[2]
- Management review: as for any management system, the effectiveness of the EMS should be subject to a management review in order to assess whether the system and procedures in place are appropriate and sufficient. A management review gives the opportunity for any weaknesses detected by the audit to be addressed and any necessary improvements to be made on a regular basis. It also ensures that the commitment to continual improvement is being upheld.

Formalized standards for environmental management

There are currently two formally recognized standards for EMS: the European EMAS regulation and the internationally recognized ISO 14001.

EMAS

The EC Eco-management and Audit Scheme (EMAS) was introduced in April 1995. The scheme was established to improve the quality of environmental management within European businesses and, in so doing, to help them to gain a competitive advantage. A voluntary scheme, EMAS is aimed at industrial sites in the EU, although in the UK, local authority sites can also obtain the standard. It is quite prescriptive regarding issues to be covered by the initial environmental review and the audit, and requires companies to publish regular performance reports which, it is argued, pushes organizations to meet their targets (ENDS, 2000).

ISO 14001

In September 1996 the International Standards Organization (ISO) published *ISO 14001: 1996, Environmental Management Systems – Specification with Guidance for Use*. This standard offers the advantage of being applicable to any business sector or activity and is recognized across the world. ISO 14001 registration can also apply to a whole organization or an individual site, so it has greater flexibility than EMAS in this respect. These and the other notable differences between EMAS and ISO 14001 are summarized in Table 7.1. Key criticisms of ISO 14001 are the lax requirements for external reporting, compliance with regulations and demonstrations of continuous environmental improvement (ENDS, 2000).

Table 7.1 *Main differences between EMAS and ISO 14001*

Elements where differences occur	EMAS	ISO 14001
Geographical area of recognition	EU	Worldwide
Applicable sectors	Industrial Local authorities (UK only)	All
Organization level to which registration applies	Site basis	Whole organization or site
Initial environmental review	An explicit requirement	An 'initial' review is not specified but is likely to be done as information required for the environmental policy
Frequency of EMS audit	Three years maximum	Not specified
Environmental statement	An externally verified environmental statement is required detailing environmental effects identified by the review, environmental policy and programme	Environmental statement not a requirement, though environmental policy should be publicly available

Table 7.1 implies that ISO 14001 offers more flexibility than EMAS on a number of issues. By May 2001, the number of companies registered under EMAS was 77 in the UK and 3120 within Europe. By comparison, the number of companies accredited to ISO 14001 was around 2000 in the UK and over 10,000 in Europe (ENDS, 2001b). Table 7.2 shows that the airport sector demonstrates a similar propensity for ISO 14001, with 32 of the 38 airports either certified to, or progressing towards, the international standard.

EMAS-2

In order to encourage more companies to opt for EMAS, the scheme has recently been relaunched. EMAS Regulation 761/2001 came into force on 27 April 2001, and with it came the opening up of the standard to all types of organization and the lifting of the restriction to site-based registrations. Annual validation of environmental

Table 7.2 *List of environmentally certified European airports*
as of 19 November 2001

Airport	Certification	Status
Amsterdam	EMAS ISO 14001	Certified
Athens	ISO 14001	Certified
BAA airports (Gatwick, Heathrow, Stansted, Aberdeen, Edinburgh, Glasgow, Southampton)	EMS developed in accordance with ISO/EMAS	Performance against EMS targets is externally verified
Barcelona	ISO 14001	Certified
Bologna	ISO 14001 EMAS BS 8800	In progress In progress In progress
Brussels	ISO 14001 (EMAS)	Certified
Dublin	ISO 14001	Certified
Frankfurt	EMAS	Certified
Fuerteventura	ISO 14001	In progress
Geneva	ISO 9000	In progress
Göteborg Landvetter	ISO 14001	Certified
Granada	ISO 14001	In progress
Helsinki	Some certification	In progress
Ibiza	ISO 14001	Certified
Karlstad	ISO 14001	Certified
Lanzarote	ISO 14001	In progress
La Coruna	ISO 14001	Certified
La Palma	ISO 14001	In progress
London Luton	ISO 14001	In progress
Lyon	ISO 14001	In progress
Madrid	ISO 14001	Certified
Manchester	ISO 14001	In progress
Menorca	ISO 14001	Certified
Milan Malpensa	ISO 14001	In progress
Munich	EMAS	In progress
Oslo	EMAS	In progress
Palma de Mallorca	ISO 14001	In progress

Table 7.2 *List of environmentally certified European airports
as of 19 November 2001 (Continued)*

Airport	Certification	Status
Prague	ISO 14001	In progress
Roma Ciampino	ISO 14001	In progress
Roma Fiumicino	ISO 14001	Certified
Salzburg	EMAS	Certified
	ISO 14001	Certified
Sevilla	ISO 14001	In progress
Stockholm Arlanda	ISO 14001	In progress
Stockholm Bromma	ISO 14001	No information
Tenerife Sur	ISO 14001	Certified
Umea	ISO 14001	Certified
Valencia	ISO 14001	In progress
Zurich	ISO 14001	In progress

Source: ACI Europe, 2001

statements remains, but there is greater flexibility now regarding the information that can be included in the statements. The requirements for the scope of the initial environmental review and the auditing procedure have also been made less prescriptive.

The main advantage offered by these formalized EMS standards is that a company can follow a customized set of procedures to set up their EMS and, if successful, gain accreditation, which can then be used to enhance public image, impress stakeholders and increase competitiveness (CTC, 2000). It has been suggested that achieving registered status in this manner may also improve a company's standing with environmental regulators and could pave the way for a certain amount of deregulation, although such developments are still at the exploratory stage (ENDS, 2001a). Used as evidence that a company is serious about environmental management and reducing its environmental liabilities, a certified EMS can result in more favourable consideration for loans and insurance (Howes et al, 1997; Sheldon and Yoxon, 1999). Certainly, there is evidence that some lending institutions are increasingly influenced by the environmental, social and ethical policies of companies when determining loan suitability, the Cooperative Bank being most notable in the UK (Smith, 2000).

Informal systems

Companies interested in establishing an EMS do not have to go down the route of applying for EMAS or ISO 14001, since they are both voluntary schemes. They may find it simpler and just as valuable to set up an EMS without any formal accreditation. A company wishing to do this may refer to the wide array of published literature on 'how to set up an EMS', probably even following the framework of the formalized approaches. They would be advised to involve external auditors to verify their systems and performance and to publish regular environmental reports to demonstrate their commitment (Zackrisson, 2000). An informal EMS may be most appealing to smaller companies; certainly, it avoids the costs of registration and reduces the pressure where staffing and monetary resources may already be overstretched.

The fact that a company does not have an accreditation certificate does not necessarily make their EMS any less valuable. In fact, some companies have deliberately opted to go it alone, concerned that the formalized approach is open to abuse. For example, because EMS is focused upon continual improvement, a business with a poor, albeit improving, environmental performance can gain accreditation and use this as a marketing tool even when its competitors may have a much better environmental record but are not accredited. B&Q, the UK's largest do-it-yourself (DIY) retailer, is one of the more notable companies with its own informal EMS. It published its first environmental policy in 1990 and since then has made significant improvements in its own environmental performance and that of many of its suppliers. In April 2001, it was awarded a Queen's Award for Enterprise in the sustainable development category (B&Q, 2001) – evidence enough that an EMS does not have to be formally accredited to be successful.

Within the aviation industry, BAA is an example of a company that has opted for an informal EMS. The company has an integrated environmental, health and safety management system covering all of its businesses. BAA publicly supports the concept of sustainable development and, in promoting this, it publishes annual reports, sets environmental objectives and targets, and has its environmental audits and reports independently verified (BAA, 2001). This approach is consistent with ISO 14001 guidelines; and yet the EMS is not formally registered. Furthermore, the EMS underpins the achievement, monitoring and recording of the environmental improvements that are highlighted in the company's annual corporate environmental report. Significantly, the most recent version of this report was identified in a UNEP/Sustainability Ltd survey (2000) as the best in the world. This success demonstrates an important link between EMS and corporate environmental reporting, with the former providing a means of systematically addressing environmental threats and opportunities, and thus the framework for the comprehensive and increasingly quantitative reports that have emerged during recent years, at least among the leading reporters.

Corporate environmental reporting

Reasons for environmental reporting are rarely explicitly explained in environmental reports themselves. However, key justifications for the investment of time and resources in this process include the following (Naimon, 1993):

- reassuring neighbouring communities that the operations and activities carried out by the business pose no threat to them, and/or that any current impact is in the process of being alleviated;
- the desire to disseminate environmental intentions to staff and management;

- the need to make a clear statement to investors that environmental factors are seen as a business opportunity rather than a potential liability that could constrain future investment and growth;
- displaying environmental progress to environmentalists, non-governmental organizations (NGOs), policy-makers and regulators.

Given these incentives, corporate environmental reporting has become increasingly prevalent in the business world, with the last ten years witnessing a dramatic improvement in both the quality and quantity of the reports produced. *The Global Reporters* survey (UNEP/Sustainability Ltd, 2000) highlighted the following trends in the evolution of reporting best practice:

- clear evidence of top management support for environmental improvement and, more specifically, the 'triple bottom-line' agenda;
- an emphasis on the business case for sustainable development, in which the scale of investment in environmental reporting is recognized and justified, along with the potential commercial returns from environmental improvement;
- increasing standardization of reporting practice as reporting standards and guidelines are more widely adopted (see Table 7.3);
- the dominance of companies from Organization for Economic Cooperation and Development (OECD) countries among the lead reporters, resulting in only rare references to the developing world sustainability agenda;
- increasing use of key performance indicators that provide the qualitative support for continuous improvement efforts, the development of broader policy commitments, and attempts to strengthen public accountability;
- a recognition of the importance of validation to the reporting process; external verification, wider evidence of quality assurance (eg accreditation to ISO 14001) and 'perspective' from leaders in the sustainability field have all been used;
- a willingness to be more open and accountable in engaging in the public policy debate surrounding the delivery of sustainable development;
- an increasing role for electronic communications (eg the Internet, intra-nets and extra-nets) in providing information tailored to the needs of specific stakeholder groups.

Table 7.3 *Corporate reporting and measurement guidelines and standards*

Year	Programme	Governing body	Website
2000	Global Reporting Initiative (GRI)	Global Reporting Initiative	www.globalreporting.org
2000	Measuring Eco-efficiency: A Guide for Companies to Report Performance	World Business Council for Sustainable Development (WBCSD)	www.wbesd.org
1999	AccountAbility 1000 (AA 1000)	Institute of Social and Ethical Accountability (ISEA)	www.accountability.org.uk
1999	ISO 14031	International Standards Organization (ISO)	www.iso.ch

Table 7.3 *Corporate reporting and measurement guidelines and standards (Continued)*

Year	Programme	Governing body	Website
1998	CEFIC Responsible Care HSE Reporting Guidelines	European Chemical Industry Council (CEFIC)	www.cefic.org
1997	Social Accountability 8000 Standard (SA 8000)	Council on Economic Priorities Accreditation Agency (CEPAA)	www.cepaa.org
1996	Ballagio Principles	International Institute for Sustainable Development (IISD)	www.iisd1.iisd.ca
+	International Accounting Standards (IAS)	International Accounting Standards Committee (IASC)	www.iasc.org.uk
++	Greenhouse Gas Protocol Initiative	Multistakeholder, convened by World Resources Institute (WRI) and WBCSD	www.ghgprotocol.org

Source: UNEP/Sustainability Ltd, 2000
+ various years of publication
++ ongoing publication

Overall, the picture that emerges is one of a more comprehensive commitment to improvements in environmental and social performance. This trend is also reflected in the evolution of reporting activity within the aviation industry. If the airline sector is considered, for example, by 1990 only two major airlines had produced corporate environmental reports (CERs). By the mid 1990s, seven airlines had produced environmental reports of some description and by 2001 this had risen to 17, of which at least ten companies have embarked upon a continuous programme of regular (if not annual) reporting (Dobbie and Hooper, 2001). Along with this growth in the numbers of reporters, quality has also been seen to improve with:

- an increasing range of issues covered in the reports;
- more widespread use of quantitative indicators and the development of accountancy principles;
- the inclusion of verification/assurance statements in some reports; and
- the use of the Internet to supplement the information provided in the stand-alone corporate environmental reports.

AVIATION – HARNESSING THE POTENTIAL OF EMS?

Previous sections have demonstrated the growing influence of the environment on corporate agendas, including those of leading airlines and airports. In order to assess the impact on a wider sample of airlines, IATA commissioned an environmental activities survey of all of its 272 members in 2000 (Dobbie and Hooper, 2001, and IATA, 2001, largely incorporate the survey findings originally presented in Hooper, Maughan and Thomas, 2000). The responses received from 32 per cent of the membership revealed that more than 70 per cent of the respondents had adopted detailed environmental policies or strategies. The significance of this strategic commitment to environmental protection was further emphasized when approximately three-quarters of all respondents identified company policy, corporate image and operational efficiency as the key motivators for reducing their environmental impacts. Thus, there appears to be a significant minority of airlines motivated to 'beyond compliance' levels of environmental performance, which are underpinned in many cases by a systematic approach to identifying and evaluating environmental threats and opportunities. For example, nearly three-quarters of the respondents indicated that their companies undertook some form of environmental monitoring and had prepared environmental reviews for key operational activities (eg maintenance and ground operations). However, this strategic treatment of environmental issues has yet to encourage widespread adoption of formal environmental management systems, as only a quarter of the respondents indicated that such a system was in place.

As with any survey, care must be taken when interpreting these results; nevertheless, at least amongst the respondents, there are some positive signs that beyond compliance environmental behaviour is becoming the norm; thus, the adoption of EMS, whether formally accredited or not, can be expected to increase. The position in the airport sector, where larger companies predominate, is more positive, with almost one half of European airports having formally recognized environmental management systems, with a further 47 per cent working towards either ISO 14001 or EMAS certification (ACI Europe, 2001). However, if non-European airports or smaller airlines are examined, the picture that emerges is much less encouraging. Similarly, in nearly all categories the medium- and small-sized airlines were seen to be less proactive than their larger counterparts.

CONCLUSIONS

This chapter has highlighted the potential of environmental management systems to help deliver environmental improvements and, more broadly, to assist in addressing the wider sustainability agenda. Evidence has been provided to indicate that, at the lead edge, the aviation sector has been proactive in harnessing the potential of management systems and engaging with stakeholders through the publication of corporate environmental reports. However, the 17 airline corporate reporters identified by Dobbie and Hooper (2001) represent less than 10 per cent of the IATA membership. Furthermore, despite the positive indications emerging from the IATA membership survey, it must be remembered that this only represented one third of the population of airlines and a disproportionate representation of larger companies.

Overall, therefore, if the aviation sector is to genuinely make an attempt to contribute to sustainable development by compensating for its growth and, more immediately, to satisfy a growing band of stakeholders demanding environmental improvements, there is a need to diffuse the good practice that exists in the sector. The influence of stakeholders is gaining momentum as local community groups, customers, trading partners and investors and insurers ensure that environmental responsibilities are kept to the forefront of the corporate agenda. The challenge for the aviation sector is to make more effective use of tools such as environmental management systems in order to enhance responses to both liabilities and opportunities and, thereby, to ensure future competitiveness and capacity for growth.

NOTES

1 Following a meeting of 16 scientists, economists, government officials and business people in 1994, convened by the Wuppertal Institute for Climate, Environment and Energy in Germany, the Carnoules Declaration was published calling for a tenfold increase in resource productivity to reverse growing environmental damage. Environment ministers of Austria, Sweden and the Organization for Economic Cooperation and Development (OECD), along with the World Business Council for Sustainable Development (WBCSD) have called for the adoption of Factor 10 goals.

2 It is important to differentiate between these reports that are explicitly associated with EMS and the corporate environmental reports published by a number of leading companies in order to highlight their environmental credentials (see the section on 'Corporate environmental reporting').

REFERENCES

ACI Europe (2001) *List of Environmentally Certified European Airports as of 19 November 2001*, ACI Europe, Brussels

BAA (2001) *BAA Annual Report 2000/01*, available at www.BAA.com

B&Q (2001) 'B&Q scoops prestigious Queen's award', B&Q Press Release, 21 April 2001, www.diy.com

Cairncross, F (1991) *Costing the Earth*, Business Books, London

CTC (2000) *Environmental Management Systems, Clean Technology Systems*, www.cit.ie/rd/cleant/CleanTech/NETBACKU/Ems.htm

DETR (2000) Press Notice, vol 144, 1 March 2000

Dobbie, L and Hooper, P D (2001) *Airline Environmental Reporting: 2001 Survey*, IATA, Montreal and Geneva, p48

EC (1996) 'Council Directive 96/61/EC of 24 September 1996 concerning integrated pollution prevention and control', *Official Journal* L 257, 10 October, pp26–40

ENDS (2000) 'How effective are environmental management systems?' *ENDS Report 311*, December 2000, pp27–29

ENDS (2001a) 'Commission issues guidance on environmental reporting', *ENDS Report 317*, June 2001, p35

ENDS (2001b) 'EMAS-2 opens for business', *ENDS Report 316*, May 2001

Hawken, P, Lovins, A B and Lovins, L H (1999) *Natural Capitalism: The Next Industrial Revolution*, Earthscan Publications, London

Heaton, G, Repetto, R and Sobin, R (1991) *Transforming Technology: An Agenda for Environmentally Sustainable Growth in the 21st Century*, World Resources Institute, London

Hooper, P D and Gibbs, D, (1995) 'Cleaner Technology: A Means to an End, or an End to a Means?' *Greener Management International*, no 9, pp28–40

Hooper, P D, Maughan, J A and Thomas, C (2000) *IATA Members Environmental Survey December 2000*, unpublished research report commissioned by IATA

Howes R, Skea, J and Whelan R (1997) *Clean and Competitive? Motivating Environmental Performance in Industry*, Earthscan Publications, London

IATA (2000) *Environmental Review 2000*, IATA, Montreal and Geneva, October

IATA (2001) *A Flight Plan to Environmental Excellence*, IATA, Geneva

Intergovernmental Panel on Climate Change (IPCC) (1999) *Aviation and the Global Atmosphere*, Special Report, Cambridge University Press, Cambridge

International Standards Organization (ISO) (1996) *ISO 14001: 1996, Environmental Management Systems – Specification with Guidance for Use*, ISO, Geneva

IWM (1998) *Environmental Management Systems: An Implementation Guide for the Wastes Management Industry*, Institute of Wastes Management, Northampton, www.iwm.co.uk

Meadows, D H, Meadows, D L and Randers, J (1992) *Beyond the Limits: Global Collapse or a Sustainable Future*, Earthscan Publications, London

Naimon, J (1993) 'Lifting the veil', *Tomorrow*, n1, pp58–66

Pringle J, Leuteritz K J and Fitzgerald M (1998) *ISO 14001: A Discussion of Implications for Pollution Prevention*, National Pollution Prevention Roundtable ISO14001 Workgroup White Paper, 28 January 1998, Washington, DC

Sheldon, C and Yoxon, M (1999) *Installing Environmental Management Systems: A Step by Step Guide*, Earthscan Publications, London

Smith, V (2000) *Environmental and Ethical Policies within the Banking Sector*, unpublished Manchester Metropolitan University undergraduate research project, Manchester

WCED (1987) *Our Common Future*, Oxford University Press, Oxford

UNEP/Sustainability Ltd (2000) *The Global Reporters*, Sustainability Ltd, London

Von Weizsäcker, E U, Lovins, A B and Lovins, L H (1997) *Factor Four: Doubling Wealth, Halving Resource Use*, Earthscan Publications, London

Zackrisson, M (2000) cited in *ENDS Report 311*, December 2000, pp27–29

Chapter 8

The potential for modal substitution

Milan Janic

INTRODUCTION

This chapter assesses the most promising options for the possible substitution of air transport services by surface transport services. The chapter consists of five sections. Following an introduction, the second section briefly describes the main characteristics of high-speed (HS) transit systems in Europe. The third section addresses the potential relationships between existing HS systems, particularly high-speed rail (HSR) and air passenger transport (APT). The fourth section analyses the potential for substitution between particular HS systems and related effects, and the final section draws some conclusions.

The aim of modal substitution is to provide conditions for further sustainable development of transport systems in the regions in question. In Europe, a realistic and emerging option is to partially substitute APT with HSR. During the past decade, HSR has become an important player in the short- to medium-distance intercity passenger transport market of Western Europe. Apart from the currently non-existent magnetic levitation transport system (MAGLEV), both APT and HSR represent alternatives that can operate exclusively or simultaneously in particular markets. When operating exclusively in niche markets, they are related only at the ends of particular routes or corridors. However, when operating simultaneously in the same markets, APT and HSR are in dynamic interaction and can be either in competitive or complementary relationship. Within the same mode, both competition and cooperation may take place between particular HSR and APT operators or carriers.

At short to medium intercity distances (between 400–800km), APT and HSR can compete effectively if there is a sufficient volume of transport demand where the infrastructure for both alternatives exists. In the absence of these conditions, only one alternative will be economically feasible. Generally, HSR has been considered a 'positive' substitute for APT rather than a complementary alternative – first, as socially and environmentally preferable and, second, as an economically feasible alternative.

On long-distance routes (over 800km), APT dominates the transport market as an exclusive high-speed mode; but there is opportunity for complementarity in terms of providing 'feeding' traffic for long-distance flights by HSR. In Europe, the latter are long continental and intercontinental flights that could be fed by HSR short-distance services instead of equivalent short-haul air services (flights). This kind of multimodal interrelationship requires multimodal integration. This should include through-ticketing, competitive prices compared to the prices of unimodal services, integration and balance of timetables at intermodal points and common baggage processing. In order to determine the distance thresholds for substitution and integration of complementary services, both alternatives need to be assessed with respect to their ability to satisfy specified needs. These may be the needs of users, such as passengers' need for an adequate service, the need of transport operators for a profitable business, or the public need for a reduction of the overall environmental impact of the transport system. With respect to the assessment and comparison of particular effects, a market and spatial boundary needs to be defined by which to determine the relative merits of particular high-speed systems in order to guarantee fulfilment of both local and global, individual and collective objectives.

HIGH-SPEED TRANSPORT SYSTEMS

It can be said that the intention to increase transport speed has been a widespread obsession of modern times. Since most people have generally had a fixed time and money budget for travel, they have generally intended to buy the maximal distance with it. Moreover, in line with increases in personal income, they have tended to buy faster transport services, and thus travel further. Therefore, it could be considered that transport speed has been increasing as a consequence of a progressively expanding per-capita income and increased travel opportunities in terms of scale and scope (Ausubel and Marchetti, 1996). Travelling at high speed has provided overall benefits for users (passengers) by allowing them faster and deeper market penetration, complete substitution of conventional transport modes, and improved spending of time and money budgets. At present, three transport systems – air passenger transport (APT), high-speed rail (HSR) and trans-rapid MAGLEV (TRM) – can be considered as high-speed systems.

Air passenger transport (APT)

APT emerged as the earliest high-speed travel option during the 1950s. Over time, it has been permanently modernized through aircraft capabilities, airline strategy and government regulation (Boeing, 1998). The development of aircraft capabilities such as speed, payload and take-off weight has been of the greatest importance, as these have most affected the other two sub-processes, and vice versa. Increases in both speed and payload have contributed to enormous increases in aircraft productivity of more than 100 times during the last 40 years (Horonjeff and McKelvey, 1994).

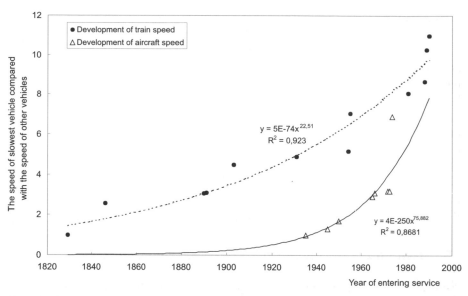

Note: the slowest passenger train speed is 47 km/h (1829) and the slowest passenger aircraft speed is 238 km/h (1934).

Figure 8.1 *Evolution of train and aircraft speed*

In particular, the development of speed has been relatively fast, as is illustrated in Figure 8.1 by relating the speed of various commercial aircraft to the speed of the slowest one, the DC3 (238 km/h). The dotted line shows a significant and relatively fast (exponential) technological progress over time, which has for the time being been completed by launching supersonic aircraft Concorde in 1974 (Boeing, 1998; Horonjeff and McKelvey, 1994). In addition, 'airline strategy' and 'governmental regulation' have increased system efficiency and safety, together with a permanent and stable long-term traffic growth in terms of scale and scope. In particular, the aircraft manufacturers and airlines have been among the leaders of this progress. They have made a continuous effort to develop and deploy new aircraft with increased efficiency in terms of fuel consumption, noise emissions and emissions of gaseous pollutants. In addition to spatial expansion, the airports have intended to use modern equipment and procedures to serve growing demand more efficiently and safely. Air traffic control has always intended to provide safe, expeditious and efficient aircraft movements between airports by using innovative and new technologies and operational procedures. Governmental institutions have created legislation to liberalize and privatize the air transport industry and particular markets. Consequently, in Europe, the sector has grown at an average annual rate of 5 per cent (ATAG, 1996a).

High-speed rail (HSR)

HSR was launched at the beginning of the 1980s. Generally, the development of railway speed has been much slower than that of air transport, and has spread over a period longer than a century and a half. During that period, train speed has increased more than ten times, from about 50–500km/h (see Figure 8.1). Probably the most

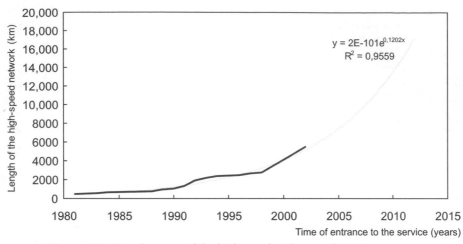

Figure 8.2 *Development of the high-speed rail network in Europe*

significant institutional attainment has been the decision of particular European Union (EU) member states to build the trans-European HSR network. The length of this network is planned to be about 29,000km, of which 12,500km will be new lines, 14,000km upgraded lines and 2500km connecting lines. The total cost is estimated to be about 240 billion Ecu, of which 207 billion Ecu were allocated to rail infrastructure and 33 billion Ecu to rolling stocks.

Figure 8.2 shows the development of the HSR network in Europe. As can be seen, the length of the network has increased over time more than proportionally, which would correspond with plans to complete the whole network by 2010 (CEC, 1995). The development of this network has proceeded through several phases. Development started by prioritizing national projects.[1] Latterly, via trans-European transport networks (TENs), international and cohesive projects have been developed.[2]

Figure 8.3 shows close relationship between the development of HSR infrastructure and the volume of traffic during the period of 1981–1993. This growth is likely to continue as a result of the implementation of new projects (CEC, 1995).

Trans-rapid MAGLEV (TRM)

TRM is based upon Herman Kemper's idea of magnetic levitation dating from the 1930s. The system is still under development and is not in commercial use anywhere. At present, two versions of a MAGLEV train are under testing, TR07 in Germany and MLU0002 in Japan. With respect to propulsion, vertical suspension and lateral guidance, MAGLEV represents a new technology, since the technological heart of the system, contact-free support, guidance and propulsion by means of electromagnets is neither modelled upon, nor comparable to, any other transport technology (Geerlings, 1998; Kretzschmar, 1995). Essentially, without physical contact with the dedicated guide-way, MAGLEV will be able to run at a speed of 400–500km/h. Thus, a travel distance of between 500–800km would take approximately one to two hours. Such performance would allow MAGLEV to be both a competitive and a complementary system to the other two high-speed systems on the related distances. MAGLEV

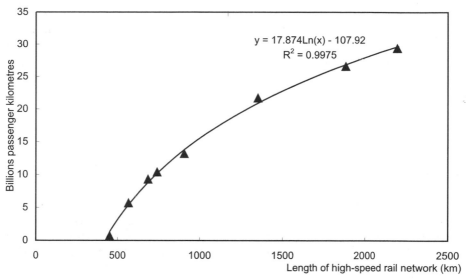

Figure 8.3 *Dependence of HSR traffic upon the length of the HSR network in Europe*

will be able to link the major cities and airports on one side, and to provide an inter-modal connection with air, HSR and urban-metro transport systems, on the other. However, as in the case of HSR, both national and/or international infrastructure networks for MAGLEV may take decades to develop to the level of having a significant global impact upon the transport market (Kretzschmar, 1995).

THE INTERACTIONS BETWEEN HIGH-SPEED TRANSPORT SYSTEMS

While operating in the same market corridors of Western Europe, HSR and APT are in permanent dynamic interaction with different internal and external impacts, as follows:

- In terms of type of interactions, HSR and APT may either compete or be complementary to each other. Both relationships may contribute to a redistribution of existing transport demand and generation (induction) of new demand, may improve the internal efficiency of each transport system, and thus of the whole transport sector, and may revitalize both regional and national transport networks through their better integration in the trans-European transport networks (TENs) (EC, 1998a, 1998b).
- Both HSR and APT have significantly influenced the micro and macro spatial, socio-economic and political development of particular Western European regions. In general, the most evident have tended to be changes in the structure and spatial distribution of the existing and new socio-economic activities.
- In addition to telecommunications and information technology, by covering much wider areas in much shorter time than the conventional systems, HSR

and APT have been particularly successful in enhancing globalization, internalization and integration of the regional and national economies and societies.

- Finally, both HSR and APT have been shown as promising options for further sustainable development of the European transport sector through increased safety and security, diminished air pollution, noise, land use and congestion, on one side, and by an efficient way of meeting growing transport demand, on the other.

In the following sub-sections, only competition and complementarity as the options for substitution between two HS systems are considered.

Competition

Competition between HSR and APT can take place in the high-volume passenger-transport market corridors, where there is the sufficient origin/destination demand to support feasible frequent services of both modes. For such competition, it is not necessary for airports at the ends of corridors to be included in the HSR network. The user/passenger makes a choice of available transport options based upon perceived utility, which is usually expressed by generalized travel cost.[3] Consequently, the mode offering a higher individual utility (ie lower generalized cost) will be selected. However, different types of passengers (business and leisure, old and young, male and female, etc) usually have different utilities, leading to each HS mode having at least some market share. Under such circumstances, HSR and APT continue to compete by modifying the factors mostly affecting the generalized travel costs, such as departure frequency, fares, internal quality of service and safety.

Experience and research carried out to date shows that HSR has mostly affected APT on the origin/destination passenger market corridors of lengths between 400–800km. It has been possible to make such impact because HSR has been able to run services at a speed of 300km/h, which together with competitive departure frequency has produced a total station-to-station travel time of about 2 to 4–4.5 hours.

Figure 8.4 illustrates some research findings on APT/HSR competition (Janic, 1993). Dependent upon the level of generalized user cost, three types of relationships between HSR and APT can be observed:

- general preference of HSR in the origin/destination (O/D) market corridors of length between 150–400km;
- competition between the two modes in the O/D market corridors of length between 400–1200km; and
- general preference for APT in the O/D market corridors longer than 1200km.

In addition, the changes of generalized travel cost resulting from variation in price, frequency, service reliability and punctuality significantly affect the individual choice between the two modes over the wide spectrum of travel distances. Nevertheless, it should be mentioned that particular individual choices are not perfectly homogeneous, which allows each mode to keep some market share.

Figure 8.5 shows an aggregate figure modal split between particular transport modes dependent upon the origin/destination travel distance. As can be seen, on short distances up to 400km, the market share of APT is about 10 per cent; of rail

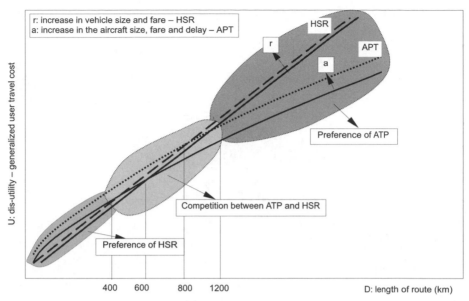

Source: compiled from ITA, 1991; Janic, 1993

Figure 8.4 *Dependence of the generalized user cost on the length of corridor/route*

(both conventional and HSR) about 20 per cent; and of individual car about 70 per cent, which is a position of virtual monopoly of individual car. On travel distances between 1200–1600km, air transport dominates, with market share varying between 50–80 per cent. On the intermediate distances between 400–1200km, both conventional rail and HSR compete with APT and individual car. In total, they have between 20–30 percent of market share, of which HSR has between 10–15 per cent (CEC, 1995).

Figure 8.6 provides examples of the impacts of HSR on APT in particular origin/destination market corridors in Germany and France. The period of 15 years, between 1980 and 1995, has been disaggregated by journey length (EC, 1998b). In the French origin/destination corridors (see Figure 8.6a), three types of mutual influence between HSR and APT can be observed. First, there has been a 'strong' impact of HSR on APT, manifested by significant diminishing of APT in the short-haul markets (up to 400 km) during the period of five years after introduction of HSR. In these cases, HSR has simply taken over the traffic from APT. Second, there is the 'weak' impact of HSR on APT, which has taken place in the markets of length between 400–700km. In these cases, HSR has only managed to reduce the rate of growth of APT (ie to temporarily slow it down). The last type is the 'counter' impact of APT on HSR, when APT has recovered after having been severely affected by HSR. In this case, APT has responded to HSR competitively by increasing the flexibility of services in terms of flight frequencies carried out by smaller aircraft, and reducing airfares, both of which have contributed to reducing generalized user cost.[4] Similar types of impacts of HSR on APT, except a 'counter' one, have been observed on particular corridors in Germany as shown in Figure 8.6b.

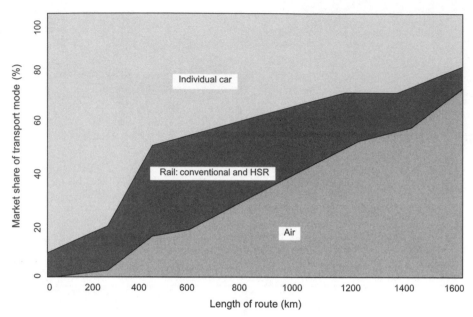

Source: compiled from CEC, 1995

Figure 8.5 *Market share of particular transport modes dependent upon the origin/ destination travel distance*

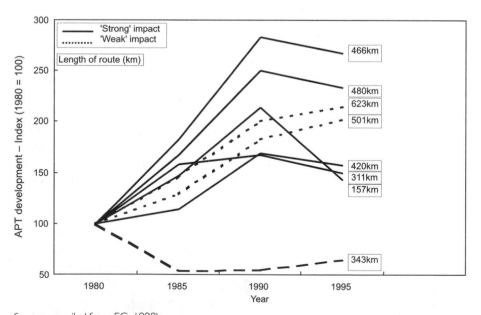

Source: compiled from EC, 1998b

Figure 8.6a *The mutual influence of HSR and APT in selected French market corridors*

As can be seen, traffic volumes have been significantly redistributed between two modes on the short routes. Despite such changes, no mode has lost traffic completely, and only partial substitution of APT by HSR services has taken place.

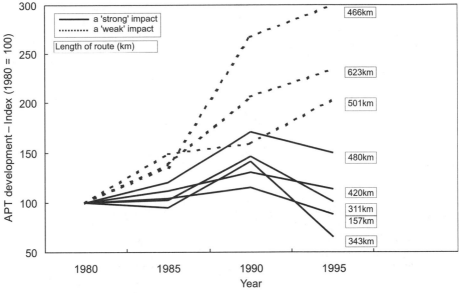

Source: compiled from EC, 1998b

Figure 8.6b *The mutual influence of HSR and APT in selected German market corridors*

Complementarity and cooperation

In general, an airport can be connected to different levels of rail service. At the first level, an airport can be connected with a catchment area by dedicated local rail links. In terms of infrastructure requirements, this type of connection needs the railway station at the airport and rail lines. At the second level, an airport may be connected to the national conventional rail network. Such type of connectivity allows exchange of passengers between air and rail at the wider scale, from regional to national. The infrastructure requirements are similar to the case of local train connections, but the rail station and links should be adapted to the type of services spread much beyond the airport catchment area. The third level of connectivity of airports is provided by HSR links. Similar infrastructure is required, as in the case of conventional rail, but the rail stations and links should be modified to the HSR requirements. In all of the above cases, the rail and air mode operate more or less independently in terms of time, frequency and capacity of particular services, and applied ticketing/pricing scheme.

Connection of airports by rail links may create benefits in terms of improving flexibility of airport surface access systems, as an alternative to congested road links and an enhancement of the overall air/rail intermodality through complementarity.[5] In particular, complementarity emerges as a convenient option of air/rail intermodality once the HSR stations and their links are present at airports. Inherently, complementarity includes cooperation between two modes: APT and HSR. In particular, complementarity can be established at the airports with a relatively high volume and proportion of connecting (transit/transfer passengers) and linked by HSR. In Western Europe, these airports are the hubs of large airlines, which operate strong hub-and-spoke networks (Amsterdam Schiphol, Franfurt Main and Paris Charles de Gaule are some

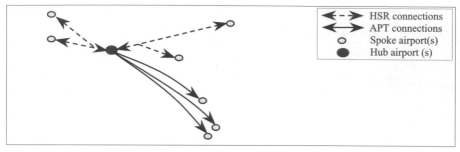

a) Collection and distribution of passenger flows to/from a single hub airport by HSR and APT

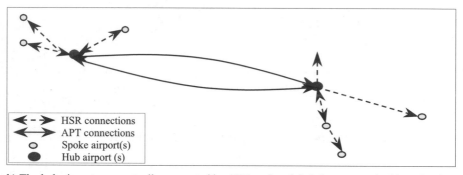

b) The hub airports are mutually connected by APT, and each hub is connected with spokes by HSR

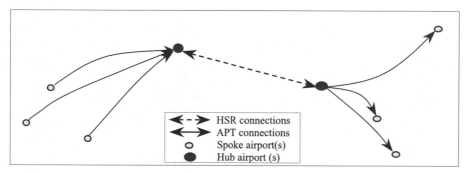

c) The hub airports are mutually connected by HSR, and each hub is connected with spokes by APT

Source: compiled from ITA, 1991; EC, 1998b

Figure 8.7 *Generic schemes of possible complementarity between HSR and APT*

examples). In these networks, pairs of hub-incoming and hub-outgoing interconnected flights serve particular origin/destination passenger flows. Under conditions when it is possible to replace some cheap short-haul feeder flights by the equivalent HSR feeder services, it is said that 'complementarity by substitution' takes place. In depending upon the development of HSR infrastructure at airports, and the mutual conectivity of airports by HSR lines, various network complementarity schemes can be established. Some of them are shown in Figure 8.7 (ITA, 1991; EC, 1998b).

As can be seen, three types of complementary networks operated by HSR and APT may take place. First, HSR partially replaces APT in collecting and distributing passenger flows between a single hub airport and particular spokes. Some spokes are connected with the hub exclusively by HSR. The others are connected exclusively by APT services. Second, HSR provides exclusive surface-access service from spokes to particular hub airports, and vice versa. APT exclusively connects hub airports to another. In the third case, APT connects hub airports with spokes and HSR provides exclusive surface connections between hub airports themselves.

In order to establish one of the above types of complementarity networks, several conditions should be fulfilled: First, there should be multimodal terminals at hub airports within the complementary network. Second, the timetables of particular HSR and APT services should be coordinated. Third, through-ticketing across different modes should be provided. Finally, convenient checking and transferring of passengers and their baggage between two modes should be provided.

Multimodal terminals

Currently, at many European airports rail stations are either under operation or construction/planning, which enables them to function either partially or fully as multimodal terminals. For example, 32 of 70 EU airports, which accommodate more then 2 million passengers per year, are connected by rail links with their surroundings. In terms of type of service and distance, there may be five types of these connections. These are high-speed trains, long-distance trains, local trains, underground trains and tram/light trains. Table 8.1 illustrates the present situation (EC, 1998b; 1999).

As can be seen from Table 8.1, large airports have already been included, or are planned to be included, in the HSR network. In terms of 'type of connections', three options can be identified such as 'city centre to airport', 'a rail system at the airport' and 'airport to airport'. 'City centre to airport' connection assumes that there is the rail system connection, in which the city-centre station is often the main railway station. Local trains, underground and tram/light rail links provide this type of connection. 'A rail system at the airport' implies that the connection of an airport is to the city centre, where the city-centre rail station remains the main station. Local, long distance and HSR links provide this type of service. 'Airport to airport' links connect two rail stations located at airports, where either the change of train or mode (train/air) may take place. The HSR between Paris Charles de Gaule and Lyon Satolas airports, for example, illustrates this type of connection.

Coordinated timetables and through-ticketing

Table 8.1 *Examples of rail infrastructure at particular EU airports*

Type of rail link	Number of airports	Airports
High-speed rail	1	Lyon Satolas
High-speed rail + local trains	4	Paris Charles de Gaule, Stockholm Arlanda, Frankfurt, Oslo Gardermoen
Long-distance trains + local trains	5	Amsterdam Schiphol, Brussels, Copenhagen, Berlin Schonefeld, Birmingham
Local trains	18	London airports (Heathrow, Gatwick, Luton, Stansted), Manchester, Newcastle, Paris Orly, Malaga, Pisa, Rome, Milano Mapensa, Düsseldorf, Munich, Stuttgart, Vienna, Friedrichshafen, Barcelona, Madrid Barajas
Underground trains	4	London Heathrow, Newcastle, Paris Orly, Madrid Barajas
Links under construction	4	Nuremberg (metro), Hanover, Dresden, Cologne

Coordinated timetables are based upon the adjustments of arrival and departure times of HSR and APT at the airport and the rail station located at the airport, which allows smooth and efficient exchange of passengers and baggage. This includes establishing the interlinkage between particular services of different transport modes – in this case, HSR and APT – to achieve minimum connection times. Typically, this time should be similar, as in the case of unimodal services (ie sufficiently long to allow smooth and efficient transfer of passengers and their baggage from incoming to outgoing service). In addition, only one ticket should be used for a trip between origin and destination independent of the mode used. Although there have not yet been clear examples of complementarity of any type between HSR and APT in Western Europe in terms of coordinated timetables and through-ticketing, some recent plans and real-life cases undertaken by particular actors within the air and rail industries seem to be promising. These are as follows (BM, 1999; Monox, 1999):

- The airline British Midland has offered through-ticketing to business passengers on Heathrow Express rail – the new high-speed rail service connecting Heathrow Airport with central London – on its flights from Heathrow Airport.
- French Railway (SNCF) is considering an option to become the first 'non-airline' member of Star Alliance,[6] which will include coordination of timetables and through-ticketing for airline passengers from major French airports to the rest of the country by using the Train à Grande Vitesse (TGV) high-speed network. The rail operator already has a limited deal with United Airlines for connections from Lyon Satolas airport.
- Lufthansa (Star Alliance member) and Deutsche Bahn (DB) launched in the year 2000 a pilot project to allow airline passengers to transfer from air to the Frankfurt Stuttgart Intercity Express (ICE) rail route, which is expected to replace some

short hauls. In addition, from 2001, the project will include through-baggage transfers and through-ticketing.

- Before British Airways reduced the scale and scope of its second hub – London Gatwick Airport – the airline, as a shareholder of Eurostar services, had pressed to connect its London hubs (Gatwick and Heathrow) by HSR link in order to be able to replace short hauls to/from cities such as Paris (Monox, 1999).

The potential for substitution and effects

General effects

The above analysis has shown that potential substitution between HSR and APT can be carried out under competitive and complementarity conditions.

As far as competition is concerned, market forces dictate the scale and scope of substitution. Consequently, both HSR and APT survive in the market but with a different scale and scope of operations dependent primarily upon market conditions. In such cases, passengers and transport operators are expected to mostly benefit through increased frequencies, reduced prices and, thus, lower generalized travel costs.

In the case of complementarity, particular HSR services may completely substitute for some APT, usually short-haul services. This may have a twofold effect. On one hand, it requires building the HSR infrastructure at, and between, airports, which may be very expensive. On the other hand, complementarity generally improves the efficiency of airport surface accessibility, as well as surface (rail) connectivity between particular airports, and thus contributes to further development of integrated air/rail systems at the European scale (EC, 1998b). In this case, passengers, operators and the public are expected to mostly benefit. Direct added value of such substitution for transport operators and public can be summarized as follows:

- alleviating air congestion by replacement of the frequent short-feeder APT services by equivalent HSR surface services;
- using the slots of previously short-haul, less-valued flights for scheduling more valuable long-haul continental and intercontinental flights; and
- reducing the overall negative impacts of the short-haul frequent services on the environment in terms of the type and level of noise and air pollution.

Specific effects

Related 'savings' can express specific effects of the substitution of particular APT services by equivalent HSR services, independent of the manner of substitution. The savings may be assessed with respect to evolution of different criteria related to given O/D travel distance in both qualitative and quantitative terms. These can be infrastructure cost, operating costs, energy consumption, user time-to-distance costs, noise, air pollution, land use, etc.

Infrastructure costs

Infrastructure costs of APT roughly increase with rising traffic volumes, particularly at congested airports, since they have to be expanded to conveniently accommodate growing demand. However, this cost may be considered negligible compared to the cost of building new HSR lines. Typical investment cost of HSR line has been about 7 million Ecu per kilometre (MEcu/km) (CEC, 1995; Janic, 1999b). Consequently, savings in infrastructure cost are in favour of APT, since the airport and air traffic control infrastructure already exists, while the HSR network has to be built as a whole.

Operating costs

Operating costs of APT per unit of output (seat-km) are shown to be generally higher than HSR, assuming that traffic volumes are sufficiently high to justify running HSR services. Moreover, for APT, this cost decreases with increase in travel distance, while it is approximately constant for HSR. Consequently, under such circumstances, in terms of potential savings, HSR appears to be preferable compared with APT. Some typical values of operating costs of APT and HSR are 0.042 Ecu/seat-km and 0.055 Ecu/seat-km, respectively (Janic, 1999b).

Energy consumption

Energy consumption has a different pattern for APT and HSR. For APT, it is higher during take-off and climb-out, 'economically' acceptable at optimal cruising altitudes, and less intensive while approaching and landing. Contrarily, energy consumption for HSR is proportional to cruising speed. This means that it is lower during the accelerating/decelerating phase of the trip and higher but constant during cruising at maximum speed. Expressed per unit of output, energy consumption per unit of output (seat-km) decreases more than proportionally for APT and is roughly constant for HSR as route length increases. For example, on average, the Airbus A 320-200 consumes 0.425 kilowatt hours per second-kilometre (kwh/s-km) on the route of 300km, and 0.248kwh/s-km on the route of 1200km. On average, the HS TGV train consumes between 0.106 and 0.141kwh/s-km on travel distances between 200 and 1200km, respectively (ITA, 1991). As can be seen, with respect to the savings of energy, HSR is favourable to APT on the whole range of travel distances.

User time-to-distance cost

User time-to-distance cost for APT decreases with increase in travel flight distance. In such a case, users take the advantage of higher speed while cruising on longer distances in comparison to the relatively time-consuming procedures, which take place at arrival and departure. For example, depending upon travel distance, the overall speed may significantly vary between 400–800km/h (Geerlings, 1998; ITA, 1991; Janic, 1993). However, this is not relevant while using HSR, particularly when there are no intermediate stops along the line. The typical overall speed of HSR varies between 250–300km/h. Consequently, savings in the time-to-distance cost are in favour of HSR compared with APT on the shorter travel distances, and in favour of APT compared with HSR on the long travel distances.

Noise

Noise has also a quite different pattern for APT and HSR. For APT, noise emission is very high in the vicinity of airports during landing and taking-off, and generally has a negligible impact while cruising. For HSR, the level of noise increases with increase in speed and can be heard along the whole line as the train passes by. Typical noise values for APT and HSR are very heterogeneous and depend upn vehicle (aircraft/train) type and phase of trip. For example, for different aircraft types, the certificate noise levels vary during landing and take-off between 46.5 and 92.5 decibels (dB(A)). Typical noise levels of the German HS train ICE vary between 72 and 92dB(A) at cruising speeds of between 96 and 320km/h, respectively. The French HS TGV train generates noise of 97dB(A) at a cruising speed of 320km/h (Geerlings, 1998; Levison et al, 1996). Consequently, savings in noise energy on the ground are in favour of HSR when compared to APT at the beginning (departure) and end (arrival) of the trip. However, these savings are in favour of APT during the cruising phase of the trip, particularly if HSR trains pass nearby populated areas.

Air pollution

Air pollution differs for APT and HSR. In absolute terms, APT is relatively highly polluting during take-off and climb-out, and less high during cruising, approach and landing. Moreover, the spatial distribution of APT air pollution is of particular importance at both local and global scales (ATAG, 1996b; Janic, 1999a).

The air pollution generated by HSR is less than that generated by APT in absolute terms, and with respect to spatial pattern, for moving a given number of people a given distance. The quantity of pollutants of carbon monoxide (CO), nitrogen oxide (NO_x), sulphur dioxide (SO_2), methane (CH_4), and carbon dioxide (CO_2) emitted by HSR depends upon the train speed and power source. For the German ICE, for example, typical air pollution is equal to 14 and 25 grams per second per kilometre (g/s-km) at cruising speeds of 200 and 300km/h, respectively. This pollution is spread near the ground, around the electricity production plants and along track lines. The air pollution emitted by APT is much higher. For example, the aircraft A320-200, flying at speeds lower than 600km/h, generates approximately 140g/s-km of air pollutants. These pollutants are spread both on the ground around the airports and along cruising altitudes. In both cases, the quantity of CO_2 dominates in total air pollution (Geerlings, 1998; Levison et al, 1996). Consequently, savings in air pollution are in favour of HSR relative to APT for the whole travel distance. In particular, these savings are much higher during arrival and departure than for the cruising phase of the trip.

Land use

The pattern of land use is also quite different for APT and HSR. For APT, land is primarily used for building airports. Generally, land use increases with traffic volumes, which require spatial expansion of airports. For HSR, land use is mostly dependent upon the length of the HSR line and is not influenced by the volume of traffic. HSR typically uses a land increment of size 3.2ha per kilometre of track. Total land use is then dependent upon the length of the line multiplied by this increment. The land use for airports is highly variable, but depends primarily upon the number, length and configuration of runways. The typical land increment for airport land use is about 30ha per kilometre of air-side infrastructure dedicated to aircraft movement (runway, taxi way, etc) (Horonjeff and McKelvey, 1994). In addition to the area of acquired land, intensity of land use may be relevant to measuring potential substitution savings. Some studies have shown that the intensity of land use is quite comparable for APT and HSR: 0.31 and 0.35ha/million passenger-kilometres, respectively

(CEC, 1993). Consequently, savings in land use are in favour of APT compared with HSR, since while most of the airports already exist and only require expansion, new land would need to be acquired to build a completely new HSR line.

The above analysis shows that substitution of particular APT by HSR services may produce a wide spectrum of significant savings, mainly in terms of operating cost, energy consumption, user time-to-distance cost, noise and air pollution. The savings in infrastructure cost and land use appear not to be in favour of HSR compared with APT, even though relatively short distances are concerned.

CONCLUSIONS

This chapter has addressed the problem of potential substitution of air passenger transport (APT) by high-speed rail (HSR) services. Such substitution should be expected to take place strongly on short-haul routes from 300–600km. The relationships between the two modes have been analysed and it has been shown that there is opportunity for substitution through competition, as well as for complementarity.

In fact, such competition has, indeed, taken place and has been justified in the market corridors with high volumes of passenger demand. In these cases, depending upon the competitive power, the market share of particular modes (ie modal split) has changed. On shorter station-to-station travel distances, HSR has managed to take a significant portion of traffic from APT. On longer routes, HSR has managed only to slow the growth rates of air traffic. In some specific cases, APT has recovered after significant loss of market share by increasing flexibility of services. However, these processes have occurred during the medium-term period.

Complementarity between HSR and APT has been shown to be at a rudimentary stage in Western Europe, despite some recent promising developments. One reason has been the need for building expensive HSR infrastructure at large hub airports with high volumes of connecting (ie transit/transfer) traffic. In addition, some schemes for further development of complementarity between HSR and APT have been elaborated.

Substitution of particular APT by HSR services, particularly on the shorter distances, has seemed to be able to provide specific added value for airport and airline operators, as well as overall savings for particular actors, users/passengers, operators and the public. These savings are proportional to the volume of traffic and are mainly achieved in operating cost, energy consumption, user time-to-distance cost, noise and air pollution.

NOTES

1   The French railways launched the first high-speed rail (HSR) service in 1981 on the Paris–Lyon line. One of the main reasons for starting the HSR in France was the oil crisis in 1973, which resulted in huge fuel deficits. It was expected that the electrically powered HSR would reduce the dependence of the transport sector upon crude oil and reduce overall fuel consumption by substituting for aviation in particular market segments. In addition, HSR services were launched in other countries. In Spain, Talgo has operated since the 1970s; in Britain, the advanced passenger train was planned to enter

the service in 1981 but it did not get past the trial stage; in Italy and Sweden there were the ETR 450 and 460 (Pendolino) and X-2000, respectively. These have all used passive and/or active tilt-body technology, which allowed the trains to run at high speed on the existing, but slightly improved, tracks. After the full success of the French TGV on the Paris–Lyon line, the TGV Atlantiqué was introduced between Paris and Bordeaux in 1989. In 1991, German Inter-City-Express started operation. In Spain, the high-speed train Alta Velocidad Espagñola (AVE) was launched in 1992 on a route connecting Madrid and Seville (ITA, 1991; CEC, 1995).

2   Eurostar, the first French–British joint venture, started service between Paris and London in 1995. The TGV Thalys, running between Paris and Brussels, and later Amsterdam, was introduced in the middle of 1996 as the second international HSR service in Europe (CEC, 1995).

3   Generalized travel costs are frequently used to measure the utility of an individual user or a group of similar users while choosing transport mode. In general, this includes the cost of travel time ('defer time' and in-vehicle time), the fare paid for travelling and the cost of other conveniences offered to the user while en route between origin and destination (Janic, 1993).

4   The development of competition between HSR and APT on the Paris–Lyon route illustrates the way in which APT can recover after years of significant stagnation. This occurred after Air France had established a hub at the Paris Charles de Gaule airport and offered more frequent and price-competitive services on the route (EC, 1998b).

5   The two transport modes will be regarded as complementary for a user when their successive utilization is either necessary or simply preferred to the utilization of a single transport mode for carrying out the journeys between intercity origin and destination. This definition focuses on the successive utilization of HSR and APT services (EC, 1998b).

6   Star Alliance is formed by 11 European and non-European airlines: Lufthansa, Scandinavian Airlines (SAS), United Airlines, Air Canada, Thai Airways, Varig, Singapore Airlines, All Nipon Airlines, Air New Zealand, Anset Australia and Mexicana.

REFERENCES

ATAG (1996a) *European Air Traffic Forecast 1980–2010*, Air Transport Action Group, Geneva, Switzerland

ATAG (1996b) *Aviation and Environment*, Air Transport Action Group, Geneva, Switzerland

Ausubel, J H and Marchetti, C (1996) 'Elektron: Electrical Systems in Retrospect and Prospect', *Daedalus*, vol 125, no 3 (summer), pp139–170

BM (1999) *Timetable*, British Midland, Derby, UK

Boeing (1998) *Evolution of the World Fleet: Time Line*, Boeing Aircraft Company, www.boeing.com

CEC (1993) *The European High-Speed Train Network: Environmental Impact Assessment*, Executive Summary, Commission of the European Communities, Directorate General for Transport, Brussels, Belgium

CEC (1995) *High-Speed Europe*, High-Level Group, the European High Speed Train Network, Commission of the European Communities, Brussels, Belgium

EC (1998a) *Integrated Strategic Infrastructure Networks in Europe*, Final Report on the Action COST 328, EUR 18165, European Commission, Luxembourg

EC (1998b) *Relationships between High-Speed Rail and Air Passenger Transport*, Final Report on the Action COST 318, EUR 18165, European Commission, Luxembourg

EC (1999) *Transport in Figures: Statistical Pocket* Book, EU Transport, European Commission, Directorate General DG VII, Brussels, Belgium, p135

Geerlings, H (1998) 'The Rise and Fall of New Technologies: MAGLEV as Technological Substitution?', *Transportation Planning and Technology*, vol 21, pp263–286

Horonjeff, R and McKelvey, F X (1994) *Planning and Design of Airports*, fourth edition, McGraw-Hill Book Company, New York, US

ITA (1991) *Rail/Air Complementarity in Europe: the Impact of High-Speed Rail Services*, Institute du Transport Aèrien, Paris, France

Janic, M (1993) 'A Model of Competition Between High-Speed Rail and Air Transport', *Transportation Planning and Technology*, vol 17, pp1–23

Janic, M (1999a) 'Aviation and Externalities: The Accomplishments and Problems', *Transportation Research-D*, vol 4, pp159–180

Janic, M (1999b) 'Multicriteria Evaluation of High-Speed Rail, TRANSRAPID MAGLEV and Air Passenger Transport in Europe', Fifth NECTAR Conference, Delft, the Netherlands, October, p30

Kretzschmar, R (1995) 'Transrapid Maglev: Prospects for Fast Regional Transportation Service', Paper presented at the First European Workshop on High Speed MAGLEV Transport Systems: European Prospects, University of Padua, Italy, p20

Levison, D, Gillen, D, Kanafani, A and Mathieu, J M (1996) *The Full Cost of Inter-City Transportation – A Comparison Of High Speed Rail, Air and Highway Transportation in California*, Institute of Transportation, University of California, Berkeley, Research Report, UCB-ITS-RR-96-3, US, p231

Monox, J (1999) 'Star Alliance Pursues French and German Rail Options', *Flight International*, July, p11

Chapter 9

Air freight and global supply chains: the environmental dimension

David Gillingwater, Ian Humphreys and Robert Watson

INTRODUCTION

There can be little doubt that the enhanced mobility of people and goods that has so characterized life in recent decades is profoundly altering the structures upon which the competitiveness of nation states, regions and localities around the world depend (Capello and Gillespie, 1993). This multifaceted phenomenon, more often than not referred to simply as 'globalization', brings with it some complex consequences – none more perplexing than those associated with environmental impacts. In terms of the movement of goods, a clear example is provided by the advent of advanced physical distribution systems. Based upon the principles of supply chain management and logistics (Bowersox and Closs, 1996), it is supporting corporate strategies geared towards developing new sources of competitive advantage globally.

As logistics operations have become ever more global, and as new agile production systems such as 'just in time' (JIT) have come to dominate, supply chains have required more rapid responses; thus, the movement of goods by air has become ever more important. As a result, air-freight volumes have increased dramatically, with many supply chains now highly dependent upon this mode of transport. A recent study conducted for the UK government calculated that in 1996 the contribution of air freight to the UK economy was of the order of UK£4.99 billion of gross domestic product (GDP) (DETR, 2000).

A significant part of this contribution has resulted from the development of innovative logistics services, such as those fulfilling the requirements of e-commerce – typically on the basis of order and delivery within 24 hours. To meet such time-sensitive movements, providers are becoming increasingly dependent upon the use of all-freighter air-freight services. Common to both is a set of environmental consequences that flows from the fact that such operations typically make use of older Chapter 2 aircraft types, such as the narrow-bodied Boeing 727 or older variants of the wide-bodied 747 and MD11 (together accounting for 57 per cent of UK air-freight uplift in 1998; DETR, 2000), and which are flown predominantly at night.

All modes of transport have negative environmental impacts, some immediate and direct (for example, noise and air-quality impacts), while others (for example, effects on climate change) are more distant and their significance still debated (Whitelegg, 1997; Royal Commission, 1995; IPCC SPM, 1999). The particular concern of this chapter is with the shorter-term quality-of-life issues associated with the local impacts of aircraft noise as a result of air-freight operations and the nuisance these cause to communities around airports. After identifying current predictions for the growth of air freight, the nature of this nuisance is considered and its significance to logistics operators and their customers is discussed through case studies. A discussion of strategies for the future explores how conflicts of interest might be resolved, ideally to the mutual satisfaction of the air-freight operators, supply-chain customers and local communities. Finally, a case study of strategies both proposed and implemented is considered for an airport that has experienced dramatic growth of night-time aircraft movements associated with air freight.

GROWTH IN AIR FREIGHT

Although at first sight the recent annual growth rate for the world's air cargo market of 5–6 per cent may not seem spectacular, a different picture begins to emerge when it is realized that this is ahead of world economic growth by a factor of almost two. The majority of air freight has, since the start of aviation, been 'belly-hold' freight (where freight travels in the hold of a passenger aircraft on a scheduled flight across an airline network). Industry forecasts predict that this form of air freight will more than treble over the next 20 years (DETR, 2000; Boeing, 2001).

Over the last decade, the role of 'belly hold' has been challenged by the integrated carriers (carriers who offer a predominantly 'one-stop' door-to-door service using, as far as practicable, their own resources, including their own freighter aircraft). They now have 9.2 per cent of the global air-freight market and a 5 per cent share of freight tonne kilometres (FTKs), compared to almost zero two decades ago. They have, on average, been expanding at an annual rate of around 24 per cent since 1992 (Boeing, 2001; Kingsley-Jones, 2000). Key players in this sector are DHL, FedEx, TNT Express and UPS, who – between them – account for almost 83 per cent of the integrator market place (Jones, 2001). Of these four, DHL leads the international market with 38 per cent. Integrated operators are now forecast to grow on average by 13 per cent per annum and to take a market share of 31 per cent by 2019; in addition, it is assumed that most of the operations underpinning this growth will continue to be flown by aircraft that are already flying (freighter conversions of current passenger aircraft) or that are in the fleet of these air-freight operators (DETR, 2000; Boeing, 2001).

The attractiveness of using an integrated carrier is based upon their offering of a high-quality single-company point of contact for door-to-door delivery to the majority of places worldwide within 48–72 hours, depending upon the distances involved

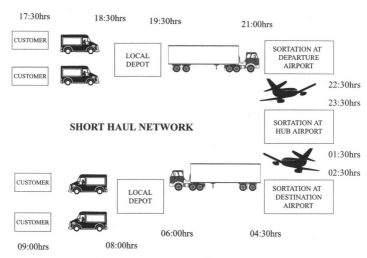

Figure 9.1 *An integrator's overnight short-haul network operation*

– compared to the average for belly-hold air freight of six days – and overnight delivery to most destinations within a continent or region. A further key attribute is their development of, and dependence upon, a global long-haul air network that is integrated with regional short-haul air/truck networks, which are, in turn, integrated with local truck networks. A typical short-haul schedule for an integrator operating in Europe is shown in Figure 9.1.

A trend towards integrators carrying a wider range of products, offering warehouse services and locating account managers directly in production plants has facilitated improvements in global supply-chain capabilities, as well as fuelling their continued growth. For example, 15 years ago planned deliveries as part of an integrated supply chain accounted for 25 per cent of DHL's business; today it is over 70 per cent (Macbeth, 2001). DHL currently offer a service where it personally runs the distribution function of major clients, including Dell Computers, Rolls-Royce, Sony and Toyota; it now claims to carry 31 per cent cargo sold as general freight against 69 per cent sold as its express document and package services (Macbeth, 2001). This has partly been achieved as a consequence of the maximum weight of consignments carried being increased beyond the traditional limit of 50kgs (Peters and Wright, 1999).

It is the integrators who have contributed substantially to the growth in and dominance of 'just-in-time' production on an international scale by offering supply-chain services to and from suppliers in the global market place. The speed and, increasingly, the reliability of these service providers have facilitated the concentration of production at locations around the world where costs are favourable and economies of both scale and scope can be realized, and where transport can be relied upon. The result is a remarkable collapse in the time–space geography of the world's principal market places that could not have happened without such innovative developments in freight transport operations (Humphreys, Gillingwater and Watson, 1999). Industry forecasts of the kind produced by Boeing show no sign of change in this upward trend (Boeing, 2001).

Within these forecasts it is anticipated that there will be two main drivers of future growth: firstly, a continuation of the processes of globalization mapped out at the beginning of this section and, secondly, dramatic growth in the market for e-commerce-based activities. For companies such as DHL, FedEx, TNT Express and UPS, e-commerce and the e-tail revolution are seen as possibly the biggest potential for growth for their services. An estimated US$1.6 trillion worth of business per year is forecast to be transacted via the Internet by 2003 (Bates, 2000). Delivery speed and convenience are seen as vital requirements by e-business, and integrated carriers often provide the favoured delivery solution with their global reach, time-definite and rapid-delivery services (Bates, 2000). However, these anticipated developments are not cost neutral; their associated social and environmental costs are described in the following section.

EMERGING ENVIRONMENTAL PROBLEMS

While the integrators have substantial road-based truck fleets at their disposal, it is considered that aviation will play an increasingly significant role in their ability to meet increasingly tight delivery schedules and pick-up deadlines. To maximize the efficiency of their service, this inevitably means aircraft operating from airports that are close to centres of commercial activity and, hence, close to centres of population – and the nature of integrator operations means that these aircraft will be operated almost exclusively during the night. Currently, around 100 aircraft distribute over 2000 tonnes of packages across Europe every night of the working week; in recent years, such aircraft movements are also beginning to occur at weekends (Kingsley-Jones, 2000).

Communities around airports receive the benefits of income and employment associated with the direct, indirect and induced effects of air-freight activity. In the UK, this has been calculated as somewhere between 60,000 and 82,500 jobs (DETR, 2000). In Europe, it has been estimated that 400,000 people depend upon the integrators directly for their employment (Jones, 2001). The precise number of those employed indirectly as a consequence of the integrators' activities is unknown, but is likely to be in the order of a further 200,000.

However, since the first international aircraft noise regulations were imposed in 1972, there has been considerable growth in the level of public opposition to the disbenefits of aviation – namely, aircraft noise exposure, air pollution, vortex damage, surface travel congestion and deterioration of water quality (Moxon, 2000; Caves and Gosling, 1999; Archer, 1993; Bannister and Button, 1993; Royal Commission, 1994). Unsurprisingly, night-time noise and sleep disturbance are perceived to be much worse than day-time disturbances (Smith, 1989; Pedoe et al, 1996). In general, it appears that the main effect of environmental restrictions to date has been to force the integrated carriers to reorganize their networks to avoid noise-sensitive airports and to encourage them to invest in quieter aircraft. At a stroke, environmental regulations can remove any competitive advantage that an integrator may have achieved as a result of locating at a particular airport, and may threaten the delivery capability of the supply chain.

The night-time noise impact of such cargo aircraft operations upon local communities is becoming of increasing significance; so much so that public opposition to such operations has led to the imposition of night-time curfews at airports. Proliferation of local noise regulations has developed: whereas London Heathrow, Amsterdam Schiphol and Madrid Barajas each have a quota count system to restrict night-time operations, Brussels uses a different quota system and the Italian government recently considered a proposal to ban all night-time operations.

A series of recent cases illustrates the implications of stricter noise regulations for the operations of the integrated carriers. Stringent noise restrictions at one individual airport location may solve a problem locally, but without an upgraded air fleet will only shift the noise burden to another airport. TNT Express moved its main European hub across the border from Cologne in Germany to Liege in Belgium because of night-time noise restrictions that banned operations of its ageing Boeing 727s – the typical workhorse of the integrated carriers. When it began to operate at Liege in 1998, it was confronted by a 5000-strong demonstration against its relocation (De Wulf, 1998); as a consequence, TNT Express is under constant pressure to operate newer, quieter aircraft.

Nuremburg in Germany subsequently banned Boeing 727 operations, which led to DHL rescheduling and re-routing cargo away from the airport. It has been estimated that, as a result, the locality lost over 400 jobs at DHL and the airport (Jones, 2001). DHL tackled the problem by re-routing and redistributing traffic across its European network, with the direct effect of a lowering of delivery service levels. This has been cited by DHL as one of the key factors for a major production plant halving its production (Jones, 2001).

Brussels National, where DHL currently has its main European hub, has tightened noise regulations and plans to impose severe restrictions on night-time operations. Regulation has become more severe since 1994, and in 1999 the minister for transport tried to close down the night-time operation altogether with little notice period (De Wulf, 2000). The irony of this situation was that the Belgian government had given DHL a number of incentives to locate its main hub at Brussels during the late 1980s. The current situation will mean the removal of all Boeing 727 operations, the mainstay of the airline's fleet, by January 2003 (Ewers, 2001). Permission to continue using Brussels at night was only granted on the basis of DHL's investment of US$1.3 billion in 44 newly converted Boeing 757 aircraft that meet the proposed noise restrictions.

In response to pressure on its main Brussels hub in 1995, DHL began to develop sub-hubs and today these are at Bergamo, Copenhagen, Vitoria, Metz, Cologne and East Midlands, which provide them with alternative routings for cargo and less dependence upon Brussels. Extra pressure for capacity at previously less-utilized points in the integrator's network has placed new challenges on the airports selected as sub-hubs in DHL's network and has provided new challenges to maintain supply chain networks. A case study of the East Midlands sub-hub highlights some of the issues faced by integrated carriers and provides insight into some of the strategic responses that are being considered.

CASE STUDY: DHL AT EAST MIDLANDS AIRPORT

Restrictions at Brussels Airport have led to growth for DHL being re-routed via sub-hub points such as East Midlands Airport in the UK. The data tells its own

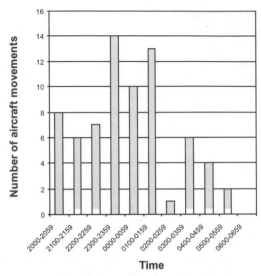

Figure 9.2 *Air-freight movements at East Midlands Airport: 20:00–07:00hrs*

story. Freight uplift through East Midlands has grown from 11,116 tonnes in 1990 to 178,770 tonnes in 2000 (CAA, 2001), a staggering 1500 per cent increase compared to the UK average of 95 per cent for the same period. The vast bulk of this uplift is due to the overnight activities of DHL, although TNT Express, UPS and the Royal Mail are also major operaters.

In order to cater for current and further growth, and in a joint finance venture with East Midlands Airport Limited (the first of its type in Europe), DHL opened a new 50,000m² sortation hub facility in April 2000 at a cost of UK£70 million with a new 165,000m² cargo apron at a cost of UK£15 million to accommodate 18 aircraft stands. Although capacity is available to meet forecast growth of throughput up to over 1000 tonnes per night, this facility currently copes with a cargo throughput of 400–500 tonnes per night with 48 daily aircraft movements. The pattern of air-freighter movements for all freight operators based at the airport is shown in Figure 9.2. Of the 63 movements between 21:00–06:00hrs, DHL's operations typically account for 40 of these.

The growth of night freight operations at the airport has prompted increased pressure from local residents concerned about noise nuisance and sleep disturbance. It is also a major focus of deliberations for the East Midlands Airport Independent Consultative Forum. In order to address these concerns, DHL has entered into close partnership with the airport company to introduce noise-related operational restrictions. Strategies that the airport and DHL are developing in response to these concerns include:

• introduction of noise-preference routes to ensure that aircraft overfly the least number of people possible;
• installation of aircraft noise and track-monitoring equipment;
• differential charging between day and night-time cargo operations;
• restrictions on flight operations to avoid overflying local villages;

- a new noise insulation scheme, as part of which night freight operators are charged more for operating at night;
- a community fund to be set up to receive charges from airlines that operate aircraft beyond agreed noise criteria; all proceeds go to the local community, environmental projects and insulation of homes within a defined noise contour;
- recruitment from the immediate community;
- noise-preferential routes for truck access.

The airport company has been keen to point out that an estimated 1700 jobs depend upon night-time activities at the airport, including around 500 employed directly by DHL (Spooner, 2001). Proposals to restrict night-time operations by the airport's local planning authority, North West Leicestershire District Council, provoked a response of 53 per cent in favour of restrictions and 47 per cent against. This highlights the uncertainty of the planning system because this authority did not object to the proposed development of the sortation hub when the planning application was submitted and approved in 1998. As discussed above in the context of events at Cologne and Nuremburg airports, such restrictions could potentially have a major negative impact on DHL's ability to deliver a network operation by increasing supply-chain times and costs for all of the firms that depend upon DHL's service standards. The actual implications of this proposal have yet to be quantified but are likely to be national and international in scale, given the role of East Midlands as a key hub in DHL's intra-European and European–North American network operations.

The issues identified and discussed above can now be brought together and synthesized in order to understand the different possible operational conditions that the integrators may have to face in the near future. What follows is a set of four contrasting and conjectural visions of possible outcomes to resolving the conflicts between integrators' operations and community concerns.

VISIONS OF THE FUTURE

Visions of the future (1) – regulation of night-time operations

Night-time bans already apply at many airports and, as discussed above, there is growing pressure to implement them elsewhere. It is therefore quite possible to envisage the equivalent of the London airports' 'quota count system' being applied to airports such as East Midlands. Such a system (based upon London Heathrow) combines five components: the determination of a night period (eg 23:00–07:00); the definition of aircraft noise levels according to an agreed metric (eg effective perceived noise level – or 'EPNdB'); their categorization into a set of discrete bands (eg six bands between <90 and >102 EPNdB); a weighting scheme for each noise band (eg an aircraft with a noise level of >102 EPNdB carries a penalty 16 times greater than an aircraft emitting between 90 and 92.9 EPNdB); and, finally, an agreed annual noise quota (eg 9750). For aircraft with a weighting of 1 (eg emitting 90 to 92.9 EPNdB), the maximum number of movements permitted would be identical to the agreed noise quota – 9750; however, if all aircraft were operated with a penalty weight of 4 (eg emitting 96 to 98.9 EPNdB), the equivalent maximum number of movements would be reduced to 2438. In addition, it is a simple administrative task to exclude operations by the noisiest aircraft types during the night period. Any aircraft classified with a weight of, for example, 8 or 16 may not be scheduled to land or take off between 23:00 and 07:00hrs.

What would this mean for an airport such as East Midlands and an operator such as DHL? If the airport's noise regime was regulated as per the London airports by government through its UK Department for Transport, Local Government and the Regions (DTLR), it is clear that many of DHL's and other operators' movements could run contrary to an agreed noise quota scheme – and with it the probability of these operators having to withdraw. But what would be the implications for the logistics industry and its customers? Clearly, it would require an in-depth strategic re-evaluation of supply chains. Very many supply chains are focused upon next-morning delivery as a *sine qua non*. It may be no bad thing to require proper end-to-end reassessment of whether this is really so essential (Whitelegg, 1997). The trade-off between speed and overall supply chain cost could be reconsidered and the road versus air mode decision re-evaluated. Given that it costs some ten times more to carry cargo by air than by truck, maybe more freight could be trucked (Macbeth, 2001), a move that may actually lower supply-chain costs.

This amounts to asking what the consequences would be for the supply chain if the integrators no longer operated at night time but were forced to operate by day. How much would this slow down the supply chain? Perhaps reliable delivery is really the critical factor rather than 12-hour delivery times? What would be the impact of shifting the air-freight element of the supply chain outside of the night-period time window? Could genuinely time-critical material be flown in smaller, less noise-sensitive aircraft? Of course, consideration of these options would need to take account of increased journey times and transaction costs, as well as the environmental implications of an increase in truck journeys across congested European road networks.

Visions of the future (2) – the polluter pays

An alternative market-based scenario is that night-time operations are permitted to continue, but that those responsible for generating the noise nuisance are charged the full social cost for the nuisance they cause. There is already a precedent for this, with the noisiest aircraft being charged additional landing fees. However, to date there is little agreement as to what this full-cost recovery approach would amount to and there is no agreed formula for calculating either its incidence or the likely additional cost (Whitelegg, 1997; Royal Commission, 1994; Maddison et al, 1996). In addition, there is no guarantee that the monies accumulated would be hypothecated and redirected to those directly affected by the noise nuisance in the form of direct or indirect monetary compensation. If a market-based full-cost recovery solution is proposed along the lines indicated above, then that solution must be a complete market-based solution where some of the benefits are returned directly to those in distress. The scheme proposed at East Midlands and outlined above goes part way in this direction and is likely to set a trend as one of the first to link the generators of noise (airlines) to the sufferers of the noise financially – albeit indirectly.

Clearly, this approach would increase the cost of night flights and, hence, would increase the cost of time-sensitive delivery. This would again require many supply chains to be reassessed, this time via the market mechanism of the increased costs of current operations being absorbed directly by those responsible for generating the external costs in the first place and compensating those affected.

Visions of the future (3) – relocation of the noise burden

As has been seen from the case studies, the integrators under discussion have already had to move airports and it is likely that more relocations will be required. In fact, they have a long history of moving between airports, with an average stay of around five to seven years at any one site in the UK. They have also been remarkably reluctant to commit capital in the form of sinking their own funds into infrastructure. (This partly explains why DHL's decision to invest its own capital in a new sortation hub at East Midlands took the industry by surprise.) No doubt, the search will continue to find new intermodal hubs for their operations at an airport and a local community that will tolerate the downside of these types of operation. Indeed, there continue to be airports – often ex-military airfields such as Alconbury (north of London) and Finningley (in south Yorkshire) – that indicate that they would welcome night flights. However, such locations are becoming fewer as every year passes and, by definition, are relatively remote from the population and business centres whom they aim to serve.

In such circumstances, and given such uncertainties about their ability to sustain their operations, the impacts on integrators' network robustness and schedule designs become increasingly sub-optimal and operating costs rise. Every move typically involves increased road transport distances and, hence, increases the cost (and time taken) of the services offered. In addition, as shown by the East Midlands Airport case study, while the welcome may initially be warm for the job opportunities offered and the economic activity created, local communities quickly become disenchanted when their sleep is disturbed as night-time operations intensify.

Visions of the future (4) – managing the local community interface

Given the absence of either direct regulatory intervention and control over night-time flights or the use of market mechanisms to compensate those directly affected, it is hardly surprising to find that local communities are beginning to question why they have to put up with the actions of those who are directly responsible – in this case, the integrators. After all, it is they who fly their aircraft into and out of local airports, intensively at night, and using typically 'older' and noisier aircraft than those that fly during the day. On a network-wide basis, but particularly at the busiest network points such as East Midlands and Brussels, there is a growing need for integrators to work directly with both the airport and the local community to manage relations more effectively than hitherto.

Until now, those operating aircraft have tended to assume that it is the airport owners' responsibility to maintain 'good neighbour' relationships. Several European airports such as Manchester have consistently demonstrated 'good practice' in this area over a long period, prioritizing environmental mitigation, and signing up to environmental targets agreed and set in close partnership with the surrounding community (Pedoe, Raper and Holden, 1996; Caves and Gosling, 1999).

The East Midlands case shows that partnership with its local community regarding night-time operations is now being seriously pursued, and it is likely that this model may be applied more widely. It is better for the operators to develop a dialogue and to engage with their local communities rather than face confrontation, which may result in draconian measures to appease local political sensitivities. Direct interaction between integrators and their communities could lead to a better understanding of the problems facing both, and to local solutions being found to reduce nuisance while not significantly interfering with operations. In this context, further research could explore how, for example, noise monitoring and mapping techniques could be developed in partnership with the affected community to try and uncover ways of facilitating the expansion of supply-chain operations in a more socially responsible and environmentally acceptable manner.

In turn, the local community may benefit from being more clearly informed of the value of integrator activities in terms of employment and the wider economic repercussions of a slower supply chain. That said, a core problem is that the local community suffers the noise, while at present the benefits do not accrue to them exclusively even if they do contribute on a national scale.

Conclusions

It is clear beyond doubt that if night-time air-freight operations are to continue at airports with nearby residential populations, then 'business as usual' is simply not an option for future growth. The implication is that, just as the actual operational capacity of an airport is always less than its design capacity, mitigating the effects of night-time noise nuisance will constrain operational capacity further. In the UK, there are administrative mechanisms whereby any airport can, in principle, be designated under section 80 of the Civil Aviation Act 1982 for the purposes of section 78 of the act: that is, 'for the purpose of avoiding, limiting or mitigating the effect of noise and vibration' connected with aircraft taking off or landing. This designation process results in the present noise curfews in place at the three London airports and, with it, the application of the quota count system. This is the primary weapon that the government currently has in its armoury against aircraft noise – but it is a weapon that it chooses to use sparingly and as a last resort. If airports and integrators wish to avoid the prospect of its application to their airports and their operations, then they must act jointly to resolve locally what is a local issue.

Although central government has the policy responsibility for aviation, its policy instruments are relatively blunt and unyielding in the context of intervening in local circumstances. However, government policy does provide broad guidance on what it envisages as appropriate policy objectives in such situations; these objectives are to:

- strike a balance between the need to protect local communities from excessive aircraft noise levels at night and to provide for air services to operate at night where they are of benefit to the local, regional and national economy;
- ensure that the competitive factors affecting UK airports and airlines and the wider employment and economic implications are taken into account;

- encourage the use of quieter aircraft at night; and
- put in place arrangements that will bring about further improvements in the night noise climate around the airport over time (DETR, 1999).

If it proves impossible to strike a balance between the need to protect local communities and the ability of integrators to continue operations, then the continuation and growth of JIT systems that the integrators facilitate is under severe threat, which could lengthen delivery times by as much as 100 per cent. Reduced night-time operations, an increased emphasis on the polluter paying and relocation of operations are all unattractive options for integrated carriers; this makes it critically important for the managements of integrators, airports and other supply-chain stakeholders to come together more effectively with the local community through joint dialogue. This, in turn, raises questions about the ways in which formal consultation and participation arrangements function, as well as issues regarding their effectiveness. It is clear that in helping to strike a balance between different and irreconcilable interests, it is necessary to recognize that no one group of interests will be entirely satisfied with the decisions taken (DETR, 1999) – in which case some mechanism must be found whereby benefits accruing to one party (eg airlines) can compensate for the costs imposed on others (eg local communities) (Goodwin, 1993).

While the relative significance of the four visions described here will depend upon the particular context, it is clear that the cost in terms of time and money will be borne by the supply chain to an ever-increasing extent in order to reflect the social and environmental implications for communities affected by the operation of aircraft at night. Currently, the problem is seen narrowly as an airline-noise nuisance issue. Further research is needed to assess the precise economic impact of the supply chain continuing to deliver in its current form, and the opportunity cost of restricting future growth, particularly for sectors such as e-commerce.

Once these are known, then government and planners can take a more informed view about the balance between the value of night operations and their environmental and social externalities. Without the economic side of the argument, politicians may be swayed by the rising complaints of residents and the true value of the integrators' operations may be missed, perhaps with economic consequences to the very people who are complaining!

Prior to permitting development, planners need to issue clear guidance to integrators regarding where it is acceptable to operate and the limits, in terms of night noise, in the form of planning conditions and obligations that may be attached to the granting of planning permission. Authorities should not, as in the East Midlands and Brussels cases, gain the social, economic and political advantages of attracting additional employment and then try to restrict the modus operandi of a company with regulations that effectively bring its operations to a halt.

If the achievement of reduced delivery times is to continue, then much will depend upon the ability of the integrators to forge partnerships with local communities to implement measures that will meet the ground rules of corporate responsibility in the 21st century, particularly in the UK and Europe. Meeting shareholder expectations is still crucial, but is now only one part of the 'triple bottom line', where financial probity is now conjoined with the need to meet social and environmental obligations.

ACKNOWLEDGEMENTS

The authors wish to express their thanks to the following for their input to this research: staff at DHL; East Midlands Airport Limited; and members of the East Midlands Airport Independent Consultative Forum.

REFERENCES

Archer, J (1993), *Aircraft Emissions and the Environment*, Oxford Institute for Energy Studies, Oxford

Bannister, D and Button, K (eds) (1993) *Transport, the Environment and Sustainable Development*, E and F N Spon, London

Bates, J (2000) 'Cashing in on the e-tail revolution', *Airport World*, vol 5, no 5, pp47–51

Boeing (2001) *World Air Cargo Forecast 2000/2001*, Boeing Commercial Airplane Group, Seattle

Bowersox, D and Closs, D (1996) *Logistical Management*, McGraw Hill, London

CAA (2001) *UK Airport Statistics*, Aviation Data Unit, Civil Aviation Authority, London, Table 13.2 'Freight 1990–2000', www.caa.co.uk/erg/erg_stats/sgl.asp?sglid=3

Capello, R and Gillespie, A (1993) 'Transport, communications and spatial organisation: future trends and conceptual frameworks' in Giannopoulos, G and Gillespie, A (eds) *Transport and Communications Innovation in Europe*, Belhaven Press, London

Caves, R and Gosling, G (1999) *Airport Strategic Planning*, Elsevier, London

De Wulf, H (1998) 'Overnight parcels carriers face noisy opposition', *Flight International*, vol 153, no 4620, p11

De Wulf, H (2000) 'Noise limits will stymie Brussels cargo hub', *Flight International*, vol 157, no 4716, p10

DETR (1999) *Night Restrictions at Heathrow, Gatwick and Stansted (revised restrictions with effect from 31 October 1999)*, 22 June, Department of Environment, Transport and the Regions, London

DETR (2000) *UK Air Freight Study Report*, Department of Environment, Transport and the Regions, London

Ewers, G (2001) 'The Belgian presidency and airports – a clear and present danger?', *Airport Business Communique*, April/May, p21

Goodwin, P (1993) 'Efficiency and the environment: possibilities of a green-gold coalition' in Bannister, D and Button, K (eds) (1993) *Transport, The Environment and Sustainable Development*, E and F N Spon, London

Humphreys, I, Gillingwater, D and Watson, R (1999*)* 'Globalisation and logistics service providers: a strategic position analysis', *Managing Enterprises*, Proceedings of the 2nd International Conference, Newcastle University, Newcastle, NSW

IPCC SPM (1999) *Aviation and the Global Atmosphere Summary for Policymakers*, Special Report of IPCC Working Groups I and III in collaboration with the Scientific Assessment Panel to the Montreal Protocol on Substances that Deplete the Ozone Layer, J E Penner, D H Lister, D J Griggs, D J Dokken and M McFarland (eds) Intergovernmental Panel on Climate Change, Geneva

Jones, T (2001) 'Aviation and the environment: the impact on express logistics operators', *Global Aviation, Aviation and the Environment*, Conference Proceedings, Euromoney, Amsterdam

Kingsley-Jones, M (2000) 'Express delivery', *Flight International*, vol 158, no 4747, pp43–46

Macbeth (2001) *DHL Network Strategy*, Presentation at East Midlands Airport Hub, March

Maddison, D, Pearce, D, Johansson, O, Calthrop, E, Litman, T and Verhoef, E (1996) *The True Costs of Road Transport*, Earthscan Publications, London

Moxon, J (2000) 'Environmental effort', *Flight International*, vol 158, no 4738, pp116–128

Pedoe, N, Raper, D and Holden, J (eds) (1996) *Environmental Management at Airports*, Thomas Telford, London

Peters, M and Wright, D (1999) *International Air Express Distribution*, Cranfield University, Cranfield

Royal Commission (1994) *Transport and the Environment*, 18th Report, Royal Commission on Environmental Pollution, Oxford University Press, Oxford

Smith, M (1989) *Aircraft Noise*, Cambridge University Press, Cambridge

Spooner, J (2001) 'Consultation results show balanced views', News Release, 17 April, East Midlands Airport Limited, Castle Donington

Whitelegg, J (1997) *Critical Mass: Transport, Environment and Society in the Twenty-first Century*, Pluto Press, London

Chapter 10

The potential offered by aircraft and engine technologies

Jacquetta Lee[1]

INTRODUCTION

Almost 100 years ago, Orville Wright took to the air at Kitty Hawk, North Carolina, in the Wright Flyer. Since then, airframes and engines have developed at an amazing pace. The first gas turbine propulsion system, developed by Whittle and Von Ohain in the 1930s, has evolved from turbo jets through turbo props to today's high by-pass ratio engines, and the propulsive efficiency and reliability of the system has improved enormously. Over the last 40 years alone, the industry has dramatically improved fuel efficiency and reduced noise and emissions. Engine and airframe weights have been significantly reduced per passenger kilometre, and safety and reliability have improved by more than a factor of ten during the last 25 years, allowing the development of twin-engine long-range transport with potentially lower associated emissions (Birch, 2000).

While aviation has an impressive record in reducing its environmental impacts, it faces an interesting future where the environment is likely to play an increasingly important role. It has been suggested that the predicted growth of 5 per cent per annum in passenger traffic, and still higher for freight transport, will outstrip the improvements in fuel consumption, emissions and noise that can be expected through evolutionary engine and airframe design (IPCC, 1999, p11). Thus, the environmental burden resulting from air transport is likely to increase. In addition, achieving further reductions in fuel burn, emissions and noise is also set to become increasingly difficult as trade-offs between these key impacts become more acute.

The near-term future offers a range of evolutionary solutions for both engine and airframe; their application depends upon a dialogue with all stakeholders to ensure that potential improvements do not unduly focus on one aspect to the detriment of

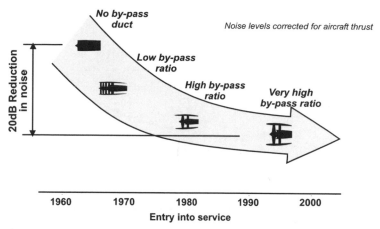

Source: Birch, 2000

Figure 10.1 *Aircraft noise*

any other. The long-term future has the potential to offer revolutionary solutions that may significantly reduce the environmental burden of the aviation industry. For these solutions to play a part in the industry of the future, a number of key factors need to be considered. First, drivers need to be put in place to stimulate the industry to develop these revolutionary concepts. This motivation could come from a wide range of sources – from environmental concerns and legislation to increased aviation fuel prices. Second, the ability to develop from a concept to a product, and third, the opportunity to make changes (Birch, 2000). A variety of alternative solutions are currently being evaluated, from innovative engine/airframe configurations, active laminar flow[2] and advanced combustion technologies to alternative fuel systems. The ability of these technologies to meet expectations, individually or in combination, will determine the future effect of aviation on the environment and, ultimately, the part it will play in the transport system of tomorrow.

Noise

Noise has traditionally been a key design issue for air transport systems, especially for communities around airports, and is subject to international noise legislation. The industry has cut noise levels by 20 decibels (dB) during the last 30 years (Air Transport Action Group, 1999, p11), as is shown in Figure 10.1.

Despite the growth in air traffic in recent years, noise exposure to communities living in close proximity to airports has been decreasing. This has been due to the retirement of older, noisier aircraft and the development and incorporation of noise-reducing technologies within the remainder of the fleet. However, in the coming years it is expected that noise levels will start to rise again as the continued growth of the fleet will outweigh further reductions in the average noise levels – see Figure 10.2 (Walsh, 2000).

Future noise control must be achieved by a combination of source noise reduction, developments in operational procedures, such as take-off and landing corridors, and improved land-use planning systems.

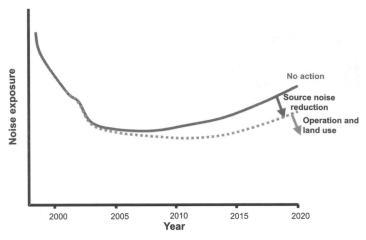

Source: Walsh, 2000

Figure 10.2 *Noise trends*

Fuel efficiency

The fuel consumption of modern aircraft gas turbines is now less than half – per passenger kilometre – of what it used to be when the Comet was introduced during the 1960s. Over 60 per cent of this saving is due to engine improvements (Rolls-Royce plc, 1999, p15), as is illustrated in Figure 10.3. Increased engine efficiency comes from a combination of increased core thermal efficiency (mainly through increased core temperatures and pressures) and propulsive efficiency (through the use of high by-pass ratios, defined as the ratio of total air flowing through the engine to the air flowing through the core).

In addition, changes to aircraft pressurization and air-conditioning systems have reduced the requirement for engine bleed flow, thus improving engine efficiency. The aerodynamic efficiency of the airframe has increased through the use of advanced computational fluid dynamics (CFD) and improved wind-tunnel testing techniques. Modifications to the shape of the engine nacelle inlet section have also reduced drag and increased efficiency.

One feature that has significantly helped reduced fuel consumption is weight, with both airframe and engines showing a continued decrease. Lower weight leads to a lower work requirement for each aircraft mission. For example, a reduction of 1 unit of engine weight can lead to between 1.5 and 4 units of aircraft empty weight (IPCC, 1999, p229), particularly through reduced structural requirements and lower fuel volume. The lower power required for take-off means less noise, and the reduced fuel burn leads to fewer emissions. Today, engines are approximately 30 per cent lighter than their equivalent ancestors 30 years ago (Beesley, 2000). This has contributed to an overall reduction in operating empty weight (OEW) per seat of approximately 50 per cent (Daggett, 2001). These weight reductions have been achieved by the incorporation, in both the engine and airframe, of lighter and stronger materials, such as aluminium and titanium alloys, and the use of composites for non-load-bearing structures.

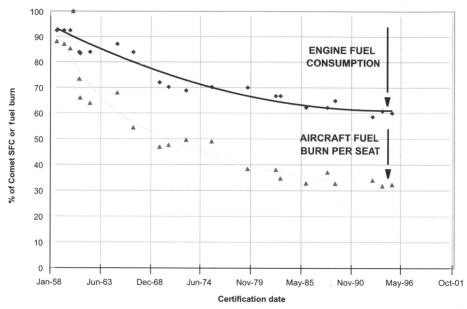

Source: Rolls-Royce data
Note: Since the introduction of jet-powered airliners the improvement in fuel burn has been dramatic. This chart shows the trends in engine fuel consumption and fuel burn per passenger over a 1000 nautical miles (nm) mission relative to a specific De-Havilland Comet 4 powered by Rolls-Royce Avon engines. The markers in the figure represent specific aircraft on a standard 1000nm mission, subject to typical international reserve rules for fuel, and using three class seating. The vertical scale is normalized to the correct date. Data for the newest aircraft was unknown at the time. It could be argued that this fuel consumption improvement is much better than other modes of transport, and that the fuel is an important part of the cost of flying. The emissions of carbon dioxide (CO_2) and water vapour will be reduced by a corresponding amount, but note that this will not necessarily help the contrail issue. The emissions levels of carbon monoxide (CO), hydrocarbons (HCs), nitrogen oxide (NO_x) and smoke have changed at different rates.

Figure 10.3 *Fuel efficiency and specific fuel consumption (SFC)*

Emissions

The combustion products from engines consist of unburned hydrocarbons (UHCs), carbon monoxide (CO), nitrogen oxide (NO_x), sulphur dioxide (SO_2), water vapour, carbon dioxide (CO_2), soot (particulate emissions) and smoke (combustion emission particulates that contribute to a visible plume), some of which augment ground-level smog and local air pollution. CO_2, water vapour and SO_2 are related directly to the fuel consumption at the various flight stages; but NO_x, CO, UHCs and soot are significantly influenced by the engine power setting and engine inlet conditions. CO and UHCs result from incomplete combustion, and are mostly produced at low power levels. This has been effectively controlled by optimized air/fuel-mixing systems, and hence emissions at ground level have been substantially reduced to relatively low levels. NO_x and soot, however, are mainly produced at high power levels.

NO_x emissions are more difficult to control, as the quantity of NO_x released is dependent upon the temperature at which the fuel is combusted, and the time held at a particular temperature. The higher of either of these two factors, the more NO_x is formed. Continuous design improvements to the combustor over the last 20 years have ensured that NO_x formation has been reduced by nearly 50 per cent, despite engine temperatures rising by approximately 300°C (Ruffles, 1998). Aircraft NO_x emissions, as well as UHC, smoke and CO, are currently regulated through the landing and take-off (LTO) cycle, but the regulatory authorities are investigating the possibility of extending this to cover NO_x emissions during cruise.

FACTORS AFFECTING DEVELOPMENT

Market growth

Average passenger air transport (revenue passenger kilometres) has been growing at a minimum of 5 and 6 per cent over the last 40 years. Projections of future traffic indicate growth rates for passenger traffic of around 5 per cent and higher for freight transport (Rolls-Royce, 2000). This expected growth will impact upon a number of areas, such as increased congestion at airports and the need to expand existing capacity, but also operational issues such as flight path management and air traffic management systems. Communities local to airports are more involved in airport planning procedures, and can be expected to increase their involvement in the future, perhaps demanding restrictions on night-time traffic, local air quality assurances or improved access to the airport before consenting to airport expansion plans.

The expected effect on the aviation growth rate by the revolution in electronic communication is not yet clear. It could lessen the need for business travel through Internet-based business transactions or, conversely, increase business travel because web-based advertising reaches a wider target audience, resulting in more face-to-face contact. Other transport systems such as high-speed rail and fast ships can offer alternative travel arrangements for some journeys currently undertaken by air, such as short-haul flights.

Global climate change

Climate change is a major concern, and the Intergovernmental Panel on Climate Change (IPCC) has accordingly issued the special report *Aviation and the Global Atmosphere* (IPCC, 1999). This report highlights the major contributing factors to climate change that are believed to result from aviation – factors that are discussed in more detail elsewhere in Chapter 5. While it is understood that there remains some considerable uncertainty about the radiative forcing effects of aircraft emissions, it is clear that CO_2, NO_x and contrails play a significant part. As a result, existing international legislation covering emissions is likely to become more stringent, and it is becoming clear that attention will focus not only upon emissions produced during landing and take-off, but also at cruise, and will apply to both engine combustion and acoustic emissions (Birch, 2000).

The reduction in fuel consumption and NO_x over the past 30 years has been driven by economic and environmental factors. However, the environment and, more specifically, global climate change should have a significant effect on the future development of the aviation industry.

Local regulations

Local regulations are becoming more commonplace. Most major airports have noise limits, which, if contravened, can result in fines levied against offending aircraft operators. Some airports, such as Washington, simply do not allow aircraft above a certain noise threshold to land. More recently, Zurich Airport has started to apply NO_x limits. While these regulations limit noise emissions near the airport, there are some concerns over their influence on the goal of reducing the total impact of aviation over all flight stages. Increasingly stringent local regulations may have the effect of driving airframe and engine design away from the optimum configuration for fuel efficiency, as airlines request aircraft that do not incur local fines for either noise or emissions.

CURRENT DESIGN LIMITS

The dominant engine/airframe configuration, a classical swept wing with podded underwing engines, first emerged in the form of the Boeing B-47 Stratojet bomber in 1947. Since then, advances in materials, structures and aerodynamics have improved and refined the design to what we commonly see today. However, some limits to future developments are now being approached.

The three main environmental issues that result from engines are fuel burn (and, hence, CO_2 and water vapour emissions), other gaseous engine emissions (most notably NO_x) and noise. These issues need to be considered alongside optimum and/or desired range, cost and aircraft payload.

Within the environmental issues alone, trade-offs between fuel burn and NO_x exist. In simplistic terms, increasing the combustion temperature and operating pressure leads to conditions that give increased NO_x formation. The converse of this, combustors designed to reduce NO_x through efficient mixing of fuel and air prior to combustion, can impede increases in overall pressure ratio (OPR) and turbine entry temperature (TET) aimed at increasing fuel efficiency. Noise and fuel efficiency also conflict; reducing noise through the development of extremely large by-pass ratios increases fuel burn through increased weight and drag, and reducing noise by noise shields increases OEW and, thus, fuel burn. An additional issue to consider is the effect of engine exhaust temperatures on contrail formation where there are indications that modern, efficient aircraft may be more likely to form contrails (Schumann, 2000).

Other issues need to be resolved. For example, the optimum configuration for a long-range aircraft would be for minimum fuel consumption and weight to achieve range targets that can exceed 8000nm. Good climb performance, an advantage in crowded airspace, can be achieved but at the expense of cruise fuel consumption or high maintenance costs. Some aerodynamic losses are inevitable, and the potential for improving lift to drag ratio (L/D) with fully turbulent boundary layers for the current aircraft configuration is thought to be limited.

FUTURE EVOLUTIONARY OPTIONS

The continued development of both engine and airframe technologies will produce more efficient, cleaner and quieter aircraft; however, it is unlikely that these evolutionary developments will provide the large reductions in environmental impact that have been seen during the last 30 years. This can be seen in Figures 10.1 and 10.3, where the levelling out of the trends would suggest a technology floor is being reached. Perhaps more importantly, predictions by both the IPCC report and the Royal Commission for Environmental Pollution (RCEP) have indicated that to become sustainable, CO_2 emissions need to be reduced by 60 per cent from current levels (RCEP, 2000, p2).

Engine

Specific fuel consumption

The overall efficiency of an engine is the product of thermal and propulsive efficiency. Figure 10.4 shows how the thermal efficiency of an engine can only be significantly improved if both OPR and TET are raised together.

To date, the increases in OPR and TET have been achieved through advances in technology with the development of smaller high-speed cores, materials with improved temperature properties, and turbine components with better cooling characteristics. For thermal efficiency to increase further by this route, these associated improvements must also continue. If not, then any gains in thermal efficiency will be eroded through increased cooling requirements and component scale effects. An estimated 3 per cent gain in thermal efficiency can be achieved over the next 20 years, provided advances in materials and cooling technology continue.

The most practical option available to increase the propulsive efficiency of the engine is to reduce the jet velocity. This has been achieved through the introduction of progressively larger by-pass ratios. Modern engines have by-pass ratios in the range of five to nine; however, increases much beyond this will lead to the need for a gearbox between the power turbine and the fan, increasing weight and reducing the benefits in efficiency gained through having the larger by-pass ratio. Above a by-pass ratio of about 15, the duct must be removed otherwise drag and weight penalties become severe. Very large by-pass ratio engines cannot be accommodated on existing subsonic aircraft, as there is insufficient space to hang the engine below the wing.

A possible development to increase the propulsive efficiency of an engine is to improve the mixing of the propulsor and main flows in the duct before the exhaust nozzle. It has been estimated that efficiency gains in the order of 1 per cent could be achieved in this way (IPCC, 1999, p233).

Noise

At take-off, engine noise dominates, but at landing the noise from the engine and the airframe is similar. The main noise sources in the engine are the fan and the front compressor stages, the low-pressure turbine stages and the exhaust flow. While the most significant reductions in noise have been achieved through the introduction of

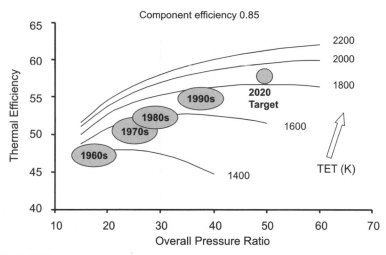

Source: Birch, 2000

Figure 10.4 *Thermal efficiency variations*

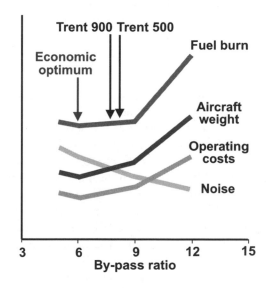

Source: Birch, 2000

Figure 10.5 *Trade-off between noise and fuel efficiency*

high by-pass ratio engines, continued increases in by-pass ratio can lead away from the optimum engine design. Figure 10.5 shows the trade-offs that exist between increasing by-pass ratio and fuel consumption.

Additional noise reducing techniques can be employed, such as reducing fan tip speed and careful shaping of fan blades to reduce fan noise. Noise from turbo machinery can be minimized by optimizing the number of rotating parts and careful rotor/stator spacing. The addition of acoustic liners to the inlet and exhaust sections of the nacelle can also reduce noise, but this can add weight to the aircraft, thus creating a trade-off with fuel consumption. Figure 10.6 shows areas of research in this field.

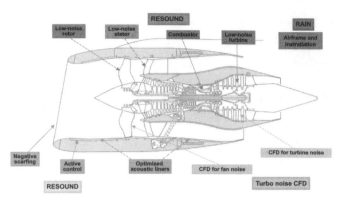

Source: Walsh, 2001

Figure 10.6 *Noise reduction programmes and technologies*

Research is continuing into reduced noise from aircraft engines with programmes in both the US and Europe. The National Aeronautics and Space Administration (NASA) has set noise reduction targets of 10dB within ten years and 20dB within 25 years. Within Europe, a similar target has been set to reduce noise by 10dB within the next decade and a range of European Union (EU) funded projects are currently underway.

Emissions

International limits are currently imposed for UHCs, smoke, CO and NO_x, measured during a standardized take-off and landing cycle. At ground level, all emissions except NO_x have been reduced to relatively low levels. The development of the modern combustor and its effect on NO_x emissions is shown in Figure 10.7. Figure 10.7 also shows the legislation currently enforced for NO_x emissions (CAEP 2). The International Civil Aviation Organization (ICAO) and the Committee on Aviation Environmental Protection (CAEP) have set ever tighter legislation on emissions: CAEP 1 took effect in 1986, CAEP 2 has applied to new engine types since 1996 and all new engines manufactured from 2000, and CAEP 4 is due to take effect from 2004.

Whereas the latest international regulation accounts for high operating pressure ratios, the local regulations in Switzerland give no consideration to those engines operating with a high OPR. This means that at high OPR, even the newest combustor design cannot meet the most stringent NO_x production level, and will thus be subject to landing charges at those airports. The most common combustor currently found in engines today is the single annular combustor. The latest development, the double annular combustor (DAC), provides a reduction in NO_x emission of approximately 12 per cent against the single annular for OPRs of between 25 and 30. However, for higher OPRs, it appears that the current DAC can offer little in the way of lower NO_x.

The future of combustor developments is currently focused upon improving fuel/ air mixing prior to combustion, reducing the peak combustion temperature and thus reducing NO_x formation. Some of the features resulting from research aimed at the next generation of supersonic transport are being incorporated in NO_x reduction programmes for subsonic aircraft. Such programmes are aiming for a 40 per cent

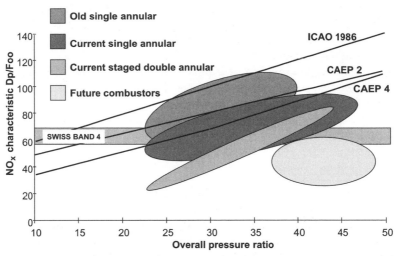

Source: Birch, 2000

Figure 10.7 *Development of combustor technology*

reduction in NO_x relative to CAEP 2 requirements. More radical research programmes in the US are aimed at ultra-low NO_x technology, with targets of a reduction of 70 per cent relative to CAEP 2 requirements.

A new concern that has only recently come to the attention of the industry is the effect of engine exhaust plumes (water vapour, soot and SO_2) at altitude and, specifically, their ability to form contrails that can, given particular atmospheric conditions, form persistent cirrus clouds. Currently, research is being carried out to identify the mechanisms for contrail formation and to determine their environmental impact. The results of this research will feed back into engine and airframe design considerations for future developments.

Airframe

Evolutionary improvements to the airframe can be separated into derivatives of existing features and new developments (but which could still be applied to the conventional airframe shape).

Laminar flow

Achieving laminar flow over the whole of an aircraft frame is extremely difficult, and passive control concepts, such as slotted aerofoils, suction and actively heated/cooled surfaces, are currently being explored. The potential for laminar flow to reduce drag is considerable and is estimated to be up to 80 per cent for long-range aircraft (Poll, 2000, p322), giving a factor of between two and three in specific air range. However, some of the benefits from this will be outweighed by increasing weight and power off-take requirements, needed to drive the suction system. While the concept is sound, some issues need to be considered. The application of laminar flow techniques may lead to an increase in the fuel reserve needed for long-range aircraft in order to counter the effect of potential loss of laminar flow due to degradation of the surfaces during flight. This would reduce the benefits in fuel consumption gained by reduced drag.

Hybrid laminar flow has also been considered. These systems aim to keep the flow attached to the aerodynamic surfaces by sucking ambient air through porous skins. This type of system continues to be evaluated as it raises a number of safety issues. Cleaning of the skin surface would also increase maintenance costs. Application of this technology is believed to have the potential to raise the performance of long-range aircraft, but may be only marginally beneficial or even detrimental for short-range craft.

Other aerodynamic concepts

Other aerodynamic possibilities exist. Riblets (tiny grooves in the direction of air flow) reduce viscous drag and could contribute to a substantial fuel saving if applied over the aircraft surface. However, degradation of the adhesive plastic film bearing the grooves could present a problem. This may reduce not only the manufacturers' enthusiasm to apply the technology, but also that of the airlines. Advanced wing-tip devices reduce induced drag and could contribute significantly to reducing the total airframe drag. Advanced manufacturing methods, improving the surface smoothness of the fuselage and wings, would also reduce drag.

Weight

The weight of the airframe is expected to continue to reduce through the application of lighter alloys for primary structures. Introduction of new alloys requires much testing before eventual certification, a costly and time-consuming process. For non-structural parts, composites are being applied. Weight savings can range from 10 to 30 per cent, with an associated fuel burn saving of between 10 and 15 per cent (Aeronatique Astronautique, 1998, pp34, 44–48, 71–75).

Other weight reduction options exist, such as reducing seat pitch, in-flight entertainment systems, galleys or the elimination of windows. Given the current health concerns regarding seat pitch and the requirements and desires of customers, it is unlikely that these options would be implemented. However, there is the potential to save approximately 2 tonnes of operating empty weight (OEW), which corresponds to an increase of 1 per cent in fuel efficiency (IPCC, 1999, p227).

Noise

Noise is also generated from the airframe in take-off and landing situations, originating from the undercarriage, tail-plane, flaps and wings. Noise reduction programmes, such as RAIN, now nearing completion, have concentrated on reducing airframe noise and are intended to contribute to the EU Framework 5 Technology Platform programme. SILENCER, a new research programme, is due to start in April 2001.

REVOLUTIONARY OPTIONS

It is believed that the reductions in environmental impact from evolutionary improvements in engine and airframe design are likely to be outstripped by growth in air travel. To meet the challenges of the future, innovative configurations, fuels and technologies are being considered as potential directions for the long-term future of the aviation industry. While many evolutionary concepts can be easily separated as applying to either the engine or the airframe, many of the revolutionary ideas require consideration as a fully integrated system.

Some of the options can be applied not only to more radical designs, but also to existing airframe/engine configurations. Such developments include the application of extended 'fly-by-wire' or 'fly-by-light' control systems, full hybrid laminar flow control, geared fan engines, or alternative liquid fuels. Other options can only be applied to radically different airframe/engine configurations.

Innovative developments for existing configurations

Aircraft systems

Extension of existing fly-by-wire and the development of fly-by-light (using fibre optics) technology to include wing load alleviation and pitch stability augmentation has a potential to improve fuel efficiency by 1–3 per cent. Active centre-of-gravity control, reducing tail-plane area by up to 10 per cent, could offer an increased fuel efficiency of 1–2 per cent. On the negative side, flight safety improvements could lead to an increase in OEW, thus counteracting some of the savings created (IPCC, 1999, p228).

Replacing the auxiliary power units (APUs) with advanced fuel cells could reduce noise, fuel burn and emissions at ground level, but could add weight, thus reducing fuel efficiency when in the air. Aerodynamic integration of the interface between the engine and airframe, with the aim of passing the airframe boundary layer through the propulsor, thus eliminating the airframe wake, could provide an increase in propulsive efficiency of up to 5 per cent (IPCC, 1999, p233).

Innovative engine configurations

One potential way to improve the efficiency of the engine is to move from a simple Joule thermodynamic cycle to an inter-cooled recuperative cycle (ICR). This has the potential to substantially improve the thermal efficiency of the engine, while at the same time reducing NO_x emissions. A study has been carried out on the feasibility of such an engine (Plohr, 1999). While the addition of heat exchangers adds to the weight of the engine, it was estimated that this technology could contribute up to a 10 per cent reduction in specific fuel consumption and reduce NO_x emissions by up to 35 per cent. The ongoing CLEAN programme for the European Commission's (EC's) fifth framework programme is aiming to demonstrate this technology.

The More Electric Engine (MEE) and More Electric Aircraft (MEA)

The More Electric Engine (MEE), as seen in Figure 10.8, features electrical generators attached to the engine shafts from which electricity is generated. This can be used in the engine to improve operability or to improve relight capability. Additional features include replacing mechanically operated accessories by those driven by electricity,

Pylon/aircraft-mounted engine systems controller connected to engine via digital highway

Air for pressurization/cabin conditioning supplied by dedicated system

All engine accessories electrically driven

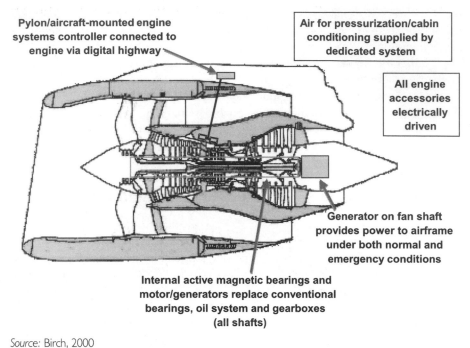

Generator on fan shaft provides power to airframe under both normal and emergency conditions

Internal active magnetic bearings and motor/generators replace conventional bearings, oil system and gearboxes (all shafts)

Source: Birch, 2000

Figure 10.8 *The More Electric Engine*

providing weight savings. Future development could also include removing the need for lubrication through the installation of magnetic bearings.

If the MEE were combined with the More Electric Aircraft (MEA), shown in Figure 10.9, further savings could be made. Potentially, the electricity generated by the engine could eliminate, or at least reduce, the pneumatic and hydraulic aircraft systems. Control actuation and wing anti-icing are also candidates for the use of engine-generated electricity. These technological advances could lead to a more efficient aircraft with reduced fuel consumption during flight and ground-based operations.

Alternative fuels

Jet-fuel composition is tightly controlled, which ensures that exhaust emissions are constant. The one exception to this is sulphur. The effect of removing sulphur entirely from jet fuel would be a small increase in CO_2 emissions resulting from the increased hydrogen required during the refining process, and a possible consequence for the lubrication of fuel pumps.

The introduction of a new fuel type raises many issues, from airport infrastructure changes to compatibility with materials in existing engines and fuel systems. Nevertheless, many alternatives to fossil-derived kerosene have been considered, including alcohols, methane, hydrogen and, more recently, fuels derived from vegetable oils such as soybean or rapeseed and other biomass-derived fuel. Many of these alternatives have been discounted for technical reasons and, currently, only two options appear to have any potential.

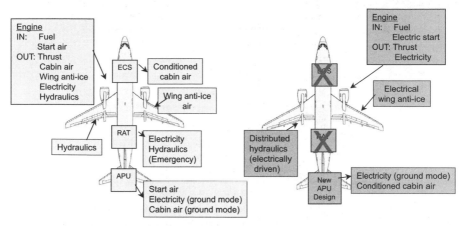

Source: Birch, 2000

Figure 10.9 *The More Electric Aircraft*

Biomass-derived fuel is a prospective candidate, but still has several obstacles to overcome. The Fischer-Tropsch synthesis process (F-T) can successfully create sulphur-free kerosene from natural gas, coal and biomass sources. The use of biomass as the source for the fuel significantly reduces the net amount of CO_2 released into the atmosphere, as that released during the combustion of the fuel will have been previously absorbed when the biomass was growing. However, biomass-derived fuel cannot be completely CO_2 neutral, as energy is required to operate the F-T process. Additional benefits are that existing engine configurations would not need to undergo large modifications to use the fuel, and airport infrastructure could be easily upgraded to cope with the new fuel. Synthesised kerosene is already produced in South Africa by SASOL, indicating that this has commercial potential as an alternative fuel.

The synthesis of biomass-derived fuel could offer a short-term, easily integrated, solution to CO_2 emissions from aircraft. It may be possible that biomass fuel would provide a 'breathing space' to allow more radical technology to be fully developed. However, biomass-derived kerosene requires additional research in order to evaluate the potential CO_2 savings, to determine the land area required to grow sufficient biomass, and to assess the environmental effects associated with the increased agricultural requirements (such as increased use of fertilizers, their manufacture and their effects on groundwater).

Hydrogen-powered aircraft potentially offer a solution to one of the major environmental problems facing aviation: global climate change through the emission of CO_2. With respect to weight, liquid hydrogen has 2.8 times more energy than kerosene, (Klug, 2000), and the major product of its combustion is water. Some of this energy advantage will be lost because of the increased complexity and weight of the fuel system, and especially because of the large tanks required to store the fuel. These large tanks lead to an unusual configuration of a hydrogen-powered aircraft. For large passenger craft, the most common solution is a traditional configuration with the fuel tanks placed on top of the fuselage, increasing drag. Other options are available for smaller aircraft for short-haul flights.

The engine will also need to be modified. One potential problem is that the stoichiometric temperature[3] of hydrogen is about 100°C hotter than kerosene. This has implications not only for the materials in the combustion and turbine area, but also for the formation of NO_x. However, it is believed that the low flame-out limit of hydrogen will enable lean burn, allowing lower temperatures in the combustor, thus limiting NO_x production and keeping engine efficiency at its current level.

There are a number of environmental concerns with using hydrogen as a fuel for aircraft. The consequent water-vapour emissions in the upper atmosphere could exacerbate contrail formation, which would tend to warm the Earth's surface. Although it has been indicated that hydrogen offers a significant reduction in greenhouse potential at all altitudes (IPCC, 1999, p257), studies on the upper atmosphere are continuing and uncertainty still remains. In addition, the energy requirement to mass produce sufficient quantities of liquid hydrogen is considerable, but could be overcome should renewable energy be used. At the current time, however, such renewable energy sources are not widely available. The final impediments to the introduction of hydrogen are the costs and logistics of developing the required infrastructure to support switching to the new fuel.

It is believed that liquid hydrogen can only offer an environmental benefit if it is produced using renewable energy. The technology currently exists to do this; but, currently, it is not economically competitive with kerosene. It is, however, the only alternative fuel that would completely eliminate the direct production of CO_2 from aircraft.

Innovative configurations

A huge range of alternatives to the traditional fuselage and podded engines exists. These have included multi-hull layouts, span loaders, tandem wing layouts, flatbed layouts and the use of canards (Jenkinson et al, 1999). Indeed, one Russian design has incorporated some aspects of all the potential new designs. At the current time, the blended wing body concept (BWB) is receiving most attention.

The BWB concept could offer a significant improvement in the operational and environmental costs of air transport. It offers a potential reduction in fuel burn of up to 27 per cent (Daggett, 2001) through improved lift/drag ratios and reduced weight achieved through incorporating more composites in the aircraft structure. The novel design also provides more opportunities to integrate novel propulsion systems. For example, locating the engines above the wing would have two benefits: sufficient ground clearance to allow the use of large fan engines, and reduced noise as the aircraft itself would act as a shield reflecting noise upwards. Ducted and unducted prop-fan concepts, which were first developed during the early 1980s, may provide a suitable propulsion system for this type of aircraft. These options have substantially better fuel burn than modern engines, but cause the aircraft to fly more slowly. An additional consideration is the potential for BWB to use hydrogen for fuel as the aircraft shape lends itself to storing the cylindrical tanks that are necessary. Some concerns exist with respect to passenger transport of this kind, including the time needed to evacuate the aircraft in an emergency and how passengers would take to flying in an aircraft with no windows.

CONCLUSION

It is clear that the conventional airframe/engine configuration can offer reduced environmental impacts, even where these impacts appear to be in conflict with one another. However, it is also clear that in the long term, alternatives to this configuration need to be carefully evaluated. For example, a blended wing body, fuelled by hydrogen, with engines mounted on the top side and with hybrid laminar flow, could represent the ultimate technological solution. The key to continued air transport is, of course, an integrated system incorporating many of the concepts given here, alongside non-technical options such as planning and operational issues.

The decision as to which technologies are finally developed rests on the market, and includes legislative bodies, non-governmental organizations (NGOs), technology developments and, perhaps most importantly, the concerns of the public who ultimately decide what they want, and do not want, through consumer spending power and votes. While, at the current time, it is hard to envisage a world in which environmentally benign transport is the only acceptable form of transport, the aviation industry must be ready to face this challenge should the need arise.

NOTES

1   It should be recognized that the views expressed in this chapter are those of the author and do not necessarily represent the policy of Rolls-Royce plc.
2   Laminar flow is an expression used to describe air flowing smoothly over a surface (eg a wing). It usually refers to the flow close to the surface, known as the boundary layer. When the flow is smooth, the boundary layer is said to be laminar. The opposite is a turbulent boundary layer, where the flow is of an irregular, eddying nature. Friction between the surface and the moving air is much greater when the boundary layer is turbulent. (Shevell, 1989, p167; Allen, 1982, p136).
3   Stoichiometric temperature is the temperature resulting from the combustion of a fuel/air mix at a ratio where all the oxygen is consumed.

REFERENCES

Aeronautique, Astronautique (1998) *Proceedings of the 3rd Aerodays*, Toulouse, 27–30 October 1997

Air Transport Action Group (ATAG) (1999) *Aviation and the Environment,* ATAG, Geneva

Allen, J E (1982) *Aerodynamics: The Science of Air in Motion*, second edition, McGraw-Hill, New York

Beesley, C (2000) *The Impact of Product Stewardship on Materials Selection,* ICETS, Beijing, July 2000

Birch, N (2000) '2020 Vision: The Prospects for Large Civil Aircraft Propulsion', *The Aeronautical Journal*, volume 104, no 1038, August, pp347–352

Daggett, D (2001) 'Airplane Energy Reduction Technology', *Aviation and the Environment*, conference, Amsterdam, 30–31 January 2001

IPCC (1999) *Aviation and the Global Atmosphere,* Intergovernmental Panel on Climate Change, Cambridge University Press, Cambridge

Jenkinson, L R, Simpkin, P and Rhodes, D (1999) *Civil Jet Aircraft Design*, Butterworth-Heinemann, London

Klug H (2000) *Cryoplane – Hydrogen Fuelled Aircraft, Background and Status*, The Royal Aeronautical Society Fedden Lecture, Cranfield University, November 2000

Plohr, M (1999) *The Gas Turbine Heat Cycle and its Influence on Fuel Efficiency and Emissions,* NATO/RTO Air Vehicle Technology Symposium, Ottawa, October 1999

Poll, I (2000) 'Aerospace and the Environment, What Contribution can Aerodynamics Make?', *The Aeronautical Journal*, volume 104, July, pp321–324

Rolls-Royce plc (1999) *Powering a Better World, Environment Report for 1998,* Rolls-Royce plc

Rolls-Royce plc (2000) *The Outlook*, Rolls-Royce plc

Royal Commission on Environmental Pollution (RCEP) (2000) *Energy, the Changing Climate*, 22nd report, RCEP, HMSO, London

Ruffles, P (1998) *Power and the Environment,* 46th Hatfield Memorial Lecture, Sheffield University, Sheffield

Schumann, U (2000) 'Climate Sensitivity to Contrails for Increasing Propulsive Efficiency. Aviation, Aerosols, Contrails and Cirrus Clouds (A^2C^3)', *Proceedings of European Workshop*, Seehiem, Frankfurt, Germany, 10–12 July 2000

Shevell, R S (1989) *Fundamentals of Flight,* Prentice Hall, Englewood Cliffs, New Jersey

Walsh, P (2000) Internal Rolls-Royce communication

Chapter 11

Climate policy for civil aviation: actors, policy instruments and the potential for emissions reductions[1]

Andreas Pastowski

INTRODUCTION: THE ROOTS AND PACE OF AVIATION'S SUCCESS STORY

Since the first flight of the Wright Brothers in 1903, air transport has become technically feasible, but its contribution to total transport activity remained insignificant. World War II brought about an enormous advance in aircraft technology and, thus, the potential for an economically viable civil aviation industry. In 1945 a commercial transatlantic flight with several stop-overs took place between New York and Bournemouth for the first time. Even though that flight was still rather costly and time consuming, it opened up the rapid development towards ever faster, safer, more comfortable and less costly aviation services (Holloway, 1999, p32). Technological change, in general, and particularly in jet engine efficiency has been the main driving force for increasing aircraft productivity and, hence, reductions in unit operating cost and ticket prices (Doganis, 1995, pp1–4).

Global passenger transport activity by air has reached roughly 50 times the volume it had 50 years ago. This has contributed 10 per cent and 30 per cent to the overall increase in passenger kilometres (ie from all forms of transport) in Europe and the US respectively during that same period. An average European flies around 2.5km per day, resulting in 15 seconds of daily travel time. US citizens on average spend 70 seconds flying per day, while the so-called jet set may reach up to 30 minutes per day (Ausubel et al, 1998). Even though enormous efforts were made for improving fuel efficiency, exponential growth in demand has resulted in a substantial increase in fuel burn.

Moreover, political support to the aviation industry has played an important role in its success. Airlines that are state owned still serve as symbols of national economic success and power (Ragumaran, 1997, p240). Such a role may be particularly vital in some developing countries. However, it still persists in developed countries, as illustrated by the way in which Swissair was perceived as the 'flying Swiss identity' (Anon, 2001, p30). This role of aviation, as well as airlines owned by governments, seems to be no longer appropriate given the rising adverse environmental effects of aviation.

THE CHALLENGE OF LIMITING GHG EMISSIONS FROM CIVIL AVIATION

Climate policy generally is in a situation where there is a high degree of negotiating activity, while the results obtained so far appear to be somewhat limited. Tackling greenhouse gas (GHG) emissions from civil aviation seems to be even more tricky and cumbersome owing to a lack of well-established and agreed scientific basis and the diversity of interests involved. Although some uncertainties remain, the scientific basis has been significantly improved since the special report, *Aviation and the Global Atmosphere*, prepared by the Intergovernmental Panel on Climate Change (IPCC) (Penner et al, 1999) on behalf of the International Civil Aviation Organization (ICAO). However, just as with climate policy in general, the diversity of interests of the various actors and stakeholders involved remains a decisive obstacle. In fact, the situation regarding aviation is worse, as the issue of limiting the climate change consequences of civil aviation has not yet reached the stage of international negotiations.

In the context of the United Nations Framework Convention on Climate Change (UNFCCC), it has been recognized that there is a lack of mechanisms for addressing international GHG emission sources. Article 2, paragraph 2, of the Kyoto Protocol states that the parties included in Annex I (developed countries) shall pursue limitation on, or reduction of, emissions of greenhouse gases not controlled by the Montreal Protocol from aviation, working through the ICAO. In the national GHG inventories, emissions that directly result from international civil aviation (combustion and evaporation of fuels) are to be excluded from other national GHG emissions of the transport sector and are to be reported separately according to the IPCC's *Greenhouse Gas Inventory Reporting Instructions* (IPCC, 1995, p1.5). A review of the national emission inventories submitted has revealed that, in particular, with regard to emissions from international civil aviation, there are significant inconsistencies in current reporting practices as to the definition of fuels used for international transport and coverage of GHG other than carbon dioxide (CO_2) (Det Norske Veritas, 1999). At the same time, there is an ongoing debate as to whether these emissions should be allocated to individual countries or international bodies.

As long as the problems associated with the assessment and allocation of GHG emissions from civil aviation persist, individual countries will have little interest in reducing emissions. Moreover, in contrast to the technological options that are possible in principle for stationary sources of pollutants, the potential for individual countries to apply technological solutions is more limited for globalized sectors. For

GHG emissions from steadily growing civil aviation, a technical fix that is relatively easy to implement – such as that for ozone-depleting substances regulated by the Montreal Protocol – does not exist. Even if hydrogen produced from renewable energy sources were used for jet aircraft, this would not achieve zero GHG emissions due to the climate impact of water vapour.[2]

Taking into account these obstacles and the time that will most likely be required to integrate the aviation sector into a binding global climate regime, the question arises as to how the challenges ahead might be accommodated in the meantime. The lack of effective policy for global environmental issues is an important aspect of the contemporary critique of globalization. One might argue that some of the phenomena embraced by the phrase 'globalization' are not new and are difficult to track empirically, even for international trade and direct investment where economic integration is primarily taking place within and between the predominant economic unions such as the European Union (EU) and the North American Free Trade Area (NAFTA) (Kleinknecht and Wengel, 1998, p645). Nevertheless, civil aviation is a global industry and is of key importance for globalization in that it allows for rapid travel over the globe. Moreover, with the exception of contrails and cirrus clouds, its climate impacts are global in character.

THE POTENTIAL FOR REDUCING THE CLIMATE IMPACT OF AVIATION

As today's transport operation normally involves various technologies, tackling emissions from transport has often focused upon technology forcing. In principle, it is imaginable that technology might be used for achieving zero GHG emissions from aviation. This necessarily requires other fuels than kerosene to be considered. So far, aircraft fuelled by hydrogen have only been taken into consideration with modified jet engines that come with the disadvantage of radiative forcing from emissions of water vapour at altitude, resulting in the formation of contrails and cirrus clouds (Lewis and Niedzwiecki, 1999, pp257–258). Aircraft that would emit no GHG might use hydrogen in a fuel cell, with the hydrogen produced from renewable primary energy sources. The electricity generated might propel electric motors and the water resulting from the chemical reaction in the fuel cell would have to be disposed of into the atmosphere in a way that safely prevents the formation of contrails and cirrus clouds. Within the framework of a general conversion of human primary energy use to renewables, and provided such aircraft are technically feasible, this would be the first, best long-term technical option. It is actually unclear whether such aircraft will become technically feasible and at what price. Taking into account the development of the required new airframe and other aircraft components, the relatively long lead times of aircraft development and the average economic lifetime of aircraft of around 30 years, significant contributions to reducing radiative forcing cannot be expected within 50 years. Unfortunately, stabilizing the climate cannot wait that long and therefore non-technical options need to be considered for the short and medium term.

Even though technology necessarily plays an important role, it cannot be expected to provide the emission reductions needed for sectors that, in the long term, display substantial growth in output. In such cases, policy-making needs to take a broader view with regard to the principal potentials available for limiting emissions. In general, direct passenger and freight transport GHG emissions can be explained and estimated by the following equation, which also identifies the main potentials for emission reduction (Schipper et al, 2000, p10):

$$G = A \times S \times I \times F$$

In this identity, (G) denotes the GHG emissions from transport. (A) is total passenger or freight transport activity (in passenger kilometres or tonne kilometres respectively), (S) is a measure of the shares of the transport modes used, (I) is a measure of the energy intensities of the respective modes, and (F) identifies the volumes of fuels burned by those modes during operation. Further to this, emissions may indirectly result from the construction, maintenance and scrapping of vehicles and infrastructure and the production of fuels.

This general approach for modelling and estimating the total emissions from transport operation may translate into the following equation if GHG emissions from civil aviation are considered:

$$G = A \times I \times F$$

Activity (A) can be explained by the variables 'frequency of travel' and 'average distance travelled for passenger transport' or 'volume and average distance transported for freight transport' respectively. The energy intensity variable (I) can be subdivided into a technical determinant that depends upon aircraft technology and an operational determinant that comprises operation-oriented design specifications of individual aircraft (distance range), flight operation, air traffic management and utilization of aircraft capacity. The variable (F) for the fuel used is of limited value for reducing aviation's GHG emissions as long as no fuels other than kerosene are considered. Another important variable for aviation's impact upon the climate that is related to flight operation and is independent from the total volume of emissions is flight altitude for radiative forcing caused by water (H_2O) and nitrogen oxide (NO_x) emissions.

Demand has so far been the most important single factor influencing fuel use and related carbon emissions from aviation. This can be expected to continue in the future in a business-as-usual scenario owing to the potential savings in travel times offered by air travel. Average travel time budgets have been found to be fairly constant over time and across different cultures (Schafer and Victor, 2000, p174–175). Thus, growth in overall travel is primarily dependent upon increases in travel speed, prices for transport services and available income. In many developed countries, car use no longer allows significantly increased travel speed, and high-speed rail also offers limited potential for travelling faster. Therefore, aviation has the greatest potential for growth in personal high-speed, long-distance travel. Growth in demand for air travel is influenced by a variety of technological, economic, political, social and psychological factors (Nielsen, 2001). Many of those are important only owing to the advantages in travel time that air travel offers and the fact that it has become affordable to an ever-growing number of humans. However, in dealing with growing demand, policy must address all relevant determinants as it cannot be expected that historic trends of increasing speed and affordability of air travel will be reversed.

Consequently, if emissions of GHG and radiative forcing from civil aviation are to be reduced, the following options are available in the short and medium term:

- influencing the development of demand for aviation services in terms of lower frequency and shorter average distance of air travel;
- increasing the technical efficiency of aircraft in use;
- increasing the operational efficiency of air traffic; and
- optimizing cruise altitude in a manner that reduces the effects of emissions on the climate.

Deploying any of these options in isolation may result in partially counteracting or rebound effects in the development of other variables (see Table 11.1). One might expect, at least, reductions in demand to provide for unambiguous effects on GHG emissions. However, reducing demand beyond what the aviation industry has planned for may limit their capacity to achieve high load factors and may slow down the take-up of more environmentally efficient technology.

Table 11.1 *Likely rebound effects of options for reducing aviation's climate impact*

Effect of on	Reduced air travel frequency	Reduced air travel distance	Increased technical efficiency	Increased operational efficiency	Optimized cruise altitude
Air travel frequency		+	+	+	ne
Air travel distance	+		++	++	ne
Technical efficiency	−	−		ne	ne
Operational efficiency	short term −	− −	ne		−
Optimized altitude	ne	ne	ne	ne	

Note: The effects of deploying the options in the columns on those in the rows are indicated by the abbreviations: (ne) no effect; (+) increase; (++) substantial increase; (−) decrease; (− −) substantial decrease.

In so far as improvements in the mentioned determinants of energy intensity of aviation go hand in hand with cost reductions that are passed on to customers, this will result in induced demand, the volume of which depends upon price elasticity. Figure 11.1 shows for Swissair how technical and operational improvements have reduced energy use per tonne kilometre of payload and how the influence on overall fuel use was counteracted by increases in demand driven by the simultaneous effects of decreasing ticket prices in real terms and growing incomes. Thus, additional efficiency gains and cost savings induced by kerosene taxes or emission charges may leave the growth trend in demand nearly unchanged (Brosthaus et al, 2001, p138). Estimates for efficiency gains in air traffic management suggest that the overall effect on carbon emissions, including demand induced by reduced travel times and lower ticket prices, may be a negligible decrease in emissions or even higher emissions (Freire et al, 2000, p8).

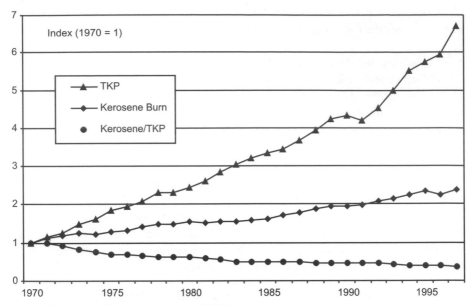

Note: Unified tonne kilometres performed (TKP) for passenger and cargo operation.
Source: Swissair, 2000, pers comm. Even though Swissair suffered from severe financial problems during 2001, it remains a good example of an airline with outstanding operational efficiency.

Figure 11.1 *Long-term relative changes in transport activity, fuel consumption and unit fuel consumption for Swissair*

Reduced air travel frequency may induce longer air travel distances to the extent that air travel expenditures remain constant and demand concentrates on longer trips and vice versa. Reductions in overall travel demand either through reduced trip frequency or trip distance may partly sacrifice further achievements in technical and operational efficiency. Development and take-up of more environmentally friendly aircraft technology may be delayed and airlines may face problems in maintaining high load factors in the short or medium run. Increases in technical and operational efficiency that allow airlines to cut costs and, hence, ticket prices may activate latent air travel demand. Optimized (lower) cruise altitude may give rise to higher fuel burn and, hence, CO_2 emissions as far as this incurs increased aerodynamic drag. With the exception of the negative effect of reduced air travel frequency on operational efficiency, which may disappear after adaptation of airlines to a decrease in the number of passengers, the rebound effects mentioned can be expected to be lasting. In order to keep rebound effects to a minimum, a balanced policy approach that most effectively combines all relevant options for reducing emissions will be necessary.

Actors influencing GHG emissions from civil aviation

Generally, environmental problems arise from certain activities performed by governments, industry and consumers, as depicted in Figure 11.2. Governments often provide for infrastructure that encourages industry and consumers to perform activ-

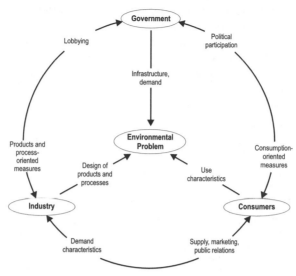

Figure 11.2 *Main actors in causing environmental problems and environmental policy*

ities that are harmful to the environment. The construction and maintenance of such infrastructure also often negatively affect the environment. At the same time, governments demand products and services for their own operations that negatively impact upon the environment. Taking consumer preferences as given, industry influences environmental problems through the design characteristics of products or services and the production processes deployed. Taking supply of goods and services as given, consumers put strains on the environment via the manner in which they make use of the products and services bought on the market or that they produce for self-supply respectively. Knowing that neither consumer preferences nor supply of goods and services are given, an important interdependency exists between industry and consumers that works via the market. While industry influences consumer demand through the scope of alternatives supplied, the price, and marketing and public relations activities, consumers make their choice of which products and services are profitable.

One area of environmental policy is focused upon the supply of relevant infrastructure and government operations in general (eg procurement). Political action is predominantly directed at the interrelationship of industry and consumers, on the one hand, and the government, on the other. Industry is subject to governmental policies relating to the design of goods and production processes. At the same time, governments are targeted by industry through related lobbying activities. Governments also address consumers via policies designed to render consumption more environmentally sound, while consumers influence government decision-making through political participation of various kinds. Environmental non-governmental organizations (NGOs) have become an important element of political participation, which is expressed not only via a relationship with government, but also via influence on production and consumption decisions beyond narrow product specifications and price. Additional pressure may come from capital markets, as far as these factor environmental accountability and related risks of sectors and individual companies into investment decisions.

In the past, environmental policy was often focused upon measures and instruments implemented by governments that were aimed at industry. In particular, it has become obvious for the transport sector that addressing the transport industry alone will be insufficient if the volume and structure of demand are important factors for the level of environmental degradation caused (Pastowski, 2000, p359). Therefore, environmental policy necessarily needs to be broader with regard to the actors addressed and involved.

Table 11.2 lists the main actors and relationships regarding options for reducing aviation's impact on the climate. The main, directly relevant, actors for reducing the GHG intensity of air traffic are the aircraft industry, which is important for introducing new technology, and the airlines, which have some influence on the technology used and a greater influence on operational practices. In addition, operational efficiency is influenced by airports and air traffic management and control. Activity is determined through demand exerted by travellers, the tourism industry and shippers.

Table 11.2 *Objectives, options, direct actors and climate policy in civil aviation*

Overall objective	Stabilizing the global climate					
Sectoral objective	Limiting GHG emissions from civil aviation					
Determinants/ options	Emissions per seat-kilometre		Aircraft operation		Demand for aviation services	
Intermediate determinants	Aircraft technology	Modernity of fleets	Efficiency of air traffic operation		Frequency	Distance
Direct actors Involved	Aircraft industry	Airlines	Airports	Air traffic control	Traveller, tourism industry, shipper	
Policies: governmental bodies at various levels; international organizations;	Actor-oriented policies					
NGOs	General sector-oriented policies					

GLOBAL DISPARITIES IN THE DEMAND AND EFFECTS OF AVIATION

As evidenced in environmental policy-making in the EU, disparities in perceptions of polluting activities and their effects can work as decisive barriers against the implementation of internationally harmonized policies (Neumann and Pastowski, 1992, pp80–83). A situation where national policies are dependent upon international coordination or harmonization with widely varying interests may result in a joint decision trap, where decisions taken are most likely based upon the smallest common denominator (Scharpf, 1988, p251). Diversity in the interests of the parties involved cannot

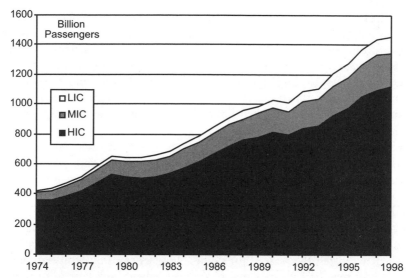

Note: acronyms are explained as follows – high-income countries (HICs); medium-income countries (MICs); low-income countries (LICs).
Source: World Bank, 2000

Figure 11.3 *Domestic and international passengers by income per capita group of country of departure*

always be overcome in the short term and may require a balanced policy approach that allows for taking sufficiently harmonized or coordinated measures, while at the same time providing incentives for innovative approaches and leadership.

Disparities at the global scale relating to policy-making in this field exist at least with regard to the following issues:

- the current geographic distribution of demand for aviation services;
- the expected geographic distribution of the negative impacts of climate change;
- the significance of tourism dependent upon aviation for gross domestic product (GDP); and
- the international structure of the aviation industry.

Not surprisingly, the geographic distribution of demand for aviation services shows a similar pattern to GDP per capita. So far, demand for aviation services has been the domain of people from developed countries travelling for leisure and business purposes. Figure 11.3 depicts the distribution of passengers at airports in high- (HICs), medium- (MICs) and low-income countries (LICs). It needs to be noted that these figures are somewhat biased in favour of high-income countries because a significant share of airport passengers in medium- and low-income countries is comprised of citizens from high-income countries. With growing income per capita, it can be expected that demand will grow faster in today's populous medium- and low-income countries, per-capita income growth being one of the main determinants of the enormous potential for additional demand for aviation services at the global scale.

While the causation of climate change is primarily located in the developed countries, the expected impacts reveal a different pattern. This also applies to aviation-related climate change, except for some effects of contrails and cirrus clouds that are concentrated in northern latitudes where most air traffic takes place. According to the third assessment report of the IPCC, the regional incidence of vulnerability to impacts from climate change varies with regard to physical exposure to adverse effects and adaptive capacity for dealing with such effects (IPCC, 2001). Vulnerability of most less-developed regions is particularly high owing to the sensitivity of their economies to climate change hazards and their limited resources available for adapting to such hazards (McCarthy et al, 2001, p16).

Ironically, climate change to which tourism-related air travel contributes may have severe repercussions on the attractiveness of many of today's popular tourism destinations. As far as the regional effects of climate change can already be estimated, coastal regions may substantially suffer or simply disappear (eg the Maldives) owing to a potential sea-level rise. Increased sunshine and temperatures may turn sunny regions unacceptably hot (eg Australia), warmer temperatures may allow some tropical diseases to spread into areas that, so far, were unaffected (eg malaria), and reduced snowfall may shorten the seasons for skiing. Winners of rising temperatures in the tourism sector may be countries that so far were subject to relatively unfavourable weather conditions for tourism purposes (eg the UK) (Agnew and Viner, 1999, p3).

The development of international tourism has brought about a specialization of certain countries and regions in supplying tourism services based upon natural beauty, climate, opportunities for certain sport activities, current manmade structures and cultural heritage. The US is both a major contributor to GHG emissions from civil aviation and the most important international tourist destination of the world without being substantially economically dependent upon such tourism. Other countries, however, are in a rather different situation. For instance, the Republic of Maldives is both heavily dependent upon civil aviation for its tourism industry and – like some other so-called small island states – extremely vulnerable to a sea-level rise that may result from climate change, owing to its low elevation (Agnew and Viner, 1999, p17). In 1999, travel and tourism in the Maldives directly and indirectly accounted for 85.7 per cent of GDP and were equivalent to 72.9 per cent of exports (WTTC, 2001, p2). Even though these figures are very high for the Republic of Maldives when compared to other small island states, these economies are generally heavily dependent upon tourism (Nurse and Sem, 2001, p862). Apart from small island states, there are many other developing countries with significant contributions of tourism to GDP. Even within the EU there are various countries that have specialized in tourism and have become somewhat economically dependent upon it.

As results of a survey amongst international airlines suggest (Koehn and Pastowski, forthcoming), the structure of the aviation industry reveals certain patterns that have implications for greenhouse gas emissions. The modernity of the aircraft in use is highest for West European scheduled airlines, with some other regions of the world significantly lagging behind. Aircraft used for non-scheduled and, in particular, for cargo operation generally are older than those used for scheduled services. Non-scheduled services still allow for a superior level of operational efficiency through very high load factors. Many aircraft exclusively used for cargo traffic have been converted from passenger operation and, therefore, are rather old. The main challenge associated with the international structure of the aviation industry, for internationally coordinated policies, concerns the regional variance of the average age of aircraft in use. Airlines from some regions or countries combine older aircraft and, hence, lower capital costs with lower labour costs; in this way, they compensate for the cost disadvantages of lower operational efficiency and higher fuel use. Airlines from other regions or countries face high labour costs and therefore apply the latest aircraft technology in order to be competitive. Furthermore, above average modernity of the fleet can be communicated to customers in terms of safety and environmental considerations. Any policies that, in effect, discourage the use of older aircraft for environmental reasons pose a threat to the competitiveness of airlines using such aircraft while fostering the competitiveness of airlines with a relatively modern fleet.

The disparities mentioned necessitate a balanced policy approach that includes national and regional measures that are well ahead of what may be a global compromise, wherever such flexibility exists, in order to harness further progress in technology and operational practices. At the same time, globally harmonized policies are needed where the global operation of airlines requires this. For instance, the quality of aircraft fuel needs to be harmonized globally for technical reasons. Furthermore, some transfer of technology and capital may help airlines with outdated aircraft to achieve a better environmental performance without compromising competitiveness.

STRATEGIES AND POLICY INSTRUMENTS FOR CLIMATE POLICY IN CIVIL AVIATION

Environmental problems are sometimes limited in terms of the:

* geographical spread of causation and impacts;
* number of directly relevant actors who determine the environmental effects of a certain activity; and
* number of nations and political levels that need to be involved in mitigating emissions.

Opposed to this, current environmental problems are often trans-national or global in character. This is particularly the case for GHG emissions from civil aviation. In the past, aviation was primarily a concern in the vicinity of airports for its emissions of air pollutants and noise. However, owing to the sector's dynamics and its influence on the manmade greenhouse effect, civil aviation can be regarded as the prototype of a completely globalized sector. Clearly, combined with the tremendous growth in forecast demand, this poses a challenge for environmental policy-making that necessitates a political strategy that goes beyond national policy-making.

Policy-making for reducing GHG emissions from aviation starts from the ultimate objective of stabilizing the global climate. Limiting GHG emissions from aviation will contribute to this objective. Given the growth in demand forecast and the technological improvements to be expected, it is obvious that a permanently negative contribution from the aviation industry will result from a business as usual development path. While increases in fuel efficiency of aircraft have been substantial during the last decades, they have never been sufficient to offset the effect of growing demand. Determining the level of emissions reductions required of civil aviation in order to stabilize global climate is a subject that requires serious discussion. Equity, as well as economic efficiency, are relevant considerations. This will be subject to political deci-sion-making and negotiations.

In order to keep the complexity of the political discussion to a minimum, it is often focused upon single policy instruments. This may be appropriate as long as sin-gle policy instruments implemented at the national level work well in solving the respective environmental problem. However, a limited set of instruments most likely will prove insufficient in mitigating aviation's climate impact due to the:

- new and partly still-preliminary evidence on aviation's climate impact and its likely future dynamics;
- relatively large number of actors involved;
- varying economic dependency of countries and regions on aviation services;
- significant variation in operational conditions within the aviation industry at the global scale; and
- need to take globally coordinated or harmonized measures.

In order to deal with these obstacles, a patchwork policy approach that considers both the full range of options available for reducing aviation's climate impact and a broad range of policy instruments, to be implemented at the various political levels, may be most suitable. Only a patchwork of policy instruments will be able to cover the different political levels involved, and will account for the high level of coordina-tion needed between national and regional approaches and what are likely to be only moderately strict individual instruments implemented at the international level. Such an approach may also allow for more flexibility on the part of individual governments or certain regions and, hence, help attain more ambitious emission-reduction targets at the global scale. Moreover, single policy instruments may come along with signif-icant rebound effects. Therefore, a comprehensive policy package may help to avoid undesired countervailing effects (ECMT, 1997, p117). An optimum patchwork would combine policy instruments that are mutually reinforcing. Moreover, com-plementarity in terms of options used, actors influenced and timing of phasing-in would yield the biggest overall effect. Table 11.3 provides an assessment of the strengths and weaknesses of various policy instruments.

In Table 11.3, the assumed strictness of individual policy instruments and the assessment of their effects reflect existing barriers to implementation and can there-fore be regarded as an outcome of a political compromise. The assessment of the effects differentiates between effects on the level of general aviation activity and effects on GHG intensity of operation. To the extent that strong effects on intensity give rise to cost reductions, this may result in rebound effects in the form of induced demand. Some rebound effects on emission intensity may also occur in the form of higher fuel burn owing to a reduction in flight altitude. Table 11.3 also shows which instruments address which direct actors. The assessment of the timing differentiates between the time that will most likely be required to introduce an instrument and to attain the full effect, respectively. Regarding the geographical scope of implementa-tion, political levels for implementation are suggested. The last level (global) is the optimum level for reasons of environmental effectiveness and undistorted competi-tion. However, policies may start at national or regional levels in a stepwise process of implementation in order to gain momentum.

Table 11.3 *Assessment of various instruments for climate policy in civil aviation*

Policy instruments	Main effects		Influenced direct actors					Timing		Political
	Activity	Intensity	Aircraft Ind	Airlines	Airports	ATM/C	Traveller	Introduc.	Effect *	levels
Information/voluntary action										
Public awareness campaigns	–	–					X	st	mt	n, r, g
Voluntary agreements		–		X				st	mt	r, g
Research and development										
Aviation's climate impact	–	– –	X	X		X	X	st	mt	n, r, g
Improved aircraft design	(+)	– –	X	X				st	mt, lt	n, r, g
Economic instruments										
Phase-out of subsidies	–		X	X	X		X	st	st, mt	n, r, g
Kerosene tax	–(+)	– –	X	X			X	mt	mt, lt	r, g
Emission charge	–(+)	– –	X	X			X	mt	mt, lt	n, r
Trust fund charge		–	X	X				mt	mt, lt	g
Emissions trading	–(+)	– –	X	X				mt	mt, lt	n, r, g
Regulation and guidelines										
Privatizing airlines/airports	–			X	X			mt	st	n, r
SEA for airport capacity	–				X			mt	mt, lt	n, r
Optimization of flight altitude		– –(+)		X		X		st	st, mt	r, g
Emission standard (NO$_X$)		–	X	X				mt	mt	g
Environmental reporting		–	X	X			X	mt	mt, lt	r, g
Optimization of ATM/C	(+)	– –				X		mt	mt, lt	r

Key: + = increase, + + = substantial increase, – = decrease, – – = substantial decrease, (+) = potential rebound effect; st = short term, mt = medium term, lt = long term; n = national, r = regional, g = global; * = full effect after introduction

As evidence about aviation's impact on the global climate is relatively new, public awareness campaigns may both influence decisions on demand and increase the acceptability of stricter measures. Hand in hand with this, a public consultation process on the future of aviation similar to that being performed in the UK may increase the public perception of the challenges ahead and foster a common understanding of the measures and instruments available for policy-making (DETR, 2000). Voluntary agreements may be considered as a short-term measure until economic instruments are implemented.

Publicly financed research into aviation's climate impact is a necessary prerequisite for appropriate public awareness measures, as well as for industry investment decisions on new technologies and aircraft. Refocusing of research and development (R&D) funding, with more emphasis on improved aircraft design in terms of lower GHG emissions, is complementary to other policy instruments aimed at increased technical and operational efficiency.

Even though some progress has been made in the EU regarding the abolishment of state aid to airlines and of duty-free sales on intra-EU flights, the phasing-out of environmentally perverse subsidies is not yet on the agenda. The most prominent tax exemptions are those for excise duties on fuels and value-added tax (VAT) on tickets for international travel. A wide definition of subsidies would include a tax on kerosene similar to excise duties imposed on other fuels used for transport purposes. However, existing bilateral air-service agreements preclude the introduction of fuel taxes and would need to be renegotiated. While a fuel tax would primarily work as an incentive for increasing fuel efficiency, an emission charge may be designed in a way that covers all GHG emissions from aviation. A trust fund charge with a low charge rate, the proceeds of which are recycled for financing additional climate-change mitigation measures inside and outside the aviation sector, may ideally be suited for implementation at the global level. Despite a low rate and related direct incentives for emission reduction, the combined effect may be significant (Leifert et al, 1997). Emission trading is increasingly under discussion for the aviation sector. Normally emission-trading schemes for climate policy are restricted to CO_2 emissions. However, as with an emission charge, other important GHG from aviation need to be included in emission trading. Otherwise, in an open trading regime the sector may become a net buyer of emission permits from other sectors, resulting in an increase in total radiative forcing (Lee and Sausen, 2000, p2).

Regarding regulations and guidelines, privatization of airlines and airports may help to separate governmental and commercial interests in relation to air traffic operation and airport capacity planning, and avoid quasi subsidies from capital holdings. In contrast to infrastructure planning for other modes of transport, there is currently no federal planning for airport capacity in Germany because there is no federal money spent on such projects. This results in planning decisions being uncoordinated between regional and local authorities and in relation to growth in airport capacity.

Strategic environmental assessment (SEA) for transport infrastructure, currently underway within the EU, may help to better spatially coordinate airport capacity planning and, hence, eliminate excess capacity and supply-side driven growth in demand. Taking account of the influence of cruise altitude on radiative forcing, regulations for flying at somewhat lower altitudes than are currently usual may allow for a substantial reduction in aviation's effect on the climate. An international agreement may be required to ban the development of a supersonic fleet beyond the limited number of Concorde aircraft currently in service that cruise at higher altitudes than subsonic aircraft and have a significantly bigger climate impact per passenger kilometre travelled.

NO_x emissions from aircraft are still under discussion for their ambiguous effects on radiative forcing through ozone formation and a decrease in methane concentration (Penner et al 1999, pp6–7). Further technical reductions in NO_x emissions may help to reduce radiative forcing because the effect from ozone formation seems to be more profound. ICAO engine-emission standards were first introduced in 1980 and the latest standards adopted will be applicable to new engine designs after 2003 (ICAO, 1999). However, stricter standards for new engine designs, as well as minimum requirements for existing aircraft, may be introduced.

Environmental reporting is decisive for benchmarking the environmental performance of airlines. Investors, tour operators, travellers and shippers who also want to base their decisions upon environmental considerations need comparable data on the emission characteristics of individual airlines. To date, environmental reporting is only carried out on a voluntary basis by a rather limited number of airlines. Besides, the data on fuel use and emissions is often generated using different methodologies and is therefore inconsistent (Koehn and Pastowski, forthcoming). Introducing mandatory environmental reporting under the umbrella of ICAO at the global level would be a solution. Existing voluntary reporting would greatly benefit from adopting a unified methodology for calculating and presenting the data on GHG emissions that might be developed in an ICAO working group.

For historic and military reasons, air traffic management and control are often restricted and fragmented to an extent that precludes efficient air traffic operation. The technologies applied are partly outdated and incompatible and lag behind standards of modern aircraft. Regulations and internationally agreed guidelines that are partly underway may foster more coherent regional systems of air traffic management and control, as well as the application of latest technology. In addition to more efficient air traffic operation, positive side effects from such efforts can be expected for safety of air traffic operation.

CONCLUSION

The instruments listed above provide for a broad range of policy measures, many of which can be regarded as being mutually reinforcing and complementary. However, this also means that the economic instruments contain some redundancy, as is evident in their identical patterns of effects. In particular, once a comprehensive emission-trading regime is implemented, an emission charge might no longer be required. Even though some of the instruments discussed may be implemented at the national level, it is obvious that policies that address the highly globalized sector need to be sufficiently coordinated or harmonized. Further policy instruments that are inherently international in character have been developed in the context of the Framework Convention on Climate Change and the Kyoto Protocol and may be adapted to the civil aviation industry. These instruments comprise international emissions trading, joint implementation (JI) and the Clean Development Mechanism (CDM) as project-oriented measures. Further to these, direct international transfers, in terms of financial resources or technology, may be implemented between countries that have committed themselves to quantitative emission-reduction targets and those which have not adopted any such targets under the Kyoto Protocol (Bashmakov and Jepma 2001, pp424–430).

NOTES

1   This contribution builds on some results of a research project entitled 'Potentials for Reducing GHG Emissions from Civil Aviation'. The author is grateful to the Volkswagen Foundation for financial support.
2   The climate impact of water vapour emitted at altitude is 2.6 times more than that of combusted kerosene (Lewis and Niedzwiecki, 1999, p257). Moreover, such technical solutions are a long-term matter.

REFERENCES

Agnew, M and Viner, D (1999) *Climate Change and Its Impacts on Tourism*, Climatic Research Unit University of East Anglia, Norwich
Anon (2001) 'Wieder ein stolzes Flaggschiff fuer die Schweiz', *Neue Zuercher Zeitung*, Zurich, 26 April, p30
Ausubel, J H, Marchetti, C and Meyer, P (1998) 'Toward Green Mobility: The Evolution of Transport', *European Review*, vol 6, pp137–156
Bashmakov, I and Jepma, C (2001) 'Policies, Measures and Instruments' in Metz, B, Davidson, O, Swart, R and Pan, J (eds) *Climate Change 2001: Mitigation, Contribution of Working Group III to the Third Assessment Report of the Intergovernmental Panel on Climate Change*, Cambridge University Press, Cambridge, pp424–430
Brosthaus, J, Hopf, R, Koehn, A, Kuhfeld, H, Limprecht, B, Pastowski, A, Petersen, R, Schallaboeck, K O, Schmied, M, Schneider, J, Sonnborn, K S, Weyrauther, G and Winter, G (2001) *Massnahmen zur verursacherbezogenen Schadstoffreduzierung des zivilen Flugverkehrs*, Umweltbundesamt (Federal Environmental Agency), Berlin (executive Summary available at www.umweltbundesamt.org/fpdf-k/1955.pdf)
Det Norske Veritas (1999) *Methods Used to Collect Data, Estimate and Report Emissions from International Bunker Fuels, Draft Report Prepared for the UNFCCC Secretariat*, Det Norske Veritas AS, Hovik, Norway
DETR (2000) *The Future of Aviation*, Department of Environment, Transport and the Regions, www.aviation.detr.gov.uk/consult/future/index.htm
Doganis, R (1995) *Flying off Course*, second edition, Routledge, London and New York
ECMT (1997) CO_2 *Emissions from Transport*, European Conference of Ministers of Transport, Paris
Freire, D, Cowart, W A and Noland, R B (2000) *Air Travel Passenger Demand Responses to Free Flight Technologies and the Impact on Carbon Emissions*, paper submitted to the 80th Annual Meeting of the Transportation Research Board
Holloway, J C (1999) *The Business of Tourism*, fifth edition, Longman, New York
ICAO (1999) *ICAO Adopts New Aircraft Engine Emissions and Noise Standards*, ICAO Press Release PIO 02/99, Montreal
IPCC (1995) *Greenhouse Gas Inventory Reporting Instructions*, vol 1, IPCC WGI Technical Support Unit, Bracknell
IPCC (2001) *Climate Change 2001: Impacts, Adaptation and Vulnerability*, Grid-Arendal, Norway

Kleinknecht, A and Wengel, J (1998) 'The Myth of Economic Globalisation', *Cambridge Journal of Economics*, vol 22, pp637–647

Koehn, A and Pastowski, A (forthcoming) *Handlungspotenziale zur Minderung der klimarelevanten Emissionen des zivilen Luftverkehrs*, Wuppertal

Lee, D S and Sausen, R (2000) *The Potential Atmospheric Impacts of Controlling only Aviation CO_2*, paper presented at the NASA 2000 conference on the Atmospheric Effects of Aviation

Leifert, V, Pastowski, A, Wilkinson, G, and Winter G (1997) *Air and Maritime Transport Emission User Charges*, study commissioned by the Global Environment Facility, Wuppertal Institute for Climate, Environment and Energy, Wuppertal

Lewis, J S and Niedzwiecki, R W (1999) 'Aircraft Technology and its Relation to Emissions' in Penner, J E, Lister, D H, Griggs, D J, Dokken D J and McFarland, M (eds) *Aviation and the Global Atmosphere, A Special Report of IPCC Working Groups I and III*, Cambridge University Press, Cambridge

McCarthy, J J, Canziani, O F, Leary, N A, Dokken, D J and White, K S (2001) *Climate Change 2001: Impacts, Adaptation and Vulnerability, Contribution of Working Group II to the Third Assessment Report of the Intergovernmental Panel on Climate Change*, Cambridge University Press, Cambridge

Neumann, L F and Pastowski A (1992) 'Rahmenbedingungen, Probleme und Perspektiven der Umweltpolitik in der Europaeischen Gemeinschaft' in Jarrass, H D and Neumann, L F (eds) *Umweltschutz und Europaeische Gemeinschaften*, Springer, Berlin

Nielsen, S K (2001) 'Determinants of Air Travel Growth', *World Transport Policy and Practice*, vol 7, pp28–37

Nurse, L A and Sem, G (2001) 'Small Island States' in McCarthy, J J, Canziani, O F, Leary, N A, Dokken, D J and White, K S (eds) *Climate Change 2001: Impacts, Adaptation and Vulnerability, Contribution of Working Group II to the Third Assessment Report of the Intergovernmental Panel on Climate Change*, Cambridge University Press, Cambridge

Pastowski, A (2000) 'Umweltpolitik und Verkehr im Spiegel sozialoekonomischer Konzepte' in Jens, U and Romahn, H (eds) *Sozialpolitik und Sozialoekonomik*, Metropolis, Marburg

Penner, J E, Lister, D H, Griggs, D J, Dokken D J and McFarland, M (1999) *Aviation and the Global Atmosphere, A Special Report of IPCC Working Groups I and III*, Cambridge University Press, Cambridge

Ragumaran, K (1997) 'Airlines as Instruments for Nation Building and National Identity: Case Study of Malaysia and Singapore', *Journal of Transport Geography*, vol 5, pp239–256

Schafer, A and Victor, D G (2000) 'The Future Mobility of the World Population', *Transportation Research Part A*, vol 34, pp171–205

Scharpf, F W (1988) 'The Joint Decision Trap', *Public Administration*, vol 66, pp239–278

Schipper, L, Marie-Lilliu, C and Gorham, R (2000) *Flexing the Link between Transport and Greenhouse Gas Emissions*, International Energy Agency, Paris

World Bank (2000) *World Development Indicators 2000 on CD-ROM*, International Bank for Reconstruction and Development, Washington, DC

WTTC (2001) *Year 2001 Tourism Satellite Accounting Research Maldives*, World Travel and Tourism Council, London, available at www.wttc.org/ecres/pdfs/md.pdf

Part 3

Multisector Commentaries

Chapter 12

Multisector commentaries on sustainability and aviation

INTRODUCTION

Major built developments and transport infrastructure are often politically contentious. Forecast aviation growth will inevitably require airport expansion internationally and will also increase greenhouse gas emissions. Part 3 allows commentators from different sectors and perspectives to express their opinions on these and other matters more succinctly than in the preceding chapters. The purpose of this chapter is to show the contested nature of sustainability and aviation and provide readers with a further range of opinion on the subject. Sustainability is subject to many competing definitions and its relationship with aviation – as with any other human activity – will remain as political as it is technical.

ECONOMIC ASPECTS OF SUSTAINABILITY AND UK AVIATION

Simon Bishop, Institute for Public Policy Research

Sustainable development is generally held to involve meeting the needs of the present without compromising the ability of future generations to meet their needs (WCED, 1987). This lofty principle boils down to the task of reconciling social, environmental and economic objectives to improve the quality of life for all. In relation to the aviation industry, the challenge is formidable – balancing the benefits of growth in air transport (trade, travel and employment) with the costs (congestion, noise, air pollution and the use of natural resources).

The task is made all the harder by the growth in air transport demand forecast to 2030. The number of passengers using UK airports could more than double by 2020 and triple by 2030. Unconstrained growth in air freight is forecast to be higher still, rising at a rate of 7.5 per cent to 2010, compared with 4 per cent annual growth in passengers. The additional capacity of Heathrow Terminal 5 could be soaked up within ten years.

In the UK government's current review of aviation policy, maintaining high and stable levels of economic growth is one of the economic criteria for deciding on the right level of capacity (DETR, 2000). One way of spurring economic growth is to ensure that investment finds its way to sectors that make best use of capital and labour. The aviation sector has an above-average level of labour productivity, a fact mistakenly used to explain its positive contribution to overall economic growth. A more representative measure would also consider how productively it used capital. Highly capital intensive compared to other sectors, the effect is to lower aviation's overall contribution to economic growth.

There are other ways in which the availability of efficient global air transport networks may increase investment and productivity in the wider economy. Increased accessibility allows markets to enlarge. Lower transport costs facilitate increased specialization in international markets, enabling each country to exploit its comparative advantage in global production. In principle, greater exposure to competition helps to ensure that people, products and ideas move to where they are most efficiently utilized.

Forecasting these linkages is more difficult. An industry-sponsored report by Oxford Economic Forecasting (OEF) suggested that capping air transport at today's level would result in a whole year's worth of economic growth being lost by 2015 (OEF, 1999). It did so while failing to prove a link between air transport and economic growth and ignoring environmental costs. No attempt was made to consider that future investments in transport infrastructure could have diminishing or even negative economic returns.

In areas where congestion is already a problem, the marginal costs of more people and goods getting to and from airports could outweigh the benefits of growth. Three-quarters of international air travel is for pleasure not business, and leisure spending by UK residents when abroad is greater than spending by overseas visitors in the UK. The UK£7 billion deficit in spending by UK air travellers (OEF, 1999) is growing as long-distance air travel becomes cheaper per kilometre than more sustainable local travel, and incentives to travel further and faster accelerate.

Tax exemptions and subsidies worth an estimated UK£6 billion a year are part of the reason behind low air-travel prices and high demand (Sewill, 2000). There is no tax on aviation fuel, no value-added tax (VAT) on tickets, duty-free sales and cross-subsidy of airport charges by retail activity. If aviation were to pay its way, then growth would be much more modest, with passenger numbers rising from 160 million in 1998 to 240 million instead of 400 million by 2020 (Sewill, 2000).

Raising charges for airport access would make flying more expensive, possibly hitting those on low incomes hardest. Even if tax exemptions and subsidies were removed, there would still be around 80 million or 50 per cent more passenger air trips by 2020 than there were in 1998 (Sewill, 2000). There are likely to be more, not less, people flying in the future. Leisure flights are discretionary, while the same cannot be said for the environmental costs associated with air travel. With growth unchecked, the adverse impacts of aviation will be meted out faster than the industry can mitigate them. In the vicinity of airports, more people will be exposed to the harmful effects of noise and air pollution.

Aviation's global contribution to climate change will also grow from a 1992 level of 3.5 per cent to over 15 per cent by 2015, as a percentage of total anthropogenic carbon emissions (IPCC, 1999). The figure will be greater still if the emissions from international flights remain outside the Kyoto Protocol while other industries come under an emissions cap. The Royal Commission on Environmental Pollution (RCEP) recommend a 60 per cent reduction in greenhouse gas emissions by 2050 to avoid the catastrophic consequences of climate change (RCEP, 2001), while unconstrained aviation could be adding anything up to 150 per cent on current levels. Including aviation in the Kyoto treaty is a priority; removing tax advantages and subsidies is another. Targets should be set for air pollution and noise, met with a mix of charges and regulations to guarantee compliance.

References

DETR (2000) *The Future of Aviation Consultation*, HMSO, London
IPCC (1999) *Aviation and the Global Atmosphere. Summary for Policymakers*, Special Report for the Intergovernmental Panel on Climate Change, Geneva; http://www.ipcc.ch
OEF (1999) *The Contribution of Aviation to the UK Economy*, Oxford Economic Forecasting, Oxford
RCEP (2001) *Response to the Future of Aviation*, Royal Commission on Environmental Pollution, London
Sewill, B (2000) *Airports Policy – A Flawed Approach*, Friends of the Earth, Gatwick Area Conservation Group (GACG), Aviation and Environment Federation (AEF)
WCED (1987) *Our Common Future*, World Commission on Environment and Development, Oxford University Press, Oxford

SUSTAINABLE AVIATION: IMPLICATIONS FOR ECONOMIES IN TRANSITION

Delia Dimitriu, TAROM Romanian Air Transport

Introduction

The world has realized the need to be eco-friendly while developing; but sustainable development will never be achieved if one out of every five people on Earth continue to live in poverty. This conclusion is evident at all United Nations Commission on Sustainable Development meetings. Agenda 21 – the environmental plan of action agreed by the world's governments at the Earth Summit in Rio – stressed that all aspects of environmental protection must be taken into account, including economic and social aspects. All countries use the global set of resources. Traditionally, it has been the developed countries of the North who used the bulk of those resources, and where most consumption occurred. The developing world has its right to development, and these countries rely very much on tourism and trade. This commentary provides a perspective relevant to European economics in transition, in Central and Eastern Europe, and the less-developed world, where revenue and employment are as much a priority as environmental protection.

The importance of tourism

Aviation and tourism can be considered a tool for developing and improving quality of life at a local level, promoting a more balanced form of national development. Mass tourism requires mass transportation and, as a consequence, there is a need to remember that cheap air travel results in environmental consequences. Sustainable tourism could be a key positive contributor to sustainable development in the 21st century. It could contribute to more than 10 per cent of the global gross domestic product (GDP), capital exports and jobs. It could also lead to social evolution by creating jobs, replacing declining industry and underpinning developments in emerging markets. Thus, the result of increasing the cost of air travel on emerging markets must be considered. If managed in a sustainable manner, aviation can contribute considerably to achieving sustainable development and can play a crucial role in the economic and social development of developing countries.

It should be realized that while aviation is currently a problem, it could become a part of the solution to sustainable development problems. The potential for environmental issues to constrain future aviation growth poses a great challenge for aviation stakeholders worldwide. One way forward is to use national evaluations of aviation as the basis for an analysis of air transport's strengths, weaknesses, opportunities and threats. The result may lead to suggestions for possible new policies, aimed at solving several problems. These may include promotion of air transport's ability to enhance regional accessibility, acceleration of the trend to use aircraft with reduced field requirements, and research into the possibilities for novel technological solutions to environmental and capacity problems. All of these are contemporary issues facing aviation decision-makers worldwide.

According to the Commission on Sustainable Development's ninth session on transport, 16–27 April 2001: 'in view of the different contributions to global environmental degradation, States have common but differentiated responsibilities (agenda item 5). Financial resources and mechanisms play a key role in the implementation of Agenda 21 and decisions concerning transport issues should reflect the sustainability balance' (UN, 2001). The commission notes in Decision 9/3, paragraph 8, the need for a sustainable transport system, especially in developing countries where accessibility and affordability are important for eradicating poverty. Article 11(b) encourages international financial institutions to make transport for sustainable development a priority.

Economic power via environmental regulation

How can countries from the developing world develop their own transport and aviation systems while having severe financial constraints and, at the same time, being required to meet environmental standards set by global institutions? Looking carefully at the involvement of economies-in-transition (EIT) countries in the European Union (EU) enlargement process, one can see limited potential for improvement in aviation-related infrastructure and fleet renewal processes. This is due to high European standards, which sometimes, in terms of the environment (particularly noise), can be more stringent than International Civil Aviation Organization (ICAO) regulations.

Governments from the Central–Eastern European region, taking into account their respective national priorities and circumstances, are encouraged through the support of the international community to promote sustainability by integrating economic, social and environmental considerations within decision-making in the transport sector. Yet, the enlargement process is challenging European transport policies through forecasts of strong, associated transport growth. Current trends in the transitional economies show tremendous modal shifts from large market shares of rail and public transport, which are environmentally preferable, to growing car use and road freight. There is clear evidence that current trends are not sustainable in the transport sector of these regions; but aviation has changed tremendously since the early 1990s.

It can be logically argued that environmental issues associated with aviation are key limiting factors for future growth of the industry. For economies in transition within Central–Eastern Europe, this gives rise to a clear contradiction. There is a need to develop aviation in order to compete more fully in the global economy and also to assist the process of the EU enlargement. However, environmental measures and standards prescribed by European legislation and ICAO requirements have to be demonstrably achieved. This has clearly been a difficult challenge because aviation within EIT countries has been often characterized by an old and inefficient aircraft fleet. There is universal recognition that, globally, air transport is undergoing radical change and that EITs must adapt accordingly in terms of airline deregulation and compliance with new and stringent environmental regulations, and the adoption of cost-effective measures.

New, environmentally sound infrastructure will be needed. By including environmental and health considerations early in the planning process, the likelihood of finding good solutions increases dramatically. In working towards sustainable transport and aviation for Europe, it is important to recognize differences between member states – for example, with regard to environmental problems and sensitivities; policy objectives and responses; behavioural responses to policies; and geographical location and economic development. A solution could be the restructuring, regrouping and integration of airlines to enable them to meet the challenging regulatory and economic developments currently taking place in the international air transport arena.

It is clear that the modernization and development of air transport in the Central–Eastern European region is a priority; but are these governments able to fulfil this demand, knowing that aviation is a very expensive sector and that the investment is long term? For the last ten years, Central–Eastern governments have tried to meet the challenge by phasing out all Chapter 2 aircraft and buying new Chapter 3 aircraft. However, the possibility of Chapter 4 aircraft in a very short period of time has left these countries with little hope of developing national fleets, due to financial constraints. Nevertheless, this represents an environmental gain, as fewer flights will be operating in the region.

My own view is that, at present, aviation is environmentally sustainable in the Central–Eastern region. To meet the demand for mobility by air, Western airlines can, and do, service this part of Europe, while airport infrastructure is developing within the Western standards framework. Current trends in European aviation are based upon a simple premise: that aviation can only be managed in a sustainable way if many countries give up the national pride of having their own fleet and integrate with the regional economy. Similarly, on a larger scale, the future for the developing world could well take the form of an acceleration of the globalization process, in which stronger aviation alliances meet demand for growth, while fewer flights are operated in a more efficient way. The developing world's need to foster trade and tourism using aviation could probably be met in this way. All aviation stakeholders are talking about the economic and social benefits this sector brings in a sustainable global economy. Unfortunately, the relevant literature shows scenarios and data from the developed world, mainly the US and Western Europe. It seems to be quite difficult to 'sell' the concept of sustainable aviation based on such examples, knowing the need for development in the low-income countries and transitional economies. More research in this area is needed in order to develop regional and alternative scenarios of sustainable aviation.

The Future

It is to the aviation industry's advantage to initiate a full societal evaluation of air transport. It is essential that the demand for air transport is managed in a way that is compatible with wider social and environmental objectives. Substitution of air travel wherever possible with less damaging modes of transport, together with new fuels for air and surface power plant, are likely to be part of the solution. Air transport provision is currently based upon the 'predict and provide' scenario. Yet, it may be that international bodies should adopt the role of creating a global demand management strategy for air travel, taking into account the arguably excessive use of air transport by 'developed' nations (US and EU). Will aviation ever be sustainable? The debate will go on and on.

References

UN (2001) *Commission on Sustainable Development: Report of the Ninth Session*, 5 May 2000 and 16–27 April 2001, Economic and Social Council, Supplement No 9, pp19–24

KEY ISSUES IN AVIATION ENVIRONMENTAL POLICY-MAKING

Léonie Dobbie, Partner, GreenAscent (former Director, Aviation Environment, IATA, 1996–2002)

Introduction

Aviation environmental policy-making is significantly more complex and costly than for some other industries and transport modes.[1] This situation derives from the diversity of the issues and trade-offs involved and because of the special nature and characteristics of the industry itself.[2] This commentary reviews some of the key issues and choices involved in designing and implementing policy to address aviation's atmospheric effects and its contribution to climate change. Its underlying thesis is that aviation environmental policy-making tends to weaken the delivery of appropriate policies based upon the accepted definitions of sustainable development.

Aviation growth

Much of aviation environmental policy-making begins with the premise that the proportional and absolute environmental impact of aviation on climate change (also on local air pollution, noise and human health) is likely to increase in line with the growth in demand for aviation. Thus, the key assumption driving policy development is that if the environmental impact of aviation is to be limited, aviation should not grow as before.

This perception arises from the fact that, historically, aviation has experienced the highest demand rates of all modes of transport, expanding as the world economy has grown, thereby making aviation one of the fastest growing global industries. Between 1970 and 1995 there was a 360 per cent growth in revenue passenger kilometres worldwide – from 551 billion to 2537 billion (IPCC, 1999). Passenger traffic grew at an average of 9 per cent per year (in revenue passenger kilometres) until the mid 1990s, stabilizing at an average 5 per cent a year thereafter, as the industry matured. Freight traffic (80 per cent of which is carried by passenger aircraft) grew at an average annual rate of 11 per cent over the same period (IPCC, 1999).

Looking ahead to 2050, the Intergovernmental Panel on Climate Change (IPCC) assessed the potential climate and ozone changes due to aircraft under different scenarios representing the plausible growth for aviation. These include a high-range scenario that projects annual growth of 4.7 per cent on average between 1990 and 2050, a mid-range scenario that projects annual growth of 3.1 per cent on average, and a low-range scenario that projects annual growth of 2.1 per cent on average (IPCC, 1999). For the range of scenarios, the range of an increase in carbon dioxide (CO_2) emissions from aviation to 2050 would be 1.6 to 10 times the value in 1992, reflecting a growth in CO_2 emissions of 4–15 per cent (most probably 5–6 per cent) by 2050 (IPCC, 1999). The IPCC also observed that the effect of CO_2 emissions from aviation is indistinguishable from that of other sources, and is difficult if not impossible to identify.

More recent research has confirmed that there is considerable uncertainty with regard to future levels of emissions and climate response, and that continuing research will be needed in order to provide guidance for policy decisions. Scientific uncertainties are largest for the complex impact of oxides of nitrogen (NO_x) and methane (CH_4), for contrails and, especially, for the indirect effects of aviation on cirrus cloud cover and changes in cirrus properties (European Commission, 2001).

The IPCC scenarios are not predictions of the future and are inherently uncertain because they are based upon different assumptions about the future. Each scenario reflects unconstrained growth. The factors acting to constrain growth include those relating to limits in the supply of aviation infrastructure, including airspace, aircraft and airport availability; in fossil fuel; and the maturity of the aviation market. The factors most likely to sustain growth relate largely to the fact that traditional patterns of supply and demand are giving way to global supply chains and a trend towards more liberalized and deregulated economic activity, especially in transitional economies.

Policy-making focus

In some of its earlier forms, aviation environmental policy-making was characterized more by an apparent intent to contain aviation growth per se than by a full understanding of the effects on the atmosphere of cruise altitude emissions from aircraft (Barrett, 1991). Almost all policy-making since then tends to give emphasis to controlling aviation's apparent 'negative' environmental outputs through a combination of technological, operational, regulatory and market-based policies (such as economic instruments and demand management). Application of these policies has had the effect of drawing attention away from the 'positive' contributions that aviation makes to social and economic development.

Paradoxically however, policy-making generally appears to recognize that access to aviation is one of the key foundations of the global economy and a powerful driver (and beneficiary) of economic and social progress (Environment Agency, UK, 2001). In many countries, civil aviation policy is directed towards encouraging economic growth, competition, trade and investment. Today, aviation is perceived by many to be as necessary to most economies as the railway was a century ago. It has created a unique world of business connections, economic opportunities, travel and tourism. Its contribution to the creation of global wealth and eradication of poverty is seen as a solution to global environmental issues, particularly in the developing world where travel and tourism are the only common service exports. These countries access the global trading arena through the medium of air transport, and most of them cannot benefit from the global market without air transport links (Dobbie, 1999).

Policy-makers are now being led to believe that the environmental burden of aviation may jeopardize this contribution, and that the widely accepted link between aviation growth and economic gross domestic product (GDP) growth should not be taken for granted. In 'decoupling' aviation growth from that of GDP in this way, it becomes possible to justify tougher environmental commitments for aviation, even though the environmental impact from aviation is less than proportionally related to its economic effects.

More fundamentally, policy-making approaches of this kind implicitly understate aviation's economic and social contributions to society. They also do not take into account the way in which the global air transport system largely functions as a public transport system, both in the developed and developing world. Under this interpretation, the facilities and services offered to society by aviation thus constitute a public good, just like telecommunications, postal, security or health services. Similarly, whether they travel or not, many people benefit from the facilities and services provided by aviation.

Current policy-making appears to work against, even undermine, the delivery of appropriate policies based upon accepted definitions of sustainable development as enshrined in policy-making theory and law (Brundtland, 1987).[3] The established definitions of sustainable development include three interdependent and equally important components: economy, environment and society. This relationship implies that complex trade-offs may be required in order to achieve the desired level(s) of sustainability or sustainable development. Moreover, there is a clear distinction between the concepts of environmental protection and sustainability, which, although linked, are not identical. Whereas the notion of environmental protection gives precedence to the idea of preserving natural resources because of their intrinsic value, central to most definitions of sustainability is the notion of responsibility towards future generations. Because resources (both natural and manmade) can sometimes be substituted, the obligation to future generations does not necessarily require that specific resources should be left untouched, provided that suitable substitutes are provided for the well-being of future generations (Solow, 1991).[4]

In line with established definitions, aviation might be considered sustainable on account of its contribution to the development of a sustainable global economy, meeting today's needs while investing in the future. This means that aviation activity is sustainable to the extent that the global socio-economic benefits it provides are not denied to future generations and its environmental impact is kept within limits acceptable to society (ATAG, 2002).

Current policy-making tends not to emphasize this theme. Rather, it is oriented more towards the premise that the continued growth in aviation activity per se is unlikely to be sustainable without major improvements in environmental performance, particularly when compared to other modes of transport. As long as this perception persists, aviation environment policy-making will continue to focus upon reducing the level per unit of aviation activity of resources consumed, materials used, wastes generated and pollutants released.

Risk management

Clearly, aviation has a range of atmospheric and climate change impacts that should be accounted for in the assessment of sustainable development options. Because these impacts are not well understood, but could cause potentially serious and possible irreversible changes in the atmosphere and in the global climate, two well-established principles of international law (though much less accepted in the US than in Europe) drive environmental risk management and subsequent policy-making. These are that, first, prevention of environmental damage is better than the remedy (irrespective of whether there is full scientific proof) and, second, the polluter should pay and damage should be rectified at source (UNCED, Rio Declaration, 1992).[5]

The so-called precautionary and polluter pays principles have become the foundations of environmental policy-making generally, but only address the environmental dimension of sustainability. Measures based upon these principles are meant to reflect a comprehensive, systematic analysis of the problems being addressed, including the feasibility and (as regards the precautionary principle) the cost effectiveness of any appropriate measures. They are also meant to give due regard to any potential distortion to the public interest, international trade and investment (the polluter pays principle). Any resulting policies should be in proportion to the identified damage; non-discriminatory; consistent with existing measures; and subject to periodic review.

In practice, these elements have received the least attention at policy-making level. Instead, the precautionary and polluter pays principles have become a 'catch all' for environmental policy-making overall, especially in matters of impact prevention and mitigation. In particular, they have explicitly encouraged the development of policies designed to address the external effects of specific economic activities.

Externalities from aviation

During the last decade, a number of scientific studies have sought to quantify the external costs attributed to carbon dioxide emissions from aviation (Brus, 2001). Most of these have been published since 1995 and are indicative of the increasing political interest in designing policy for this area on the basis of classical economic theory applied to externalities.

If policy design is to be effective, and if abatement measures are to be justified, robust values for the totality of aviation's external costs and benefits need to be calculated (IATA, 2002).[6]

This exercise is made more complex by the uncertainties associated with the prediction of the climate change effects attributed to aviation (such as the potential climatic effects of contrail formation). Also, there are difficulties in properly identifying and calculating these costs (whether under damage cost or prevent cost or marginal cost approaches) for externalities that may be based upon direct or indirect causes, or both (IATA, 2002).

Current policy approaches call for the internalization of aviation's environmental costs, yet do not take into account other externalities and the benefits from aviation, which are assumed to be captured by the market (CE Delft, 2002). This approach appears to be in evident contradiction to the fundamental principles of sustainable development (see above).

Application of externalities policies to *all* transport modes in a non-discriminatory manner could facilitate a comparison of the overall efficiency of air transport with other transport services (COWI, 2000). It could also allow the travelling public to make informed choices about which transport mode to use, especially where alternative transport modes exist (INFRAS, 2002).[7] Whether or not application of externalities approaches would help determine the appropriate balance for the development of aviation is open to discussion; it would depend also upon an associated development of integrated transport, or intermodal, policies.

Conclusion

Aviation, in common with any economic activity or industrial sector, has particular effects on society and the economy but must deal with environmental issues deriving from its unique mix of ground and air operations, such as its attributed global atmospheric and climate change effects. Most policy-making is predicated on the dual premise that aviation's overall environmental impact is increasing on a year-by-year basis and that aviation makes a disproportionate contribution to climate change. Even though aviation's impacts upon the global atmosphere are not well understood, policy-makers assume that aviation's environmental effects could cause potentially serious and irreversible changes to the atmosphere and to the world's climate. Therefore, irrespective of whether there is full scientific proof of environmental degradation or damage, these risks should be managed through policies aimed at the prevention or rectification of environmental damage at source, and which seek full compensation from the polluter.

These policy approaches have an inherent weakness in that they address only one aspect of the conundrum – the environmental – and do not satisfactorily take into account the role of aviation in delivering economic, social and environmental goals in a mutually reinforcing way to the benefit of present and future generations. As a result, most policy-making appears to work against, if not undermine, the delivery of appropriate policies based upon the accepted definitions of sustainability that, by implication, allow society to make the final choice as to when and where resources should be consumed, substituted or preserved.

Notes

1   Throughout this commentary the terms 'policy-making' and 'policies' refer to the development of longer-term guidance or principles that may accommodate a range of different positions and opinions.

2   Aviation activity is characterized as much by its traffic growth as by its poor financial performance. Total IATA international scheduled traffic, measured in revenue tonne kilometres (RTKs), rose by 9.5 per cent in 2000, an increase of 2.1 percentage points over 1999. (Revenue tonne kilometres are the revenue load (passengers and cargo) multiplied by the distance flown.) Capacity, as measured in available tonne kilometres (ATKs), rose at a lower rate than traffic, rising 7 per cent during 2000. (Available tonne kilometres are the number of tonnes of capacity available for the carriage of revenue load (passengers and cargo) multiplied by the distance flown.) This led to an increase in the overall weight load factor of 1.5 percentage points to 65.5 per cent. Despite the strong growth, the increase in operating revenue of 6.9 per cent to US$157.2 billion (from US$147 billion in 1999) was almost matched by the rise in operating expenses over the period to US$151.0 billion. The margin between operating revenues and expenses increased by only US$0.3 billion. Revenue was held back by yields (US$ per RTK), falling in 2000 by 2.6 per cent; with insignificant movement occurring in the cost per ATK (after interest), the required break-even load factor (after interest) was 64.4 per cent. The increase in the net result (US$0.4 billion) was marginally higher than the increase in the operating result (US$0.3 billion).

All 2002 forecasts are being considered against a 2000 baseline, given the exceptional circumstances in 2001, and the central scenario is for 2002 passenger volumes to improve to perhaps 5–10 per cent below 2000 levels by the year end. The air-freight market is expected to lag behind 2000 levels by around 10 per cent.

3   The definition of 'sustainable development' in the Brundtland Report remains the most widely accepted. This reads: '[S]ustainable development meets the needs of the present without compromising the ability of future generations to meet their own needs'. This concept was brought into mainstream government and business thinking at the United Nations Conference on Environment and Development (UNCED) in Rio in 1992 and has been incorporated in various treaty obligations, such as the Amsterdam Treaty (1997), which has made sustainable development an explicit goal of the EU.

4   Solow (1991) considers 'sustainability' 'as a matter of distributional equity between the present and the future…a problem about the choice between current consumption and providing for the future'. He considers, also, that the connection between environmental and sustainability issues is not necessarily intrinsic and that 'current environmental protection contributes to sustainability if it comes at the expense of current consumption. Not if it comes at the expense of investment.'

5   In both cases, the decision as to what is an 'acceptable risk' is a political, rather than a societal, responsibility. The precautionary principle was enunciated in Principle 15 of the UNCED Rio Declaration (1992). It reads: 'in order to protect the environment, the precautionary approach shall be widely applied by States according to their capabilities. Where there are threats of serious or irreversible damage, lack of full scientific uncertainty

shall not be used as a reason for postponing *cost-effective* measures to prevent environmental degradation.' Although originally developed by the Organization for Economic Cooperation and Development (OECD), the polluter pays principle was transposed as Principle 16 of the UNCED Rio Declaration (1992). It reads: 'national authorities should endeavour to promote the internalization of environmental costs and the use of economic instruments, taking into account the approach that the polluter should, in principle, bear the cost of pollution, with due regard to the public interest and without distorting international trade and investment'. As originally drafted by the OECD, the polluter would not be held to pay for the cost of pollution but, rather, the cost of measures taken to prevent or control pollution.

6   A policy principle of crucial importance to aviation is that of fair treatment between all transport modes. From an economic perspective, the selective introduction of external costs to aviation alone could create diseconomies and inefficiencies rather than eliminate them. Therefore, in order to avoid competitive distortions, economic measures to internalize externalities, if introduced, should apply to all competing economic activities in the same sector.

7   This study, carried out for the Air Transport Action Group (ATAG), assessed all external costs related to transport by air, road and rail on five selected European corridors. It confirmed that all transport modes produce external costs and that, in certain circumstances, rail transport may have higher external costs than air transport. It also demonstrated that rail transport generally has the best performance in terms of external costs on short distances between major centres and in terms of ground access to airports. The study also showed that when compared to road transport, rail access to major airport hubs may help to improve aviation performance in that it reduces delays, accidents and local emissions.

References

ATAG (2002) *Aviation and Sustainability – Partnerships to Meet Society's Growing Mobility Needs*, Air Transport Action Group, Geneva

Barrett, M (1991) *Aircraft Pollution – Environmental Impacts and Future Solutions*, WWF, Gland

Brundtland, H (1987) *Our Common Future*, World Commission on Environment and Development, Oxford University Press, Oxford

Brus, D (2001) *The Costs of Carbon Dioxide Emissions by Aviation*, ICAO Discussion Paper, Montreal

CE Delft (2002) *External Costs of Aviation – Main Report*, CE Delft, the Netherlands

COWI (2000) *Civil Aviation in Scandinavia – An Environmental and Economic Comparison with Other Modes of Transport*, COWI, Denmark

Dobbie, L (1999) 'Airline Environmental Performance', *ICAO Journal*, vol 54, no 7

Environment Agency, UK (2001) *Response to Consultation by DETR on the Future of Aviation*, EA, London

European Commission (2001) *European Research in the Stratosphere 1996–2000*, DG Research, Brussels

IATA (2002) *General Remarks Concerning the CE Delft Study – External Costs of Aviation*, IATA, Geneva

INFRAS (2002) *External Costs of Corridors – A comparison between air, road and rail*, INFRAS, Zurich

IPCC (1999) *Special Report on Aviation and the Global Atmosphere*, Intergovernmental Panel on Climate Change, Cambridge University Press, Cambridge

Solow, R (1991) 'Sustainability: An Economist's Perspective', Paper presented at the Eighteenth J Seward Johnson Lecture to the Marine Policy Centre, Woods Hole Oceanographic Institution, Woods Hole, Massachusetts

UNCED (1992) 'Rio Declaration On Environment and Development', Annex 1, *Report of the United Nations Conference on Environment and Development*, Rio de Janeiro, 3–14 June 1992, available at www.un.org/documents/ga/conf151/aconf15126-1annex1.htm

TOWARDS SUSTAINABLE AVIATION?

Brian Graham, University of Ulster

Recent academic analyses of internal air transport markets have been dominated, firstly, by a shared focus on the effects of liberalization and competition and, latterly, by the impacts of globalization. More widely, however, the contemporary debate on transport and social change as a whole is concerned increasingly with issues of sustainability, and the mounting recognition that present and projected trends in mobility cannot be pursued indefinitely. These broader sustainability issues have had relatively little impact on the academic study of air transport, either in European or North American contexts. Moreover, the thrust of current policy-making for the industry, particularly by the agencies directly charged with the conduct of the air transport industry, is largely concerned with the regulation of imperfections in the liberalized, competitive and increasingly globalized market place.

The air transportation sector worldwide has experienced dramatic changes over the last 20 years. Perhaps the most sweeping has been in the institutional environment, where long-established regulatory regimes have been modified, and in some cases abolished, as a result of policies of liberalization or deregulation, resulting in mergers, acquisitions and/or strategic alliances among the largest carriers. Together with technological improvements and economic dynamics across all industries, these forces have furthered the process of globalization, which is fundamentally altering the volumes, patterns, directions, ownership, and control of air transport flows around the world. It can be argued that the combination of strategic alliances and network restructuring is the most potent manifestation of globalization processes in the airline industry.

Globalization, in general, is partly a result of economic shifts that have encouraged free trade and increased competition, achieved through worldwide processes of deregulation and the removal of trade barriers. In this present context, deregulation involves the exposure of air transport to *laissez-faire*, or free-market, forces, achieved through the removal of most regulatory controls over pricing, while permitting carriers to enter and leave markets at will. The thrust of air transport policy in the US and European Union (EU) has been driven by the shared concern to introduce and implement a competitive market place. Nevertheless, as is a characteristic of all transport modes, such policies do not encourage individual restraint in the use of environmental resources on the part of any one airline.

It has been argued that sustainability as applied to transport has three basic conditions:

- The rates of use of renewable resources do not exceed their rates of generation.
- The rates of use of non-renewable resources do not exceed the rate at which sustainable renewable substitutes are developed.
- The rates of pollution emission do not exceed the assimilative capacity of the environment.

Air transport, as currently practised, fails outright to satisfy the first two conditions and, probably, also the third. In the longer term (perhaps 2050+), global air transport is not sustainable on any basis because there is, as yet, no feasible substitute for oil, hydrogen-based fuels being the only apparent possibility.

Public opposition to aviation, which is situationally determined, tends to focus primarily upon noise. Whereas modern aircraft are quieter than their predecessors, it is the volume of traffic – both airside and landside – that compounds public exposure to noise, particularly for residents who live near major airports. In general terms, internationally negotiated and implemented noise controls have largely realized the potential returns from aircraft engine noise reduction, and the principal future gains are likely to come from advances in airframe technology. Noise, however, dominates at the scale of the individual airport and its relationship with its local community, leading to a plethora of, often stringent, local operating regulations constraining aircraft operations.

It is becoming more widely recognized, however, that the most serious sustainability impacts of air transport are from atmospheric pollution at both global and local scales. These include the, as yet, poorly understood effects of contrails in the upper atmosphere, and carbon dioxide (CO_2) pollution and nitrogen oxide (NO_x) emissions, all of which contribute to global warming. It has been estimated that because of aviation's growth and the lack of alternatives to fossil fuels, the sector's current 3 per cent contribution to global warming may increase to between 10 and 20 per cent of the total by 2005. In addition, ground-level emissions at airports, both from aircraft and surface vehicles, are increasing – the trend exacerbated by the development of airports as major activity economic centres and intermodal transportation hubs. In general terms, although again technology has been successful in reducing atmospheric and ground emissions per aircraft and vehicle, the technological returns are diminishing and being offset by aviation's growth.

It must be emphasized, however, that in addition to concerns with environmental carrying capacity, sustainability also invokes connotations of long-term economic development, social needs and equity. Such targets, especially when applied to more peripheral or disadvantaged regions, demand accessibility to core regions as measured by time and cost, while the access of isolated areas to wider networks is a basic social equity objective. Firms also require accessibility to factors of production and markets. However, the infrastructure created to enhance accessibility also encourages mobility, which is essentially a behavioural attribute and, moreover, one easily manipulated by price. Arguably, it is mobility provision, best exemplified here by low-cost airlines, which provides the basic challenge to sustainability.

In the US, the sustainable transport initiative has largely been confined to strategies that mitigate the environmental impacts of transportation without infringing upon the individual freedom to travel. Most of the effort has targeted motor vehicles and their impacts at the metropolitan scale. Interest in air transport and sustainability has focused upon impacts from new and expanded airports, with much less concern being expressed about aviation's overall environmental consequences. In sustainability terms, the EU looks to a transport strategy, which reconciles a curb on mobility with competing demands for accessibility related to competitive efficiency, geographical location and social equity for all of its citizens.

Even at this most cursory level of analysis, it is apparent that a complex mesh of tensions and contradictions is produced by the relationships between air transport globalization, liberalization and sustainability. Policies and strategies that might curb or diminish the environmental externalities of air transport are likely to be swamped by those promoting its development. Although air transport is almost entirely a derived demand, one result of liberalization and privatization is that its provision is increasingly dominated by the interests of private companies, particularly the airlines. Their market strategies may impact directly and negatively on sustainability and its achievement. These tactics strive to achieve precisely the opposite effect to the curbs on movement inevitably intrinsic to sustainability. They are aimed, instead, at enhancing air transport demand and increasing volumes of traffic. Airlines as businesses in the globalizing, liberalized market place have no rational alternative but to cater to existing demand in ways that are most profitable, while fostering future demand. In that conundrum lies the principal dilemma compromising the entire idea of sustainable aviation.

AIRCRAFT NOISE: THE NGO PERSPECTIVE[1]

Tim Johnson, Aviation Environment Federation

An inadequate regulatory framework

In October 2001, the European Court of Human Rights (ECHR) ruled that the UK government had infringed the human rights of residents living near London's Heathrow airport by failing to protect them adequately from night-time aircraft noise.[2] The court decided that in setting night-time noise restrictions for Heathrow in 1993, the government had failed 'to strike a fair balance between the UK's economic well-being' and the applicants' right to enjoy 'their homes, their private and family lives'.

While at the time of writing the UK government has appealed, and the Grand Chamber of the ECHR will reconsider its earlier decision, an important question to consider is why this case went to the ECHR in the first place. Quite simply, the piecemeal way in which aircraft noise is regulated in the UK, and in Europe, meant that it was the only route available to residents. Ever since the 1920s, civil aviation legislation in the UK has protected aviation from anyone wishing to take an action for nuisance resulting from aircraft noise.[3] At the time that it was enacted, the rationale was that aviation was a fledgling industry which needed protecting. Yet, some 80 years on, with the industry in a relatively mature stage of development, this protection has never been repealed. Furthermore, it has meant that aircraft noise remains exempt from the provisions of more recent legislation such as the Environmental Protection Act. This industry protection is, of course, not unique to the UK. The majority of countries worldwide have similar long-standing legislation, or have hastily introduced it in recent decades. Japan, for example, was forced to introduce legislation after the widespread introduction of commercial jet airliners during the 1960s and 1970s led to hundreds of civil law suits that almost brought operations to a standstill.

So, instead of being able to rely on the statutory nuisance powers that apply to many other sectors, airport neighbours have been forced to look to the town planning system and other discretionary government powers to provide the necessary environmental safeguards. While the ability of the planning system in the UK to impose operational conditions or enter into legally binding conditions, with a view to limiting noise, has had its successes, its application is limited in scope and fails to deal with many day-to-day problems. Many airports benefit from either established use rights or permitted development rights that do not always present local planning authorities with an opportunity to impose controls; others have been granted planning consents that did not necessarily envisage the type or level of traffic currently being handled and, consequently, fail to provide an effective set of controls. This 'hit-or-miss' approach to environmental regulation has, without any doubt, reinforced local opposition to proposals for new airport development.

Where environmental problems at airports persist, the UK government prefers to see them resolved at a local level. This is an obvious starting point, and discussions between an operator and the local community can yield benefits, especially in areas such as operational procedures and on-airport activity. But where problems relate to more fundamental issues, such as the number of noise events, it is unlikely that an airport will ever agree to voluntarily restrict or limit traffic. Such decisions can only realistically be taken by regulators. In this respect, the UK government has several discretionary environmental powers available to it, but these have rarely been used. To date, only London's Heathrow, Gatwick and Stansted airports have been designated by the government despite the fact that there are other UK airports that have either more night flights than Heathrow, or more people affected by aircraft noise than Stansted.[4] Consequently, many residents feel that the existing controls at UK airports are not effective and that the industry, to a large extent, remains self-regulated at a time when other sectors are facing increasing environmental legislation.

Of course, the contribution of progressive technological improvements should not be underplayed; but these benefits have often been offset by the introduction of larger aircraft, more frequent movements, often at sensitive times of the day (or, to be more accurate, at night), and growing community expectations. What are those expectations? Ideally, most would like to see an end to the noise problem, but in Europe there is a 'bottom-line' expectation that, at the very least, noise levels will not deteriorate following the completion of the Chapter 2 phase-out in April 2002. This expectation is not unfounded: many European regulators, including the European Commission, the European Civil Aviation Conference, and various European states, have already stated that their wish is to prevent any increase in the number of people affected by noise at airports after 2002. Furthermore, over 57 countries have signed the World Health Organization's (WHO's) Charter on Transport, Environment and Health. This incorporates elements of the WHO's guidelines for community noise exposure, which state that day-time noise levels above 55 Leq decibel noise units (dB(A)), and night-time levels in excess of 30 Leq dB(A) (interior noise level), should be avoided. Given that most airports exceed these values every day, these guidelines could be regarded as ambitious; but they also serve to remind us of the challenge we still face if we are to reduce noise to levels that experts regard as acceptable. The charter is not legally binding, but it nevertheless raises the expectations of airport neighbours in those countries who are signatories.

ICAO responses

In this context, are existing measures sufficient to meet these expectations? To date, the response of regulators, in addition to the measures discussed above, has been to pursue the reduction of noise at source, working through the International Civil Aviation Organization (ICAO).[5] Although there has been no improvement (until last year) to the current Chapter 3 noise standard since its introduction in 1977, a decision by some countries (namely, European states, the US, Canada, Japan, New Zealand and Australia) to phase out the operation of Chapter 2 aircraft by April 2002 has resulted in a reduction in noise exposure levels at some airports despite a growth in traffic. However, as the benefits of this phase-out programme have now been fully realized, it is highly questionable whether airports can continue to maintain this trend. In fact, as ICAO's own analysis highlights, without any further action, the number of people affected by aircraft noise in the countries implementing the Chapter 2 phase-out will increase by 21 per cent between 2002 and 2020. Yet, not all regions will be impacted in the same way. This significant increase hides the fact that the number of people affected by noise in Europe and, in the Australia, New Zealand and Japan region, will increase by 42 per cent and 169 per cent respectively during this period, while the increase in the US and Canada will only be 3.5 per cent.

Presented with this evidence, there were few amongst the industry who doubted the need to look at further improvements in the stringency of the existing noise certification standards. This led ICAO's Committee on Aviation and Environmental Protection (CAEP) to recommend that a new certification standard should be introduced for all new subsonic jet aircraft entering service from 1 January 2006 (to be known as Chapter 4). The recommended standard, later adopted by ICAO's council, improves on the existing Chapter 3 standards by a cumulative margin of 10 dB(A).

At face value, this may appear a significant step forward, and one that local communities should embrace. Yet, closer examination reveals a different picture. Noise certification of aircraft requires three measurements: one measured on approach, one on take-off and a third at a sideline measurement point. The new Chapter 4 standard is based on the sum of the improvements at these three measurement points. In other words, the average reduction at each of the three measurement points is a little over 3 dB(A). Against average background noise levels, changes of this magnitude can be very difficult to perceive for the average person. By the time the new standard comes into force, it will have been nearly 30 years since the introduction of the current Chapter 3 standard. Is this really the best we can expect from an industry that prides itself on its rate of technological innovation? Quite simply, the answer is no. Many aircraft in service today already improve upon Chapter 3 standards by cumulative margins in excess of 20 dB(A), while over 95 per cent of the current in-production aircraft are already capable of meeting the new standard, and around 75 per cent are capable of meeting an improvement of at least 14 dB(A).

Nevertheless, this recommendation may still have met with some acceptance from airport neighbours if it had been accompanied by a decision to phase out the worst-performing Chapter 3 aircraft. Recent experience, as noted above, has shown the benefits of phasing out Chapter 2 aircraft, and a decision to extend this policy further to some, or all, Chapter 3 aircraft would have been extremely popular amongst local communities. A few disproportionately noisy movements are frequently responsible for the majority of noise complaints at airports. Hence, it is common sense that removing some of the worst-performing aircraft from the fleet would have brought a clear environmental benefit. Instead, CAEP's analysis failed to show any overall cost-effective benefit from a phase-out, and no agreement was forthcoming on implementing a phase-out strategy.

From the perspective of airport neighbours, this outcome was disappointing and totally unacceptable, and is likely to lead to increasing pressure for local airport restrictions, opposition to new developments and a deterioration in the often fragile relationship between airports and their communities. The environmental and community groups are not alone in this view. The Airports Council International (ACI), the voice of airports worldwide, has expressed similar opinions, and had pressed CAEP members, without success, to adopt a more stringent standard.

Of course, there are other important ways to reduce noise: CAEP did endorse a 'balanced approach' to noise management, which involves the contribution of effective land-use planning, operational improvements and operating restrictions, in addition to noise reduction at source. Yet, applying the 'balanced approach' would appear to be new terminology for a relatively old concept. Certainly, land-use planning and improvements to operational procedures have been practised at many European airports for years. While there is probably room for marginal improvements in these areas, they are unlikely to deliver a step improvement in noise exposure levels (unless more radical efforts are made by airport operators to buy out those who are adversely affected by aircraft noise). This leaves us with the option of airport operating restrictions. Seen by many within the industry as a last resort, they would appear to offer the only real alternative to noise reduction at source.

European responses

While Europe has been keen to work within an ICAO framework and avoid the sort of disputes that followed the introduction of its regulation on hush-kitted aircraft, now is the time to adopt measures that are capable of meeting the shortfall between what the ICAO can deliver and what Europe requires. Yet, the ability to take effective regional action is being increasingly compromised. The recent European Union (EU) directive on operating restrictions on marginally compliant Chapter 3 aircraft (the introduction of which has permitted the EU to repeal the hush-kit regulation, thus ending the dispute with the US) is a good example. Its biggest flaw is that it will only apply on an airport-by-airport basis, although this requirement was necessary to comply with ICAO guidance. While this approach is justified on the basis that only those airports with a noise problem need consider restrictions, the reality poses some serious difficulties for its widespread application. For example, how willing will authorities be to impose restrictions on one airport if it has competitive advantages for another? Equally, from an environmental perspective, such an approach is also likely to result in some airlines switching to an airport that is free of restrictions, forcing a rapid increase in the number of aircraft at the noisier end of the spectrum at that airport. While this may subsequently trigger the need to apply restrictions at that airport as well, measures need to be preventative rather than reactionary.

The future: tighter noise regulation

An increasing role for the EU should not conceal the fact that the industry needs to be more forward looking. In our view, immediate steps need to be taken to support the introduction of a phase-out of Chapter 3 aircraft, thereby keeping pressure on both ends of the aircraft noise spectrum. To give the airlines some flexibility in this respect, it is suggested that this is done in two phases: aircraft that are within a 5 dB(A) margin of the existing Chapter 3 standard should be phased out within a period of four years; all other aircraft unable to meet a Chapter 4 standard should be phased out by 2020 at the latest.

But the industry and ICAO also need to develop long-term objectives for aircraft noise reduction. Environmental organizations believe that a cumulative reduction of 30 dB(A) compared to Chapter 3 by 2012 is a realistic target, and one that is consistent with some internal industry targets. For example, Rolls-Royce's Noise Reduction Target is to develop engine technology by 2010 that will reduce noise by half relative to 1998 levels. Long-term goals can help manufacturers and airlines to plan for the future with a degree of confidence, especially in respect of research and development (R&D) programmes. Environmental targets are also required at the airport level: an environmental capacity approach to noise management needs to be developed, with particular attention given to the most emotive issue: night flights.

The long-term objective has to be to continually reduce the number of people currently exposed to excessive noise levels. Failure to do so will guarantee that actions similar to the Heathrow case will become commonplace, and that airport environmental policy will become increasingly fragmented. Such an outcome, based upon variable standards and uncertainty, is in no one's best interest.

Notes

1   This commentary is based on an article for *Issues in Aviation Law and Policy*, 2001.
2   Case of Hatton and Others versus the UK (application no 36022/97), Judgement of the European Court of Human Rights, Strasbourg, 2 October 2001
3   Currently Section 76 of the Civil Aviation Act 1982
4   The range of measures introduced at these airports includes the setting of departure noise limits, noise insulation schemes for residential properties (except for Stansted, which applies a voluntary scheme) and night-noise restrictions.
5   ICAO sets noise certification standards for aircraft, and these are contained within Annex 16 to the Chicago Convention. With regard to subsonic jet aircraft, aircraft certified before 1977 are generally referred to as Chapter 2 (or Stage 2 in the US), while those meeting the more stringent post-1977 standard are referred to as Chapter 3 (the term 'chapter' is a reference to the relevant section of Annex 16).

ENVIRONMENTAL AND ECONOMIC FACTORS
IN AIRPORT CAPACITY

Joop Krul, Schiphol Airport

Introduction

All major institutes expect that air traffic in Europe will double during the next 15 to 20 years. There will be an ongoing concentration of the major alliances on a limited number of hubs. However, hub capacity in Europe is scarce, and airport development on most of these hubs is seriously lagging behind. Delays of air traffic due to airport restrictions will get worse and their share in total delays will be growing. So, capacity problems in the air, caused by the patchwork of European air traffic control, will increasingly become a problem caused by lack of capacity on the ground. Substitution to high-speed trains will become important, but offers no real capacity relief for European airport capacity. Trains might, in the future, substitute only 5 to 10 per cent of total European air traffic. This means that creating airport capacity for future demand, mostly on existing hubs, will become the biggest challenge for airport operators and airlines in the present decade.

Getting political approval for new runways, terminals and other major facilities in Europe can take 10 to 15 years and, in some cases, even longer. Extensive consultation, public inquiries and environmental studies and reviews are required, and even then it may take much more time before the new runway or facility can be built, due to long-lasting land purchase procedures. Moreover, all big airports in Europe are environmentally constrained. This problem is, however, not exclusively European: worldwide, the number of airports with some form of environmental constraint is fast growing. According to the comprehensive Boeing database, airports worldwide impose over 350 restrictions, varying from curfews, to quota, charges, levies and budgets.

There is no evidence that this might change. On the contrary, creating airport capacity for the growing demand of air traffic is, in general, only possible if at the same time airports can prove that the environmental impact for the community will not be worse or, in most cases, will become better. If the social and economic effects have proven to be positive, further development may be possible.

To keep this balance positive, airports have to play in a complex setting with many actors, many decision-makers, strong opinion leaders and often opposing communities involved. While for expansion and development the focus is mostly on the hardware (planes, engines and runways), compensation and mitigation is generally found in extending the software (procedures, standards and measurements). However, the real problem is in the *mind ware*: the image, the perception that the local people and their politicians have regarding further growth of the airport and their reaction towards its expansion.

There are also some serious economic threats to continuing airport expansion. In the first place, there is the decreasing value of large-scale hubs, especially when they have reached a scale where people begin to question if further capacity will still add value to their community. This is especially the case when more capacity and more noise lead to more transfer traffic, and communities do not see a direct interest for their economy. In the second place, when airports are important for their region in attracting new kinds of industries and economic activity, the opportunities also grow for alternative sources of income with lower environmental costs than air transport. Third, with growing economic activities, there is an increasing need for land and competing land use for other activities of the local communities, which in the end can lead to severe constraints on further airport development. Last, there is the welfare paradox: the wealthier people get, the more they want to fly, but also the more they want a healthy environment and, hence, the more restrictions they put on air traffic. Only ongoing improvement in environmental performance can meet both needs.

The Schiphol case: airport development and the need for noise capacity

Management of the noise impact around Schiphol Airport during the past 20 years has been relatively successful. As at most airports, the total area with the same noise impact shrank by one third. The total number of noise-impacted houses dropped from 24,000 in 1982 to 10,000 in 2000. However, in the perception of its neighbours, the situation got worse, and in 1998 affected individuals filed a record number of complaints. These complaints were related to major public events, airport development and a major accident.

Since 1998, Schiphol has been a fully noise-coordinated airport. It has a total noise volume budget, which is also the maximum noise capacity for the airport. The total number of yearly slots has to fit within this budget, so the only way to grow is to make less noise per aircraft movement. There is also a network of measuring points within built-up areas, each with its own maximum noise limit. Fixed land-use planning zones for noise have been designed to ensure that the number of houses cannot rise through new-build as the noise impact has dropped. There is also an external safety zone, defined in relation to a maximum standard for third-party risk and a fixed number of houses. National law enforces the total noise impact of the airport. The airport is responsible for operating within the total noise budget. The air traffic control (ATC) for the operations (routes) and the airlines can be penalized if the airlines (without ATC permission) do not follow prescribed routes.

The most effective way to enable growth within those noise limits is ongoing reduction of the noise at the source: all other measures are trivial compared with the effect of phasing out the noisier aircraft. However, the phase-out of Chapter 2 aircraft is practically complete, so at Schiphol we have to begin phasing out marginal Chapter 3 aircraft to enable growth within the fixed noise budget. This year, Schiphol started with a dynamic surcharge and operational (night) restrictions for Chapter 3 aircraft. Other measures, such as quieter flight procedures and preferential runway use, do help in reducing noise hindrance but have no effect on the total noise volume budget. This is contrary to reduced night flights, as each night flight equals ten day-flights with respect to the noise budget. In 2003, the opening of the new fifth runway will give important noise relief and therefore not only generate more runway capacity, but also new noise capacity.

In 2000, total traffic demand and the required runway capacity could be roughly handled within the available noise budget, thanks to the total phase-out of Chapter 2 aircraft. In 2003, the opening of the fifth runway will enable further growth to

600,000 movements in 2010. However, in a business-as-usual scenario, noise capacity will fall short. In 2020, when traffic demand has doubled, the situation repeats: a new runway is needed, but this investment is only justified if we can dispose of the corresponding noise capacity. This means that at Schiphol the noise performance of the overall fleet in 2020 has to improve by 3.75 decibel noise units – dB(A). This will be roughly the same for other airports with comparable traffic figures. In terms of reaching this, the majority (72 per cent) of the present fleet operating at Schiphol will need to consist of planes not older than ten years. As the phase-out of Chapter 2 has already been completed, we will have to phase out almost all marginal Chapter 3 aircraft before 2010 (eg older 737s, A300, MD80, 747-300). For the period after 2010, new technology is urgently needed. These conclusions can also be drawn for other airports.

The present international situation: CAEP 5

On the basis of the general assumption that world air traffic will double in the next 15 years, the Airports Council International (ACI) proposed and passed a policy of increased noise stringency of minus 14 dB(A), with at least minus 4 dB(A) at each measuring point. The ACI proposal also included the phase-out of substandard Chapter 3 aircraft by 2005 and immediate operating restrictions for those aircraft. With regard to this proposal and the problematic situation at most airports, the results of CAEP 5 in January 2001 were rather disappointing. The Committee on Aviation and Environmental Protection (CAEP) proposed a stringency of minus 10 dB(A), which will not be effective until 2006. It is only applicable for new aircraft and there will be no phase-out of Chapter 3 aircraft. This means that the proposed stringency will be insufficient and too late for most airports that want to develop new capacity. As phase-out of substandard Chapter 3 aircraft is strongly needed, the CAEP decision will lead to further differentiation in policies between states and regions.

If ICAO–CAEP wants to be the primary international regulator – a role that is needed – then it needs at least to reconsider its noise policies in order to:

- sustain further growth with at least the same level of noise, but preferably an improvement;
- provide relief at noise-sensitive airports;
- prevent regional proliferation of different rules; and
- permit airport capacity development for meeting future traffic demand.

POTENTIAL IMPROVEMENTS TO AIR TRAFFIC MANAGEMENT

Arthur Lieuwen and Ted Elliff, EUROCONTROL

Introduction

This commentary briefly describes some current EUROCONTROL initiatives that are designed to improve European airspace management. Further details can be found on the organization's website (www.eurocontrol.be/). EUROCONTROL is the European Organization for the Safety of Air Navigation, currently with 30 member states, and with the primary objective of developing a seamless pan-European air traffic management (ATM) system. Accordingly, EUROCONTROL develops, coordinates and plans for implementation of short-, medium- and long-term pan-European ATM strategies and their associated action plans in a collective effort involving national authorities, air-navigation service providers, civil and military airspace users, airports, industry, professional organizations and relevant European institutions.

Air transport is a growth industry, and it must balance increasing demand with responsible and responsive measures to mitigate its impact on the environment. This goal is recognized in the EUROCONTROL Air Traffic Management (ATM) Strategy for the years 2000+, of which a key objective is the reduction of air traffic-related effects of aviation on the environment. Reducing the impacts of noise and emissions from aircraft operations are the most important contributions that air traffic management can make to mitigate the environmental impact of aviation. Whether through improvements to airspace organization or the introduction of communications, navigation and surveillance (CNS) technology, the implementation of the ATM 2000+ Strategy, encompassing the entire spectrum of flight activities, gate to gate, will help aviation meet environmental objectives.

The need for ATM improvement

Although the global volume of controlled civil air traffic was virtually static between 1975 and 1985, since then there has been sustained growth of between 5 per cent and 12 per cent every year. By the year 2015, forecasts suggest a probable doubling of 1997 traffic figures. In Europe, the European ATM Programme (EATMP) has managed to find an additional 40 per cent capacity from within existing ATM systems by improving communications and procedures designed to eliminate air traffic bottlenecks. Yet, more will be needed to cope with the forecast growth; an entirely new approach to ATM is required.

Although airport congestion in Europe and North America has posed a problem for some time, airport ATM-related operations have never been integrated fully within the overall system. Besides, airspace is still organized largely according to national boundaries, and the levels of services provision in Europe are uneven; the lack of uniformity in en-route and airport operations has effectively prevented the optimization of resources and is environmentally inefficient.

A composite network is needed in order to unite the three key players in aviation: aircraft operators, the airports and ATM, which is itself made up of three parts: air traffic control (ATC), air traffic flow management (ATFM) and airspace management (ASM). The European Civil Aviation Conference (ECAC) ministers adopted this point of view in 1997 and commissioned the drafting of a comprehensive gate-to-gate ATM strategy. Furthermore, they stressed the growing importance of taking environmental issues into account when considering future developments.

The major objective of the EUROCONTROL ATM 2000+ Strategy is to realize a long-standing ambition for European aviation: a uniform airspace for Europe, one that encompasses airspace at, and around, airports as well as en route. This, applied in conjunction with emerging technologies, will give maximum freedom of movement to users, providing them with distinct cost–benefit results and increased environmental efficiency. The strategy stresses the necessity for consistent, high-quality management processes; it advocates systematic collaboration of all partners and focuses on transparent decision-making.

The existing route structure sometimes imposes mileage penalties compared to the most economic routes (generally great-circle routes), taking into account wind, temperature and other factors, such as aircraft weight, charges and safety. Use of a fixed-route network results in concentration of air traffic flows at major intersections, which can lead to a reduction in a number of routes and available flight levels. Studies on penalties to air traffic associated with the European air traffic system (ATS) route network suggest that ATM-related problems add an average of about 9 per cent to the flight-track distance of all European flights en route and in the terminal area (TMA). Insufficient international coordination in the development of ground ATC systems and of maximizing airport and airspace capacity exacerbates these problems.

EUROCONTROL environmental policy and strategy

Article 1 of the revised EUROCONTROL convention gives the agency a clear mandate to play a central role of ECAC ATM-related environmental issues. In order to comply with the revised convention, environmental objectives have been fully integrated within the EUROCONTROL ATM 2000+ Strategy. The strategy considers that ATM-related environmental considerations are an essential part of the ATM decision-making process and that, wherever possible, the most environmentally efficient solutions should be adopted.

The EUROCONTROL ATM 2000+ Strategy was approved by the ECAC ministers of transport in January 2000 at their sixth meeting on the air traffic system in Europe (MATSE/6). It has a number of strategic objectives, covering safety, economy, capacity, national security and defence requirements, uniformity, quality and human factors. The reduction of air traffic-related effects of aviation on the environment is also one of the major strategic objectives of ATM 2000+, as stated below:

> ...to work with ICAO and its Member States to obtain improvements in ATM, in particular the accelerated implementation of CNS/ATM concepts, procedures and systems which help to mitigate the impact of aviation on the environment.

Furthermore, at that meeting, the ECAC ministers:

> Reaffirmed [their] commitment to develop air traffic services so as to maintain safe, cost-effective and environmentally sustainable air transport, which will benefit European economic development and, in particular, airports, airlines, the travelling public and other users of Europe's airspace.

In response to this commitment, EUROCONTROL's member states unanimously adopted a proposal for an Environmental Policy and Strategy (2001), which aims to:

- permit aircraft operations with a minimum environmental impact;
- comply with international standards and regulations; and

- support actions contributing to the management and mitigation of aviation noise and emissions.

Furthermore, the strategy provides an overall framework for increased cooperation on environmental issues between EUROCONTROL and its key stakeholders, including the International Civil Aviation Organization (ICAO), the standing European Civil Aviation Conference (ECAC), the European Commission (EC), airlines, airports and other relevant international and national bodies.

Conclusion

As aviation activity in Europe increases, the pressure on aircraft operators, airports and the ATM system to increase capacity will intensify the debate on the environmental impact of aviation. In particular, it must be determined whether it is possible to achieve an environmentally sustainable air traffic system throughout ECAC, while simultaneously meeting demand.

EUROCONTROL is now in the process of putting its environmental policy and strategy in place. It has already contributed significantly to ICAO efforts through its support for CAEP, as well as ECAC–ANCAT (the Committee on Abatement of Nuisances Caused by Air Transport of the standing European Civil Aviation Conference). The approved environmental policy and strategy confirms EUROCONTROL's joint commitment with its stakeholders to ensuring that environmental concerns are built into the ATM decision-making process.

MAKING AVIATION LESS UNSUSTAINABLE: SOME POINTERS TO THE WAY AHEAD

Caroline Lucas, MEP

…an unquestioning attitude towards future growth in air travel, and an acceptance that the projected demand for additional facilities must be met, are incompatible with the aims of sustainable development (RCEP, 1994).

The problem

Flights to Dublin for less than a pint of beer, trips to Athens for the price of a meal for two…air travellers have never had it so good, and more people than ever before are taking to the skies. But, at the risk of sounding like Cassandra warning of gathering gloom on the horizon, trends like these simply cannot last.

Consider the facts. Aviation is the fastest-growing source of greenhouse gas emissions and looks set to be a major contributor to climate change. Air traffic is forecast to almost double during the next 15 years. Government air traffic forecast figures show total passenger numbers at UK airports rising from 160 million in 1998 to 400 million in around 20 years' time. If we were to try to apply a predict-and-provide model to that level of demand, that increase of 240 million passengers would require the equivalent of four new airports the size of Heathrow or eight new airports the size of Gatwick.

By 2020, the forecasts indicate that demand will be rising by about 15 million a year, equivalent to a new Gatwick Airport every two years.

Clearly, the political as well as the environmental consequences of such expansion would be totally unacceptable. These projections only serve to show the nonsense of assuming the possibility of continuous exponential growth. The old 'predict-and-provide' model is simply not going to work and has to be abandoned.

Most significantly, climate scientists have concluded that improvements in aircraft and engine technology and in air traffic management will not offset the projected growth in aircraft emissions. That means that, in order to reduce the growth in aircraft greenhouse gas emissions, we will have to slow, and then reverse, the growth of air travel.

The European Commission's *Communication on Air Transport and the Environment* (COM(1999)640-C5-0086/2000) comes to a similar conclusion:

> *The air transport industry is growing faster than we are currently producing, and introducing technological and operational advances which reduce the environmental impact at source. The overall environmental impact is bound to increase since the gap between the rate of growth and the rate of environmental improvement appears to widen in important fields such as emissions of greenhouse gases. This trend is unsustainable and must be reversed because of its impact on climate and the quality of life and health of European citizens.* (EC, 1999)

Some solutions

We are not short of policy instruments to begin to curb the growth of aviation. Key among them would be:

- a European-level charge on aviation, based on emissions;
- an end to all public subsidies to aviation and to all its tax exemptions;
- investment in less-polluting travel alternatives; since 70 per cent of European air trips are less than 1000km, there is huge scope for transfer to alternatives;
- research into, and promotion of, further alternatives to business air travel, including video-conferencing, telepresence, etc;
- optimization of air traffic control, which alone could reduce aviation's carbon dioxide (CO_2) emissions by 6–12 per cent over 20 years;
- changes to land-use planning law, requiring all applications for airport development to give full consideration to climate change, health, external costs and alternative job creation; and
- a public education programme on the negative economic and ecological consequences of air transport.

The new bottom line

The Intergovernmental Panel on Climate Change (IPCC) is calling for cuts of at least 60 per cent in CO_2 emissions by 2050. Aviation needs to play its part in achieving that goal: this is the new bottom line. And this is where sustainable development becomes not just a matter of political negotiation but a profound challenge to the way in which we live our lives.

Much will need to change as we shift away from our dependence on a carbon economy. Cost internalization and energy taxes will have a key role to play in the move to relocalize our economies. That doesn't mean putting an end to all international trade; but it does mean limiting the unnecessary transport of goods by trying to meet as many of our basic needs as possible from closer to home.

And individual habits will have to change, too, as we weigh the economic benefits of aviation against its longer-term environmental (and hence, ultimately, also economic) costs, and squarely address the argument that air travel has undoubtedly brought a new freedom to many people.

But democratic government is, in the last analysis, about drawing lines between different freedoms. Against one person's freedom to fly, we have to balance another's freedom to be free of noise and nuisance and pollution – and, ultimately, the freedom to act in the knowledge that there will be a healthy future not only today, but in years to come.

References

EC (1999) *Air Transport and the Environment*, Communication from the Commission to the Council, the European Parliament, the Economic and Social Committee and the Committee of the Regions, Brussels, 1 December, COM (1999) 640

RCEP (1994) *Transport and the Environment*, 18th Report of the Royal Commission on Environmental Pollution, Cm 2674, RCEP, London

SUSTAINABLE AVIATION: WHAT DO YOU MEAN?

Mark McLellan, Partner, GreenAscent

sustainable (adj):
1   *Capable of being borne or endured; supportable, bearable.*
2   *Capable of being upheld or defended; maintainable.*
3   *Capable of being maintained at a certain rate or level* (Simpson and Weiner, 1989).

Every now and then, environmental policy adopts a new word. E O Wilson's 'biodiversity' (Wilson, 1987) irritated many life science professionals in the 1980s; but since there was no other word to describe 'the whole variety of life on earth', it resonated in the media, persisted and is now mainstream. Like the word or not, biodiversity is useful shorthand with a clear meaning.

Compare biodiversity's word journey to that of 'sustainability'. The *Oxford English Dictionary* meaning of the word and its synonyms is clear enough (Simpson and Weiner, 1989), but when linked to 'development', or to emerging environmental and social policy, confusion sets in. Far from being defined, sustainability is subject to a wide range of general and specific interpretations (Upham, 2000). The current debate on the future of aviation is a good example of how the semantics of sustainability deny clarity. The future of aviation in the UK is already based on a policy of 'sustainable aviation'; but the recent formal consultation in the UK (DETR, 2000) has produced a spectrum of interpretation as to what this actually means.

The UK government, in its strategy for sustainable development (DETR, 1999), has four main aims:

- social progress that recognizes the needs of everyone;
- effective protection of the environment;
- prudent use of natural resources;
- maintenance of high and stable levels of economic growth and employment.

This political interpretation is related to the metaphor of a balanced 'three-legged stool' of economic growth, social progress and environmental protection. This interpretation is favoured and cited by many aviation industry respondents to the UK consultation. For example, on the question of limiting growth by establishing environmental limits, several airlines argue that this would put environmental issues above economic factors and social considerations, which is at odds with government sustainability policy.[1]

However, several other versions of sustainability are present in the consultation responses and elsewhere in the aviation debate. Before examining some examples, it is worth reminding ourselves of the brief history of sustainability.

This term and its synonyms began to appear widely in policy documents after the Brundtland Report (WCED, 1987), which addressed forecasts of depletion of global natural resources, coupled to human population growth statistics. The report concluded that planetary supply could not meet the demand of predicted human populations; that development at predicted rates was *simply unsustainable*; and that a new approach was necessary through *sustainable development*.

Brundtland's sustainable development was 'development that meets the needs of the present world without compromising the ability of future generations to meet their own needs' (WCED, 1987). To some extent, this was a challenge to the old hegemony of 'sustainable growth', which demanded a 'rise in per capita real gross national product for a long time' (Schumacher, 1969); but did it really contain and embody the first principles long espoused by environmental and social justice campaigners?

For many of us, that vital resources limit species population growth and homeostasis was O-level biology, and evident neglect of the planet in favour of national gross domestic product (GDP) league tables was A-level geography. As an environmental undergraduate in 1980, it was evident that a new language was necessary to hitch economics to ecology:

> *The laws of supply and demand are fundamentals not just of economics, but also of planetary ecology. Some human cultures have been able to forge an equilibrial relationship with their local ecologies for vast periods of time. They have been able to derive their necessary sustenance, without disrupting the ability of the earth to replenish itself. Translating this ability from local to global is the modern human challenge. To achieve it, there needs to be a wholesale re-engagement of people to planet, and a global ecology that*

defines the rules of human exploitation and development. This might be called 'ecological development' (McLellan, 1980).

Much earlier, in 1969, E F Schumacher coined the terms 'healthy and unhealthy development' (Schumacher, 1969). Unhealthy development for Schumacher leads to a degradation of people and ruination of the environment. Healthy development leads to an upgrading of people and their environment on the widest possible scale (Schumacher, 1969).

For Schumacher and me, Brundtland's 'sustainable development' was an insipid dilution of ecological principles, open to abuse by traditional economic philosophy and technocratic progress. But it did offer the opportunity to wrestle environmental principles to the fore in new arenas. Those of us who believe in the full integration of economic, social and environmental issues prefer the analogy of a 'three-egged omelette' to a 'three-legged stool', and there is little doubt that a sustainability omelette is more palatable to industry than a raw environmental egg.

As debate and study continued, some useful core principles of sustainable development were published. The offspring phrase 'environmental sustainability' began to appear, containing such principles as those adopted by the World Bank:

- The rate of use of renewable resources must not exceed their rate of regeneration.
- The rate of use of non-renewable resources must not exceed the rate at which renewable substitutes are developed.
- The rate of pollution emission should not exceed the assimilative capacity of the environment (Daly, 1990).

Several organizations have developed these and similar principles (Upham, 2000), and some technologies have been more amenable than others to sustainability analysis. Certainly, the contemporary debate on what is, and what is not, sustainable aviation flounders for logic and consistency.

At the first SCAN-UK International Conference in April 2001 (SCAN-UK, 2001), references to the 'unsustainable growth in aviation' or 'the commitment of the industry to the principles of sustainable development' abounded. Those preferring a rhetorical use outnumbered speakers who prefaced their remarks with an interpretation of what they meant by their 's' words.

Strange arguments were propounded. I give just two examples, but there are many others. Some industry representatives proposed that if environmental costs can be internalized and the proceeds used to address environmental issues, then growth is 'sustainable'. However, there is no consensus that the internalization of external environmental costs constitutes sustainability (though it may be an important component of achieving it).

By contrast, environmental campaigners cited the forecast growth statistics of aviation, calculated the airport infrastructure provided, and pronounced this to be 'unsustainable'. Some went further and compared the forecast rate of growth with forecast improvements from technology on noise and pollution abatement, demonstrated that these would not tally, and thereby invoked 'unsustainability'. Again, there is no consensus to support this conclusion, although a possible principle of sustainable aviation may be to counter any growth with technological improvement in order to keep overall impacts from rising.

I call for the following measures:

- As a rule of debate, the use of 'sustainable' or its synonyms by participants must be qualified with an explanation of interpretation.
- A comprehensive study should assess aviation under all current definitions, interpretations and analytic systems of sustainability.
- Arising from this study, a brokered consensus on definitions, components and indicators of sustainable aviation should be attempted.
- New descriptive language and component terms should be developed to include 'accountable', 'acceptable', 'justifiable' and 'responsible' aviation.

From here to sustainability? In the case of aviation, there is a long way to go; but first, let us develop a useful lexicon.

Note

1   Responses were inspected at the UK Department for Transport, Local Government and the Regions (DTLR) library, London, January 2002.

References

DETR (1999) *A Better Quality of Life: A Strategy for Sustainable Development for the United Kingdom*, Department of the Environment, Transport and the Regions, Cm 4345, HMSO, London

DETR (2000) *The Future of Aviation: The Government's Consultation Document on Air Transport Policy*, Department of Environment, Transport and the Regions, HMSO, London

Daly, H E (1990) 'Toward some Operational Principles of Sustainable Development', *Ecological Economics* vol 2, pp1–6

McLellan, M R (1980) 'Ecological Development: The Modern Human Challenge', Essay submitted to School of Applied Biology, University of Hertfordshire (unpublished)

SCAN-UK (2001) *Environmental Capacity at Airports*, UK Sustainable Cities and Aviation Network First International Conference, 2–3 April 2001, Manchester Metropolitan University

Schumacher, E F (1969) 'Healthy Development', *Resurgence*, vol 2, no 8/9

Simpson, J A and Weiner, E S C (eds) (1989) *Oxford English Dictionary*, second edition, vol XVII, Clarendon Press, Oxford, p327

Upham, P (2000) 'Scientific Consensus on Sustainability: The Case of the Natural Step', *Sustainable Development*, vol 8, pp180–190

WCED (1987) *Our Common Future*, World Commission on Environment and Development, Oxford University Press, Oxford

Wilson, E O (1987) 'An Urgent Need To Map Biodiversity', *Scientist*, vol 1(6), 9 February, p11

SUSTAINABILITY AND AVIATION:
PROBLEMS AND SOLUTIONS

Beatrice Schell, T&E[1]

The problems

Aviation produces local air pollution, noise and climate change. In the European Union (EU) it also contributes to the economic inefficiencies of our transport system and harms the quality of life of vast numbers of European citizens. While it is still common to promote aviation's so-called benefits (freedom, mobility, prestige, etc), the benefits that we all take for granted are being increasingly outweighed by the costs that the air transport sector poses to our society.

The problems are hardly minor. Aviation noise is creating health and psychological problems, hindering learning and globally exposing several millions of citizens to significantly disturbing noise levels. Local air pollution, to which aviation contributes, is a cause of health problems and can trigger fatality in vulnerable people. Perhaps most ominous, aviation is the fastest growing source of greenhouse gases and thus contributes to climate change.

These impacts should not come as a surprise. Their associated costs are referred to by economists as externalities because the people who cause them don't have to pay for them. More than this, aviation has benefited during the last 50 years from many direct and indirect subsidies generously and indifferently granted by most countries' governments. What other sector is experiencing 5 per cent per year growth[2], growth which is inevitably off-setting environmental efficiencies and having major negative effects? The aviation industry and its defenders argue that major efforts have already been made to improve the fuel efficiency of the sector. They also point out that noise and other standards have already brought about improved technology to deal with environmental problems; and that they are currently very active in developing instruments that can help tackle some of the environmental problems aviation causes. To be fair, it is true that noise standards have become more stringent over the years and that much is being done in and around airports to tackle some of the problems of air pollution. Yet, in terms of carbon dioxide (CO_2) emissions, the right technology is not yet available and the fuel efficiency improvements are insufficient to even limit the growth in emissions.[3] Much more is needed to deal with this serious problem – including curbing the strong growth of the sector.

Decision-making for solutions

Citizens have been complaining for a long time about noise and health problems created by aviation, waiting for their elected governments to act. Until recently, they have had little support; but now a number of environmental organizations have become active in political discussions about aviation's impact on the environment. My organization was one of the first. There are many different levels for decision-making when it comes to aviation and its environmental impact, and here environment impact is taken to mean climate change.

Because climate change is a global problem, and aviation is a global sector operating in dozens of countries, tackling the problem needs to happen at a global level. Yet, the difficulty of getting agreement among lots of countries is often given as the reason for the lack of action to date, and meanwhile no agreement means no action.

Are appropriate solutions likely at the global level? Perhaps. Countries often negotiate international protocols and conventions to tackle environmental problems, and the United Nations Framework Convention on Climate Change (UNFCCC), signed by 160 countries at the 1992 Earth Summit in Rio, is the classic case of an attempt at global cooperation. The same countries signed the Kyoto Protocol in 1997. Most countries agree on the need to develop policies and implement measures to tackle climate change, but they differ in the way that this can be done. Discussions have taken place over the years on how to deal with emissions from aviation that occur over the oceans – so-called 'international bunker fuels' – and which are therefore not allocated to any particular nation.

Since there has been no political agreement on this thorny issue, the International Civil Aviation Organization (ICAO) has asked countries to try to find solutions. Yet, forcing ICAO and UNFCCC to work together has been something of a culture shock, especially for ICAO. Both are agencies of the United Nations (UN), but there the similarity ends. While the UNFCCC is looking for solutions to an environmental problem, ICAO exists to protect the economic interests of an industry. While the decisions in the one are transparent and involve mostly environmental ministries, the other is run by transport ministries. Although tackling climate change is being seriously addressed by the ICAO, there are many barriers to it producing an appropriate response.

What, therefore, should be done? There is another level of trans-national decision-making: the European Union (EU). The EU treaty has as one of its major principles the integration of environmental protection within all sectors, as well as sustainable development. Not responding to the problems caused by aviation would thus mean acting against the European Union treaty. This has been recently reinforced by concrete messages from the Gothenburg European Council, which put sustainable development and its three pillars (economic, environmental and social) at the core of European Union policy.[4]

At the EU level, there are some simple actions that could be implemented with a little political will, and which would begin to tackle the environmental impact of aviation:

- An environmental charge for European aviation would be both feasible and effective (Wit and Bleijenberg, 1998).
- Intra-European flights need to contribute to the overall emission reduction target agreed by the EU in Kyoto.
- An emissions-trading system needs more study and analysis.
- All greenhouse gas emissions – not just CO_2 – need to be taken into account when developing a programme on emissions.[5]

It will obviously be necessary to have a global solution to a global problem for a global industry; but the first step towards that could be an example set in Europe showing how action can take place, and within a short time span. This could easily be done within the EU.

Notes

1   T&E is the European Federation for Transport and Environment, the principal umbrella for around 40 non-governmental organizations (NGOs) in 21 countries in Europe working on transport and environment issues. T&E is also the official CAEP/ICAO observer on behalf of ICSA. ICSA stands for the International Coalition for Sustainable Aviation and is an informal coalition of NGOs, which include the Aviation Environment Federation, the Centre for Clean Air Policy, the Clean Air Coalition, Friends of the Earth, the German League for Nature Protection, the Dutch Society for Nature Conservation, the Natural Resources Defence Council and the World Wide Fund for Nature.

2   The IPCC *Special Report on Aviation and the Global Atmosphere: Summary for Policymakers*, states: 'Global passenger air travel, as measured in revenue passenger km is projected to grow by about 5 per cent per year between 1990 and 2015, whereas total aviation fuel use – including passenger, freight and military – is projected to increase by 3 per cent per year over the same period, the difference being due largely to improved aircraft efficiency' (IPCC, 1999, p 4).

3   Article 2.2 for the Kyoto Protocol states that the 'Parties included in Annex I shall pursue limitation or reduction of emissions of greenhouse gases not controlled by the Montreal Protocol from aviation...working through the International Civil Aviation Organisation' (UNFCCC, 1997).

4   The EU's sustainable development strategy is based upon the principle that the economic, social and environmental effects of all policies should be examined in a coordinated way and taken into account in decision-making. 'Getting prices right' so that they better reflect the true costs to society of different activities would provide a better incentive for consumers and producers in everyday decisions about which goods and services to make or buy. Furthermore, 'a sustainable transport policy should tackle rising volumes of traffic and levels of congestion, noise and pollution and encourage the use of environment-friendly modes of transport as well as the full internalization of social and environmental costs. Action is needed to bring about a significant decoupling of transport growth and GDP growth' (EC, 2001).

5   IPCC (1999, pp8–9) states: 'Over the period from 1992 to 2050, the overall radiative forcing by aircraft for all scenarios in this report is a factor 2 to 4 larger than the forcing by aircraft carbon dioxide alone'. The other gases are ozone, methane, water vapour, contrails, cirrus clouds, sulphate and soot aerosols.

References

EC (2001) *A Sustainable Europe for a Better World: European Union Strategy for Sustainable Development*, COM(2001)264 final communication from the Commission, Commission of the European Communities, Brussels, 15 May 2001, available at www.europa.eu.int/eur-lex/en/com/cnc/2001/com2001_0264en01.pdf

IPCC (1999) *Special Report on Aviation and the Global Atmosphere: Summary for Policymakers*, Intergovernmental Panel on Climate Change, Geneva

UNFCCC (1997) *Kyoto Protocol to the United Nations Framework Convention on Climate Change*, UNFCCC Secretariat, Bonn, Germany. text available at www.unfccc.de/resource/docs/convkp/kpeng.pdf

Wit, R and Bleijenberg, A (1998) *A European Environmental Aviation Charge: Feasibility Study*, Centre for Energy and Environmental Technology, Delft, the Netherlands

AIRLINES AND SUSTAINABLE DEVELOPMENT

Hugh Somerville, British Airways

Introduction

In May 1999, the UK government strategy for sustainable development was published (DETR, 1999) and provides a useful benchmark against which to examine aviation. According to the UK government, sustainable development involves 'a better quality of life for everyone, now and for generations to come' (DETR, 1999). This brief interpretation is relatively easy to support, though some might argue that it could be more demanding. There is little doubt that aviation can improve the quality of life. Discussion centres on the selective nature of access to aviation and the balance of costs and benefits. While the real cost of aviation has reduced over the years, it is still only accessible to a minority of the global population. No one should contest the need for a favourable balance of benefits against undesirable environmental and social effects. Quality of life and sustainability cannot be delivered by individual companies but, rather, by society as a whole.

The UK government identifies four objectives for sustainable development and these can be used as a framework for considering aviation.

Social progress that recognizes the needs of everyone

Aviation is an essential part of the world's communication and economic system. Directly and indirectly, it provides jobs throughout the world. Leisure and business travel, and air cargo provide benefits to economies, both of developed and less-developed countries. By bringing people together, airlines contribute to business, to political understanding and to cultural interchange. Leading companies in aviation are publicly reporting on relevant social issues. However, business and society, as a whole, still have a long way to go to realize aspirations respecting human rights.

Effective protection of the environment

Aviation has invested consistently in clean technology, through acquisition of newer aircraft emitting less noise, using less fuel and emitting less of polluting exhaust gases. Many airlines now track progress in minimizing effects on the environment through targets and indicators, which are reported to the public. There is an open and expanding programme of reporting on environmental performance and engaging in dialogue with key stakeholder groups.

Prudent use of natural resources

Leading airlines measure and report the consumption of natural resources and set targets for improvement. Although remarkable progress has been made, there is still a long way to go. We believe that efficiency is an essential first step on the route to long-term sustainability.

Maintaining high and stable levels of economic growth and employment

Aviation has shown a consistent pattern of overall growth in economic and employment terms over the last few decades. This pattern will continue, although the rate of growth may slow. While there is a need to identify the external costs of aviation, their levels will depend upon scientific determination of impacts and upon development of appropriate costing mechanisms. In the meantime, minimizing the impacts is the best route to reducing these costs.

The fundamental question for transport organizations is whether clean technology, efficiency and environmental responsibility will be sufficient to attain long-term sustainability in the eyes of society, as a whole. There are three elements commonly taken as contributing to sustainability, outlined below, and these raise a number of issues and questions that should be asked of an airline.

Environmental

Is there a commitment to reducing the harmful impacts of aviation? How can airlines improve performance and work with others on noise, emissions, waste management and sustainable tourism?

Economic

This is the basic requirement without which environmental and social programmes are virtually meaningless. What do airlines offer the world in terms of trade flow, jobs, shareholder returns and communications infrastructure? What benefits do their passengers bring to their destinations and points of departure?

Social

What is the quality of airline relationships with staff, customers and shareholders, as well as suppliers, partners, communities, regulators and other stakeholders? Who is excluded from the prosperity they generate, and who are the victims? Do they meet their fundamental responsibilities to our employees and our customers in terms of wealth creation, safety, security and fair play? Do they respect human rights?

Airlines will only add value in the eyes of their stakeholders if their image and supporting activities address all three areas and are relevant, not necessarily equally, to all stakeholder groups.

Climate change – the long-term view

There is a further factor that merits discussion in relation to airlines and sustainability – namely, the major issue of climate change (IPCC, 1999). The first imperative is to pursue fuel efficiency coupled to best available technology. Emissions trading based on conversion to carbon dioxide equivalents is the best medium-term solution for aviation. Such trading must be linked to other industries and to mechanisms for offsetting carbon dioxide emissions, and progress towards this must be made on a global basis. In the meantime, it is essential that priority is also given to developing a better understanding of the fate and effects of nitrogen oxide (NO_x) and water vapour exhaust emissions at cruise altitudes. With this understanding, the industry will be able to identify any relevant radical changes in technology. Already, Boeing is working on the concept of fuel cells powering aircraft during cruise; direct use of hydrogen is another possibility. British Airways is a member of a group looking at the potential of alternative sources of energy for aircraft, including hydrogen fuel cells and the possible use of fuel from biomass. However, new fuel technologies are more likely to apply first to terrestrial transport.

Conclusion

It is possible to build pictures in which aviation is a part of a sustainable society; but it is far too early to be definitive. Aviation has a long history of environmental innovation and outstanding improvements continue to be made. There is still substantial uncertainty over the effects of engine exhaust emissions, particularly in relation to global warming. Priority should be given to determining these effects. The industry is not unwilling to consider control measures, but has a strong view that they must combine environmental benefit with economic reasonableness. There is no reason why aviation should not continue to grow within the overall context of sustainable development. Governments, in particular the UK government, face tough decisions in this regard.

References

DETR (1999) *A Better Quality of Life: A Strategy for Sustainable Development for the United Kingdom,* Department of the Environment, Transport and the Regions, Cm 4345, HMSO, London, Available in full at www.environment.detr.gov.uk/sustainable/quality/life/index.htm and in brief summary at www.environment.detr.gov.uk/sustainable/consult2/index.htm

IPCC (1999) *Aviation and the Global Atmosphere,* Cambridge University Press.

THE CASE FOR 'NO GROWTH'

John Whitelegg, Liverpool John Moores University[1]

Introduction

The aviation industry and its future prospects are central to whether or not sustainable development can really make a difference to traditional political and business decision-making. Currently, the industry is locked into ambitious growth plans that are progressed in the absence of any indication or measurement of what level of flying is consistent with sustainable development objectives. More interestingly, the industry has embraced the language and rhetoric of sustainable development/sustainable aviation, while at the same time being deeply committed to the most unsustainable form of behaviour. A commitment to growth without limit is fundamentally unsustainable, and the aviation industry is hostile to any suggestion that growth should slow and then be reversed. This short contribution to the debate argues the case for a no-growth aviation industry.

Aviation has some very special characteristics. It is the fastest growing consumer of energy in transport, and transport is the fastest growing consumer of energy in all sectors of the economy. Aviation pays no tax on fuel, receives large subsidies in the form of state expenditures on infrastructure and grows at a rate that in the UK requires another Heathrow airport every five years. Every airport has an expansion plan (more runways and more terminals), every business has an eye on expansion through logistics and the opportunities presented by globalization (air freight), and every poor region of the world thinks that tourism (air passengers) will bring income and wealth. This is a powerful cocktail of forces working towards higher and higher levels of kilometres flown and tonnes of freight carried by air.

Demand for air transport

The number of passengers carried by global aviation in the year 2000 was 1.6 billion. Contrary to the impression given by this very large number, only 5 per cent of the world's population have ever flown. Thus, the growth potential of this industry – assuming capacity problems at airports and in airspace can be overcome – is enormous. Over the past 20 years, the number of passengers carried into and out of UK airports has trebled and air transport movements and freight have doubled. This is also a global phenomenon, with growth rates in the Asia and Pacific regions being greater than in the UK. The industry itself estimates that global air travel will increase threefold by 2020 on a 1999 base. Since this growth is stronger than aircraft fuel-efficiency gains (currently about 1 per cent per annum), the aviation industry cannot avoid significant increases in greenhouse gas emissions over the next 20 years. On this simplest of measures of what is sustainable, the aviation industry is not currently sustainable.

Greenhouse gas emissions

The relationship of aviation to climate change is reported elsewhere in the book. While this will not be repeated here, it remains one of the most pressing reasons for curbing aviation growth. Suffice it to say that, year on year, increases in energy consumption and greenhouse gas emissions are not compatible with national and international strategies to reduce greenhouse gas emissions. International discussions aimed at reducing the greenhouse gas emissions of aviation continue within the International Civil Aviation Organization (ICAO); but nothing has emerged that can even begin to deliver aviation's contribution to reducing greenhouse gases in the UK by the 12.5 per cent of the Kyoto agreement or by the 20 per cent 'domestic goal'. The implication of this 'no-go' area in greenhouse reduction targets is that other sectors of the economy must make greater proportionate reductions in order to create the space for aviation to continue on its upward growth trajectory. This is once again a departure from the principles of sustainable development; it is unfair and it is inefficient from an economic perspective. There is no evidence that society, as a whole, gains from the expansion of aviation under these privileged circumstances (no greenhouse gas (GHG) reduction targets and no tax on fuels). If anything, the evidence on externalities, environmental costs and human health shows that aviation is a drag on economic performance.

Health impacts of aviation

Evidence on the health impacts of aviation is currently biased towards the impact on those who live near airports or under flight paths. Air pollution around airports is severe enough to damage human health. A US Environmental Protection Agency (USEPA) study in 1993 (USEPA, 1993) concluded that 11 per cent of the cancer cases in south-west Chicago could be attributed to aircraft emissions from Midway Airport. Emissions from cars, trucks, buses and trains contributed 25 per cent of the cases. The aviation industry in the UK frequently draws attention to the 'tiny' contribution of aviation emissions to total potentially harmful emissions. The USEPA study shows that this is not the case, with aviation emissions running just under half of all land transport emissions. The expansion of Heathrow Airport with Terminal 5 will expose 250,000 residents in Hounslow, Hillingdon and further afield to increased levels of toxic emissions and health-damaging noise. Aircraft noise is a long-standing problem and is discussed elsewhere in the book.

Mitigation

The aviation industry is fundamentally and unsurprisingly committed to the year-on-year growth of its output, with growth rates large enough to cancel out gains in the noise performance of engines and in the fuel efficiency of aircraft (engines, weight, materials and aerodynamics). Given this, one has to ask whether sustainable aviation can really exist. Governments around the world have accepted two sets of interrelated arguments about aviation. First, it is difficult or impossible for a national government to intervene because, by definition, aviation is an international industry and, second, aviation is good for the economy and if we try to interfere the only result (in Europe) would be a shift of pollution and GHG production from Heathrow (for example) to Paris Charles de Gaule, Frankfurt or Amsterdam Schiphol. Both sets of arguments are fatally flawed.

Aviation is a polluting, classic 'dirty' business and on clear public health, environmental protection and sustainability grounds (especially climate change) should be subject to strong environmental controls and intervention. These include the following:

- Introduce fuel taxation and/or emission charges and the full internalization of all external costs.[2]
- Apply the 'environmental bubble concept', as developed in Zurich, so that an individual airport assembles a complete inventory of all emissions and is legally obliged to keep its emissions within a predefined limit or 'bubble'.
- Develop attractive rail services (not necessarily high speed) between key UK destinations now used by air passengers (eg all London airports to Manchester, Newcastle, Glasgow, Edinburgh and Aberdeen). This should include sleeper services, night services and high-quality coaches. There should be a presumption in planning and regional development strategies that aviation is inappropriate for flights between main UK cities.
- Develop attractive, direct-rail services from the same UK cities to Paris, Brussels, Amsterdam, Cologne, Frankfurt and Milan. With the full implementation

of internalization of external cost principles, the cost of rail services would fall rapidly and the cost of air services would rise.

- Bring an immediate end to all the subsidies going into aviation, including grants and soft loans from the European Union (EU) to fund airport expansion, road-building and road-widening costs, the costs of railway stations and metro lines. All of these costs should be borne by the industry and the passengers themselves and not supported out of general taxation.
- Introduce full road pricing on all road routes to airports. Car journeys should pay their own full external costs.
- Encourage all government departments, local authorities, universities, regional assemblies, regional economic development agencies and companies to use video conferencing and telematics as alternatives to international flights for meetings and conferences, etc.
- Exclude air travel from those expenses that can be set against tax in business.
- Encourage businesses to adopt targets for their use of air transport (eg a 10 per cent reduction in total kilometres travelled by air by 2010 on a 1999 base).

All of these measures can be introduced at the EU and UK level. The legal basis for doing this already exists. The existence of international agreements on aviation (eg the Chicago Convention) does not bind national governments or the EU to non-intervention in this area.

Conclusion

Aviation has successfully held on to a very privileged position amongst a wide range of businesses and industry. It enjoys significant taxation advantages (no tax on fuel); airports are not regulated in terms of emissions in the same way that large industrial plants are; international aviation is not counted as part of any reduction target for greenhouse gas emissions; and large amounts of public cash are poured into supporting airports through new roads, motorway widening and new metro lines. The result of this very artificial and privileged position is that demand for air transport is rising very steeply, with severe and negative health and environmental consequences. This is not acceptable in the 21st century. If international and national commitments to sustainable development and public health are real, then aviation cannot remain a 'no-go' area for public policy. The 50-year exemption is now over and aviation should grow up and play its full role in delivering a responsible and intelligent sustainable development plan for the future. At the core of this plan will be less flying, less freight carried by air and an end to airport expansion plans.

Notes

1   The author's affiliations are the School of the Built Environment, Liverpool John Moores University, Clarence St, Liverpool L3 5UG, and Eco-Logica Ltd, Lancaster.
2   The expression 'internalization of external costs' (a variant on the polluter pays principle) refers to a policy already in place in the UK and in the EU that activities such as transport should bear the full cost of all the damaging consequences that they generate. Air travel, in the form of the price paid for a ticket, should bear the full cost of all climate change problems; health damage from noise and air pollution; all costs associated

with noise protection in homes, offices and schools; and all costs associated with public transport, air traffic control, emergency services, government administration, accidents, etc. Many of these costs are routinely quantified and can be applied on a kilometre-flown basis for a passenger and on a tonne carried for freight.

References

DETR (2000) *The Future of Aviation. The Government's Consultation Document on Air Transport Policy,* Department of Environment, Transport and the Regions, HMSO, London

IPCC (1999) *Special Report on Aviation and the Global Atmosphere: Summary for Policymakers,* Intergovernmental Panel on Climate Change, Geneva

USEPA (1993) *Estimation and Evaluation of Cancer Risks Attributed to Air Pollution in SW Chicago Final Summary Report,* EPA Region 5, Chicago, Environmental Protection Agency, Washington, DC

WHO (1993) *Community Noise,* Environmental Health Criteria Document, World Health Organization, European Office, Copenhagen, Denmark

Chapter 13

Conclusion

Paul Upham

CONCLUSION

Are trends in contemporary aviation sustainable? How should one answer this as an academic analyst, if sustainability has a strong ethical and, hence, value-laden component? To answer our own question, the approach taken by the editors has been twofold: to present our own individual viewpoints and those of other academics, but also to emphasize the further diversity of opinion on the subject.

The collective answer from the authors and commentators is that the *environmental* sustainability of the aviation industry is at least in doubt. However, a consensual answer across the industry and its observers should not be expected. For the industrial contributors, in particular, aviation is performing well, especially across the social and economic dimensions of sustainability. Whether academics acknowledge their own values in this arena explicitly or not, impartiality in terms of questions asked is not possible – hence, the emphasis in this book on including a wide range of opinion.

On the economic side, while there is no doubt that aviation is delivering economic and social goods, a key economic question is how these would compare to those obtained via alternative use of the same resources (Grayling and Bishop, 2001). In other words, comparative factor productivity is the key economic criterion, not simply the level of contemporary aviation productivity (Grayling and Bishop, 2001, p11). In response, the aviation industry could question whether those resources would be any more likely to be used in socially and economically desirable ways.

On the environmental side, the aviation industry can point to the growth in absolute environmental impacts from other transport modes. Levels of transport in the European Union (EU) are constantly increasing, particular for those modes (road and air) seen as least sustainable by the European Environment Agency (EEA) (EEA, 2001). Transport is a core activity of the tourism sector, which is itself becoming the primary service sector of the European economy (EEA, 2001, p4). Thus, the EEA reports that demand for transport fuels is growing faster than overall energy demand. The average growth rate of total passenger kilometres in the period 1980 to 1998 was 2.8 per cent per year, slightly higher than that of gross domestic product (GDP). Only a slight decoupling from economic growth is expected by 2010 (EEA, 2001, p4). In the EU since 1990, while there has been a decoupling of emissions of acidifying substances and ozone precursors by transport, emissions of greenhouse gases continue to rise (EEA, 2001, pp6–7).

Despite these wider trends, it is both possible and necessary to envision practicable and relatively environmentally sustainable transport networks – both surface and air. These will involve lower carbon fuels and engine technologies, policy measures such as carbon trading, emissions charges/taxes and regulation, all designed to achieve substantial absolute reductions in the primary environmental problem of greenhouse gas emissions.[1] The Swedish Environmentally Sustainable Transport research programme (Brokking et al, 1997) is an example of such an envisioning approach. Similarly, the Organization for Economic Cooperation and Development (OECD) forecasting project Environmentally Sustainable Transport takes a targetled ('backcasting') approach to detailing policy measures for environmentally sustainable transport.

Still, major reductions in transport greenhouse gases by countries or regions can only be judged to be sustainable if the rest of the industrialized world follows suit, and if emissions by the industrializing world decrease after a necessary initial increase (for detail on global carbon emissions contract-and-convergence scenarios, see www. gci.org.uk). Discussion of aviation and sustainability should be cognizant of this wider context.[2]

So, where should aviation go from here? While arguably insufficient in terms of environmental and, hence, community protection, commentators advocating the use of policy instruments to curb the growth of at least the marginal (per aircraft) impacts of aviation (eg Grayling and Bishop, 2001) are probably hitting the middle ground of observer opinion. In addition, it has also been observed above that it is not the policy context of aviation alone that needs reform, but that aviation is 'only' one particularly visible driver of some forms of environmental deterioration. Whatever one sees as priorities for research and action, and whatever one's understanding of sustainability, there can be no doubt that this field will remain – live and contentious – for many years to come.

NOTES

1   For people exposed to undue aircraft noise, gaseous emissions may well be seen as a secondary issue. Nevertheless, it will be acknowledged that climate change will affect all citizens wherever they live, now and in the future.

2   For OECD environmentally sustainable transport (EST) documents, see www.oecd.org/ EN/about/0,,EN-about-518-nodirectorate-no-no-no-8,00.html.

REFERENCES

Brokking, P, Emmelin L, Engström, M-G, Nilsson, J-E, Eriksson, G and Wikberg, O (1997) *An Environmentally Sustainable Transport System in Sweden – A Scenario Study*, KFB-Rapport 1997:3, KFB, Swedish Transport and Communications Research Board, Stockholm

EEA (2001) *Environmental Signals 2001: Summary*, Office for Official Publications of the European Communities, Luxembourg, available at www.eea.eu.int

Grayling, T and Bishop, S (2001) *Sustainable Aviation 2030 – Discussion Document*, Institute for Public Policy Research, London, available at www.ippr.org.uk/research

Index

Page numbers in *italics* refer to figures,
tables and boxes

Advisory Council for Aeronautics Research
45
Aer Rianta *31, 33*
Aeromexico 27
Africa 4, 11, 20, *30*
Agenda 21 117, 201, 202
Air Afrique 22
air crashes 48, 57, 59, 65, 68–70, 77, 99
Air France 22, 27
Air New Zealand 22, 52
air pollution
at airports 4–5, 12, 59, 66–8, 145, 152,
212, 236
health issues *8,* 36, 48, 49, 59, 66–8,
229, 236
high-speed rail systems 145
technological developments 68, 167, 212
see also emissions
air traffic management 5, 101, 133, 183,
193, 220–3, 224
Air Transport Action Group (ATAG) 10
Airbus A380 25, 26, 29, 90, 92
aircrew 48, 49, 53, 54–6, 61, 67
airlines *see* aviation industry
airports
air pollution 4–5, 12, 59, 66–8, 145,
152, 212, 236
in alliances 28, 30, *31,* 33
commercialization 28–9, 30, 31–2, 33
compensation payments 44–5, 102–3, 111
economic issues 29–33, 37–9, 40, 44–5,
70, 102–3, 218
environmental impact 9–10, 11, 12–13,
21, 33, 42, 43, 218

environmental management systems
123–4, 128
expansion 28–33, 43–4, 101, 234–5
local community involvement 11, 15,
21, 42–3, 98, 166, 218
growth in aviation affects 20–1, 29, 166,
199, 200, 221, 223
health issues 48, 57–70, 236
and high-speed rail systems 139–43, 146,
219
hub-and-spoke networks 21, 23, 24–6,
140, 218
infrastructure costs 11, 143, 146
land use planning *8,* 9–10, 12, 102, 107,
145, 216, 224
local community involvement
in expansion 11, 15, 21, 42–3, 98,
166, 218
noise issues 102–3, 105–10, 157–8,
163, *164,* 212, 213–17, 219
noise
controlling 45, 97, 100–3, 106–11,
213–17, 219–20
freight traffic causes 22, 150, 152–3,
154–7, 158–9
health issues 57–66, 70, 98–9
local community affected 102–3,
105–10, 157–8, 163, *164,* 212,
213–17, 219
measuring 99–100, 144, 215
privatization 28–33
safety issues 23, 37, 68–70
social issues 32, 36, 40, 58, 70, 111, 152,
159
and sustainable development 6, 9–10,
11, 12, 108, 212
Airports Council International (ACI) 216,
220

Alitalia 26
American Airlines 25, 27, 28
American Society of Heating, Refrigerating
   and Air-Conditioning Engineers
   (ASHRAE) 49
Amsterdam 33, 68
Asia 4, 20, *30,* 235
Athens Airport *31*
Australia 24, 30, *31,* 33, 215
Austria 30
aviation industry
   alliances 26–8, 33
   climate change impact 14–15, 90, 115,
      186, 188, 190–2, 223, 233
   economic issues 6, 10–11, 21, 22–8,
      232, 233, 239
   emissions responsibility 15–16, 115,
      186, 188, 233, 235–6, 237, 240
   energy consumption 6, 9, 12, 15, 144,
      232, 235
   environmental issues 5–6, 115–16,
      185–6, 226, 229, 232, 233, 239–40
   environmental management 5, 125,
      127–8, 193
   globalization 19, 20, 22, 26–8, 33, 211,
      212–13, 235
   health issues of aviation 49, 51–2, 53, 54,
      56, 236
   liberalization of aviation 22–4, 33, 133,
      205, 211, 212–13
   modal substitution 131–2, 135–9,
      143–6, 236
   noise response 104, 105, 215, 217
   social issues 37–8, 39–40, 42, 44, 159,
      206–7, 232–3, 239
   sustainable development challenge 10–11,
      23, 45, 100, 108–10, 116, 213, 227,
      232–7 *see also* airports

BAA plc 30, *31,* 32, 33, *123,* 125
Barajas Airport, Madrid *123,* 153
Birmingham International Airport *31,* 43, 67
Boeing 4, 25, 68, 90, 151, 153, 218, 233
Brazil 24
British Airways 21, 22, 27–8, 39, 49, 52,
   142–3, 233
British Midland 142
Brundtland Report 116, 117, 227
Brussels Airport *123,* 153, 157, 159

Canada 30, 215

carbon dioxide (CO_2)
   in air pollution 49, 145, 165, 167
   climate change impact 4, 9, 12, 14, 79,
      166, 205, 212
   radiative effect 87, 91, 166
   reducing 9, 14, 90, 175, 224–225, 229,
      230, 233
   technological improvements 90–1, *165,*
      174, 175, 229
   trading 7, 90, 192, 233, 240
carbon monoxide (CO) 49, 66, 77, 145,
   165, 166, 170
Caribbean 20
Cathay Pacific 27
Charles de Gaulle Airport, Paris *29,* 68, 107
China 4
China Airlines 22
cirrus cloud formation 78, 80, 81, 87–9,
   91, 171, 181, 205
Civil Aviation Act (1982, UK) 158
Civil Aviation Authority (CAA) 38, 40, 49
climate change
   emissions cause 15, 77–8, 79–80, 90,
      115, 200–1, 223, 229 *see also* carbon
      dioxide; nitrogen oxides
   government policies 13–15, 166, 180–1,
      186, 189–94, 201, 208, 229
   growth in aviation impact 6, 115, 200–1,
      204–5, 212, 223–5
   industry impact 14–15, 90, 115, *186,*
      188, 190–2, 223, 233
   measuring 78–9, 91
   radiative forcing 78, 79–81, 87, 88,
      91–2, 166
Committee on Aviation and Environmental
   Protection (CAEP, ICAO) 90, 170, 171,
   215–16, 220
Concorde 68, 77, 133, 193
contrails 78, 80, 81, 87–9, 91, 171, 181,
   205, 212
Copenhagen Airport *31,* 101

Delta 25, 27
Denmark 30
developing countries and aviation 39–40,
   41–2, 180, 187–8, 202, 204, 234
DHL 22, 28, 42, 150, 151, 152, 153–5,
   156, 157
Dulles International Airport, Washington
   30, 167

East Midlands Airport 153–5, 156, 157, 158, 159
EasyJet 24
Eco-Management and Audit Scheme (EMAS, EC) 121–2, *123–4*, 128
economic issues
  of airports 29–33, 37–9, 40, 44–5, 70, 102–3, 218
  of aviation 4, 12–14, 40–2, 149, 206–8, 239
  compensation payments 44–5, 102–3, 111
  environmental costs 6, 11, 12–14, 37, 90–1, 159, 206–8
  for industry 6, 10–11, 21, 22–8, 232, 233, 239
  for local communities 41, 44–5, 102–3, 111
  of noise 4, 13, 44–5, 99, 102–3, 104, 111, 159
  of sustainable development 10, 11, 15, 199–201, 202, 206–7, 239
economies in transition and aviation 105, 201, 202–4, 205
emissions
  climate change impact 15, 77–8, 79–80, 90, 115, 200–1, 223, 229
  environmental impact 4, 12, 15, 45, 66, 67, 145, 165, 167
  industry responsibility 15–16, 115, *186*, 188, 233, 235–6, 237, 240
  measuring 81–4, 182
  radiative effects 78, 80–1, 84–5, 87, 88–9, 90, 91–2, 166
  reducing
    policy instruments 14–15, 166–7, 170, 180–1, 189–94, 230, 236, 240
    quotas 6, 14–15, 90, 180
    technological developments 91, 170, 171, 173, 181–4, 240
  see also individual emissions
employment 10, 11, 37, 39, 40, 99, 103, 233
environment
  air traffic management benefits 101, 183, 220–1, 222–3
  airports impact 9–10, 11, 12–13, 21, 33, 42, 43, 218
  economic issues 6, 11, 12–14, 37, 90–1, 159, 206–8
  emissions affect 4, 12, 15, 45, 66, 67, 145, 165, 167

environmental management 5, 117–28
government policies 7, 12–15, 184–6, 204, 205–9, 213
growth in aviation constrained 115–16, 202, 203, 205
growth in aviation impacts 6, 100, 115–16, 149–50, 152, 162, 172–3, 200
industry relationship 5–6, 115–16, 185–6, 226, 229, 232, 233, 239–40
and resource consumption 7, *8*, 9, 37
substitution benefits 6–7, *8*, 9, 131–2, 204, 208, 224, 236
and sustainable development 6, *8*, 9–10, 12, 206–7
technology development affects 26, 45, 90–1, 104, 162–3, 168, 229, 233 *see also* climate change
Environmental Protection Agency (EPA, US) 77, 235
EUROCONTROL 220–3
Europe
  air traffic management 220–3
  airports 15, 29, 105–8, 111, *123–4*, 128, 140–3, 157, 217–18 *see also* individual airports
  economic issues of aviation 38, 39
  environmental management systems 120, 121–5, 128
  growth in air transport 20, 29, 179, 221
  health issues of aviation 55–6, 68
  high-speed rail systems 131, 132, 134–6, 137–9, 140–3, 144–5, 146, 218
  liberalization of airlines 22, 23
  noise issues 57, 105–8, 170, 213, 214, 215
  sustainable transport 131, 136, 202–3
  technological development 90, 170, 172, 173, 188
  see also economies in transition; European Union
European Commission (EC) 9, 15, 90, 91, 99–100, 106, 111, 173, 224
European Environment Agency (EEA) 6, 11, 12, 239–40
European Union (EU)
  climate change intervention 91, 192, 230
  environmental regulations *122*, 186, 192, 202, 203, 230
  high-speed rail systems 134
  liberalization of aviation 23, 211
  noise regulations 45, 99–100, 106–7, 111, 170, 172, 202, 217

sustainable transport 212, 239–40
tourism 188, 239–40

Federal Aviation Administration (FAA) 38,
    39, 40, 49, 55, 57
Fedex 22, 28, 150, 152
Frankfurt Airport *29, 33*
freight traffic 4, 22, 28, 149–59, 166, 199,
    205, 235

Gatwick Airport, London *31,* 43, 214
Germany 30, 91, 192
Go and Buzz 24
government
    airport ownership 29, 31, 32, 180
    aviation policies 21, 22, 23, 224, 229,
        234, 236–7 *see also under* UK
    climate change policies 13–15, 166,
        180–1, *186,* 189–94, 201, 208, 229
    emissions reduction 14–15, 166–7, 170,
        180–1, 189–94, 230, 236, 240
    environmental policies 7, 12–15, 184–6,
        204, 205–9, 213
    health issues of aviation 62–3, 66
    liberalization of aviation 27, 28, 133,
        211, 213
    noise response 105, 152–3, 155–6, 157,
        167, 212 *see also under* UK; US
    safety issues 37, 68, 133
    sustainable development strategies 12,
        23, 108–10 *see also under* UK
greenhouse gases *see* climate change; emis-
    sions
growth in aviation 3–4, 33, 48
    airports affected 20–1, 29, 166, 199,
        200, 221, 223
    climate change impact 6, 115, 200–1,
        205, 212, 223–5
    constraints imposed
        by environmental impact 115–16,
            202, 203, 205
        by noise 7, 21, 98, 103, 106, 111, 115,
            159, 212
    environmental impact 6, 100, 115–16,
        149–50, 152, 162, 172–3, 200
    freight traffic 4, 22, 149, 150–2, 154,
        166, 199, 205, 235
    passenger traffic 4, 19–20, 166, 179,
        187, 200, 205, 234–5
    speed as driver 132–3, 149, 152, 179,
        182

sustainable development relationship 6,
    100, 116–18, 199, 207, 234–7
from tourism 3, 20, 187, 200, 239–40

health issues
    of air pollution *8,* 36, 48, 49, 59, 66–8,
        229, 236
    of airports 48, 57–70, 235–6
    deep vein thrombosis (DVT) 48, 49–52
    disease 48, 49–54, 55, 62, 64–5, 67, 188
    government involvement 62–3, 66
    industry involvement 49, 51–2, 53, 54,
        56, 235–6
    jet lag 48, 61
    of local communities 48, 57–70
    long-haul flights 49–50, 51, 61
    of noise 4, 12, 36, 48, 57–66, 70, 98–9,
        229
    safety issues 48, 68–70
Heathrow Airport, London *31,* 33, 61, 67,
    142, 153, 155, 213, 214
    Terminal 5 21, *29,* 38, 43, 107–8, 199,
        236
high-speed rail systems 131–2, 133–4,
    135–46, 166, 218
Hochtief and Bechtel *31,* 33
Hong Kong Airport 30, 98, 101

INCA project (EU) 91
India 23, 30
integrated carriers 22, 28, 42, 150–2,
    153–5, 156, 157, 158, 159
Intergovernmental Panel on Climate
    Change (IPCC) 79, 80, 81, 188, 205, 224
    Aviation and the Global Atmosphere (1999)
        4, 78, 86–7, 88, 89–90, 91–2, 166,
        168, 180
International Air Transport Association
    (IATA) 22, 26, 51–2, 118, 127, 128
International Civil Aviation Organization
    (ICAO)
    climate change issues 4, 7, 77, 170, 193,
        230, 235
    environmental issues 193, 202, 203, 222,
        223
    noise regulations 97, 103–4, 105, 106,
        215–16, 217, 220
International Commission on Radiation
    Protection (ICRP) 55
ISO 14001 43, 121, 122, *123–4,* 125, 128
Italy 30, 33, 153

Japan 30, 213, 215
Japan Airlines 52
JFK Airport, New York *29, 31*
Jordan 23

Kansai Airport *30,* 101
Kenya Airlines 22
KLM 25, 26, 27, 49, 52
Korean Airlines 27
Kyoto Protocol 90, 180, 193, 194, 201,
    230, 235

La Paz Airport *31*
Land Compensation Act (1973, UK) 44
Latin America 20
local communities
    airports relationship
        expansion issues 11, 15, 21, 42–3, 98,
            166, 218
        noise issues 102–3, 105–10, 157–8,
            163, *164,* 212, 213–17, 219
    compensation payments 44–5, 102–3, 111
    economic issues 41, 44–5, 102–3, 111
    health issues 48, 57–70
    noise affects
        around airports 102–3, 105–10,
            157–8, 163, *164,* 212, 213–17, 219
        freight traffic 22, 150, 152–3, 154–7,
            158–9
        health issues 57–66, 70, 98–9
    social issues 36, 58, 70, 111, 152, 159
low-cost airlines 24
Lufthansa 25, 27, 52, 142

Malaysia 30
Maldives 188
Manchester Airport 42–3, 61, 157
Maui, Hawaii 37
Mauritius 33
methane (CH$_4$) 79, 80, *81,* 84, *85,* 86–7,
    91, 145, 205
Mexico 30
Middle East 20, *29*
Munich Airport 21, *31,* 98, 101

NASA 89, 90, 170
Netherlands 68
New Zealand 30, *31,* 215
NGOs 11, 105, 109, 126, 177, 185, 214,
    217, 229 *see also* individual NGOs
night flights

noise issues 22, 58, 62, 152–3, 154–6,
    158–9, 213, 217
    restrictions 22, 62, 101, 153, 154–7,
        158–9, 213
nitrogen oxides (NO$_x$)
    in air pollution 12, 66, 67, 77, *83,* 145,
        165, 167
    climate change impact 12, 86–7, 89,
        166, 205, 212, 233
    ozone formation 84–7, 90, 91, 92, 193
    radiative effect 84–5, 91, 92, 166, 193
    technological improvements 90–1,
        165–6, 167, 170–1, 176
noise
    at airports
        controlling 45, 97, 100–3, 106–11,
            213–17, 219–20
        freight traffic causes 22, 150, 152–3,
            154–7, 158–9
        health issues 57–66, 70, 98–9
        local community affected 102–3,
            105–10, 157–8, 163, *164,* 212,
            213–17, 219
        measuring 99–100, 144, 215
    annoyance factor 12, 57, 58–61, 63, 66,
        99
    compensation payments 44–5, 102–3,
        111
    economic issues 4, 13, 44–5, 99, 102–3,
        104, 111, 159
    government response 105, 152–3, 155–
        6, 157, 167, 212 *see also under* UK; US
    growth in aviation constrained 7, 21, 98,
        103, 106, 111, 115, 159, 212
    health issues 4, 12, 36, 48, 57–66, 70,
        98–9, 229
    high-speed rail systems 144–5
    industry response 104, 105, 215, 217
    local communities affected
        around airports 102–3, 105–10,
            157–8, 163, *164,* 213–17, 219
        freight traffic 22, 150, 152–3, 154–7,
            158–9
        health issues 57–66, 70
    measuring 36, 57–8, 59, 62–3, 99–100,
        144, 215
    night flights cause 22, 58, 62, 152–3,
        154–6, 158–9, 213, 217
    regulating 98, 101–2, 167, 212, 220 *see
        also under* European Union; Interna-
        tional Civil Aviation Organization

sleep disturbance 4, 57, 58, 59, 61–4, 66, 98, 99, 154
social issues 58, 99, 104, 111, 159
stress 57, 58, 59, 62, 63, 64–5, 70, 98, 99
technological developments 45, 100–1, 103, 163, 167, 168–70, 172, 219–20
non-governmental organizations *see* NGOs
non-methane volatile organic compounds (NMVOCs) 12, 66, 67, 68
North America 20, *29–30,* 221
Northwest Airlines 27

OECD 7–10, 240
Oneworld 27
ozone (O$_3$) 49, 66, 67, 77–8, 84–7, 89, 90, 91–2

Pacific region *30,* 235
PARTEMIS project (EU) 91
particulates 12, 66, 67, 88, 91, 165, 166, 170
passenger traffic
growth in 4, 19–20, 166, 179, 187, 200, 205, 234–5
health issues 48, 49–54, 61
PAZI project (Germany) 91
Pearson International Airport 60
Philippines 30
pollution *see* air pollution; noise; water pollution
Portugal 23

Qantas Airways 27, 49, 51
Qualifier 27

RAIN project (EC) 172
Rolls-Royce 217
Royal Commission on Environmental Pollution (RCEP) 14–15, 168, 201
Ryanair 24

Sabena 27
safety 11, 19, 23, 36, 37, 48, 68–70, 133, 189
SAS 27
Schiphol Airport, Amsterdam 7, *29, 31,* 67, 68–9, 98, 107, 153, 219–20
SILENCER project 172
Singapore 30
Singapore Airlines 22, 27, 52

SkyTeam 27
smoke *see* particulates
social issues
of airports 32, 36, 40, 58, 70, 111, 152, 159
of aviation 37–8, 39–40, 42, 44, 159, 206–7, 232–3, 239
for local communities 36, 58, 70, 111, 152, 159
and noise 58, 99, 104, 111, 159
of sustainable development 10, 11, 206–7, 232, 239
Sonic Cruiser (Boeing) 25–6, 90, 92
soot *see* particulates
South Africa 30
South African Airways 22
South America 4, *30*
South-Eastern and East of England Regional Air Service Study (SERAS) 43–4
Southwest Airlines 24
Stansted Airport, London *31,* 214
Star Alliance 27, 142
Strasbourg 42
Subsonic Assessment Programme (SASS, NASA) 90
subsonic aviation 77, 81, 84–9, 90, 91, 215
sulphur dioxide (SO$_2$) 66, 67, 89, 145, 165, 171
supersonic aviation 25–6, 77, 89, 90, 92, 133, 192–3
Sustainable Aviation report (INFRAS) 10–12
sustainable development
and airports 6, 9–10, 11, 12, 108, 212
defining 5, 6, 7–10, 199, 206, 225, 226–8
economic issues 10, 11, 15, 199–201, 202, 206–7, 239
environmental issues 6, *8,* 9–10, 12, 206–7
and environmental management 116–17
government policies 12, 23, 108–10 *see also under* UK
growth in aviation affects 6, 100, 116–18, 199, 207, 234–7
industry challenge 10–11, 23, 45, 100, 108–10, 116, 213, 227, 232–7
social issues 10, 11, 206–7, 232, 239
and tourism 202
and transport 131, 136, 143, 145–6, 202–3, 211, 212, 239–40

Swedish Environmentally Sustainable Transport programme 240
Swissair 27, 180, 183, *184*
Switzerland 30, 170

TBI 33
technological development
  for air pollution reduction 68, 167, 212
  airframe improvements 167, 171–2, 173, 176–7
  alternative fuels 6, 9, 91, 174–6, 177, 179, 181, 212, 234
  for emissions reduction 91, 170, 171, 173, 181–4, 240
    carbon dioxide 90–1, *165,* 174, 175, 229
    nitrogen oxides 90–1, 165–6, 167, 170–1, 176
  engine improvements 45, 164, *165,* 167, 168–71, 173–4, *175*
  environmental impact 26, 45, 90–1, 104, 162–3, 168, 229, 232
  for fuel efficiency 26, 45, 164, *165,* 167–9, 183, 229, 234
  for noise reduction 45, 100–1, 103, 163, 167, 168–70, 172, 219–20
Thai Airlines 27
TNT Express 22, 150, 152, 153, 154
tourism
  growth in 3, 20, 187, 200, 239–40
  importance to developing countries 39–40, 41, 42, 188, 204, 235
  socio-economic issues 37, 39–40, 41, 42, 200, 201–2, 203–4
  sustainable 201–2
TRADEOFF project (EC) 90
transport
  modal substitution 6–7, 9, 131–46, 166, 204, 208, 218, 224, 236
  sustainable 131, 136, 143, 145–6, 202–3, 211, 212, 239–40
Transport and Environment Reporting Mechanism (TERM) 11, 12

UK
  air pollution 4–5, 13, 14–15
  airports 30, 32, 33, 38, 42–4, 157, 199, 223 *see also* individual airports

aviation policies 5, 12–14, 36, 37, 62–3, 158–9, 192, 200–1, 234
  economic issues of aviation 37, 38, 40, 42, 199–201
  environmental management systems 120, 121, 122
  environmental policies 12–15, 43, 120
  growth in air transport 21, 149, 154, 179, 199, 223, 234, 235
  noise issues 57–8, 61, 62, 63, 66, 158–9, 213–14
  safety issues 37, 68
  sustainable development strategy 5, 7, 10, 36, 45, 199–201, 225–6, 231–2
unburned hydrocarbons (UHCs) 77, 165, 166, 170
United Airways 21, 27, 28, 142
United Nations Framework Convention on Climate Change (UNFCCC) 90, 180, 193, 230
UPS 22, 28, 150, 152, 154
Uruguay 30
US
  airports 21, *29–30,* 33, 102 *see also* individual airports
  economic issues of aviation 39, 42, 45
  growth in air transport 4, 29, 179, 188
  health issues of aviation 52–3, 57, 63
  liberalization of airlines 22, 23, 24, 26, 211
  noise issues 57, 63, 215
  sustainable transport 212
  technological development 89, 90

Varig 27
Vienna Airport *31*
Vietnam 30
Virgin Express 24

waste production 4, 5, 7, 116
water pollution 4, 36, 115–16, 152
water vapour 78, 87, 88, 89, 165, 167, 171, 180, 233
Wings 27
World Health Organization (WHO) 48, 53–4, 58, 98–9, 214

Zurich Airport *124,* 167, 236

The Earthscan Reader on World Transport Policy and Practice

Edited by *John Whitelegg* and *Gary Haq*, Stockholm Environment Institute, University of York

Transport is now a critical problem throughout the world, and it is set to get worse. Whether it is traffic congestion, crashes (10 million killed and injured each year), noise, air pollution, landscape destruction, or greenhouse gas emissions (of which transport is the fastest-growing source), the damage and the costs from our current forms of transport are dangerously high and getting worse. Policies and practical measures that can reduce and eliminate these problems are urgently needed.

This Reader contains 16 important contributions on how to improve transport globally. They are based on sound science, sound people-centred analysis, and a strong awareness of equity and human rights. And they have been selected for their originality, the importance of the issues they focus on, the quality of their insight and their practical relevance. A further 7 commissioned chapters provide informative overviews of the transport problems specific to each region of the world, while the editors' Introduction and Conclusion frames the discussion and lays out the scale of the challenges we face.

As a whole, the Reader demonstrates what steps can be taken to improve both transport provision and use, in both the developed and the developing world, while reducing environmental and health impacts.

Paperback ISBN 1-85383-851-9 • £19.95
Hardback ISBN 1-85383-850-0 • £50.00

Orders
Littlehampton Book Services Limited
Faraday Close, Durrington, Worthing, West Sussex BN13 3RB
Tel: +44 (0)1903 828 800 • Fax: +441903 828 802
• Email: orders@lbsltd.co.uk
www.earthscan.co.uk

Urban Transport Environment and Equity

THE CASE FOR DEVELOPING COUNTRIES

Eduardo A Vasconcellos, Associate Director, ANTP (Brazilian National Public Transport Association)

Traditional transport policies in developing-world cities have been creating an unfair distribution of accessibility and environmental impact; they can divide communities, widen economic inequalities, compromise safety and threaten the health of vulnerable social groups.

Urban Transport, Environment and Equity highlights the failures of current approaches and the importance of social and political considerations for planning, policy and management to create equitable and socially sustainable urban transport. It proposes alternative approaches, develops an appropriate methodology and lays out a range of actions aimed at reversing current trends and minimizing inequities.

The book provides a thorough and practical guide for a range of professionals, policy makers, academics and students, in transport, planning, geography, environment and social science, in both developing and developed countries.

Paperback ISBN 1-85383-727-X • £24.95
Hardback ISBN 1-85383726-1 • £60.00

Orders
Littlehampton Book Services Limited
Faraday Close, Durrington, Worthing, West Sussex BN13 3RB
Tel: +44 (0)1903 828 800 • Fax: +441903 828 802
• Email: orders@lbsltd.co.uk
www.earthscan.co.uk